THE COMPASS

THE COMPASS

Janet Coleman

19 90

ALFRED A. KNOPF   NEW YORK

Grateful acknowledgment is made to the following for permission to reprint previously published and recorded material:

Shelley Berman: Extracts from recordings *Outside Shelley Berman, Inside Shelley Berman,* and *A Personal Appearance* by Shelley Berman. Reprinted by permission.

Roger Bowen: Extracts from the recording "Football Comes to the University of Chicago" by Roger Bowen from *From the Second City.* Reprinted by permission.

Severn Darden: Extracts from recordings "A Short Talk on the Universe" from *The Sound of My Own Voice and Other Noises* and "Blind Date" from *Comedy from The Second City* by Severn Darden. Reprinted by permission.

The Permanent Press: Extracts from *Rebel Without Applause* by Jay Landesman. Reprinted by permission.

Jeffrey Sweet: Extracts from interviews from *Something Wonderful Right Away* by Jeffrey Sweet. Published by Limelight Editions. Copyright © 1978 by Jeffrey Sweet. Reprinted by permission.

Library of Congress Cataloging-in-Publication Data

Coleman, Janet
  The Compass / Janet Coleman. — 1st ed.
    p.   cm.
  ISBN 0-394-52545-0
    1. Compass Players.   2. Improvisation (Acting)   3. Comedy.
  I. Title.
PN2277.C42C664   1990
792'.09773'11—dc20   89-43362
                                                          CIP

To my mother, Sally,
and the memory of my father, Jack

My curse on plays
That have to be set up in fifty ways
—WILLIAM BUTLER YEATS

CONTENTS

Photographs follow pages 82, 146, and 210

PREFACE

The Compass was an improvisational theatre, the first of its kind in the nation, unrewarded in its lifetime and barely chronicled in its posterity. It began in a storefront theatre on a main drag of a great university campus in Chicago, in the childhood of the Atomic Age.

There, a group of people, under thirty, smart, complicated, dressed in basic Bohemian black and khaki, crossed paths.

The task they set themselves was to report on their times, seven or eight times every week, with no set script and no fixed lines. They improvised much of their stage material by playing off the shouted concerns of their audience. (This one consisted mostly of unassuming eggheads—mathematicians, social scientists, physicists—whose main requirement for an enjoyable evening was cheap beer.) The intentions of The Compass Players in practicing this hair-raising exercise were serious. They did not plan to be funny or to change the course of comedy with their improvisations. But that is what happened.

THE COMPASS

1

The Hutchins Plan

The great gray neo-Gothic buildings of the University of Chicago were the gift of a Baptist, John D. Rockefeller. The spires of this gloomy medieval fortress provided the backdrop for an almost miraculously long and bright interlude in American education from 1931 to 1959, the official life span of Robert Maynard Hutchins's "Chicago Experiment," described in the official annals as the "Chicago College Plan" and popularly called the "Hutchins Plan."

One of the great exponents of liberal education in the tradition of John Dewey, Chancellor Hutchins's strategies for exposing students to the glories of the contemplative life were inspired by the medieval university of Saint Thomas Aquinas. By incorporating the scholastic principles of the Thomists into the Chicago Experiment, Hutchins hoped to produce an intellectual community of scholars capable of achieving enlightenment through a common body of ideas and information and by sharing the divine revelations of knowledge.

Like Socrates, Plato, and Aristotle, the Greeks he and Saint Thomas so admired, Hutchins had no distrust in youth. (He himself had become president of the University of Chicago at the age of twenty-nine.) Hence, he reorganized the entrance requirements for the university's undergraduate college and abolished the age requirement for students seeking a B.A. Students who could pass the entrance exam were encouraged to enter the University of Chicago after their sophomore year of high school, at fifteen or sixteen, but the entrance age was considerably lower for some whiz kids.

Hutchins felt that there was too much pressure on the American student to specialize. Prematurely habituating students to succeed in the job market, he argued, was resulting in "a trivialization of our lives." A college education, he maintained, should focus solely on the acquisition of knowledge, not on training for a vocation in an economic environment that would be completely different by the time the trainee entered it.

According to the Hutchins Plan, all undergraduates read the same great texts, including Plato, Kant, Aquinas, Shakespeare, Marx, Dante, Goethe, Aristotle, Dostoevski, Max Weber, Machiavelli, and William James. Even science was treated like a humanity: instead of clocking hours in the lab, students were required to read Archimedes, Mendel, Newton, and Einstein. It was a grueling program. An advanced course, Observation, Interpretation, and Integration (O.I.I.), was referred to by students as "Oi, oi, oi."*

After passing the fourteen excruciatingly long and difficult exams, an undergraduate was eligible for a University of Chicago Bachelor of Arts degree. By scoring well on the placement exams when they entered, or by accelerating their studies at their own pace, students could (and commonly did) complete the undergraduate program in two years. Of the class that entered in 1948, fifteen members besides Dale Aukerman (whose picture was featured in an article on *Speedy Students* that year in *Life*) were eligible for their degree in one year. Although it was often hard to satisfy the picky requirements of the specialists on other graduate faculties (many universities refused to accept the University of Chicago's "two-year degree"), it was unextraordinary for a twenty-one-year-old at the University of Chicago to have a Ph.D.

Hutchins had lured a brilliant faculty from unguarded niches throughout academia. The University of Chicago paid its faculty well and guaranteed complete academic independence, communication with top scholars in other disciplines, and funds and freedom to experiment, as well as nice Hyde Park lodgings. A prevalent professorial dialect was German-Jewish, but so was Hutchins's own plain Brooklyn accent. In 1950, the University of Chicago faculty included such eminences as Mortimer J. Adler, Bruno Bettelheim, Benno Landesberg, David Riesman, Gerhard Meyer, Har-

---

*Based on their experience at the University of Chicago, Hutchins and his colleague Mortimer J. Adler devised a similar syllabus for the *Encyclopaedia Britannica*'s Great Books of the Western World program as a means of spreading culture to the grass roots. The plan was also transplanted to Saint John's College in Annapolis, Maryland, by University of Chicago faculty members Scott Buchanan and Stringfellow Barr.

old C. Urey, Richard McKeon, Robert Redfield, Rudolf Carnap, Walter Johnson, Louis Wirth, Reuel Denney, Elder Olson, Milton Friedman, Daniel J. Boorstin, Enrico Fermi, and Rosalie Wax.

The Hutchins system called for dialogue, not for lecture. A student who wished to discuss the fine points of metaphysical agnosticism could post a notice on the dead tree in front of the Woodworth Book Store, and the resulting symposium would probably include his own philosophy professor. At a physics department picnic, it is still remembered that Enrico Fermi was enchanted by his introduction to the yo-yo. This sort of thing was not to be missed. But it was not incumbent on a University of Chicago student to show up for class.

Since independent thinking, along with reading, was intended as the principal activity of a University of Chicago education, even a twelve-year-old student did not need a note from his mother to stay up all night counting the prime numbers between one and one thousand or to spend his mornings playing Persian rummy.

"When I feel like exercising," Hutchins liked to quote the humorist J. P. McEvoy, "I lie down until the feeling goes away." Hutchins's adoration of the intellect led him to deplore the idea that the university's intellectual function might compete with the panoply of extracurricular activities traditionally associated with college, especially in the rah-rah tradition of the Midwest. He disapproved of college sports. Big Ten football was an inspiration for endowments besides a source of ticket revenue, but Hutchins viewed the game merely as an educational diversion. "If a university needs a sport, let it be horse racing," he said. "Horses don't have to study for exams." However bitterly the alumni swallowed the news, the Hutchins reign spelled the end of the Chicago Maroons.

In 1934, unbeknownst to the chancellor, the squash courts under the grandstand of the unused football field, Stagg Field, were appropriated by the research team of Enrico Fermi (whom Hutchins had helped escape from Fascist Italy) for the first demonstration of nuclear fission. Hutchins himself was considered too unreliable a security risk to be alerted on that awesome day when, just before igniting the first chain reaction, one of Fermi's associates supposedly wondered, "What do we lose if I unscrew this bulkhead?" "Chicago," Fermi supposedly said.

An unusual and elite student population was attracted to the Hutchins Plan. They were young (Marvin Peisner '51 entered at fourteen), serious (Omar Shapli '53 came to study Egyptology), and daring (Eve Leoff '59 came from a mill town in Methuen, Massachusetts, because "my grandmother told me everyone there was a Communist and everybody slept with everybody. So I took steps to go there. And it was true. Everybody *was* a Communist and everybody *was* sleeping with everybody. I signed up for every club that had the word 'socialist' in it").

After World War II, and throughout the late forties and early fifties, while most of the country was winding down for a long cold war hibernation in the suburbs, the University of Chicago campus was geared up for cultural combat. There were more Easterners and Jews than usual for a Midwestern school, past and future Nobel Prize winners, teaching fellow Philip Roth, the teenaged Susan Sontag (remembered by one admirer as "a sunflower of a girl"), and interdisciplinary research teams who were transcending the petty concerns of their own fields in order to contribute to "social science," the futuristic new field of scholarship named and created at the University of Chicago. There was an influx of older war veterans on the GI Bill who wanted to get their B.A.'s fast and make up for lost time. The more conservative in-state students, the frat rats, headed for Loyola or the University of Illinois.

The composer-lyricist Joan Hopner Wile ('52) entered the University of Chicago because she had flunked out of Western High School in Washington and couldn't bear repeating the eleventh grade. According to Wile, there was something about the premise of the Chicago college that drew people who were "incredible misfits in our civilian lives." To her, the very fact of choosing the University of Chicago was a symptom of social disharmony.

Oddballs and misfits have traditionally been drawn to Greenwich Village. "But you couldn't go *there* before finishing high school," says Wile. Here was a place that had the same kind of permissive ambience as Greenwich Village. Here in Hyde Park, on the South Side of Chicago, was a legitimate Bohemian center for the underaged.

Coming from a small provincial Massachusetts high school, where "being smart was a liability," Hunter College English professor Eve Leoff found "the place was an elixir." "People came and got drunk on the atmosphere," says Omar Shapli, now a professor of theatre at City College of New York. "It was like the University of Paris when Abelard was there." In the postwar flower of the Hutchins reign, the campus was hot with the energy of ex-GI's straight from the foxholes, brainy young women, obsessed sociologists, and geniuses, some of them only thirteen or fourteen.

Controversy attended the Chicago Plan. Conservative educators and native Chicagoans arguing for the prosecution cited the "wild behavior" of University of Chicago students loose in the city without parental supervision, but with accelerated mental energy and time on their hands.

Fraternities weren't fashionable at the University of Chicago, but, like fraternity secrets, "There were about a dozen things you were supposed to know," Leoff recalls. "To say something was *qua* something was very stylish. So was the word 'relevant.' You talked about 'dialectics.' You had to be able to compare Aquinas to Augustus. Your conversation always included a smattering of Aquinas. And Marx. It was very important whether you were Platonic or Aristotelian in your outlook. You know, letting things evolve, as Plato did in the *Dialogues*, or having an agenda, the way Aristotle did." ("Understanding myself as an Aristotelian, that's been a mainstay throughout my life," says writer Frances Gendlin ['56], who was previously the executive director of the Association of American University Presses and before that the editor of *Sierra* magazine.)

As a Chicago college student, Joan Wile realized, "There were a lot of bright kids like me who thought of themselves intellectually as the cream of the crop. We all assumed we had to be something special—nuclear physicists or leading thinkers or research stars. But there were so many real academic-type geniuses around that those of us who weren't deeply delved into physics or math or philosophy felt defeated even before we started. We could see up front that we didn't have what it takes."

In this high-powered environment, the economist Mildred Goldberger, then a graduate student in mathematics, observed that "very gifted people were ruined because the very brightest people seemed to succeed without any effort at all." On the dark side of Hyde Park were students flying off rooftops or, quoting Plato, tripping near the edge. "We might get hit by falling bodies" is the reason Eve Leoff's boyfriend gave for refusing lunch at International House, where the foreign exchange students lived.

"All that may have been true," says Leoff, "but the bare bones of intellectual inquiry were put in my hands like a baby rattle. I was enchanted by every minute of my four years."

As a Senn High School girl from the North Side of Chicago, the actress Barbara Harris heard eye-widening stories from her relatives about an even younger college crowd on the South Side. "It seemed that all they needed were the togas, these little kids talking about the Power of the Good. All they needed were the fig wreaths." As an undergraduate, the actor Severn Darden wore a cape to class. "A *cape*. It sounded almost scary. There was always talk, you know, of bringing back plaid skirts."

"Darden was very much a type of the place," Robert B. Silvers ('47), coeditor of *The New York Review of Books*, realized when he saw him later on the stage. He conjured up the kind of "big and gloomy" campus character Silvers remembered from his own student days. "That was the impression you had . . . of these shaggy figures moving about, engaged in enormous projects of reading, with rather mysterious interests. Self-dramatizing. Yet sympathetic because helplessly preoccupied."

Severn Teakel Darden, Jr., arrived from Mexico City College in the fall of 1948, after taking summer high school make-up courses with the football team from Notre Dame. He brought a black cape lined with scarlet and a smattering of Spanish, "enough to get through a car wreck or a funeral," he recalls, "but not enough to make a date for lunch."

Rooming in the house of the movement teacher Beatrice Stronsdorf, "a Baroness, formerly von Stronsdorf, and, before that, Pinky Mills," he studied hagiography (the lives of saints), and read and memorized obscure words from *The Oxford English Dictionary*. The stone floor and stained-glass windows of his room were lit by a four-burner chandelier that only burned gas. From Lake Park Avenue, he could be seen jogging out of this house in an apple-green waistcoat, tweeds, cape, and tennis shoes. He had a polished stoat skull on his cane. He referred to one of his favorite teachers, the poet Henry Rago, as "Rago the Dago." He called the eminent psychoanalyst "Brutal Brutalheim."

Like the blues, he was at home in Chicago, but he was born in New Orleans. ("You're allergic to oysters? Oh, shucks.") Down South, both "Severn" and "Darden" are familiar names. His father, Severn Darden, Sr., was the district attorney of the surreal city that is properly pronounced "New Orlinz or New Orleeyuns, but never New Or*leans*." There, where he developed an ear for the sound of crazy Southern politicians, magnolia-scented ladies with white gloves and picture hats still call him "Little Sev." The Severn River runs past the U.S. Naval Academy in Annapolis, Maryland. (He would sometimes refer to himself onstage as "Sylbert Estuary.") He portrays the Stephens on the maternal, or Rubenstein, side of his lineage as "Irish undercover Jews. And every Friday night at Sabbath, they'd close the windows, close the shades, and light up. We were about as Jewish as Bing Crosby," he says.

He spent a sickly youth at boarding schools all over the country and entered the University of Chicago (still suffering from a painful and then untreatable case of "acute dermatosis") as a premed. As a student, he was somewhat heavy, and his friend Joan Wile recalls his posture then as "sort of bent. He had terrible skin. But there was something so dazzling about him that transcended his physical appearance. We all wanted to be with him all the time. Even at eighteen, he created the feeling that if you knew him, you were on to something." In the hallway of the freshman dormitory, he introduced himself to the future classics scholar Seth Benardete by asking, "Do you know the way to supper?" "No," said Benardete. Severn said, "Let's go together then."

Once Benardete's phone rang at midnight. "Is the universe finite or infinite?" Severn asked. Benardete said, "Finite." Severn said, "Thank you," and hung up.

"He was excessive sometimes," Benardete reflects. "He could annoy people because he hadn't developed his sense of an audience. He didn't know when to stop." At the movies, Severn would consistently laugh in the wrong places until everyone in the audience began to laugh too.

He bought his first (purple) Rolls-Royce in his sophomore year for $750, from the same Rolls-Royce collector from whom the Chicago TV personality Dave Garroway shopped. It was "one shade darker than an eggplant, almost black," he says. Some people remember it as brown.

Spectators swear he drove the Rolls-Royce to the opera dressed as a maharaja. Some think that his accomplice, Benardete (who couldn't drive), was in the driver's seat. Benardete says he may have removed and unfurled the red carpet from the trunk of the car. Others say that Severn Darden threw fake diamonds to a cheering crowd. He strode through the gallery, swept up to his box (in some versions a center seat in the dress circle), and enjoyed the show.

He was a regular in the lounge at Green Hall, a women's dormitory. "Other boys would come to pick up someone for a date," recalls Joan Wile, "but he was just there. There was something about him that was so unnurtured, like an empty hole. And he had a real goodness, a beautiful nature. He never got angry, never attacked anybody, never put anybody down. You didn't have to hide anything with him. You could be anything you were. Because he didn't judge. He was always surrounded by the most attractive women, although at any other university, we'd have been the dogs."

Once he remained in Green Hall after it closed at eleven. He went into the girls' bathroom and waited up all night. In the morning, as the girls came in to shower, Severn was holding on to the shower rail. "Is this the way to Clark Street?" he said.

"Place of the wild onion," the meaning of "Chicago" in the Algonquin Indian language, refers to the garlic that once grew along the Lake Michigan shore. Indian storytellers returning to their campfires once probably relayed this useful botanical information to their tribes. Chicagophiles refer to their "oral tradition" with "the neighborhood pride mixed with self-loathing" that writer Ross Talarico says is supposed to be special to the Second City. The oral tradition is improvisational, the vented urge to tell a story, to share information, to air opinions, to breathe garlic on a crowd. It is the essence of free speech. Traditionally, it has been manifested in Chicago in Bughouse Square, "the people's park," where free speech is regularly exercised from soapboxes by lunatics and left-wingers. (Once, briefly, during Chicago's blackest police state days in the 1960s, Mayor Daley closed it down.) It lives in the Chicago blues ("Goin' to Chicago / Sorry that I can't take you"). Barhopping in Chicago, you can still hear legendary bluesmen like the great Junior Wells wail in thirty or forty bars for a two-dollar cover on almost any night. The oral tradition has been respected by Chicago's radio and television talkers: Studs Terkel, Phil Donahue, Ollie the Dragon, and Dave Garroway. It can be detected in the way that old University of Chicago students say they passed on to new students phrases like "Peace, pure and simple" and kept Robert Hutchins's thoughts rebounding off each other's lips.

By one student's estimate, there are "maybe fifty thousand" versions of Severn Darden's Rockefeller Chapel escapade. University of Chicago graduates of all ages know it as "the legendary legend."

Once the Rockefeller Chapel had been open all night long. When it became apparent to Chancellor Hutchins that "more souls were being conceived there than saved," he ordered a cutback on the hours of prayer. Its religious services were nondenominational. Its architecture and atmosphere remained Gothic. Severn Darden had become familiar with the layout on a previous occasion, when he climbed into the bell tower and set off a surprise concert on the carillon.

He entered the Rockefeller Chapel one autumn day in 1950, as the night watchman was closing up. "As he walked along the open part of the arches, I ran to the closed part," Severn says. "I followed him that way all around the oblong and unlocked the back door that he had just locked."

At midnight, he returned to the chapel, dressed in his cape and accompanied by the young lady he wished to serenade. He played Bach's cantata "Ich Habe Genug" for her on the organ, which, "of course, I don't play."

When the campus police arrived with their flashlights, they spotted the cape flapping through the arches, under a flying buttress and across the nave. In the apse, the perpetrator threw himself spread-eagled on the spot where a denominational chapel would have an altar, and began screaming, "Sanctuary!"

Under cover of his echo, he vanished through the unlocked back door. His famous escape route led to the women's dormitory, his favorite hideaway.

At sixty, Severn Darden regards himself as "a mole in the communications structure." Enigmatic blue eyes dominate his face despite the reddish hair and glasses. He bears a striking resemblance to the portraits that survive of Socrates.

The Chicago poet Paul Carroll once praised him as "the only American comic of the first rank who incorporates the wit, the scholarly, wry, outrageous and scurrilous puns of James Joyce." His translations of the darkly humorous German poems of Christian Morgenstern have been favorably compared to those of the Austrian-born Jewish-American novelist Lore Segal and the American poet W. D. Snodgrass. Shakespearean verses, Catalonian road directions, and Eskimo fish recipes sit comfortably on his tongue. But frequently, say, near a table setting that has no linen napkins, he says nothing, and twisting it into the shape of a pastry tube, exactly as he did in college, he chews his handkerchief.

What circumstances in 1950 had unleashed the desperation of Quasimodo? Why had a well-read, well-dressed fellow like himself screamed for sanctuary?

"It was just too hard. There were these veterans, these guys from Korea, and if they disagreed with you it was very scary," he says. "They'd spent three years in foxholes deciding they wanted to be physicists. And work for the government. And *nobody* was going to get in their way. That attitude wasn't only in the classrooms. A lot of serious big-money poker games were going on among the undergrads. I was certainly surprised. These were big brains. They stood apart. I thought you weren't *supposed* to have pastimes. Unless it was chess. It was a different atmosphere than you would have found, say, in Oxford in 1910, with G. E. Moore and Wittgenstein."

Severn Darden left the campus in 1951, the same year Robert Hutchins resigned: "Mr. Hutchins heard that I was leaving first."

Their sole meeting took place in a hospital elevator: "I had a friend in the hospital. Mononucleosis. She was in quarantine a long time. I had once worked in the hospital as an orderly. I was a frequent visitor on the seventh floor. I used to steal a white coat, a mask, and a stethoscope. But underneath I was dressed as a Viennese psychiatrist. I wore a Brooks Brothers jacket. Wing collar. Carried an umbrella. I had studied fencing in boarding school. The elevator stopped. I drew my umbrella and jumped in, parrying and making shrieking sounds. The elevator closed. There in the corner was Mr. Hutchins. I was only eighteen. And we smiled at each other without admitting that that was what we were doing."

Eased out of the chancellorship, he later implied, by a board of trustees ready for a more conventional chief, Hutchins went west to Santa Barbara, California, to head the Fund for the Republic, an offshoot of the Ford Foundation that funded groups concerned with civil liberties and rights. His administrative associates suspect that he decided to dispense money because he was tired of raising it, although funding liberals seemed an anticlimactic ending to his great career. He did not enter the ranks of professional humorists until 1969, long after his student Severn Darden, upon the publication of *Zuckerkandl!*, a "remorseless dissertation" on an obscure Freudian who posited the un-Freudian theory that "the only purpose of life is to get through it," and that "there is no difference between pleasure and pain." On the radio, playing himself in a Brooklyn accent, Hutchins as the Zuckerkandl authority was an amusing performer who could garner smiles, if not big yocks. He was somewhat Benchleyesque.

Severn Darden went east, to Annandale-on-Hudson, New York, and enrolled at Bard College for six weeks but "compared to the University of Chicago, it was like grade school," he says. He went down to New Orleans, where, by "sheer accident," he got his first job as an actor. In 1952, the actress Peggy Pope was touring there in *Mr. Roberts*, when she met him for the first time at a party: "Would you care to go for a run over the rooftops?" he asked. "He couldn't go out in the daylight because the sun bothered his skin. So he stayed out all night and roamed across rooftops around New Orleans. He had all these little paths. We went through apartments, climbed in and out of windows, up stairs, jumped across buildings. We went all over New Orleans that way. It was like a long walk. One bedroom we went through, the people were sleeping. As we were climbing out their window, one sat bolt upright and said, 'Who's that?' And he said, 'Don't wake up. It's only a dream.' "

In 1955, when he drove his second (black) Rolls-Royce to the South Side of Chicago to join The Compass Players, and to find his true calling in America's first improvisational theatre, his name still was on the dean of women's Ten Most Wanted List.

2

Tonight at 8:30:
Connections Are Made

"We were people who spent most of the time reading, not living. And then," it seemed to actor Jerry Cunliffe ('53), a University of Chicago freshman at fifteen, "it turned around."

In fact, the first improvisational theatre evolved from considerable theatre activity on the University of Chicago campus. Observes its creator, David Shepherd: "Compass wasn't born on the half-shell, naked."

"It didn't happen overnight," says Paul Sills, its first director. "Compass was years in the making. We were in each other's company a long time."

A vanguard theatre does not ordinarily emerge from the theatre department of an American university. In fact, lack of official involvement was one of the unique features of the University of Chicago theatre scene and one of the key factors in the success of the Compass in a bar on Fifty-fifth Street. There are different and more inhibiting rules of decorum set forth by a faculty adviser than a state liquor commission. "A theatre department usually presents an academic, or sexual, or political profile to the university community," points out David Shepherd, "and excludes it too."

It may be that the powerful surge of energy toward the theatre began in the intellectual climate of the University of Chicago because it was one of the few outlets for expressing creativity, excitement, physicality, and postadolescent sexual drive.

"We were theoretical and academic, reading all the original writers and having discussions about the great ideas of the great authors and thinkers," reflects Joan Wile. "But we never had anything where we could *do* anything. There were no hands-on courses within the college curriculum. We had no outlet to express ourselves."

Wryly, it is said that "Chancellor Hutchins cooperated with two professional schools, Law and Divinity, and then only reluctantly." The Chicago College Plan had been created to shield undergraduates from the premature pressures of specialization. Hutchins had waged a long civil war with his upper university faculties to keep his college program pure. He had also deplored the "multiplication of trivial courses in cosmetology, fishing, and tap dancing, which swell the catalogues of great American universities." He had been horrified when *Life* magazine ran an effusive article about a college course for clowns. Thus, on the grounds that it was not a vocational school, the University of Chicago college included no applied or practical courses such as creative writing, etching, or modern dance.

The closest thing to a dramatics course at the University of Chicago was Davis Edwards's interpretive reading in the school of divinity. Edwards taught acting in the guise of sermons, and would-be "dramat" students flocked to the class. The University of Chicago was almost unique among large American universities in having no drama or speech department. There was no University of Chicago Drama School. The University Theatre was considered an extension of University of Chicago ideals and standards in the humanities, a literary theatre whose director was hired through the student activities office on a seasonal basis, the way another college would have hired a football coach. In the years leading to the formation of the Compass, three men—George Blair, Otis Imbodin, and Marvin Phillips—officially held the post. They, in turn, appointed directors to supervise main-stage productions of classics like *Oedipus Rex* and *Antigone* in Mandel Hall. Less imposing entertainments were booked into smaller university theatre spaces, like the one-hundred-seat Mitchell Towers and the large echoey main ballroom of the student recreational facility, Ida Noyes Hall.

For a visionary young director like Paul Sills ('50), there were advantages to using the University Theatre as a base. Not least was a devoted audience that included Nobel Prize winners who might enjoy the work. But there seemed no likelihood of changing the bland policies of University Theatre or of a renegade eventually running it.

As an English graduate student and part-time faculty member, Marvin Peisner ('50) was hired to run the University Theatre in the summer of

1951 until a replacement could be found for George Blair, whose reign was fraught with conflicts with the students and who was unable to fulfill his term. Peisner had been active in the University Theatre from the time he entered college, at fourteen. During his tenure, more contemporary plays than usual appeared on the main stage, for example, *Winterset*; *Blithe Spirit*; *Ah, Wilderness!*; and *Death Takes a Holiday*. In the Mitchell Towers, Peisner also initiated a chamber theatre series of readings from the works of modern literary masters like T. S. Eliot and Virginia Woolf. But although his administration stretched on well into the year, his was never intended as any but a temporary assignment. Peisner had been a child actor in the flourishing Detroit radio market, playing regularly in such serials as "The Lone Ranger," "The Green Hornet," "Challenge of the Yukon," and "The Hermit's Cave." ("I usually played weird kids or old, old men," he says.) With these credits, he supported himself as a student by taking professional acting jobs in the Loop. Moreover, he was simultaneously writing his master's thesis on "The Wit and Wisdom of Henry James," and his faculty adviser, the James scholar James Napier Wilk, "gave me hell." Peisner recalls, " 'If you dropped this goddamn theatre work,' he'd tell me, 'you'd get straight A's.' "

Consider the prospects at the University of Chicago for a director like Sills: since there was no University of Chicago Drama School, there was no graduate credit given for theatre work. Since there were no voice and speech or scene study classes to teach, there was no young director invited to join the faculty. He was a Young Turk without tenure, and Chicago was not a theatre town. In New York, the trailblazing little theatre movement was acquiring the name "off-Broadway." If the visionary young director wanted to revolutionize the theatre in Chicago, he had to improvise.

The available casting recruits were student actors who did not attend an acting (or probably any other) class. A student with rehearsal time who could somehow also act the classics would be cast even in main-stage productions instead of an imported star.

Arriving on campus in the late forties, Edward Asner ('51) and Asner's idol, Fritz Weaver ('51), were the rival classic actors. A University of Chicago theatre ditty during George Blair's term was: "This is the cast of *Antigone* / The home of the thespian air, / Where Asner speaks only to Weaver / And Weaver speaks only to Blair." Students interested in a particular play might also try out for the occasional part. (In a 1948 production of *Murder in the Cathedral*, Severn Darden played one of the

Temptors. In *Antigone*, Susan Sontag played Ismene.) Directors sometimes advertised for other actors in the neighborhood papers or posted a notice on the dead tree in front of the Woodworth Book Store. The University of Chicago campus was hardly the place for would-be showfolk. In this snobby atmosphere, even nearby Northwestern University, with its prestigious drama department, was considered a trade school.

Of the considerable numbers of actors who emerged from the University of Chicago in the early fifties, few dreamed beforehand that show business would consume their lives.

Until Paul Sills "thrust" her onstage as Grusha in Brecht's *The Caucasian Chalk Circle*, Zohra Lampert ('52) thought, "I might want to become something scholarly. A librarian. Not an actor."

The late actor Anthony ("Tony") Holland ('50) described his conversion from an art historian this way: "I was in my early twenties. I was married and getting my master's in art history and already teaching at the University of Chicago. I went to a convention in Philadelphia for art historians. They were all reading their papers. I realized that this was what academic life was about, and I was appalled. I remember coming back from Philadelphia thinking, 'God, there's got to be more to life than this.' When I got back to Chicago, I just threw myself into the theatre."

Joyce Piven ('53), now the coartistic director of the Piven Theatre and Workshop, had always wanted to be a dancer, but "I was terribly torn," she says. "I decided to go to the University of Chicago and walked right into this group of people that changed the face of the American theatre. It was not your ordinary college crowd sitting around at Jimmy's or Steinway's Drugstore discussing 'Is theatre really dead?' "

Severn Darden ('52) remembers Jimmy's as the kind of place where "women stood up on tables and sang *La Bohème*." Officially, it was called the Woodlawn Tap, one of at least six neighborhood bars that flourished on or around Fifty-fifth Street. There, particularly, and at Steinway's Drugstore ("the morning place"), discussion groups or "cadres" formed and specialists in various intellectual obsessions held forth at separate tables.

The Kant table, the Hegel table, the quantum physics table, the Communist table, and the science fiction table persist in many student memories. But even those passions were upstaged by that of the theatre table. Aaron Asher ('52), the publisher of Grove Weidenfeld, found himself well sated with stage talk after a couple of mugs with his theatrical friends, but, "They could go on all night," he says. "They could talk for hours."

Some student onlookers found them frivolous. "A lot of people sit around in bars and coffee shops dreaming up a theatre," Joyce Piven reflects. "But how many actually do it?"

The first student-initiated theatre group on campus, Tonight at 8:30, had blossomed late in 1950, after differences with George Blair had reached a crescendo and a small ad for "people interested in one-act plays" was posted by a graduate student, Renaldo U. Anselmo, in the student newspaper, the Chicago *Maroon*. Several rebels, including student dropout Mike Nichols, turned out with a desire to stage plays of their own choosing at Ida Noyes Hall.

Omar Shapli, the aspiring Egyptologist from New York's Scarsdale High School, had hung around the Institute for Oriental Studies just long enough to change his mind about becoming an Egyptologist. As a student-at-large with vague theatrical ambitions, he signed on to direct a one-act play for the opening show on a triple bill with Alice Snyder and Anselmo, who respectively selected Tennessee Williams's *This Property Is Condemned* and Chekhov's *The Boor*. Shapli chose George Bernard Shaw's *The Man of Destiny*. In the lead part of Napoleon, he cast another student dropout then working the swing shift at the Ford auto plant and thirty years later Charlton Heston's successor as president of the Screen Actors Guild, Edward Asner, a true union man.

Asner had entered the University of Chicago in 1947 and dropped out the following year. His parents were immigrant Jews who had become successful in the junk business in Kansas City. They cut off his funds during his second Christmas vacation upon learning of his romance with a Gentile, an actress at University Theatre and the daughter of a famous anthropologist. A succession of blue-collar jobs financed Asner's life as one of the university's leading actors. He joined up with the rebels soon after George Blair publicly accused him of sabotaging *Antigone* by shouting his lines. (Bulldozing the actors had become a common motif at University Theatre under Blair's regime. "I had a fight with the authorities there too," recalled Tony Holland. "I wouldn't take a curtain call. I figured, why should I hang around for a curtain call? I'm on as The Watchman in *Agamemnon*. They considered me temperamental, so they blackballed me.")

Perhaps it is testimony to his versatility that Asner is remembered by other student actors as "a sweet Jewish boy from Kansas City" as well as "a powerful man who walked as if he expected to leave footprints." Holland observed that even as a young man, "He looked old enough to play all the *zayda* parts."

In Shapli's rendition of *Androcles and the Lion*, his next directorial assignment at Tonight at 8:30 the following spring, Mike Nichols played The Emperor. The curtain raiser that evening was Yeats's *Purgatory*, in which Nichols, simultaneously making his debut as a director, cast Asner as his leading man.

"Cold," "hungry," "insecure," "ambitious," "insufferable," and "brilliantly witty" are the characteristics most frequently attributed to the young Mike Nichols. "Not too many people got along warmly with Mike," says Shapli. "He had an edge about him that put people off." Another acquaintance describes Nichols's manner as that of "a princeling deprived of his rightful fortune."

"There was something about Mike that was like the abused child who turns the abuse on others. He always seemed to be vying with others for power and authority," says Heyward Ehrlich, now a professor of English at Rutgers University, then a University of Chicago student whose literary expertise led Nichols to *Purgatory*. "I liked him in those days, but you had to endure him. He was a pain in the ass." At Tonight at 8:30, Ehrlich remembers himself as an occasional and "clumsy actor, sometimes miscast in comedies, usually as a junior Sidney Greenstreet or a small Orson Welles." Besides turning up unusual plays, he also played the phonograph records offstage, inventing the use of a nail-polish spot to hold the needle on a 78 rpm in the middle of a trumpet concerto, a shiny cue mark. "Mike Nichols was not Mike Nichols in those days," says Ehrlich. "He was the person he came to satirize, and he wasn't laughing at it. He felt the world had treated him so cruelly. In some ways, the theatre was his revenge."

In an interview for *Eye* magazine in the late sixties, Nichols described a world divided into two categories of people. One consisted of "the people to whom all the good things happen in the first part of their lives—the Kennedys are the world's great example of this—and then all the terrible things happen." He pictured himself in the remaining fraction, to whom "the pretty bad things happen in the first part, and then things get better, and they get better, and then they're great."

At the time of the interview, he was thirty-seven, already the winner of three of his five Tonys (for *Barefoot in the Park*, *Luv*, and *The Odd Couple*) and an Oscar (for his second film, *The Graduate*), and hailed as the most successful stage and film director in America.

And he reflected on the "only one drawback" to the category into which he fell: "that one is poisoned forever by the bad things that happened in the beginning. So if one had a choice, I think, one would choose to be the first kind. They are the lucky ones, because they get to experience an untainted good half. Otherwise, although you can fight it and overcome it and make something joyful and pleasurable out of your life, there is always poison left from before."

As Michael Igor Peschkowsky, he had arrived in America with his younger brother, Robert, on *The Bremen* in 1939, at age seven, a Jewish refugee from Nazi Berlin. Hitler had become chancellor when he was two. As was compulsory for a Jewish child in Germany, he had attended segregated schools. He knew two phrases of English, "Please don't kiss me" and "I don't speak English." A reaction to a whooping cough injection at the age of four had left him without any hair.

Nichols's father, Paul Peschkowsky, a doctor, had settled in New York the year before. He had emigrated to Germany from Russia after the Bolshevik Revolution. In Germany, he met Brigitte Landauer, the daughter of Jewish intellectuals, and she became his wife. Mike Nichols's maternal grandmother, Hedwig Lachmann Landauer, translated the libretto of *Salome* from Oscar Wilde's play for the composer Richard Strauss. His grandfather Gustav Landauer headed the German Social Democrat party, and his execution by the Nazis precipitated the family move.

In 1938, Paul Peschkowsky changed his last name to Nichols (from Nicholaiyevitch, his Russian patronymic) and set up a successful new medical practice in Manhattan, on the Upper West Side. Among his patients was the impresario Sol Hurok, who once told Mike Nichols, "You're not as funny as your father." Nichols's view of comedy as "inborn" was inspired by his father, who "could rage, but he also told very funny stories, and he used to dance for us in his underwear."

Brigitte Landauer Nichols, who had been too sick to travel, arrived in America the year after her sons, and, with a former wife of Stefan Zweig, set up a manuscript service for German writers who were also refugees.

At ten, while both his parents worked, Nichols was sent away to boarding school. In 1944, when Nichols was twelve, his father died of leukemia. As family finances grew precarious, his mother took jobs in a bakery and in bookstores. Before and after she remarried, scholarships and an assortment of part-time jobs—including one as a riding instructor at Claremont Riding Academy—made it possible for Nichols to continue his education in New York City in progressive private schools.

He graduated from high school at fifteen and applied the next year to the only three schools that accepted students without college boards: the

University of Chicago, the University of Mexico, and New York University. He chose NYU for its prime location and dropped out after one day. The next year, with thoughts of becoming a psychoanalyst like his stepfather, he enrolled with a scholarship at the University of Chicago as a premed student. His classmate, Susan Sontag, a fifteen-year-old freshman, considered him her closest friend.

In college, Nichols promptly enrolled in psychotherapy at the Chicago Institute for Psychoanalysis, since, as a student, he says, "you could get shrunk for free." Many other University of Chicago students engaged in psychotherapy, but, says Heyward Ehrlich, "Mike was the leader of the pack. In those days, it was not something one advertised. If the secret came out, you'd say, 'Excuse me, I'm late for my therapist,' and that was the end of it. Not for Mike. He was very outspoken about it. Mike's therapy was at the top of his conversation. He publicized his handicap. He shook his tin cup."

He slept eighteen hours a day, struggled through his first year's comprehensives, and dropped out in the middle of his second year to join the ranks of "educated hoboes," in Robert Hutchins's phrase. Swept up in the excitement of hanging around at Steinway's and Jimmy's, he began to realize that, "Jesus, the world is full of possibilities."

In this intellectually rigorous company, he showed excellence at parlor games like Famous Last Lines and Botticelli and was "extremely clever in conversation, a person brilliant to talk to," says Ehrlich. "He was also extraordinarily young."

Nichols was also acknowledged by Ehrlich as "indigent" and by his rooming house mate, Aaron Asher, as "scrambling" then. Nichols took jobs he regarded as "weird." He was night manager in a nursery. He drove a delivery truck for the post office during one Christmas season and "never once delivered a package," he recalls. "I could never find the address." He stuffed envelopes for Sears. Sometimes the only way he could eat was by walking through the cafeteria line backward or stealing leftovers from abandoned plates.

Ehrlich remembers Mike Nichols living "in some godforsaken co-op, torn and tormented by pictures of himself as he might be if he was who he thought he was. He really thought the world had fucked him over. He had really gone through it. Mike had better ideas about himself, I guess because his family was of previous consequence. They had made money, lost money. He had been through several identities. He had lost his hair. He was bleeding on the inside and trying not to show it."

Mike Nichols, who was observed by one friend as "a man who would go into a White Castle and send back the hamburger," was forced by his finances to wear a cheap ratty wig. Eating the leftovers off the tables at the University of Chicago coffee shop, he had become friendly with one of the busboys, Paul Sills.

Sills was twenty-three, four years older than Nichols, and a native Chicagoan. Sills's family background, like his experience and ambitions in the theatre, were decidedly more Bohemian. "I'm not a Broadway guy," he says. "I'm a community theatre guy."

Sills had not shown up at the meeting at which Tonight at 8:30 convened. In fact, as a student actor at University Theatre, he had only played a few parts. He remembers enjoying his first appearance in George Blair's production of *Richard II*. As Faust in a one-act play by Elder Olson called *Faust: A Mask*, which Sills neglects to mention, Omar Shapli recalls that Sills was "pretty awful. Not good." It was not by Sills the player, however, but by Sills the director that all the others at Tonight at 8:30 were quickly eclipsed.

If it is true, as Marvin Peisner says, that "being experimental is part of the meaning of the word 'Chicago,'" then Paul Sills was, and is, the definitive Chicago director. Actors have variously described him as "uncorruptible," a "saint," a "purist," a "genius," a "Stalinist," a "bully," and an "inarticulate megalomaniac."

Toward actors, he is cited as having "the lion tamer's attitude," subduing them, one player says, with "a combination of praise and abuse." Nevertheless, "In their personal pantheons, many actors have a place for Sills," says Shapli. "He represents integrity." The actor Richard Libertini once nicknamed him the "Grotowski of Comedy."

"The most striking thing about Paul is that he doesn't stratify people," Mike Nichols observes. "He takes everyone equally seriously." "That was his genius," says Zohra Lampert. "It's a very unusual quality. Most people will only support what they like in others. He always saw the originality in people, even if he didn't like them."

Sills thus turned the shortage of student actors and the plethora of dropouts to his advantage. He ran weekly workshops, whose continuity enabled him to train the workshoppers to operate as a company with a common terminology and process. In his workshops, it was not necessary to have prior stage training. In fact, it appeared to one participant that "he threw out all assumptions and started from scratch."

In one workshop session, Zohra Lampert, Mike Nichols, and Sills improvised an adaptation of Thomas Mann's *The Magic Mountain*. Sills played the doctor, and Lampert and Nichols played the dying tubercular patients. The scene, which Marvin Peisner still remembers as "extremely moving," was performed in gibberish.

Even in 1950, at the fledgling phase of his career, Sills was practiced in providing the greenest of actors with a key to unlocking their gifts through a body of improvisational exercises—games—he had learned as a child from his mother, Viola Spolin, who invented them. Sills says of these games, "I used them as a group formation device, as a way of working to make an acting company. To get the actors to play together, to relax in each other's company. Wherever I have worked, they're integral, Viola's games."

3

The High Priestess

Viola Spolin has reigned as the "High Priestess of Improvisation" for fifty years. She is the author of the seminal, Biblical words on the matter, *Improvisation for the Theater*, and the creator of more than 200 amazing exercises called "theater games." At 83, her finger dexterity is wanting. Her eyes light up over an easy "foursie" in a practice hand of jacks. She says, "My games are more than just a bunch of exercises. Used properly, they are a learning system which can reach the intuitive power of the individual and release genius."

She began inventing them during the Depression, in Chicago, as tools to teach creative dramatics to ghetto children from the West Side streets. Originally, she called these exercises "problems." Only shortly before the publication of her book in 1963 were they bestowed with the uncapitalized, uncopyrighted title she calls "Spolin games." "Improvisation isn't new, for god's sakes," she says. "The commedia dell'arte improvised. The socialist political theatres in Europe improvised. They didn't *read* it anywhere. They were working on what was happening in the streets."

Theater games have provided the technical and philosophical under-pinning for a swarm of improvisational acting ensembles: the Compass, The Committee, The Convention, The Premise, The Proposition, The First Amendment, The Second City, The Third Ear, and The Fourth Wall. These companies (and hundreds more throughout the nation) have propagated a vast body of original theatre pieces, scenes and sketches, and legions of actors who improvise.

Spolin's collaborations with her son and the improvising actors of the

Compass, The Second City, Story Theatre, and Sills and Company are the main conduit between the professional theatre and Spolin's work. Sills says, "She's the only one who can do it, really. I don't come up with games. I don't revise her exercises, or fool around with them, or twist 'em, or use 'em to get funny scenes." Sills and Spolin refer to those who do so as "revisionists."

Yet Spolin's techniques have influenced avant-garde, experimental, and political theatres, comedy writers, stand-up comedians and comedy teams, Broadway, off-Broadway, Hollywood, network television, and advertising. The San Francisco Mime Troupe, the Open Theatre, El Teatro Campesino, SCTV Network, Fridays, Saturday Night Live, the Ace Trucking Company, War Babies, Chicago City Limits, Nashville, A Chorus Line, Robert Klein, Shelley Berman, David Steinberg, Stiller and Meara, Cheech and Chong, Mork & Mindy, the Blue Nun Winery, the manufacturers of the Excedrin headache remedy are all indebted to theater games.

Since its publication by Northwestern University Press, some 95,000 hardback copies of Improvisation for the Theater have been published in fourteen printings. It is sold throughout the world and has been translated into German, Dutch, and Danish. It exists in paperback in Portuguese. At Larry Edmunds Cinema and Theatre Bookshop on Hollywood Boulevard, it outsells Stanislavsky's Building a Character by more than two to one. It begins, "Everyone can act. Everyone can improvise."

Theater games are taught by this book in nursery schools, group therapies, drama schools, and universities. They are popular as "Violas" in Brazil. In Chicago, the birthplace of both the improvisational theatre and Viola Spolin, "improv" workshops are run in such profusion as to almost compose a cottage industry. Improvisations have been played in the Bellevue psychiatric ward and in prisons. In 1975, CEMREL, a government-funded educational think-tank in St. Louis, published the Theater Game File by Viola Spolin as a teaching aid, in a box, with each exercise printed on an index card, recipe-style.* Under Spolin's supervision, the entire production team of television's Rhoda was invited by its star, Valerie Harper, to learn theater games.

Still a few points shy of a high school diploma, Spolin has received an honorary doctorate from Eastern Michigan University, the first university in America to give credit for the pursuit of theater games. Although she eschews any opinions on the topic, the High Priestess has been heard to say, "I've always known this stuff about the right brain."

---

* It was reprinted by Northwestern University Press in 1989.

The left brain, the province of the intellect, the mind, is literal, sedimentary, logical, premeditated, censoring. Metaphoric, metamorphic, mystical, spontaneous and unguarded, the province of intuition, genius, is the right brain.

Both Spolin and Stanislavsky employ improvisation as a vacuum cleaner for the left brain of the actor. Both teach processes of what is called "the secondary concentration" to disconcert and free the actor from the intellect, the monkey, the predictable, the script, the word.

As used in Stanislavsky's Method, improvisation is analytical, only a dissecting tool to find life between the lines in the performance of a written play. A Method improvisation is based upon a situation or a premise: a divorced masseuse and an asthmatic Hershey bar salesman want to rent the same apartment. The characters obviously have a conflict. They also have a prior life. Each actor brings to the scene a lot of psychological baggage (memory and motivation), stored where neither the other actor nor the audience can see it, in their "inner lives," their heads. Ad-libbing, acting out the situation in their own words, the actors can maneuver their characters into a murder, a marriage, or a massage, a melodrama, a love story, or a comedy, but with so much left-brain paraphernalia that their slates have already been cluttered, their energies introverted, their minds engaged. They will always be separately occupied with the exposition of a story. Melody not harmony. A writing exercise.

Spolin's exercises were originated to assist a script, and it was in that context that they were first used by Sills. But they have a life of their own. "True" improvisation is the state of not knowing. To Spolin, playwriting is a strategy for "planning how." No content or situation is necessary in a "true" improvisation. Information and content come out of the playing. Playing will produce the play.

Theater games are executed without rehearsal, without props, without a script or situation, in front of spectators, on an empty stage.

The players observe a structure based on one or more suggestions as to *where* (a cemetery), or with *whom* (two sailors), or from *what* activity (having a picnic), object (a cuckoo clock), or topic of conversation (toxic waste) the improvisation will emerge.

The synthesizing mechanism for each game is the *Point Of Concentration* (*"POC"*) or *Focus,** a changing, moving point that players follow

---

*POC is the term used in the first twelve editions of *Improvisation for the Theater*. Spolin now prefers *Focus*. Sills and Spolin sometimes refer to *Focus* as "the meditation." Spolin also calls it "the ball," the "anchor for the mind," and the "plumb-bob into the x-area." *Focus* is called a *pokey* in Brazil.

together as jazz musicians follow the bass line or baseball players follow the ball.

The *Focus* of the game Conversation with Involvement, for example, is on two or more players continuing a conversation while eating an invisible meal.

Four players enter the stage and are given a topic of discussion. The rule is that they must talk about the topic (jogging) and not about the food. They pull chairs around an invisible table. Player A's gestures are those of someone carving turkey. He forks some turkey onto the plate extended by Player B, who hands it to Player C. From Player C's first bite, we see he has the drumstick. Player D is uncorking and pouring wine. Player C wipes greasy fingers on his napkin. He lifts his wineglass in a formal gesture that is mirrored by Players A and B and finally by the pouring Player D. Wine is sniffed, sipped, swallowed. Player A begins to butter bread. Player B is bumped while pouring gravy. Player B wipes gravy off his sleeve. Player A tosses a muffin to Player D, but it rolls off the table. The invisible muffin is retrieved under the invisible table by the player holding the invisible drumstick, Player C.

While all this is going on, the players are engrossed in the topic of discussion, jogging:

> "I jog up to seven and a half miles a day."
> "That sounds exhausting. How do you do it?"
> "I wear good jogging shoes."
> "What kind? Puma?"
> "My podiatrist recommends Adidas."
> "I wear earphones to relieve the boredom."
> "I was mugged once jogging."
> "Why didn't you run?"
> "I did run. The mugger was wearing Adidas."
> "My doorman jogs with a Dalmatian."
> "I wear Keds."

Should the concentration of the players wander, *Focus* is reinforced by a group leader or an offstage player using a technique called *sidecoaching*, which may continue (*"Keep up the conversation!"*) as needed (*"Pass the salt!"*) throughout the game (*"Keep talking!"*) without interrupting the play (*"Eat!"*).

Personality cannot be written. The way an actor fills a stage—walks, talks, winks, whistles, sings, smiles, laughs, listens to another actor—is information a writer can't supply.

Improvisation, according to Spolin, is "showing not telling." It is basically nonverbal. It does not emerge from the logical sequence of language, only from the sequence in which objects, the environment, characters, relationships, points of view, and personalities appear out of spontaneous interplay. The art consists purely of players tossing the ball to each other, communicating the invisible, sharing and transforming empty space.

There are 222 published games, including games of hearing, smelling, moving, touching, singing, storytelling, and memory, games to create an environment, a climate, a character, or a relationship, games in gibberish, games with sound effects, games with a blindfold, games in slow motion, games in no-motion, games for the eyeballs, games for the feet.

In Spolin's teaching system, 222 aspects of stagecraft are broken down into simple game language, such as Who, What, Where, and into separate, manageable parts. Each game pinpoints another outlet off the mainstream where intuition flows—not through the individual mind or ego but through human connections in physical space.

Since each game presents an acting problem with infinite solutions, there is no "right" way to play a theatre game. So the *sidecoach*, whose job, no less than the players, is to keep following the *focus*, unlike a director, has no preconceptions of an outcome in his or her head. At the spectator level, an evaluation of the playing may only be made in terms of "Did the players follow the rules?" "Was the *focus* observed?" and "Was the game played?"

Clapping and booing are extreme examples of the "approval-disapproval" syndrome Spolin shuns as authoritarian. (She considers it a minor frailty of her system that "sometimes they clap anyway.") In the nonjudgmental atmosphere required of a theater-games workshop, where group focus is always on the problem and never on the person, stage fright, inhibitions, exhibitions, mannerisms, and personal preoccupations ("What do I do now?" "How am I doing?" "This is silly." "Aren't I great?") subside and dissipate. Every aspect of the human instrument is gradually tuned into heightened consciousness—intuition—through the revelations of the games.

"People don't play, they behave" was supposedly Lee Strasberg's criticism of Spolin's theater games, as if the actor's only objective were to behave like other people, realistically. Spolin's insight is that anybody playing himself in the moment, following the ball, can learn to express himself like an actor, with intensified reality.

Situational improvisation, with its emphasis on emotional reality and conflict, has attracted the serious dramatic actor and produced a small body of heavy psychological material, such as the films of John Cassavetes, usually featuring language that is labored, repetitive, and dull. (A line of dialogue expresses a theatrical moment, as a note expresses a musical one. If the moment is blocked by conflict, the new moment, or note, or line of dialogue cannot evolve without playwriting or input from the left brain.) Improvised also was Marlon Brando's "butter" scene in Bertolucci's *Last Tango in Paris* and the strange encounters played in a bathtub and in a bonnet in Arthur Penn's *The Missouri Breaks*. Brando has stretched the possibilities of Method improvisation more than any other actor. He takes astounding risks to "not know" his lines. Using the Method, however, even Brando can only improvise a solo: he plays a one-man game.

Theater games, with their built-in ingredient of spontaneity and surprise, produce extroverted material, more elliptical observations, less Sturm und Drang, a funnier report of things. People lighten up when playing theater games.

Typically, the form draws people from the far-out corners of other fields and transforms them into actors. Paul Sills, who has trained dozens of ensembles, both professional and amateur, explains: "It's a group process. So you have these nuts. And somehow they're accepted too. Pretty soon all their loony acting out begins to disappear. Because somehow they're accepted. In fact it's necessary to have madmen and oddballs and people who can't do it in the group."

Actors who improvise experience the practice as a high, a form of bliss. Alan Alda calls it "a mental music that's played . . . that everyone shares." Mike Nichols describes it like this: "once in a while you would literally be possessed and speak languages you didn't speak . . . I don't mean to sound mystical, but such things did happen. Like doing twenty minutes of iambic pentameter that we had not thought of but just came pouring out. That was thrilling, and you'd be drained and amazed afterward, and you'd have a sense of your possibilities."

Richard ("Dick") Schaal has been called "one of the purest" practitioners of Spolin's work. (Valerie Harper, his former wife, extends the compliment. "If he's playing an electrician, you can really see his wires," she says. "There's nothing he can't do with space.") Schaal describes the difference between improvising and acting with a script as "the difference between writing a poem and working in the coal mines. Are you gonna talk about the function of theater games? I mean, they're spiritual, they're infinite, they're everything."

There were still horse-drawn fire engines in Chicago when Viola Spolin as a child "played intensely" on an empty street. Playground games, street games, traditional games (like tag), and esoteric games (like Mother, Mother, the Teakettle's Boiling) were practiced all day long by the ringleader of the Northwest Side neighborhood, composed, she recalls, of "first-generation Americans. Intellectuals. Professionals. Bohemians." At the box office of her street theatre, she charged a penny, or ten pins. She excelled at basketball and baseball and remembers "running . . . running," wearing long shorts they called plus fours. "I was a very *physical* girl," she says. "I was a player. I played and played."

At eleven, Paul Sand appeared in whiteface in a Spolin production of *The Clown That Ran Away*. Sand was trained so early to regard the stage as play space that as an adult actor, he says, "I never knew I had technique." He describes his mentor as "so feminine. A long-time-ago kind of feminine. How can I say it? Feminine in an ancient way."

At eighteen, she enrolled at the Recreational Training School run at Chicago's Hull House by Neva Boyd, later the author of *Play: A Unique Discipline*, and a revered Northwestern University sociologist. In Boyd's classes, Spolin remembers long physical workouts in large spaces: "We'd run for hours. We did Kentucky running steps. We learned all kinds of dances, starting with the pavan. I knew practically every folk dance in the whole world. I can still call squares: 'Ladies twirl, gents go home, 'round you go, ladies go home, everybody twirl.' We had to know everything about every kind of game, including table games. We learned to set up a game room. We used to go to camp for two weeks. We ran track, we shot arrows, we threw discus, we swam, we boxed. Nothing was *theory*. We *did* everything."

Poor grades had kept her out of the high school dramatics club: "Nobody ever bugged me about report cards. I signed ninety percent of 'em myself." As a Settlement House girls worker, she flourished: "I knew more games than anyone else in my class."

Her origins are Russian-Jewish. Her father, Constantin Belachakovsky, supposedly arrived in America carrying a copy of *On Liberty* by John Stuart Mill. Finding the Russian name unpronounceable, the immigration officer saw the book and directed Belachakovsky to "make it Mills." Make Mills became a Chicago police lieutenant and was assigned to head the Red Squad, the unit that scouted local radical groups. Of six children, Viola was number five. Her brother George was an Illinois state senator. The newspaperman was brother Ted. All of the Mills sisters were independent and creative women. None shared their father's politics. Irene became a social worker, Pauline a buyer in the Orient. The respected movement teacher, now Beatrice Lees, the former Baroness von Stronsdorf, is Viola's younger sister, Pinky Mills.

There was no formal theatre in her background ("I'm a great reader," says Viola, "but I never read two theatre books in my life"). Throughout Viola's young womanhood, however, a favorite Saturday night pastime of her clan was an intense and elaborately costumed rendition of the parlor game charades.

At nineteen, Viola married Wilmer Silverberg, half Irish, half Jewish, a pharmacist like his father and mother (one of Chicago's first woman pharmacists). When World War II broke out, he changed the name to Sills. Viola had two children by Wilmer, Paul and William (now a professor of mathematics at San Jose State University) and put her work aside. She did not drop charades.

Paul Mills Silverberg Sills regards improvisation as "the family business" and the Sills-Mills players as "just an ordinary family of talented and clever people from the Chicago West Side." He gets this unordinary inspiration from his mother: "It's very Eastern, very Tao: make no plans. Spontaneity. No motion: Viola's got the Taoist approach to things."

As expressed by Viola, Taoism sounds as Chinese as apple pie: "Dictatorship begins in kindergarten. It has to be gotten rid of in the schools. Approval/disapproval is outside authority determining what you should or shouldn't do. Isn't that the essence of dictatorship?" She likens her own pedagogical territory to that of "Madame What's Her Name."

Blavatsky, the Russian theosophist and mystic, was Yeats's muse. She shared Viola's view that human consciousness—the spirit—can transcend rational intelligence into a state of divine telepathy, synergy, oneness and connection with the cosmos, nature, mankind, God, and all the demons, dybbuks, metaphors, and mythologies that throb through the universal mind.

Spolin first used audience suggestion in 1939.

This hallmark technique of the modern improvisational theatre, Spolin's major contribution to the form, was inaugurated in performance at Hull House by children under fourteen years old. Their startling improvisations on subjects that concerned the Depression audience—bomb shelters and unemployment—were enthusiastically reported by the Chicago press. A 1940 headline says, "YESTERDAY'S NEWS IS TOMORROW'S PLAY."

The director of these entertainments, Viola Sills Spolin, now remarried, was a working mother, running programs in dramatics for neighborhood children at Hull House and for adults in the recreation project of President Roosevelt's WPA. Sills and his brother invariably accompanied their mother on her lecture demonstrations throughout the neighborhood. In 1938, along with other artisans and craftsmen, she had found financial and creative relief in the WPA project, to which she had been directed by her former teacher, Neva Boyd. The WPA job paid ninety dollars a month: "I tell you it was great. People were B-R-O-K-E, honey. I was so excited when I got the job, I ran around the block."

The new job had also introduced her to her new husband, Ed Spolin, whose craft on the WPA was carpentry and set design. Their combined incomes allowed Viola to rent "a darling little apartment for forty dollars a month." It was a time of great community. Ed Spolin had friends in the left-wing theatre crowd, and Viola was often seen with him in the audience and at the parties of Chicago's first and leading labor theatre, The Chicago Rep. Besides presenting agitprop and satirical entertainments to trade unions that were written by its own members (among them Studs Terkel) on such issues of the day as the right to strike and organize, the Rep company was a platform for important new plays that reflected social conditions, like Clifford Odets's *Waiting for Lefty* and Irwin Shaw's *Bury the Dead*. Their theatre had also become a home on the road for members of the Group Theatre, the dazzling group of theatre revolutionaries from New York. (Paul Sills recalls backstage handshakes as a boy with such Group Theatre luminaries as Morris Carnovsky and John Garfield.) Between their own performances, acting classes were given by Group Theatre members like Bobby Lewis and Stella Adler, who had traveled to Moscow and Paris to meet the master and learn Stanislavsky's Method firsthand. In the thirties in Chicago, Stanislavsky's Method for penetrating the creative subconscious was very much in the theatrical air.

Viola attended a Stanislavsky workshop taught by an actor she recalls as "Lew Leverett, somebody in Chicago, in the nighttime, a few times." These secondhand (and perhaps bowdlerized) exposures by Stanislavsky's disciples to his techniques have only crystallized her understanding that "their work is in the head and mine is in the space" and that "they were in the past. I believe in present time."

Of course, it was (and would continue to be) a matter of considerable controversy among his disciples as to what Stanislavsky's "true" Method was. (His complete written works were not even available in English until 1961, twenty-three years after his death.) The objective of Method work, however, is building a character, while Spolin's aim is the emergence of character as it is spontaneously manifested in the format of a game.

"On a stage, you have to be present in the moment. And that's what a game does for you," she says. "Even I didn't fully understand this when I started. But if you're not present to that ball coming, you ain't playing. Behind the bat, you can't be thinking about how you hit it last month or how you felt when you didn't hit it. You are there in the moment having to hit that ball. And you have to be in waiting for the ball to come to you. The players and the audience and the coach stand in waiting for the ball and for the outcome of the game. And that's the hard part. Nobody knows how the game is going to end. That's what they call the Buddhist thing."

Attending one of Spolin's Hull House workshops with a tape recorder and an engineer, Studs Terkel offered his radio listeners a play-by-play description of children as they improvised and remembers that "I was very taken by it. I was more than impressed."

Not all her contemporaries were admirers. Many survivors of The Chicago Rep are nonplused by Spolin's vast influence and fame, regarding the product of her exercises as "kitchen drama" ("theatre on the easiest level, the most unskilled," one former member sniffs), which indeed is the source of its strength. The Spolin theatre is not elite.

Even in its earliest stages, the accessibility of Spolin's work, and her own naïveté about business, made it fair game for profiteers. She had (and would continue to have) some bitter disappointments. After describing her system by mail to a cousin, she learned that he had taken her concept for a program she called "Instant Radio" and sold it for himself. *Life* magazine was planning a photo story on her and her Hull House children improvising in the Chicago high schools, but mysteriously (on the personal request of Henry Luce, she heard), the photo sessions were stopped and the article "fell through."

It somehow was up to her son Paul to carry her work forward. There are few such mother-son partnerships in history, unless the mother is anonymous or the son is homosexual. (For forty years, Alexandra David-Neel and her son were a partnership in searching for the true Mahayana Buddhism of Tibet. But the Lama Yongden was adopted, and Madame David-Neel outlived him.) "Paul brought my work into the world," Viola says.

4

The Great Director

In 1943, the Spolin family moved to San Francisco, where Viola joined the war effort by working in a factory as a riveter and Sills attended his first year of high school. The next year, rather than spend another year in "one of those California factories," Sills says he "wormed my way back to Chicago" to resume his interrupted scholarship studies at the Francis W. Parker School.

Tony Holland, who was also enrolled on scholarship there, described Parker as manifesting an "Isadora Duncan–like influence" and the optimistic spirit of Wilsonian democracy. At a school where one year all the students wore togas, Holland recalls his classmate's nickname as "Apollo" Sills, a teenager as handsome, popular, and athletic as he was distant, sensitive, and smart. At Parker, Sills directed a production of Jerome Chodorov and Joseph Fields's *Junior Miss*. More premonitory of his grown-up work, Holland recalled, was a student show Sills put together that made fun of the faculty.

In Chicago, Sills boarded with the family of another student, Tom De Lacey, whose father was the head violinist for the Chicago Symphony. Tony Holland found it impressive that as a high school student, Sills enjoyed such a sophisticated housing setup and such autonomy. "In Chicago, Paul didn't have a mother," Holland says.*

---

*He did have an aunt. In fact, Holland was later to study movement with Beatrice Lees, Sills's Aunt Pinky, who had developed a system of exercises for physical therapy that Holland found "marvelous." Lees, Holland observed, had "a very definite sense of mission. It was a family characteristic. Viola, Paul, and Pinky all were born pedagogues."

In 1946, Viola had moved to Los Angeles, where she built a children's theatre, the Young Actors Company, behind the Women's Club on Hollywood Boulevard and North La Brea, with the carpentry and design skills of her husband, Ed. (Among the children who were trained there were Alan Arkin and Paul Sand.)

After his high school graduation, Sills did not enter college immediately. First he sailed to China with the merchant marine. Next, after serving his stint with the army, he entered the University of Chicago on the GI Bill, at twenty, in 1948, and got his B.A. in "I can hardly remember . . . two or three years." While still in college, he married Dorothea Straus, the mother of David Michael, his only son. Heyward Ehrlich recalls that a stimulating intellectual environment was mixed with the aroma of boiling baby diapers at the Sillses' basement salon.

Even as a young man, Sills possessed an ability to set ideas and groups in motion. One friend notes that he was "a master for being a guru for a group. At a table full of people, he could really create excitement. He listened well, he talked well. Just by being in his presence, everybody got raised to a higher level. He really turned people on." Attesting to the Sills charisma, Omar Shapli recalls that "once he started a liver-for-breakfast fad."

To Sills, comedy is not supposed to be the issue when he "gives out the bat and ball." Severn Darden refers to Sills's rule to "keep away from Jewish jokes and fag jokes," not every humorist's high-minded inclination. He is praised by actor Eugene Troobnick for his "unique kind of insight and impeccable taste."

Playwrights as well as actors have credited the improvisational theatre with helping them achieve the lifelike dialogue that is the broad arrow of the contemporary style. Yet Sills seems surprised that "people really come out to do the whole business, have a smoke between the acts." For the last thirty years, Sills has directed his thoughts to pioneering forms of improvisational theatre, reaching into popular rather than literary theatre traditions, and wrestling with the mysteries of his mother's work, attempting scriptless plays. It seems to him "so old-fashioned, a regular play."

Sills is short, with a belligerent aspect and a blue-eyed, cherubic face. Except for a Celtic sweetness inherited from his paternal grandmother, Sills resembles Norman Mailer. (In 1964, in a Chicago production of Mailer's dramatic adaptation of *The Deer Park*, Sills played the part of Eitel, which Mailer in a New York workshop had attempted himself, using an Irish accent. Sills's performance, without an accent, was reported as "terrible.")

One Tonight at 8:30 actress has described Sills's as "a brilliant vision. But he had no words for it." He is still impatient with language. Words may fail to express what he wishes to see. The lucidity of his vision is evident in memories of his stage pictures as well as photographs. Sills's ensembles are without mannerism or affectation in their bearing, and, in their easy constellation, the actors share a quality of harmlessness and grace. Their visual impact is almost as great as that of the eleven-year-old actors who appear in the stills of Viola's Young Actors Company production of *The Clown That Ran Away*. The vitality and newness of his technique as a young man can only be imagined. The Chicago drama critics generally singled out his work for naturalness, energy, good-humored bawdiness, visual beauty, and wit.

The first show he directed at Tonight at 8:30, early in the winter of 1950–1951, was García Lorca's *The Shoemaker's Prodigious Wife*. About the prolific output that followed, Sills says, "Once I got started, I just kept doing it because I liked it. I was able to get a show on and get actors to work with me. That's the mark of a director. You have to at least be able to do that. In other words, I wasn't hired. I'd get an idea and the people. I'd say, 'I've got the ball and the bat. Let's play.' "

Sills's directorial debut and falling out with University Theatre occurred simultaneously the next spring, when he directed a main-stage production of John Webster's *The Duchess of Malfi*, starring Fritz Weaver as the villain Bosola, with which others on the scene suspect that George Blair was not pleased. In the snagged relationship that followed with University Theatre, Sills himself does not remember any specific watershed. "Blair wanted to light it. He was a lighting guy. I wanted to be the director. What's the difference?" Sills asks. "Everyone had arguments with everyone else. I had some arguments with Blair." As others recall it, not only was Sills's interpretation of this melodramatic Elizabethan tragedy "Brechtian," he also dropped big chunks of the text. "I cut it way down," Sills remembers. "I made the fourth act into a poem."

Sills was not invited back to direct at University Theatre during Blair's regime, creating a further rift between Tonight at 8:30 and the force that ran the main stage. The plays Sills directed during the rest of 1951 (which included a funny and bawdy rendition of Arthur Schnitzler's *Rounddance* and *Madonna Dianora*, a one-act play by Hugo von Hofmannstahl) took place under the aegis of Tonight at 8:30 in the third-floor ballroom of Ida Noyes Hall. The walls of his theatre (which was otherwise bare of theatrical equipment) were covered by murals Tony Holland remembered as "post–pre-Raphaelite" nature scenes. "Now they have little black box theatres,"

Sills remarks. "They build them in the drama schools." He and his group set up portable stages and brought in portable lights. "It was nice that we had to build our own," he says. "If we couldn't get on the main stage, we could at least do this."

By the fall of 1951, Sills had fallen under the spell of the German playwright Bertolt Brecht. Omar Shapli remembers Sills in Jimmy's waving a copy of the first American publication (in *Accent* magazine) of Brecht's manifesto, A *Little Organon for the Theatre*, "as if he had just invented it."

Sills says, "I got Brecht out of Eric Bentley. He turned our generation on to Brecht. In *The Playwright as Thinker*, he introduced Brecht and Pirandello and so on and explained why these people were smart."

Omar Shapli points out that Sills's interest in Brecht was "aesthetic, not political, if that can be imagined. He was really more Violan than 'Brechtian.'"

Shapli's observation is true, although Brecht's aesthetics detached from his politics can be imagined easily. Brecht himself, after all, was an anomaly. As a political animal, he was a Communist. As a person of background and culture, he was a bourgeois. As a man of the theatre, he was a complete iconoclast. Viola Spolin is also an anomaly: a Russian-Jewish policeman's daughter, a missionary Taoist, as Chinese as ghetto-baked apple pie.

It seems obvious that even without sharing his political ideology, Sills would embrace Brecht's ideas for making the theatre reflective of real political conditions and accessible to people who might be interested in changing them. Sills's own theatrical legacy (reinforced by his Hutchins training) combined an attraction to simple storytelling as well as to the classics, a belief in "people's theatre," and a sympathy for left-wing political attitudes. Sills would easily be drawn to Brecht's narrative approach to drama, his love of experiment, his love of fantastic premises and fables, and his penchant for remaking classical theatrical forms. Brecht was also anti-Stanislavskian, antipsychological, and nonsubjective. Thus, in several primary ways, Viola is not incompatible with Brecht.

Brecht's theories on an "epic" theatre were conceived as an antidote to the excesses of romantic German theatre. "In an age when man should not withdraw into himself, but fight his enemy," the workers' political theatre Brecht espoused was to awaken not baroque emotion but thought. As a playwright, he made it his mission to restore plot and narrative. To this end—storytelling—he wrote short, episodic scenes.

Brecht's "narrative" mode, as Bentley pointed out, is quite distinct from a "dramatic" one, which has a single Aristotelian focus and moves inevitably to an emotional catharsis. Bentley compared a Brechtian play to a Breughel painting, which "offers no solace to the eye that seeks swift strong sensation." Like the painter, Bentley said, Brecht "invites the eye to linger on this detail or that. Suspense has been reduced to a minimum." Bentley found Brecht's outlook discordant with Aristotle's theory of tragedy, "totally untragic." Finding more parallels between Brecht and Aristophanes, the master of Greek comedy, Bentley said, "To my mind, Brecht's theory of theatre *is* a theory of comedy."

To jolt awareness in place of tugging heartstrings, Brecht also set out to establish a new relationship between the actor and the audience. In "Notes on Stanislavsky," Brecht explained that to realize a didactic or thought-inducing theatre, the actor must be "relieved" of his traditional task of transforming himself into the character and the spectator relieved of his traditional "hypnotic state," in which the actor is perceived as his part. To accomplish this transformation of habit, he observed that "a definite distance between the actor and the role had to be built into the manner of playing." In contrast to the Stanislavskian actor, the ideal Brechtian actor would remain neutral to sentiment and pathos. To prevent getting carried away, he would "alienate" himself from his personal emotions and apply a writer's critical sensibility to the play. As Bentley points out, "distancing" is a technique of comedy.

Finally, in lieu of the usual methods of holding the audience, Brecht advocated attention-getting devices like placards, radio announcements, songs and music, and lantern lights. He compared the theatre to a sports arena. As much as a ballgame, Brecht thought the theatre should be fun.

Viola Spolin began creating her exercises to correct the excesses of children acting like actors, to awaken their natural behavior and movement onstage. The Spolin exercises sensitize the players' physical imaginations and thus their sense of the present. Games also teach precision. The players must know the rules.

To disabuse them of self-consciousness and ego, the improvisational actors' attentions are always directed outward toward the environment and the other players, toward the "point of concentration," the "Where," the object, the shared space. In Brechtian terms, the "point of concentration" distances the actor from his or her own subjective feelings. It is an "alienating" device.

As executed à la Viola Spolin, an improvisation does not allow for a cri de coeur. An actor participating at the high level of involvement an improvisation demands cannot get lost in a strong emotion. Improvisation requires an actor to be in touch with an emotional reality but also to move forward from it by means of an active dramaturgical response.

"Brecht influenced Paul more than any other playwright," says one of Sills's friends. "But there are two lines in him. He's never fused them. There's the Brecht thing. And there's the Viola thing: the fairy-tale thing."

In spite of their similarities, there are fundamental differences between the theatre of Spolin and the theatre of Brecht, and these transcend simple politics. If the theatre of Stanislavsky is psychological and emotional, and represents a feminine force, the theatre of Brecht is political and intellectual, a masculine force. Spolin's work, which eschews both the emotions and the intellect, is mystical and intuitive, attached to an energy that is asexual and childlike.

Brecht was foremost a playwright, Viola Spolin a director of play. Brecht was indeed a Communist, but he could have been any kind of ideologue and he and Spolin would still be mismatched. In an improvisation, the point of view emerges like a Platonic dialogue, embryonically. A playwright's point of view is planned. The Spolin games allow for no philosophical or political preconceptions whatever. Only playing, not political attachment, or propaganda, or knowledge of the outcome will produce the play.

Sills was leaving Steinway's Drugstore one morning when a University of Chicago divinity student who will be known here as John Ecks jumped out of a cab. "You're Sills!" he said, and began to talk up a woman playwright he described as a genius. Ecks could be reached at the school of divinity dormitory with the woman, Elaine May.

For thirty years, Severn Darden was under the impression that Elaine May was "born in a car trunk in Brazil or Argentina." She was born in Philadelphia as Elaine Berlin. Her early years were nomadic. Before settling with her family in Los Angeles, she toured with them all over America playing a little boy named Bennie in the Yiddish theatre, in which her father, Jack Berlin, was a director, writer, and actor. Father and daughter also played together on the radio in a parody of Fanny Brice's "The Baby Snooks Show." Noodnik was the baby's name. Ida Berlin, who performed producer's and practical functions, such as printing the theatre tickets, running the box office, and understudying, may have wielded more power and authority than her husband, reputedly "a sweet guy." During Prohibition, Louis Berlin, Elaine's older brother, went by the name of "Johnny Fogarty." He was once described as "always into deals," among them the purchase of surplus coffins and a beauty parlor to straighten kinky hair.

Jack Berlin died when Elaine was eleven, leaving her in the care of her mother, of whom she would say, "My mother's a good businessman."

A fellow actor of Elaine's early days considers her "the smartest woman I ever met. Like Samuel Beckett. Really a brain." But she had no formal schooling beyond Hollywood High School. At fourteen, in fact, she "quit going to school." To *The New York Times*, she once explained, "I didn't really like it. The truancy people came around and threatened to take me to court, but I called their bluff. I sat around the house reading, mostly mythology and fairy tales."

At sixteen, she married Marvin May, an engineer who created toys and, in at least one person's opinion, looked like Jesus. They had a daughter, Jeannie. After the marriage broke up, with Elaine electing to pursue the life that she was used to, in the theatre, she deposited Jeannie in Los Angeles with her mother, whose grandchild assumed the last name Berlin.

She considered herself foremost a writer, although she had studied acting with Maria Ouspenskaya and performed a hillbilly act in Hollywood in which she was billed as Elly May. In Los Angeles, she had written advertising copy and told her friends she liked it. In Chicago, she hoped to sell a local producer, Encyclopaedia Britannica Films, a screen treatment she was writing on Plato's *Symposium*.

Sitting in on classes at the University of Chicago became one of her pastimes. Once she tried to convince the sociologist Ned Polsky, as she had tried to convince a philosophy class, that the underlying action in Plato's *Symposium* was that Socrates was drunk.

When the director of a "pathetic, awful" Tonight at 8:30 production of Strindberg's *Miss Julie* was forced to bow out, Sills took over the job. The play had been staged in the round with Ann Sweet Petry playing Miss Julie. Mike Nichols was playing the other lead, Miss Julie's swinish seducer, Jean the Valet. Nichols will never forget how "one night there was this evil, hostile girl staring from the front row. I was about four feet away from her, and she stared at me all the way through it, and I knew she knew it was shit." Unfortunately, Nichols recalls, "There was no way to let her know" that he thought it was shit too.

The Chicago *Daily News* theatre critic, Sydney J. Harris, came to review *Miss Julie* and loved it. His review was so enthusiastic that to the company's regret the play was held over and audiences came for months.

Carrying a copy of the *Daily News* the day Harris's review appeared, Nichols saw the hostile girl walking on campus with Paul Sills. "Look at this!" he said to Sills. As Sills read the review, the girl read along, over his shoulder. "Ha!" she said, and walked away.

For two years, it would be Elaine May's only encounter with Mike Nichols, who learned that "it was unwise for people to start trouble with her" from the story of a windy day at Jimmy's when Elaine had walked in with wild hair. Someone male called out, "Hi, Elaine. Did you bring your broom today?" "Why?" she replied, without pause. "Do you want something up your ass?"

Sills intensified his friendship with Elaine May and, together with John Ecks and Ecks's friend Karl Mann (whom Ecks had met in a Chicago orphanage when they were both five and a half), spent much of their time mooning convention in the beatnik fashion, hitchhiking back and forth from New York to Chicago to Los Angeles, an exotically ragtag and Brechtian band.

In Los Angeles, they took workshops with Viola and made plans that never materialized for her to direct them in a production of Brecht's *The Good Woman of Setzuan*, in which a penniless prostitute, chosen by the gods for her goodness, is set up in a bourgeois occupation, running a tobacconist's shop, where she finds she cannot remain good and survive and instead submerges her own identity by disguising herself as her cousin, a ruthless man. The part of Shen Te, the good woman, is one her admirers think Elaine May, the former little Bennie, was born to play.

These were days that Karl Mann, a civilian in the theatre, regarded as "unsettling and wild," "highly emotional," and "acting out all the time." The group found a number of ways to scratch out an existence. "Selling aluminum siding was the least of it," muses Mann.

Sills fell in love with Elaine. He wrote a Brechtian play about two California con men, Bildad and his sidekick, Peleg, full of brilliant and poetic ideas, yet living on the fringes, scorned by the rest of society. The character Sills describes as "a featured creature," the sculptress Anora, was based on Elaine. The playwright burned a draft of *The Coming of Bildad* when the real Anora turned him down.

Before shipping out with the army in February 1952, Omar Shapli visited Sills in Los Angeles, joining him and John Ecks in the upstairs rooms of the Young Actors Company. Viola had a house in the Hollywood Hills and was working on an early version of *Improvisation for the Theater*. Sills was talking about starting a workshop as soon as he returned to Chicago that would conclude with a production of *The Caucasian Chalk Circle*, whose central story of a valley disputed by two Soviet collectives is illustrated by a parable—a play within the play—about an adopted child whose real mother, a noblewoman, attempts to reclaim it from the loyal peasant woman, Grusha, who has raised it through the dangers of a violent political revolt. The case is tried by Azdak, whose ignoble reputation in the village before becoming judge is learned through flashbacks. He settles the dispute by placing the baby in a chalk circle and inviting the two women to each grab hold of one of the baby's arms. The baby will be drawn out of the circle, says Azdak, by the woman to whom it feels maternal attraction. Azdak rules that the child be given to Grusha, because she cannot endure making the child suffer through this tug of war. Brecht concludes the play with this moral: both the child and the valley should be in the custody of whoever serves them best.

In New York, another young man with a vision, David Shepherd, had inherited some money from his stepmother, his father's childless second wife. He was planning to invest it in a nonexistent theatre he had already named Compass. While Paul Sills was in Viola's theatre dreaming of *The Caucasian Chalk Circle*, David Shepherd was dreaming alone about his.

5

David Shepherd's Dream

Creating the first improvisational theatre in America was neither the inspiration of Viola Spolin nor her son Paul Sills. Compass was the obsession of David Gwynne Shepherd (The Buckley School '38, Exeter '42, Harvard '46, Columbia M.A.). In the fall of 1952, the year that Eisenhower became president, he hitchhiked to Chicago with a $10,000 inheritance and a mission. Frivolity did not inform it. He was twenty-six. He had been in the army. He had sat at French cafés with Jimmy Baldwin while enrolled on a Fulbright scholarship at the Sorbonne. He had produced The Rolling Stage, a bus and truck company that toured resorts in the Catskills playing Molière's *The Mock Doctor*; he had decided to do this upon returning from India, where he had taught English literature to a thousand students at the University of Bombay. He had read Brecht. One of his favorite plays was, and still is, the early and, as he puts it, "really awful" *Baal*. He liked Brecht's concept of the theatre as a place where people could be entertained, and smoke and drink, and also not dress up. He was familiar with the tradition of Italian masked comedy, commedia dell'arte, and the way those traveling players improvised upon their own scenarios and entertained uneducated audiences—city and country bumpkins—with up-to-date satire, broad physical characterization, and local jokes. At Harvard, he had been impressed by a pamphlet a classmate showed him about Die Schmiere. "It means 'smearer' or something. It's a cabaret which puts everything down."

He had allotted himself five years to create an American cabaret theatre in some Midwestern stock or steel town that addressed itself to issues so real and immediate, in language so simple and straightforward, and in surroundings so low-priced, convenient, and congenial, that people from all levels of society—everyone in town—would flock to it in a mood of celebration because they saw their lives reflected there.

"I thought you should see yourself played by people who understand you, a picture of yourself on stage." says Shepherd. "I don't know why I believed that so strongly. Unless you could do that, I thought you'd be missin' a bet. It was before television took over. I just thought the theatre was a way of life."

For a while he toyed with naming it the Mirror Theatre, but he was more fixated on compasses: "My father was in the artillery. In the army, you had to know where you were." The compass image finally conveyed the same idea: a theatre that points the audience in the direction they are already facing. In 1952, they were facing a flat and unyielding Republican landscape: the cold war, the Red menace, the nuclear threat, the Lonely Crowd, Newspeak, and the spiritual conditions that support psychiatrists—alienation, anxiety, malaise, and sexual repression.

The popular theatre David Shepherd had in mind had nothing to do with a sold-out Broadway balcony, or parties of Great Neck matrons packed in after luncheon at Sardi's at Wednesday matinees, or a safe refuge for white-sandaled Times Square tourists fresh from the excitement of watching the smoke rings "o" out of the mouth of the man in the Camel sign. In its grandest moments, his vision harked back, if anywhere, to the funkier arenas of the Elizabethans or the Greeks. He was not then a gaunt and wraithlike prophet. He was twenty-six. He was serious. He was possessed. He was single. He was disgusted with Brooks Atkinson, the Harvard Club, the bourgeois culture of New York.

The Theatre World Annual notes that the 1951–1952 Broadway season featured productions of *Gigi*, *The Moon is Blue*, the Barrault company in Feydeau's *Occupe-Toi d'Amelie* (in French), a Comden and Green revue called *Two on the Aisle* starring Bert Lahr, and a revival of *The Wild Duck*. At the Holiday Theatre, real bagels were distributed at the opening of the play that ran the longest, *Bagels and Yox*.

As one imagines him at twenty-six, David Shepherd had as much taste for *Gigi* and Feydeau as would Baal, Brecht's incorrigible poet, the uncouth slob who spits Goldtroppchen Spatläese on the fawning bourgeoisie. Shepherd was repelled by plays about "love affairs in Nice which took place fifty years ago. And I thought it was obscene for a theatre to be dominated by French and English people. I mean *obscene*."

The Latin word *provisus* is the past participle of *providere*, which means "to see ahead." The words "provide" and "provident" are among the derivatives of this cautious verb. Its opposite is accompanied by a negative prefix. *Improvisus* means "unforeseen."

As a young man, Shepherd intended to provide the theatre with a formula for a political cabaret that could be replicated in "every community on the globe." In his inventor's isolation, he had not foreseen the consequences of testing his formula in a theatre where geniuses express themselves and the audience laughs.

Alone in New York in 1951, Shepherd had an already unswerving vision of a unique new theatre that presented plays about the rank and file in the audience. No more than he imagined these entertainments to cater to royalty did he intend them to titillate the bourgeoisie. Like another radical aristocrat and Harvard grad, John Reed, his curiosity has always been tenacious and abiding about the real-life problems of the working class, to which he was not born.

He was born in the Silk Stocking district of New York, on Eighty-sixth Street and Madison Avenue. His earliest recollections of the theatre, his life's most passionately equivocal involvement, are thanks to his great-aunt, Alice Gwynne Vanderbilt. Shepherd's relative was hostess of the seventy-room Italian Renaissance "cottage" in Newport called The Breakers, where in each of thirty baths there was a choice of fresh or salt bath water and "every surface that could be gilded was." Her New York mansion occupied the Fifth Avenue blockfront between Fifty-seventh and Fifty-eighth streets. When she moved uptown, the block's northeast corner became Bergdorf Goodman. Each Christmas, David Shepherd remembers—around "a forty-foot tree under thirty-foot ceilings, dig it?"—she presented the poorer Gwynne cousins tickets to the Met. *Don Pasquale.* *Parsifal.* Before he could be coaxed back out of the bright lights to the brisk country air of Katonah, the "dour nature" David Shepherd recalls having as a ten-year-old impelled his father to endure six-hour performances of Wagner so the child could "hear the orchestra crank up again and watch them all fall on their spear."

William Edgar Shepherd, David's father, an architect, was handsome, social, rich. David's grandmother, Cetty Shepherd, sold "a few acres of Ohio timberland" whenever she went broke. "Just ate it up," sighs her grandson. When Cetty came to call on Alice, the sisters would argue for hours about the winner of the Crimean War. "They could have resolved the whole thing if they had gone to the *Encyclopaedia Britannica.* But they didn't want to. They were sisters," Shepherd explains, not without some pride of family. "They just wanted to fight."

Cetty was unimpressed by Alice's desperate attempts to establish the parvenu name of Vanderbilt in society.

Bill Shepherd, the author of *The Gwynne Papers*, was the man assigned to trace the family lineage. At The Breakers, he also designed an elevator for "Aunt Alice, Mrs. Vanderbilt," said Bill's late cousin Josephine Gwynne from a nursing home in New Jersey when she was eighty-nine. "And when it broke down, he had it fixed." He sent his Aunt Alice a bill for $3,000. She returned a check for "Thirty. Thirty thousand," noted Ms. Gwynne. "So that was the last time they let her sign checks." Josephine recalled little David Shepherd as "cute" and "quiet," his father Bill as "adorable." During World War II, "I think he was decorated more than anybody else. He was in the artillery. He taught the French where to place the guns," she said.

According to his son, William Shepherd concluded after the war that architecture was "a hassle, all about making sales every Saturday at four or five cocktail parties," and chose to remain in uniform, that of an army colonel. He fought and beat his own retirement after a heart attack so he could collect his army pension. He married several times. His first wife, David's mother, who behaved strangely after her only childbirth at thirty-one, was diagnosed as schizophrenic and hospitalized in genteel and expensive sanitoria from the first year of David's life. Alone in command, Colonel Shepherd tried to raise his son appropriately or, the way David recalls it, as "a monarch," with riding, swimming, tennis, and piano lessons, a Scottish governess, penny loafers, Parker pens, dancing lessons at Arthur Murray's, a tuxedo, Brooks Brothers underwear, and proper frayed-at-the-collar Oxford button-down shirts. David balked at studying artillery formations and so, to the distress of his father, "I missed the Knickerbocker Greys."

At Exeter, Shepherd hoarded his allowance to splurge on a single blow-out week of theatregoing in the city: "For three months, I wouldn't spend a dime." At fourteen, he saw Kurt Weill's *Knickerbocker Holiday* and was smitten by "September Song." He met his mother for the first time at a Fifth Avenue apartment in the Nineties, where she was cared for by a paid companion. His father introduced them when David Shepherd was fifteen.

In college, he recalls, "I made the circuit. I went to Café Society, uptown *and* down." He heard Susan Reed and all the radical-sounding material in her repertoire, "all the songs in *The British Book of Ballads*." Twice, once in Greenwich Village and once, equally amused in an army outpost in Yaphank, Long Island, where they were both privates, he saw Zero Mostel's famous number about throwing up in an airplane.

It was expected that he would become an English professor at Harvard, both Shepherds' alma mater. As if seeking some solace or light in his mother's madness, the subject he chose for his master's thesis was "Great Mad Scenes in Elizabethan and Jacobean Drama." His classmates at The Buckley School, Derek Roosevelt, Roddy Lindsay, and Ogden Reid, showed more traditional interest in enjoying rank and power. Ogden Reid became ambassador to Israel. Roddy Lindsay, the former New York mayor's brother, "went into banks." David Shepherd says, "My classmates run New York."

At Columbia, after Paris, after India, after he began developing a *Weltanschauung*, radical Marxist notions about society, and getting involved with "a lot of socialists and intellectuals," his father observed, "David wants to be goo-oo-ood."

What did it matter to his family if he could distinguish a Schachtmanite from a Trotskyite? To the Vanderbilts, they all were Jews. Like his second cousin, Gloria Vanderbilt Stokowski Lumet Cooper, David eventually would marry and become divorced from one, Suzanne ("Honey") Stern Shepherd, a bountifully gifted actress and director. David Shepherd's second wife, the formidable African-American Constance ("Connie") Carr-Shepherd, is a deacon of the First Presbyterian Church of New York and a practicing psychologist.

In profile, David Shepherd resembles an old *New Yorker* caricature of his cousin, Alfred Gwynne Vanderbilt, who was torpedoed on the *Lusitania*, eternally thwarted in his efforts to serve the British Red Cross. Alfred, too, was sealed into a noble forehead, a worried brow, razor-sharp cheekbones, downturned and somewhat disapproving lips, and the Gwynne family's characteristic almond-shaped or "oriental" eyes.

The voices of our ancestors reside within us. Improvisation brings them out. David Shepherd's voice, calm and velvety, like a Harlem haberdasher, has an urgency, an edge. The enunciation and low room tone belong to a man who has taken a variety of backstage calls while the performance is going on. At the Compass, he remembers that the most powerful female characters emerged from Elaine May and Barbara Harris when they were playing their mothers, the people they had most carefully observed and knew the best.

Playing James D. Rockebilt, he too is liberated. Making fun of the brittle speaking mannerisms of the very rich, he is able to illustrate that "Larchmont lockjaw" is the natural expression of a greedy and unyielding jaw: "The Hunt brothers? *Nouveau riche*, my dear. The old rich leave more time for their hobbies. They might be into squash. Or they might be into chasing pussy. Some dudes are into museums. Which means, you know, stealing a lot of objects and bringing them to the United States."

It is not clear if he remembers how fortunate he was to be a young man on the way to Chicago with "ten thousand . . . I don't know, fifteen thousand" dollars. It is not clear if he thought of himself foremost as a producer, a playwright, a community organizer, or a tidy version of Jack Kerouac: his notebooks of this period were written in an exquisitely neat handwriting, without doodles, in bound ledgers, not paper bags or toilet paper. Three years before the Compass opened, he wrote:

> I think that any theatre written for the working class will have to use simpler forms than those of the contemporary theatre, which is an expression of the middle class. I don't believe you can keep a working-class audience awake during a play written in the style of Ibsen or Arthur Miller.

Even his own most vividly remembered theatre images had nothing at all to do with words. En route to New York from India, at the Red Rose, a boîte in Paris, he saw the pantomime of Marcel Marceau. The Red Rose was not expensive. The admission was no more than forty francs. Juliet Greco was also singing there. Shepherd was floored when she forgot the words to her song, not once, but three times: "I thought that was re-markable. She seemed to have no shame. No shame." "Maurice," Juliet Greco waved to her accompanist, "Maurice," she said, "once more."

Shepherd loved Marceau's "The Bee" so much he memorized it and performed it later in New York at parties for his college friends. "It's a commedia dell'arte shtick. About the bee chasing him, you know? I felt I had been bitten by the bee. I wanted my own Red Rose."

It was his intention to start "the theatre in my head" in a "culturally deprived" area of America, specifically, the stockyards of Gary, Indiana, but the left-wing labor organizers and union officials in that unlovely city were a grim, forbidding lot. His offering to Gary of a lunchtime theatre of commentary was ignored. At night, when Shepherd was out scouring the town for a welcoming committee, the left-wing politicos were listening to Saul Alinsky's speeches in the Union Theological Seminary; the Ev-anston executives and the North Shore dentists were at the Shubert Theatre watching *Bell, Book and Candle,* and the workers continued watching *I Love Lucy.*

He took a job on the assembly line at the Ceco Steel Company in Cicero, Illinois, which manufactured steel elements for construction. He roomed in a flophouse on Harrison Street.

The great pioneer of the experimental German proletarian theatre of the 1920s, Erwin Piscator, had believed in real people playing their parts. When the kaiser sent lawyers to Piscator's theatre protesting the way he was being portrayed by an actor, Piscator invited the kaiser to come down to the theatre and play himself.

Although without Piscator's context—Weimar Germany—David Shepherd also viewed actors as vestiges of capitalist theatre, as "professionals" and "narcissists," a bourgeois class. Even then, beyond contempt for slickness, he had a love of the authentic, the nonactor, the noble savage, the amateur.

But by the time they got off the assembly line, all the workers he had earmarked as actors for his theatre just wanted dinner. He was more interested than the Ceco steelworkers in finding out about their lives.

Others may have perceived, as does one of his old friends, that in spite of his fierce and independent intellect, "he was a lonely boy looking for a family." His Harvard roommate, Steve Elliston, teaching English at the University of Illinois in Champaign-Urbana, suggested that he desist in the lifelong habit the old friend calls "chasing tomorrow" and take himself, his visions, and his $10,000 or $15,000 to the University of Chicago campus, where "they had their own culturally deprived community" and, to understate it, a more sophisticated, a more Bohemian mix.

6

Shepherd Meets Sills

In late October of 1952, when David Shepherd arrived in Hyde Park, the University of Chicago had a fuzzier fringe. The prepubescent population, like the rest of the enrollment, had plummeted as the decade progressed. A reactionary mood had fallen on the nation. Dwindling support for the Chicago Plan and shrinking freshman rosters had been a major factor in hastening Hutchins's farewell. After the artificial boom created by the World War II veterans, the university was struggling to recruit new students to a big-city campus in a "changing" Hyde Park neighborhood, an uncomfortable urban reality for which Hutchins was also blamed.

Throughout the 1920s, 1930s, and 1940s, the University of Chicago had held the largest collection of anti-Negro restrictive covenants of any landowner in Illinois. In 1946, when Jane Kome Mather, now an editor of the *American Journal of Sociology*, arrived as Jane McCachan ('48), a freshman at the university, the South Side area between Cottage Grove and Stony Island and Sixty-third and Fifty-third streets was a nearly all-white island, inhabited predominantly by Russian and German Jews. On May 19, 1948, the U.S. Supreme Court ruled restrictive real estate covenants to be unenforceable in the courts. Hutchins, who was opposed to such restrictions to begin with, used the court's decision as an opportunity to divest the University of Chicago of its numerous real estate holdings north of Hyde Park. Poor black families moved into the shabby spaces that had formerly housed student veterans, into the old mansions cum boardinghouses in Kenwood and into the vintage apartment houses in Woodlawn that had been built along the Midway connecting Jackson and Washington parks in 1892 for Chicago's Columbian Exposition in 1893. By 1952, "Whether you did or didn't have black friends," says Jane Kome Mather, "you lived in a community where a black lower-class style was becoming increasingly prevalent and with a growing awareness of the nature of black people's lives."

Closer to campus, among the country's great thinkers, scientists, and scholars, in the low-rent peripheries of their ivory towers, the beat generation had also begun to emerge, as it had on the Columbia University campus, to provide a new model for American college youth, of on-the-road rebellion toward their own, the middle class. For them, as for other subspecies of Bohemians and eggheads of 1952, when a community of any kind, especially of scholars, was regarded as an incursion of the Red menace, the University of Chicago, in Adlai Stevenson's own home state, was becoming mecca.

"These kids were way ahead of the ones from Northwestern and the University of Illinois," observes David Shepherd. "These folks were young, but they had been around. Most of them had been in and out of uniform, in and out of jobs, or in and out of marriage. They already had experienced splitting up, getting fired, getting shot at, or being in a business that failed."

"Being grown up was important in the fifties," points out Fran Gendlin ('56), the Aristotelian who got married to "someone Platonic" at seventeen, in her third college year. "In the sixties, it was important to be a child."

As early as 1935, after Hutchins had firmly and eloquently frustrated the Chicago legislature in its probe of "subversion" at the University of Chicago, the Hyde Park campus had definitively asserted its intention to remain an academic "free zone." In his New Year's speech of 1936, Hutchins had announced to the university faculties and trustees that "we have routed or at least repulsed the forces of darkness. Repulsed is probably the proper word. For we cannot be sure that the ignorant and misguided will not return to the charge." Indeed, they would. By the beginning of 1953, the All-Campus Civil Liberties Committee would be reactivated in view of the coming investigations by the House Un-American Activities Committee and by the resubmission of anti-subversive Broyles Bills in the Illinois legislature. Nevertheless, throughout and long after Hutchins's chancellorship, the University of Chicago continued to be bombarded with intelligence, as Eve Leoff puts it, "in the essential meaning of the word."

Of the few classes Jerry Cunliffe ('53) attended at fifteen, he best remembered Rosalie Wax's startling lectures on the American internment camps for Japanese. "It was uncommon knowledge in the fifties," he reflects. "Not like nowadays. Most people didn't realize we had concentration camps here. At the U. of C. we knew it. Oh, we knew, we knew."

On the University of Chicago campus in the fall of 1952, it was possible to hear lectures by W. H. Auden on "Poetry and Opera," Louis Massignon on "Islamic Mysticism," and Mortimer J. Adler on "Reason and Faith." Jacques Maritain conducted a seminar on "The Responsibility of the Artist," and the student union sponsored a "Night of Sin." David Riesman and his colleagues, the poet-sociologist Reuel Denney and sociologist Nathan Glazer, were finishing research on the study that was to emerge in 1950 as *The Lonely Crowd*, a demystification of the "other-directed" or conformist American. Riesman's protégés in Presentation of Self in Daily Life packed up their notebooks and eyeglasses and went out in "the field"—the streets of Chicago—and studied weird professions. For his first important contribution as a scholar, Howard Becker ('46), who played jazz piano, chose to dissect the sociology of pot and jazz musicians. Ned Polsky ('51), who loved pool, took on the sociology of hustlers.

Theirs was no more an expression of populist revolt than were the other great American Bohemias of the 1950s. Nor was there any power attached—as there would be in the 1960s—to being "under thirty." Here was a community of outsiders to whom Dylan Thomas, not Bob Dylan, was a culture hero, in which students listened to Bartok while their parents listened to pop. Drug use on campus was limited to the traditional college upper, amphetamine, or an occasional marijuana joint.

While sizing up the animus of Hyde Park, David Shepherd mingled with twenty-two-year-old Ph.D.'s who could look back with nostalgia on the "good old days," when they were fourteen or fifteen and innocently discussing Plato and Max Weber over breakfast at Steinway's Drugstore. Instead of young veterans returning from a "war of conscience" to devour newfound educational possibilities and fulfill undreamed ambitions, here were young men of draft age dragging out their stay at the university, postponing reluctant involvements in America's first "police action" in Korea. Here were mainstream washouts with master's degrees who did not feel optimistic about living up to the idealistic dictum that Hutchins had proposed to the students in his farewell address: "Our mission here on earth is to change our environment, not to adjust ourselves to it. If we have to choose between Sancho Panza and Don Quixote, let us by all means choose Don Quixote." And now most of them were legally old enough to drink.

A campus contact recommended by Steve Elliston, David Shepherd's advocate down in Champaign-Urbana, was Ann Sweet Petry, daughter of the assistant curator of the Art Institute of Chicago, as well as an actress on the university theatre scene. She and Marvin Peisner were running one of the splinter groups of which Tonight at 8:30 was now comprised.

Peisner and Petry were preparing a production of Shaw's *Arms and the Man*, when into rehearsal appeared "this tall, rather naïve-looking guy named David Shepherd. His looks were in the Ralph Bellamy tradition: a bit of a hick, who seldom gets to kiss the girl. We weren't sure how to take him," says Peisner, "so we judged the book by its cover." He and Petry learned that Shepherd had recently been in Europe studying cabaret theatre, a tradition founded in politics, and that "this kind of political theatre was what he wanted to organize."

A casual note in Shepherd's diary marks this day as the one on which Marvin Peisner enjoined him to call a young man who seemed to Peisner a sympathetic spirit, Paul Sills.

"I was in on the poetry end of things," says Peisner, who had been "amazed" at the good turnout for his presentation of T. S. Eliot's poetry in the Mitchell Towers. "You'd be surprised at the number of people who didn't know T. S. Eliot in those days. Otherwise, our group was much more conventional than Paul's. We weren't that willing to take on the university. He was much more of a rebel than Ann and I. Paul was always on the side of the angels and revolutionaries. In doing the people that Bentley had mentioned, he was far more bold and far more advanced."

A successor to George Blair was finally found. The new man, Otis Imbodin, at last solicited an official merger with the renegades from To-night at 8:30 and a rapprochement with Paul Sills. Imbodin offered Sills a shelter in the theatre in the Mitchell Towers, where he had begun a weekly Saturday morning workshop using Viola's improvisational exercises. Joining the group was Sheldon Patinkin ('53), now chairperson of the Theater/Music Department of Chicago's Columbia College, artistic director of the National Jewish Theatre, and artistic consultant to The Second City. He was then a seventeen-year-old in his second year at the University of Chicago, beginning his apprenticeship as Sills's long-suffering and loyal assistant. As Patinkin remembers it, Sills used such Spolin games as Who Am I?, Gibberish Teaching, Camera, Contact, and the Mirror Exercise to prepare his company for a season that would include productions of *The Typewriter* by Jean Cocteau, *Leonce and Lena* by Georg Büchner, and *The Caucasian Chalk Circle* by Brecht.

Although technically it was a student club, Shepherd joined the Peisner-Petry faction of Tonight at 8:30 as an actor. In a second production of *The Man of Destiny*, Peisner played Napoleon and Shepherd played the supporting role of The Sub-Lieutenant whom Shaw had described as "a tall chuckle-headed young man of 24, with the complexion and style of a man of rank, and a self-assurance on that ground which the French Revolution had failed to shake in the slightest degree."

Sills attended the show and let it be known that he had admired Shepherd's graceful performance. He soon received a phone call from Shepherd and selected Steinway's as their meeting place.

Waiting alone for their rendezvous at the drugstore, Shepherd observed "a young lion with a head of uncombed curls. A group obviously not of engineering students were surrounding him. I figured out that he was Sills. He had completely forgotten the appointment."

When David Shepherd first saw him holding court in Steinway's in the late fall of 1952, Paul Sills was twenty-five. Now a divorced father, he and Charles M. ("Charlie") Jacobs ('53), an undergrad (later a law student), shared a fascination with modern German theatre and a cellar apartment on Kimbark Street. After a visit, Shepherd was impressed with the numbers of young actresses who slept there and by the interior decoration, which featured "gray army blankets and four or five beds."

"These guys were really entrepreneurs," he says. "They were into a lot of projects, like giving a fund-raising party for Maxwell Bodenheim. They were mavens of everything at the University of Chicago. They were established theatre types. One of their friends was Eugene Troobnick. They had another friend, a guy named Mike Nichols. They were all crazy about Cocteau and Büchner. And Brecht."

At the same time, Shepherd had taken a job with the Illinois Parks Department, working six hours a day, four days a week, earning $2.11 an hour to "excite dramatic activity among the Lithuanians." After work, on the radiator of his monk's cell off Fifty-sixth Street, he cooked macaroni dinners in a can. Saturdays, watching Sills in action at his workshop "bawling out in the darkness to the students" became manna to the civil servant Shepherd, "preferable to the front-row seat of any theatre in America."

In January 1953, Sills's "endless workshops," as Sheldon Patinkin calls them, culminated in a production of *The Typewriter*, staged in the round in the Mitchell Towers with Mike Nichols, Joyce Piven, Charlie Jacobs, Estelle Lutrell, and the director himself. Piven had found the intimacy of their six-month rehearsal period "thrilling. All we did was improvise. It couldn't have taken us six months to learn lines."

The Typewriter opened to excellent reviews, one critic reserving special praise for the concentration Estelle Lutrell displayed while blowing her nose. The following month, Sills appeared with Eugene Troobnick and Joyce Piven in Otis Imbodin's staging of *Leonce and Lena*. Ned Polsky had prepared the adaptation under the guidance of Gerhard Meyer's German scholarship. Sills has few words on this production. "I don't know what it was like. I didn't see it. I was in it," he says.

After the success of *The Typewriter*, Sills's originality could not be ignored. When Imbodin gave him carte blanche to direct at University Theatre, Sills decided to bring *The Caucasian Chalk Circle* to the main stage.

In Chicago, on May 1, 1953, as Omar Shapli imagined it from Korea, "the rebels stormed the citadel." Sills's Mandel Hall production of *The Caucasian Chalk Circle* was only the second one ever mounted* and was so inspiring that after the second—and final—weekend of performances, it was clear to Sills and his company that they were ready to move forth from the University Theatre as an independent repertory company into their own space.

Sills and Shepherd had exchanged plays with each other. Sills liked Shepherd's adaptation of *The Duchess of Malfi* (a play with which Sills, of course, had also toyed). Webster's great mad scenes in *The White Devil* had inspired Shepherd's master's thesis on madness; Webster's masterpiece now inspired this saga of land inheritance set in postwar Italy. Shepherd liked Sills's play, *The Coming of Bildad*, the Brechtian epic about two California con men based on his relationship with John Ecks and Elaine May. "The play was obscure and difficult," says the author. "It was like me." Shepherd thought, "It was a neat, rich play." "We all got to like each other," Sills recalls. And, as Shepherd perceives it, "When they discovered that I had this money, we decided to talk partnership."

*The first production of *The Caucasian Chalk Circle*, also in English, was staged at Carleton College in Northfield, Minnesota, at the Nourse Little Theatre on May 4, 1948. The play was not performed in German by Brecht's Berliner Ensemble at the Theater am Schiffbauerdamm until June 15, 1954.

7

The Playwrights Theatre Club

Investing $7,000 in the Playwrights Theatre Club was the first thing David Shepherd did to adulterate his dream. It bore no resemblance to his passionately written notions of a people's cabaret. The idea for a professional repertory had belonged to the Sills crowd—Charlie Jacobs, Eugene Troobnick, and Mike Nichols—all of them ambitious to move beyond the strictures of University Theatre and all of them "dedicated to stuff like Brecht and Shaw and Strindberg," Shepherd recalls, the very stuff that he regarded as "museum plays."

Charlie Jacobs dropped out, and, as a producing partner, Shepherd says, Mike Nichols got "cold feet." With an extensive musical background and what must have been a sure enough command of his own vocal instrument, he had secured a job through Aaron Asher "playing records and talking in between," as chief announcer for America's first all-classical FM station, WFMT. It was a position that gave Nichols considerable local celebrity.

"Even WQXR in New York wasn't FM in those days," Asher points out, and, unlike the Chicago station, "It played a lot of cocktail music." WFMT was totally highbrow, although its owner, Asher's cousin, worried about losing its FCC license when Nichols overslept and did not get to the station in time to warm up the transmitter before he took over his 3:00 p.m. to midnight shift. Shepherd still seems miffed when he remembers that Nichols claimed he needed his salary as the WFMT night man and that as far as making a full-time commitment to Playwrights Theatre Club, he couldn't afford the time.

The producing team winnowed down to three. Shepherd had the money. Sills had the actors. Troobnick had the car. They scoured the city in Troobnick's car for a suitable space, and once they found the empty Chinese restaurant on North LaSalle Street, Shepherd says, "Things happened pretty fast."

The distinguished list of former University of Chicago students who joined on as actors included Zohra Lampert (then Alton), James (later Anthony) Holland, Owen (now Jerry) Cunliffe, Edward Asner, Eugene Troobnick, Marvin Peisner, Jon Jackson, Bill Alton, Vernon Schwartz, Byrne Piven, Joyce Hiller (now Piven), Ann Sweet Petry, Mike Nichols, Donna Holabird, Creighton Clarke, Joy Grodzins (now Carlin), and Estelle Lutrell.

Their shared educational background, says Ed Asner, was "part of our strength and audacity. Individually and collectively, we used it as a shield." Thanks to the Hutchins Plan, these actors saw themselves as "more than mindless automatons spouting somebody else's thoughts and lines on the stage. We were a vitriolic group of young people who knew how to find their ass with both hands."

"We are not interested in the fine psychological delineation of character that is typical of modern realistic theatre—the Stanislavsky Method," announced David Shepherd to Beverly Fields, a reporter from *Chicago* magazine. "What we are after is a more vigorous idea—a more exaggerated idea of character—really a distortion; the kind of mask or prototype that you come across in Brecht or Jonson or Molière." In their "devotion to didactic theatre," Fields noted that "the three directors are pretty much abreast."

Following a quasi-Brechtian prototype was so unusual in the stage training of the naturalistic American actor of 1953 as to be almost nonexistent. Where else but at the Playwrights Theatre Club could a University of Chicago art history student like Tony Holland have begun to master what Omar Shapli describes as Holland's "art of the precipitous entrance"? For professional actors like Jackie Gleason, Sid Caesar, and Lucille Ball, television had just begun to supply a national stage for the practice of physical exaggeration and the antics of the larger-than-life character or prototype. Those great players, however, had gained their experience in lowbrow and decidedly nondidactic arenas of entertainment such as vaudeville, the circus, the army, the USO, the Borscht Belt, and burlesque. They did not, like these Chicago amateurs, learn their craft by cutting classes in Great Books.

Although "a thread of social criticism," as one critic called it, was intrinsic to the work of the Playwrights Theatre Club, in fact, the personality of this group was defined more by its interest in acting with Paul Sills than by any political philosophy or point of view about society. The Playwrights Theatre Club is remembered by more politically focused University of Chicago students only as "rather generally embattled," its most talented leading actors increasingly committed to a serious life in the theatre, not, as David Shepherd hoped, to provincial political ferment.

Because the club designation helped skirt or diffuse most city theatre ordinances, the audience bought entrance by subscription. No tickets were taken at the door. Thus, the Playwrights Theatre Club, like a Soho art gallery opening, was not for the groundlings but an intellectual elite composed of urban, polite, and well-read people. If its producer had wanted to start a popular theatre, Omar Shapli points out, this wasn't it.

In two years, the Playwrights Theatre Club nevertheless presented a formidable program of twenty-five productions of thoughtfully selected plays, some daring in the repressive political climate of the early fifties, all worthy in their innovative theatrical conceptions of their fellow dissidents off-Broadway. And it was during these two years that a common body of theatrical literature was—sometimes brilliantly—explored, old relationships were cemented or found wanting, and several important new "connections" to the Compass were made.

They opened on June 23, 1953, in a 150-seat theatre designed especially for them by John Holabird, the husband of Donna, one of the actresses, and director of dramatics at Sills's alma mater, the Francis W. Parker School. The producers, along with Charlie Jacobs, Sheldon Patinkin, and a young man with a pencil-thin gigolo mustache and a long overcoat named Phil Morini, made their bedrooms in the alcoves that ringed the room and had functioned in the Chinese restaurant as family dinner booths. The stage was based on the Elizabethan extension, a cross between an arena and an end stage. It projected into the house, bringing the actors into dramatic proximity with the audience. "There can be no mystery about this kind of theatre, nothing hidden. It invites and demands participation," said the membership brochure.

In the second Sills production of *The Caucasian Chalk Circle*, launched on Playwrights' opening night, the twenty-six characters in the Mandel Hall version were cut to fifteen and the assistant scenic designer, Zohra Lampert, was the star.

In the Chicago *American*, Roger Dettmer's rave review was prophetic.

Not only did he praise the production as "strongly syncopated and infec-
tiously multi-rhythmed," he perceived the group's impact on theatre-
starved Chicago as "an experience such as New York alone has been
privileged to own." He said, "The people who played last night are very
new—vigorously, crudely, wonderfully, irrationally new . . . Their love
of the stage is so overwhelming one cannot remain indifferent."

The good notices *The Caucasian Chalk Circle* received from the Chicago
press also attracted the attention of Brecht's American agent, Walter Nubel,
who was shocked by the unauthorized production and furious that Brecht's
young American admirers had no intention of paying royalties to their
idol. Apologies were made in lieu of restitution, and with plans to mount
a new play every month, Playwrights Theatre Club launched into a production schedule of dizzying speed.

Sills next directed Schnitzler's *Rounddance*, the sexual daisy chain set
in decadent prewar Vienna that had already been a big hit for him at
Tonight at 8:30. This "less raunchy" production, with Mike Nichols re-
prising his role as The Poet, still featured the Viennese-sounding music
that the distinguished musicologist Leo Treitler had adapted from rare
period manuscripts. Following soon after the American release of the
French film version *La Ronde*, Sills's new staging (with David Shepherd
as The Husband), proved such a crowd pleaser, it was held over a week.

Singled out for particular praise by Sydney J. Harris of the *Daily News*
was Eugene Troobnick, for "a mobility of expression and an innate sense
of movement that raise his parody of a 'Young Gentleman' from mere
cartooning to something approaching the level of art." The dark-haired
and beautiful Zohra Lampert immediately impressed the critics as "unquestionably the find of the summer season . . . here is a gypsy-like girl
with elfin grace and the dramatic constitution of Shirley Booth . . . her
potential for theatrical fame is high." She took on the task of leading
woman in a series of difficult plays, although she had only started acting
a couple of weeks before. After her debut as Grusha, she was The Actress
in *Rounddance*. As the unfaithful Marie in Büchner's *Wozzek*, which
Zohra now began to rehearse, Beverly Fields would remember months
later that "she helped to create some of the most compelling moments in
the play."

"I didn't know any better," the actress says. "We were kids. In one play
my costume was the suit my mother sent me to college in. If Paul or
David said, 'We're doing *Caucasian Chalk Circle* or *Wozzek* or *Rounddance*,' we'd say, 'Fine. In English? Can I play the aunt?' The significant

thing was their enthusiasm and sweetness. They didn't seem phony. And that was so important in those days. They were juicy people, those guys."

Back in Chicago after his release from the army, Edward Asner saw *Rounddance*, moved into an empty alcove, and began rehearsing for the title role in *Wozzek* the next day.

He was big and burly and sensitive, and if seen by Eugene Troobnick as "compulsively clean" in his alcove, it was only, Asner says gruffly, "compared to the other slobs." He got someone to give his nook a "not precisely Bauhausian" coat of high-gloss paint. Then he put himself in charge of the garbage detail and "persecuted us all," adds Joyce Piven, "for not doing our share."

While writing his master's thesis at DePauw University in Indiana, a young twelve-tone composer, Tom O'Horgan, created original music for *Wozzek* and most of Playwrights Theatre Club's subsequent plays. In 1967, with the production of "the first rock musical," *Hair*, it was as a director rather than as a composer that O'Horgan would make a much bigger theatrical mark. For Playwrights Theatre Club, he composed "Mickey Mouse stuff. Paul liked it. I'd use a piano, harp, a gong or two, maybe a glockenspiel," he says. On the piano during *Wozzek*, eighteen-year-old Sheldon Patinkin (who was also in charge of the membership office) "slavishly played every note that I wrote."

A week into rehearsals of *Wozzek*, Mike Nichols decided it was time to leave Chicago and his small role as The Young Soldier to seek his fortune in New York.

The same week, a newly graduated Senn High School student peeked in. In her own words, Barbara Harris at seventeen was "unformed and ex*trem*ely shy." Unlike the others in the company, she still lived at home with her middle-class family on the North Side. Her father, Oscar, an alumnus of the University of Chicago, had been a newspaperman on the Chicago *Tribune*, and, although a teetotaler, a regular at the Dill Pickle Club, a Chicago watering hole famous in his day as a newspaperman's dive. Natalie Densmoor Harris of Wisconsin, Barbara's mother, had been a music student at the University of Wisconsin and at Oberlin in Ohio. While raising her children, she made use of her musical talent by teaching the piano. Barbara was the youngest of four siblings, three of them girls. When her only brother was killed in action during World War II, the family was traumatized. Her father became a tree surgeon and later a cabdriver. Some sense of connection and balance was restored to her family life when Barbara's sister Nan married Howard Becker, who was studying jazz piano with Lennie Tristano and distinguishing himself as one of the University of Chicago's important young sociologists. In a family of academic achievers, Barbara was not a good student. It seemed to her that her family felt her abilities insignificant. When she expressed an interest in the theatre, they were relieved. Howard Becker heard about Playwrights Theatre Club from a young actor named Byrne Piven, the brother of his downstairs neighbor, who recommended it for Becker's young sister-in-law over more conventional places like the Drury Lane.

Recounting her first baby steps toward the stage, she says simply, "Reality was painful. The theatre was so exotic and intriguing. I knew I wanted to be part of it. When I saw those bright lights . . . well, it's just too corny."

"I was the first one to see her," actor Tom Erhart says. He was "alone in the theatre, sweeping or cleaning. An incredibly beautiful girl walked in. I thought I'd seen an angel. I almost fell off the balcony."

The coproducer Troobnick also remembers the day she arrived: "With the possible exception of Vivien Leigh in Gone With the Wind, she was the most exquisite creature I'd ever seen. She had that kind of beauty. And she made a beeline for Paul."

In the man's memory, the trajectory of the actress sounds easy. In fact, she was invited in by David Shepherd and incorporated into the acting company only after a long apprentice period of exercising what Shepherd reverently refers to as "support skills" for the theatre: mimeographing, licking envelopes, making coffee, and mopping the floor. Like many of the women present on the Playwrights Theatre Club scene, she recalls the genuine pleasure and sense of belonging she experienced while performing menial chores. Her first job in the theatre was to mimeograph twenty-five copies of The Fields of Malfi, the producer's play: "David said, 'Follow me and you can work.' And I did, especially that greasy machine."

She tried attracting the director's attention by inching her mop and bucket closer and closer to the stage, where Sills could often be found sleeping on the bed that was the central prop in Rounddance. Staggering out from his alcove in the morning "to take the one or two reservations," Shepherd observed Barbara bringing Sills his morning coffee to wake him up.

Because of her youth, inexperience, and bond with the director, her values, even more than those of the others, were shaped here. "This was her first life experience," points out Charlie Jacobs, "watching this whole thing unfold. To her, it was all, 'Wow, is this what the world is about?' Can you imagine coming from a typical beef and potatoes household to this kind of thing? At Playwrights, she was the youngest of a very young group."

As one of the Townspeople in *Wozzek*, she was given a walk-on and then retired from stage action after the summer to study at the Goodman Theatre during the next three productions of the Playwrights Theatre Club.

Büchner's fragmented scenario of a militarized society, as seen through the ordeals of a tormented Prussian peasant soldier, is an early example of nineteenth-century German Expressionism and, constructed from each of the author's four unfinished drafts, was directed "beautifully" by Sills, says Shepherd, as a series of blackout skits, with Brechtian slides made by the German sculptor Hugo Weber and lantern lights. In the *Sun-Times*, Herman Kogan praised "the off-beat offering" and observed that "Edward Asner's playing of the exacting title role was filled with deep understanding and genuine pathos." Except for rare occasions of illness or trips to Kansas City to see his family, Asner was thereafter relied on, in Shepherd's words, as "a workhorse," to appear, usually in leading roles, in twenty-two productions out of twenty-five.

The Coming of Bildad, the first original play staged by the company, was listed in the *Wozzek* program as "a didactical comedy about two roving con men," and directed by David Shepherd. Although Beverly Fields missed seeing the show, after reading the script, she surmised that the playwright was "a very young writer" but "not without talent. If Mr. Sills is a little over-conscious of words, there is no reason to think he will not outgrow it. The play falls into scenes that leap to the eye . . . And the dialogue seems to have been written to be spoken."

An old photograph of himself and Ed Asner in army uniform standing in front of Heyward Ehrlich's mother's house in the Bronx makes Ehrlich suspect that Asner was the fellow University of Chicago draftee who seduced him back to Chicago with the news that "something really interesting was going on." Ehrlich moved into an alcove on North LaSalle Street and "did my number," including "the same bad acting" he had done at Tonight at 8:30 and a translation of Molière that was never produced.

Besides all their theatrical endeavors, Ehrlich observed that through repertory his old friends "were trying to work out their relations with each other in a very deep sense." They ate at a food stand around the corner that featured a round-screened television set and specialized in "hot dogs with French fries on them, as well as other little things. And that was dinner—twenty-five cents—a lot of the time." They lived in the theatre. Once Charlie Jacobs took Ehrlich to task for sleeping in Jacobs's bed without taking a shower. To Ehrlich such incidents "typified the creature experience" of the Playwrights Theatre Club as it looked to a former draftee.

At 8:00 a.m., arriving at the theatre with Sondra Boikan "to wash the stage or something," Barbara Harris would see Ehrlich coming out of the bathroom "carrying his toothbrush and blowing a whistle. All the bunks were suddenly made up and shoved behind books to make it look like the alcoves hadn't been slept in, since it wasn't allowed. Heyward and Asner had just gotten out of the army. They were very militarized. Then they all had to sweep their alcoves. I think that was Asner's part. First it was blowing the whistle. Then sweeping the alcoves. Then marching around to get dressed. I'd see them behind their little curtains, fluffing up. Each alcove was decorated in a unique way. And they all had ladies come in and visit them. I'd get all embarrassed if I saw a girl sitting on a bed."

People took odd jobs to support themselves. For their work at the theatre, leading actors got ten to twenty dollars a week, minor actors no pay. But for $1.80 an hour, several University of Chicago graduates like Ehrlich discovered that three or four days a week they could rouse themselves for the 6:00 a.m. shapeup at the railroad and work until 2:30 in the afternoon at such mentally unstrenuous labor as sorting enormous sacks of mail. One Playwrights Theatre Club actor worked for the gas company. "He didn't read the meters, he just guessed," says Ehrlich, "and dallied with housewives."

The Coming of Bildad, a play for which Ehrlich was billed as a "technical assistant," he describes as "nothing. Free association. The most forgettable play. I think Paul would agree. It was silly. It was nonsense. Maybe he'd been reading *Finnegans Wake*. If anyone else had written it, it would have never gotten on." Incongruously, from an exponent of nonverbal expression, "It was three hours of puns."

Sills's play, which Sheldon Patinkin describes as "a squalid *The Rainmaker*," suggested a menage à trois between the two con men and the lady sculptor. "If you can, imagine a menage à trois about theatre people in California, trying to make it and thinking about themselves as socialists," Marvin Peisner says. Sills, who once burned the manuscript of *Bildad* because Elaine rejected him, now seemed to even the score. According to Peisner, "It was his *After the Fall*." The part of Anora, one of a very disorganized person, always dropping pieces of paper, is appraised by Patinkin as "a graphic image of Elaine."

Bildad, the mesmerizing person who comes to town, was played by Eugene Troobnick. As Peleg, his Sancho Panza, the playwright played himself. The stuffy town council, which hated the hero, were Edward

Asner, Tom Erhart, and Creighton Clarke. In her only incarnation, Anora was played disconcertingly by Jean Mowry in a traditional rather than a Brechtian style. Elaine May had been offered and had refused the un-flattering part of herself. "And the only one who could play Elaine was Elaine," says Peisner. "No one else came close."

Next came Ben Jonson's *Volpone,* in which Asner played Volpone, Troobnick played Mosca, Mike Nichols (temporarily seeking refuge in Chicago from his struggling actor's life in New York) played The Vulture, and Marvin Peisner played The Crow.

As the fall season began, a blacklisted former member of the Group Theatre, Al Saxe, dropped by the theatre looking for work. He had graying hair and wore a blue work shirt. The three producers, seemingly so in-transigent in their theatrical philosophies, were instantly willing to gamble on the stranger, who, under the name Allen Stone, directed Joy Carlin, Asner, and Troobnick in a fine production of *Widowers' House,* Shaw's antilandlord play.

As for Barbara Harris, it was Tom O'Horgan's impression that "they never let her do anything." That fall, however, she was asked to cut her hair off for her first speaking part, in Sills's staging of Shepherd's *The Fields of Malfi,* which she remembers as "a play about money and people arguing about their estate" and in which she was cast as Filippo, a thirteen-year-old Italian boy. She weighed only ninety pounds. She says, "There was nothing to me then."

She withdrew from classes at the Goodman Theatre, and Sills called in Marvin Peisner to coach her in working with her voice and hands. "She really wasn't very good," says Peisner. "She was so overlogical, and very timid, not just shy. She was so scared, that when Paul gave me this job, I was ready to leave."

Under the lights, Zohra Lampert, who played Bianca, Filippo's mother, remembers Barbara arriving onstage one night with a poodle-style perm and a pair of eyeglasses she'd found in the prop box, with little wire rims. Catching Zohra's eye, she proceeded to "break up." Too inexperienced herself to know how to respond to the burst of nervous energy Zohra hid little Filippo against the jacket of her off-to-college suit.

But when Barbara got up to sing a song in rehearsal workshop, Joy Carlin was suddenly struck by her presence: "She was just like herself, totally unaffected and pure." She unveiled her satirical gifts at *The Fields of Malfi* cast party when she and Eugene Troobnick treated the perfor-mances of Zohra and Byrne Piven to a parody.

If you ask Sheldon Patinkin, who was, with Jerry Cunliffe (Barbara's

Senn High School freshman classmate), the only other teenaged member
of the group, "Paul saw Barbara's talent long before anyone else. They
were like Cathy and Heathcliff. He drove her into being an actress. She
was his star."

But it was not Sills's decision to include, in a *Chicago* magazine feature
on Playwrights Theatre Club, two photographs by William Miller of Barbara Harris. In one, she is thoughtfully reading aloud from a script. In
the other, behind the blur of her broom, the camera captures the charming
and innocent grace that seems to flow from her utter commitment to
whisking the stage.

Too late to see Troobnick and Mowry play the roles in *The Coming of
Bildad* that Sills's friends had inspired and supposedly were "perfect for,"
Elaine May and John Ecks showed up together as a twosome at Charlie
Jacobs's new apartment at "some crazy hour," he recalls, after hitchhiking
from Los Angeles, in the fall of 1954, while *The Fields of Malfi* was on
the boards. Elaine took off again, for Washington. Ecks stayed on.

Ecks was "an interesting case," says Tom O'Horgan. "He was stunningly
handsome and had a power over people." He was "gaunt and romantic,
with piercing blue eyes and a thin sharp chin." One friend describes him
as "one of the most formidable mesmerists in the world." Sills calls him
"a match" for Elaine.

When an electrical blackout swept the city, Ecks alerted the AP services
to the news that *The Fields of Malfi* had gone on before a loyal and
fascinated audience in candlelight. Shepherd was delighted by the publicity
and impressed by the way that Ecks "knew the score."

"He knew how to flatter and cajole," recalls Bob Smith, at twenty-one
an army veteran newly returned to Chicago who had been told by Sills to
"stick around and make yourself useful and you can work." Selling ads
for Playwrights, Smith watched Ecks go into an Italian store as "Mr.
Bonifaccio" or into a Jewish store as "Hi, I'm Mr. Horowitz. We've got
a little theatre here . . ." and thus fill up his order book in a day.

For Christmas, to drum up an audience, it was decided to have Byrne
Piven direct *The Dybbuk*, S. Ansky's folk play about demoniacal possession
and exorcism among the Chassidim in an eighteenth-century Polish ghetto
because, according to Sills and Shepherd's calculations, "Seventy-five percent of the subscribers were Jewish, and it was a Jewish play."

Intending to avoid the show-biz atmosphere he had briefly experienced
as a young actor in New York, Piven had signed up for graduate work in
Shakespeare at the University of Chicago and for a day job at juvenile

court. He credits his excitement over Sills's Mandel Hall production of *The Caucasian Chalk Circle* for derailing his scholarship. At twenty-two, he was the only member of the group to have majored in drama at college, where he acquired a lot of Stanislavsky training. "I was always at war with Sills and Shepherd," Piven says. "I was interested in psychological realism while they were interested in the definitive gesture." He recalls it as Shepherd's very strong Brechtian wish "to permit the audience its head . . . never to ask them to relinquish their power of judgment to emotion," whereas Piven contended that a theatre revealing no inner expression was a "dry theatre of soulless ideas."

As the possessed young woman, Leah, Piven cast Joyce Hiller, later to become his wife. Ed Asner, Estelle Lutrell, Barbara Harris, Marvin Peisner, Sheldon Patinkin (the production manager), Bob Smith, and Phil Morini were cast in smaller parts. The music was by Tom O'Horgan, choreography by Chaika Fox. John Ecks, who is not remembered as an actor, was cast as Channon, the demon, The Dybbuk. "He was physically perfect. He was a wraith," says Piven. "And he conned me into casting him."

Shepherd and Sills let it be known that they considered *The Dybbuk* a complete sellout. It was sentimental and corny but probably hadn't been performed in English in a hundred years, and, as Ed Asner reflects, by presenting the play to the actors as "a sop to the audience," the producers were maintaining their "frontal appearance." Says Shepherd, "Those busloads from Northwestern were our bread and butter." Says Asner, "We knew you couldn't keep doing all the Brecht and alienation in the world."

In *The Dybbuk*, instead of using beards with spirit gum, Bob Smith recalls that the actors wore "horrible beards with wire hooks," which wound around their faces so tightly that their lips couldn't move. More discomfited by the knowledge that one member of the company, Richard Davidson, a "mad" poet, was a big spitter, the actors, playing double and triple parts, constantly switched beards.

Word spread through the beards of the make-believe Chassidim that Sills had invited an incredibly brilliant, mysterious, seductive woman to join the company. Sheldon Patinkin heard a weird woman in the balcony, laughing oddly and hysterically. It was her, Elaine May.

Arriving with one of Chicago's coldest winters, Elaine showed up in the theatre wearing a tight-fitting silk blouse and tennis shoes without socks. In David Shepherd's first glimpse of her, she was carrying a raggedy manuscript of a play she was writing called *Mikey and Nicky*. Tom O'Horgan, whom Barbara Harris remembers walking around with a harp, remembers Elaine was accompanied by a baby buggy. "A kind of scarifying lady," O'Horgan says. "Elaine was not clean-cut." Since a cigarette was constantly dangling from her lips, she talked out of the side of her mouth. If she had come with "incredible advance publicity," Bob Smith thought she "absolutely lived up to everything. She had the darkest smoldering eyes and the biggest tits I'd ever seen."

Men in their fifties who knew her in their twenties still seem apologetic when they confess they were "probably the only one" not chosen for an affair with Elaine May.

Her impressions on them were indelible.

Omar Shapli remembers "vividly" when he first met her, soon after his release from the army, as he was eating breakfast at Steinway's in 1954. "I became aware of a piercing, dark-eyed, sultry stare from this young woman. It was really unnerving. After we were introduced, she said, 'Omar, will you marry me?' If I'd said, 'Of course,' we would have been married that afternoon. But I went to pieces, and she wrote me off. She was quite playful, but vicious. She was like Carmen. She seemed like a potential black widow: 'You better eat your steak in the morning if you want to mess with me.' "

Marvin Peisner recalls her as a "mananizer. In some of these affairs, she destroyed the man."

The impressions of her financial situation were just as indelible. Professor of Theatre Arts at the State University of New York at Purchase, George Morrison ('49), remembers her pilfering at supermarkets. Shapli was "under the impression that she was sleeping in abandoned apartments like a vagabond." An actress who lent her a dress remembers, "She was like a gutter rat. She wore a size six. I gave her a size twelve dress. She had been writing plays on Corn Flakes boxes for a long time."

Shepherd remembers that she taught Barbara Harris how to beg.

She did not seem interested in fame or money. She was only interested in work.

She made a shoeshine box, staked out a space in front of the Ambassador Hotel, and charged a quarter for a shine.

"Elaine had a genuine beautiful madness, a raw unpolished intelligence, and an unbalanced education," remembers one of her suitors, psychologist James Sacks. "She knew everything about the theatre and psychoanalysis. She didn't know about anything else." She knew the subtleties of Scandinavian drama, but she didn't know if Mexico was north or south of the

United States. While Rollo May was in Truro or Nantucket thinking he had two subletters, she once stayed in the great psychiatrist's New York apartment with a group of eight and read everything in his library. (Her problems with her mother, whom she now referred to as "a good Chekhov man," were made explicit in *The Coming of Bildad*.) She didn't know if Eisenhower was a Republican or a Democrat.

She would sit in a director's chair in the back of the theatre on North LaSalle Street surrounded by a group of "guys hanging on every word, on every glance," telling stories about traveling with her father in the Yiddish theatre, where, dressed in a little suit and short haircut, she had played little boys. Her abduction by Aaron Lebedeff, a Yiddish musical comedy star famous for his rendition of "Roumania, Roumania," was one of her tales.

"In love with Elaine?" ponders Bob Smith. "Oh, sure. You'd have to be stupid not to have been."

She was a startlingly gifted caricaturist whose drawings of people onstage were brilliant and savage. She assessed this activity as just doodling. When her subjects asked to keep the drawings, she tore them up.

Little scraps of paper trailed her. She was always dropping things.

She ate huge numbers of apples. Many people recall that she consumed the pits and cores.

S ills and Shepherd had somewhat miscalculated the audience for *The Dybbuk*: a theatre party of nuns came and loved it. Bob Smith judged them "the best audience we ever had." It was the first play to make money as well as a hit with the critics, who compared Piven's stage images to those of Chagall.

More appropriate, nevertheless, to the group's own mythos was the following show, Sills's production of *The Threepenny Opera*, one of the great collaborations of Brecht and the composer Kurt Weill. Brecht was infatuated with Chicago, although he had never been there. Chicago to Brecht was the theatrical embodiment of capitalist excess, complete with civic corruption, an underworld of gangsters, stockyards, steel mills, and a fat and complacent middle class. *The Resistible Rise of Arturo Ui* and *In the Jungle of the Cities* take place in Chicago, as does *Saint Joan of the Stockyards* and the musical play it was derived from, Brecht, Elisabeth Hauptmann, and Weill's *Happy End*. Ironically, neither of the two Brecht plays Sills chose to direct at Playwrights Theatre Club had a Chicago setting, but he and the company injected what Brecht might have perceived as authentic Chicago spirit into both of them.

On a trip to New York, Joy Carlin was given the task of soliciting from Marc Blitzstein the free use of his translation of *The Threepenny Opera*. She recalls, "I explained that we couldn't afford it and asked him to leave us alone" and she was "naïve enough to ask" while Blitzstein, director Carmen Capalbo, and Weill's widow, Lotte Lenya, were making plans for an upcoming production off-Broadway at the Theatre de Lys. The "crazy" demand from the "struggling people's company," as Carlin was told to portray them, so incensed Blitzstein that he threw Carlin out of his office.

The producers decided to fall back on the earlier translation by Eric Bentley, who threatened to sue. Sills is remembered as "elated" by the correspondence. The return letters to his guru won Bentley over by invoking the supplicant's youth, pure intentions, and simpatico politics.

"A certain delight in cheating was in the nature of Paul," says Marvin Peisner. "He and his brother were not given much by their dad. The emissaries and the letters were prompted by another side of him—the side of him that was scared stiff."

Besides childhood deprivation, besides their burning enthusiasm to put daring new work on the stage, the founders of the improvisational theatre, so carefree and Brechtian in their outlaw appropriation of copyrighted plays, expressed indifference very early to authors of the written word.

At Playwrights Theatre Club, perhaps only a "mananizer" could have asserted her personality as thoroughly as Elaine May. The theatre visionaries of 1954 were Bohemians, not feminists. If the men found her "scarifying" and fascinating, Sills's admiration further validated her status. To one actor, Shepherd seemed "a pussycat," interested only in acting with political conscience. Sills, however, could be disdainful, uncharitable, erratic, and temperamental. Actors would put up with him since he gave out the parts. Waiting for a nod from Sills, the same actor observed that "what Elaine said was important to Paul. He had respect for her brain."

The new woman in Sills's life, Barbara Harris, sensed the pressure upon her to measure up to Elaine. "Elaine was very much into thought," she says, "and very sophisticated, and very smart. I was somehow more able to iron my clothes. Elaine was so . . . well . . . incompetent in terms of being able to get her clothes on. I was always running and getting her pins." Compared to Elaine, who was born in a trunk, Barbara felt infinitely bourgeois. Neatness counted for Barbara. Elaine let people pick up for her, and she was always dropping things. Elaine accepted weekly rent money from Sills. Barbara could—and sooner would—go home to her family.

Even so, Elaine was quite personable in the role of Barbara's mentor, with a world view as well as a technique for stealing scraps of food off unbused plates.

It was during rehearsals of *The Threepenny Opera* that she taught Barbara how to beg. They borrowed raincoats from the collection assembled at the theatre for Mr. Peachum's Beggar's Outfit Shop. "It was very theatrical, sort of a happening," Barbara reflects. "She kept saying, 'We have to do it in Brechtian style.' I said, 'What's Brechtian style?' And she said, 'I'll show you.' "

Elaine then walked up to a strange man. She said, "We're begging," as though she were looking down her nose at him, very superciliously. "We're begging, and we want some money," she said. The man was embarrassed and pulled out a quarter. "And now one for my friend," Elaine said. He gave another quarter. The two beggars bought oranges with the fifty cents and made dinner out of them.

As a teenager, Barbara assessed begging as "too easy. Elaine seemed a little more serious about it than I was. But I was getting money from home. There was no reason why I had to beg. And there was really no reason why *she* had to beg. I mean, she could have gotten a job."

As a slightly older fellow, David Shepherd could not fail to observe that his colleagues were "living out these crazy Bohemian lives" at the same time they were "accepted by Sydney Harris and other people as the most irritating but interesting young theatre group in Chicago. This was a wild scene, you know?" he says.

"I remember thinking they were very commercial," says Tom O'Horgan. "I was this serious twelve-tone composer. Writing theatre music was a comedown. But as a theatre musician, you come in, take your measurements, and go home and do the tailoring. So I seemed an absolute philistine to them."

If they pictured themselves on the cutting edge of society, Heyward Ehrlich, a self-described onlooker, perceived them as "proving something to a parent, trying to find a back door to conventional success." After all, they weren't acting like left-wing workers in Gary, Indiana. They were acting like lumpenproletariat in Brecht.

"They were conning the world all the time. The theatre was the con that worked. In the theatre, you believe in illusions more than you believe in reality. The particular quality of this group's illusions was very unromantic. Their storytelling, their folklore seemed to vibrate to that kind of material."

Sills's production of Bentley's translation of *The Threepenny Opera* starred Eugene Troobnick as Macheath, Edward Asner as Peachum, Ann Sweet Petry as Mrs. Peachum, Estelle Lutrell as Polly, Tom Erhart as Tiger Brown, Barbara Harris as Lucy Brown, and Zohra Lampert as Jenny the season before the Blitzstein version opened off-Broadway at the Theatre de Lys for its long and historic run.

Even after later playing Peachum for two and a half years in New York, when Ed Asner remembers the "Useless Song," "It's still the Bentley lyrics that persist in my head." Comparing the first time he sang on stage on LaSalle Street to his New York stint, Asner reflects that "there was a lot of truth in the bare-bones simplicity of our Chicago production" that he found "almost impossible to recover in the monorail of New York." In the Big Apple, Asner found himself trying "to get out of the rut I'd gotten into, depending on the same laughs. I tried to experiment, but two lines into my first speech, I realized that in front of three hundred people, I didn't have the same guts."

"**O**kay, we've done *Rounddance* for the North Side Bohemians and *The Dybbuk* for the Jews. Now let's do something for the goyim," Sills told Marvin Peisner, inviting him to direct *Murder in the Cathedral* by T. S. Eliot, whose poetry Peisner had presented on the University of Chicago campus several years before. Sills and Shepherd referred to Eliot's obscure symbolist tragedy about Anglican politics and martyrdom as "an ethnic play."

. At Playwrights Theatre Club, Elaine had as yet involved herself only in the workshops and in setting up a concession in the theatre lobby during intermissions where she sold candy bars. After Peisner cast her as one of the Women's Chorus in *Murder in the Cathedral*, she acted a lot. Under Troobnick's direction, she next appeared with him and Sills in Chekhov's *A Marriage Proposal*. On the same bill, she directed a production of Strindberg's *Miss Julie*. Bob Smith refers to its dress rehearsal as "one of the epic moments in Playwrights Theatre Club history." Zohra Lampert had been cast as Miss Julie, Joyce Hiller as The Cook. At Elaine's insistence, Ed Asner was chosen over an actor brought in from New York to play the role of the servant who seduces Miss Julie and destroys her, Jean the Valet.

In the literature of female sexuality, *Miss Julie* is an important document, the tragedy of an aristocratic young woman whose conflicts between propriety and desire drive her to suicide. There is no more "psychological" play. Strindberg rejected as bourgeois "the simplified view of human character as having a fixed disposition." He perceived his characters as "conglomerates of past and present cultural phases, bits from books and newspapers, scraps of humanity, pieces torn from fine clothes and become rags, patched together as is the human soul." For Strindberg, the "definitive gesture" was not where it was at. In 1888, he was convinced that "people of today are most interested in the psychological process." The playwright could (and did) explore the motives for Miss Julie's disorder in words, through exposition. (Thus, for example, we learn that the heroine's mother, a frustrated believer in woman's equality, raised her daughter as "a child of nature," an example of how a woman can be as good as a man, and to hate men.) But how to display the symptoms?

In his fascinating author's preface to *Miss Julie*, Strindberg explains that to accommodate the audience's view of the psychological process, he deliberately wrote dialogue that

> . . . avoided the symmetrical, mathematical construction of French drama and let characters' minds function irregularly, as they do in a real-life conversation where no topic of discussion is exhausted entirely, and one mind by chance finds a cog in another mind in which to engage. Consequently, the dialogue also wanders, presenting material in the opening scenes that is later reworked, repeated . . . like the theme in a musical composition.

As for monologues, Strindberg went so far as to suggest that "a talented actor, absorbed in the mood and situation, perhaps can improvise the monologues more effectively than the author . . . who cannot determine in advance how much may be spoken and for how long." Citing commedia dell'arte, he indicated sections where the actors could do dumb show, or mime, during which music and asymmetrical scenery would evoke the illusion of their inner condition.

Interpreting Strindberg, Elaine May was "a very meticulous director, very gifted," says Joyce Piven. "And very involved with minute details. She never seemed to be working on acting values, only on technical things." Piven remembers rehearsing an hour until her director was satisfied with the way The Cook removed a glass from a tray. At a sound studio made available to the company by Jerry Cunliffe's father, it took an all-night session with Tom O'Horgan for Elaine to satisfactorily record a complete track of background music and ambient sound.

One morning at three, Byrne Piven, who lived with The Cook around the corner from the theatre in the seedy neighborhood, began to worry about Joyce. He found her in the empty theatre fast asleep. Onstage, on a stool, was Asner. He was also asleep. Whispering beside him were Zohra and Elaine, engrossed in discovering the perfect way for Miss Julie to hold her pet bird, a green finch, which she has just provoked her lover, the brutal and insensitive valet, to behead.

While rehearsals for *Miss Julie* thus continued, Barbara Harris went alone to New York for an audience with Lee Strasberg, who was already teaching acting to Mike Nichols and Joy Carlin, and who encouraged her to stay. "You'll never learn anything in that Chicago theatre. Take my class," Strasberg said. But when Sills showed up in New York "on business," Barbara was persuaded to abandon the heady vibes of the Actors Studio, for the time being, for the Playwrights Theatre Club and romance. She resumed working in *Miss Julie* as one of the Townsfolk.

The dress rehearsal began at midnight and ran till dawn. "Elaine was not a natural social animal," observes Joyce Piven. "There was a creative perversity about her. She was willing to take an experiment as far as it could go."

"We did it, and it was a disaster," says Asner. Thinking himself too fat for the part, he had been very flattered to be cast as Jean. "To very little avail," he had even tried to slim down for the part. "I'm not sure why it failed," he says. "Instead of portraying neurotic people, we almost became them. I almost broke out in shingles doing it."

Although Strindberg himself had recommended improvisation for *Miss Julie*, none of the actors remembers taking any departures from the script. Byrne Piven observed that "Elaine epitomized the conflict between harmony and invention. She was always trying to find the truth of a moment improvisationally. But she insisted it be honed to its absolute condition and frozen there. Her perfectionism demanded that." Another viewer says simply, "Elaine was almost anal compulsive when it came to a scripted play."

Elaine never directed any but her own work at Playwrights Theatre Club again. She was succeeded in the next production by Raoul De Leon, whose continental get-up was "the exact opposite" of that of the other guest director, blue-denimed Al Saxe. Raoul De Leon had a pencil-thin mustache like Phil Morini and looked to Byrne Piven like "a refugee from the Mafia." When he offered his talents to Shepherd and Sills, they gave him Sartre's play about a power struggle within a Communist party group, *Les mains sales* (in this production called *Red Gloves*, literally *Dirty Hands*) to direct.

"Raoul didn't speak one word of our language," Piven recalls. "He was from another planet. We made a tacit pact to ignore him. It was a cocky experiment. I think Paul and David wanted to see of how much importance, if any, a director really was."

At twenty-four, Piven, who was prematurely balding, played middle-aged Hoederer, the true revolutionary. Troobnick played Hugo, the indecisive young intellectual assigned to be Hoederer's assassin or, as he calls it, "the Hamlet part." Mae Munro played Hugo's wife, Jessica, whose infidelity with Hoederer provokes Hugo to shoot his hero as an act of passion instead of politics (a revolutionary embarrassment). When Hoederer's reputation must be rehabilitated because of a change of Party line, Hugo finds a way to rectify his shame: by allowing himself to be gunned down by his comrades as the man who made the political mistake. Sills and Asner played Hoederer's bodyguards. Hugo's revolutionary mentor, Olga, was played by Elaine, in what would remain one of her favorite guises, that of a spy.

8

Playwrights' Second Year

B y the end of the first year, the Playwrights Theatre Club had 2,000 subscribers. *Chicago* magazine ran Beverly Fields's glowing feature in April 1954 and noted that "in a time when the commercial theatre in Chicago is distinguished by its dullness, the presence of a group that is searching for fresh approaches to theatre is like a spark in the dark."

Entering the second year, the company had an Actors' Equity contract, and had moved a few blocks closer to the Loop, into a former gambling joint on Dearborn and Division, a bigger and more presentable house. There were plans afoot for touring London and New York.

Eugene Troobnick, who was being hailed by the critics as "a young Fernandel," was relieved without rancor of his producer's duties. He was replaced by Bernard Sahlins ('43), an energetic young Chicagophile with an engineering background, a rich father, his own booming tape recorder business, and an interest in Irgun, an organization of radical Jews. Sahlins, who had been eager to participate in Playwrights Theatre Club from its inception, became its only producing partner with the "support skill" of making money.

Mike Nichols had finally settled in New York, where he was taking classes—along with Inger Stevens and Carroll ("Baby Doll") Baker—with Lee Strasberg. Baker thought it "obvious from his very first scene" that Nichols was "exceptionally gifted . . . He could make even a simple exercise hysterically funny in an absolutely genuine way." He supported himself as before, with a series of odd jobs. The one as a waiter at Howard Johnson's ended when a customer asked him the flavor-of-the-month and

Nichols answered, "Chicken." During the ensuing period, he devised a way to live entirely on mustard and cold cereal.

Barbara Harris and Paul Sills were married at City Hall.

Going into the second summer, Elaine got a job directing a play called *Out of the Frying Pan* for the Chicago Park District while simultaneously playing Hippolyta, Queen of the Amazons, in Bill Alton's staging of *A Midsummer Night's Dream*, the first play of the Playwrights Theatre Club Shakespeare Festival.

The next entry, *Henry IV, Part I*, featured Michael Kidd, a New York actor, as Prince Hal, Byrne Piven as Hotspur, and Edward Asner as the old King, in an interpretation by Sills over which Sheldon Patinkin and both Pivens still enthuse as one of the most exciting presentations they have ever witnessed of a history play.

Under Rolf Forsberg's direction, Elaine was one of the Fairies in *The Tempest*, in which Asner, as Prospero, received his greatest notices. In the *Daily News*, Sydney J. Harris called his performance "stunning . . . rich, passionate and dignified."

Ending the Shakespeare Festival was *Romeo and Juliet*, directed by Henry Weinstein, a guest from New York. He cast it by randomly choosing the first actors to show up for work. The Playwrights Theatre Club veterans, exercising their prima-donna privileges, slept late and arrived at the theatre in time for such parts as Citizens of Verona and Kinfolk, although Troobnick remembers that "Asner got Capulet." Tresa Hughes, who had moved from Ann Arbor to join the company, played The Nurse. Hughes remembers great hostility to Weinstein and his casting ("a terrible Romeo") and still thinks, "They were crazy not to cast Zohra as Juliet." By most accounts, Weinstein's show was a mess.

At the beginning of the fall season, from several translations he had collated, Sills directed Ibsen's *Peer Gynt*. In the first of her many mother roles, Elaine played Åse to Byrne Piven's Peer. The show (which featured several improvised interludes) opened with both of them bursting through the audience, Elaine chasing Piven with a broom. Elaine would scream, "You're lying!" Safe on stage, Piven would reply, "But it's true, every word!"

The actors noticed they were "not quite hitting it," until the night Sills muttered offhandedly before the curtain: "Play it like a fairy tale." Piven (who got great reviews) recalls the simplicity of the direction as a revelation as well as a portent of Sills's later preoccupation with the fairy tale.

Asner, who played an assortment of parts, including a Troll, thought the production "phenomenal." "It felt very alive, as though there was really some search for the truth by Peer Gynt," a spectator recalls. "Paul could infuse people with a certain enthusiasm," reflects Tresa Hughes, who was also a Troll, as well as Ingrid, Peer's betrothed. "In the mad scene, for instance, we certainly felt like we were in the booby hatch." The bold new view of Ibsen thrilled Bertram Jensenius, the local Norwegian critic, who saw it five times.

Early in the summer, Tony Holland had returned to school and an academic career, then traveled that fall to Philadelphia for the tedious conference of art historians at which he decided to put all his chips on the theatre. He was in everything the second year. As Treplev, the doomed son in Chekhov's *The Sea Gull*, he was cast, said Sydney J. Harris, "with amazing exactitude. He looks, speaks and acts precisely like an only son who has suffered from a mother's absent-minded affection." Madame Arkadina, the actress-mother, was "exquisitely repulsive," as played by Donna Holabird. Elaine did not perform in this Sills production, but she sat up all night sewing and helping Sills's always harried assistant, Sheldon Patinkin, he remembers, "in all kinds of ways."

During *The Sea Gull*, Patinkin's responsibilities began, in fact, to overwhelm him: he was deluged with schoolwork and had started fighting with Shepherd about the more practical ways he felt things should be done. Toward Sills, Tom O'Horgan observed, Patinkin was "mother-hennish— a crazy eighteen-year-old Jewish mother hen." At Playwrights Theatre Club, he had been variously the piano player, the membership office, the production manager, the costume designer, and the lighting man. Suddenly, to Patinkin, "It just seemed a good idea not to be there anymore."

After *The Sea Gull*, Zohra Lampert and her husband, Bill Alton, also left the Playwrights Theatre Club, she to shortly study acting in New York with Mira Rostova, Montgomery Cliff's coach. Zohra had decided to cast her lot in the theatre, even though everything in her upbringing told her that "being an actress was an unserious thing to do."

To Sheldon Patinkin, even Paul Sills seemed to have lost interest in Playwrights Theatre Club after *The Sea Gull*. Shepherd says, "He was exhausted." In a year and a half, he had directed eight plays. With the distinguished stage director Alan Schneider as his sponsor, he applied for a Fulbright scholarship to teach Viola's games in England at the University of Bristol in a workshop that would conclude with a production of *The Tempest* at the Bristol Old Vic.

Edward Asner was happy. He was amassing rave reviews. With these and an Equity card, he could face his parents. Joining the union made him feel "legitimized."

And David Shepherd was dissatisfied.

As distinguished from mass culture, which offers up junk food, Playwrights Theatre Club, according to its principal investor, presented nouvelle cuisine, plays he thought were "too highfalutin" to appeal to his target audience, Chicago's working class. This theatre did not reflect the views of the ordinary citizen in his own language in the issues of the day: the boss/worker relationship, urban renewal, taxes, elections, the Korean War.

Instead, he found himself producing middle-class entertainments like a Shakespeare Festival. ("You know, Shakespeare was *safe*.") Compared to Playwrights Theatre Club, John Ecks, who had started his own workshop, seemed revolutionary, as radical, Shepherd noted enviously, as the founders of The Living Theatre in New York, Judith Malina and Julian Beck.

Playwrights Theatre Club welcomed original American plays from the outset, as the name of the company implies. Shepherd in fact had started a writers' workshop the first fall. It was clear to writers like Jean Martin that although none of the workshoppers had one iota of experience in writing them, Shepherd was really interested in developing new plays. To the young people in the class, Carl Pederson looked like "just a boring old guy in a suit," but to their surprise, he impressed Shepherd immensely. Unlike the others, Pederson turned in plays every week. He deluged Shepherd with material. Martin remembers Shepherd as truly excited to discover the source of Pederson's productivity: his sole technique for getting subject matter was looking through the newspaper.

The writers' workshop never produced a play that was stageworthy, and after Playwrights Theatre Club had exhausted *The Coming of Bildad* and *The Fields of Malfi*, Sills never pursued the task of discovering new writers and plays. He seemed to prefer directing old texts from the European theatre. Shepherd, however, found the idea of filling the American stage with European plays so "obscene" he had even turned down the first American production rights to Samuel Beckett's *Waiting for Godot*. "I didn't see what was funny about it," he says. "I thought it was anemic, desiccated."

Rich But Happy, a play about Czechoslovakian displaced persons set in a concentration camp in Salzburg, was solicited through a playwriting contest Shepherd set up in March 1954. A teacher at Bard College, Theodore ("Ted") Hoffman, was the playwright who emerged the winner, but the air fare to Chicago ate up his one-hundred-dollar prize. Now a retired professor of theatre at New York University, Hoffman remembers his play as "pseudo-Brechtian" and "quite controversial. David directed, unfortunately, and it was a mess." It featured Tony Holland, Tresa Hughes, Vernon Schwartz, Tom Erhart, and Elaine May, "a disconcerting lady at the time, during notes, always snapping her bra." Hoffman did not realize that during *Rich But Happy*, Elaine was herself immersed in writing *Rumplestiltskin*, a children's play.

The second "Christmas show for the Jews" was a three-parter: the first act of *The Grand Prize* by Sholem Aleichem followed by *The Bespoke Overcoat* and a play about the Jonah complex, *It Should Happen to a Dog*, two one-acts by Wolf Mankiewicz, the nephew of Herman (the screenwriter of *Citizen Kane*), whom David Shepherd met in France. Isaac Rosenfeld, the *Partisan Review* writer, introduced the evening with a series of Jewish anecdotes.

The Jonah story, in which a man is hounded by God to travel to a distant wicked city to preach God's word against evil, has always intrigued David Shepherd. To the sufferer of the Jonah complex, as he interprets it, it is symptomatic that "you don't know where the voice is coming from that tells you to do something. When you figure out it's coming from God, you often decide not to go along with it. But you are forced unto pain of death to do what the voice is telling you." When Jonah sidestepped God's order to report to Nineveh, he was washed into the belly of the whale. And the longer Jonah put off his mission, the more punishments God appended. Since Shepherd has come to regard the Jonah story as "a paradigm" for his own obsession, his detour to the Playwrights Theatre Club may be seen as a two-year imprisonment in the belly of the whale, with more punishments to accrue.

Regarding Shepherd's growing disenchantment with the Playwrights Theatre Club, Heyward Ehrlich shrugs: "I never knew what he was doing there. Paul was there out of love and compulsion. Paul needed to be there. There was no other there for Paul. For David, it was sort of a hobby. It was almost as though he was Brandenburg Rasimovsky or something, and we were his musicians. I never had the feeling that in any way he needed to be there."

After the first anniversary performance, in May 1954, Shepherd had written in his journal:

> In a year and a half, I have helped build a miserable self-centered arts club which talks over the heads of its bourgeois members at the same time it licks their feet for patronage.
>
> In order for theatre to be an institution, its audience must love and hate it as they love and hate The Church and The President. Our fables must present not Wozzek, but the Chicago draftee; not Azdak, but Lawyer Jenkins; not Volpone, but Alderman Baker. We must

become obsessed not with the content of the classics, but with their technique.

For a brief moment last fall, Charlie Jacobs and Paul and I saw that the good of our theatre should be a riot in the audience. How could we forget it?

There had been at least some skirmishes.

"The theatre establishment at Goodman was not in love with us, the McCarthyites didn't love us, and the right-wing press didn't love us," says Edward Asner. To conservatives like the Chicago *Tribune* critic Claudia Cassidy ("The Medusa of the Midwest"), the mere presentation of *The Caucasian Chalk Circle* had been enough to establish Playwrights Theatre Club as pink.

In the fearful McCarthy atmosphere of 1954, critics came to view all the material onstage at Playwrights Theatre Club as deliberately provocative and troublesome.

Studs Terkel, the blacklisted Chicago personality, had assembled an evening called "Music from Elizabethan Times to the Blues," which was booked into the theatre on a Monday night, when Playwrights Theatre Club was dark. Narrated by Terkel, the program featured four singers, including a countertenor and Big Bill Broonzy. Cards were sent out to the membership. One flyer was returned with Studs Terkel's name circled in red. Also scrawled in thick red pencil were the words "Get this Red out of Chicago." On the return envelope was a sticker that said, "Fight CommUNism." Not only was the hostility unnerving, it was an expensive sticker. Asner says, "It looked like a wildlife stamp."

Such insidious political pressures from without were bound to threaten the fragile unity within the Playwrights Theatre Club membership. During the first year, as David Shepherd recalls it, two New York Communists came to Chicago "with their radical chic attitude and their boots," intending to present the actress Ann Harding in a reading of the script of *Salt of the Earth*, the great film about a strike in a New Mexican zinc mine.* Shepherd volunteered space for the reading in the North LaSalle

---

* *Salt of the Earth* was directed by Herbert Biberman, one of the Hollywood Ten. Most of the production team were also unemployable in Hollywood because of their politics. The film had been made on location against almost insuperable odds, including FBI surveillance, vigilante violence, and a congressional ban against releasing the negative abroad. It was finally ready for release at the end of 1953, when the Projectionists Union blackballed it. While the producers waited for their suit against the motion picture industry to come before the courts, the screenplay was being read to accommodating theatre groups.

Street theatre because, he says, "I believed that Playwrights Theatre Club should not only be a showcase for original plays but a sounding board for other groups."

When the announcements for the film went out to the membership, anti-Communist factions of Schachtmanites and Trotskyites bombarded the theatre with phone calls and threats to resign. Among the Playwrights Theatre Club company, "All hell broke loose."

"I don't care where you are," reflects Ed Asner, "if there is a group called 'the producers,' then actors will generally regard them as the enemy. With all the post facto love that I demonstrate toward Paul and David, there was a time there when I was part of a group of incipient mutineers." As Asner recalls the incident, "under the spell" of the mesmerizing John Ecks, the actors rebelled, more in protest of the producers' willingness to exploit them than over the actual reading of the screenplay. Even being associated with *Salt of the Earth*, Ecks pointed out, could endanger their future lives. Some actors were so indignant they threatened to quit.

Rather than exacerbate an internal political furor, Shepherd put the matter to a vote at a meeting that was specially convened.

Barbara Harris abstained. When John Ecks asked her why, she answered that she did not want to be responsible for the theatre closing down.

A majority voted that permission to show *Salt of the Earth* be revoked. "I was one of them," Asner says.

For this vote, Asner has since "tried to atone." He flew to Silver City, New Mexico, to add his weight to the celebration of the film's twenty-fifth anniversary, although, he says ruefully, "The barn door is closed."

Shepherd ended up personally renting space for the reading at a radical hangout owned by Slim Brundage, who had once run the famous Dill Pickle Club. "For a hundred and fifty dollars," Shepherd says, "I got off the hook."

Although most of them were people "so poor they were shoplifting," Shepherd felt shafted by the actors and deeply disappointed at their reluctance to share their stage with real political dissidents, even if they ran the risk of closing down.

They closed down anyway.

Ever since the Iroquois Theater Fire of 1903, Chicago theatres had been subject to complicated fire laws. By city ordinance, the only legal theatre was one with a proscenium stage. Hydraulic fire curtains were also required, and they were to be fed by twenty-six-inch water pipes. The archaic ordinance discouraged the little theatre movement and stultified its growth. "If you didn't have a Shubert or a Blackstone, you ran a weekend theatre in a church or school," says Richard Orlikoff, the Playwrights Theatre Club lawyer, who tried to have the ordinance amended in two unsuccessful battles in court.*

Thus, David Shepherd's short experience in the Chicago theatre had already included sophisticated negotiations with city inspectors. The theatre on North LaSalle Street had been "a tinderbox," and although the Playwrights Theatre Club was finally evicted, the sanitation, ventilation, and electrical inspectors had all accepted bribes. On Dearborn and Division, while waiting for the outcome of the unsuccessful legal appeal, the producers continued the time-honored local procedure of greasing palms.

It was "a quiet protest" to the mayor's office that provoked the final fire inspection. It is said that all theatres close because of fire laws. The open cans of paint were found behind the proscenium during the second production of *Rounddance*, which Rolf Forsberg staged with the sobering edge Schnitzler intended from his satire about free love in Vienna. Forsberg's version featured Barbara Harris as The Little Darling, in a performance Sills recalls as "sensational," Elaine May as The Actress, and Tony Holland as The Count.

During the first (and raunchier) Sills production, there had been no outcry, but shortly before this one, Richard J. Daley had moved into the mayor's office for his elongated tenure, and he was less indebted to Chicago's culture than to its Catholic diocese.

In February 1955, to the relief of the diners at Ballantine's, the fancy German restaurant downstairs, the fire department closed down the beatniks and their 200-seat theatre, 8,000 feet of "beautiful space" at Dearborn and Division (nicknamed "Queerborn and Perversion" for its street traffic), which had been converted the previous spring from Bill Johnson's D&D.

In his column in the Chicago *American*, George Murray observed that "no branch of government ever seemed to interest itself in Big Bill's roulette tables when he ran it in partnership for so long with Billy Skidmore, the West Side junk dealer. So a lot of folks wondered at the rash of righteousness brought to bear on the buskers. Building inspectors, electrical inspectors,

---

*Subsequently, a new ordinance was passed allowing theatres off the Loop, which would provide impetus for the growth of Chicago's little theatres. Today there are over 120 little theatre companies in Chicago, and, for experimental theatre, it is the country's national hub. In calling attention to the legal restrictions on the city's theatre, Playwrights Theatre Club was, as Orlikoff describes it, "a sacrificial lamb."

water inspectors and even Uncle Sam's T-men came like a plague of locusts."

After the Playwrights Theatre Club cleared out, over the lobby, where Big Bill's guards used to stand, remained two inches of lead.

Without its physical facility, the theatre fell apart. Shepherd continued to produce it, and under its aegis, productions continued to be staged, although they were organized by another faction, the group Shepherd refers to as "Rolf Forsberg and the Yoga crowd from the North Side."

When the end was near, Eugene Troobnick, who was now married, became an editor at Sears. Still more mainstays left Chicago for New York.

The "psychological" approach to acting had been written off by Sills and Shepherd. But actors are sensitive to their own notices. Although these were mostly supportive and glowing, the critics had made it obvious that the school of the "definitive gesture" had not provided this ensemble with the technique to play consistent Chekhov or Shakespeare.

Even after winning critical praise, Tony Holland trusted his own barometer. "I had great parts in all these wonderful plays, but it wasn't enough," he said. "Even though it was all acceptable to the audience, there was something I knew I wasn't getting. I didn't have the skills to sustain a role beyond the first three or four nights. I realized that if I wanted to be an actor, I'd have to learn to use my feelings." Immediately after *Rounddance* closed, Holland took off for New York, where he chose Lee Strasberg's classes for further study and Howard Johnson's for a job.

To others, like Ed Asner, who felt secure in his skills, Chicago was still the Second City. Instinctively, the actors were drawn to "the monorail of New York." Asner remembers, "I was quite dedicated to taking my new-found loot—the reviews and the security I had received from two years at Playwrights—and trying my luck in the Big Apple."

Their Equity cards said they were workers, but after Playwrights Theatre Club, David Shepherd would always regard professional actors with a mixture of contempt and apprehension and as the enemy.

Between productions of the Playwrights Theatre Club, he alone had persisted in his notion of the Compass, the political cabaret.

He had first tried to book an after-hours cabaret on the same bill as the Shakespeare Festival, on the lawn of Ellen Borden Stevenson, the ex-wife of the presidential candidate, Adlai, and the former First Lady of Illinois. But it was impossible to get the permits to launch such a project in Democratic Chicago without friends in high places, and, divorced from the party leader, Mrs. Stevenson had no political allies.

LEFT: *Viola Spolin with her assistant, Robert A. Martin, Hollywood, 1948.*

BELOW: *Viola surrounded by the Young Actors Company, Hollywood, 1946. Alan Arkin is third from left.*

"The University of Chicago" said Robert Hutchins, "is not a kindergarten. It is not a club. It is not an agency of propaganda. It is a community of scholars."

A favorite campus joke: "The only university in America where a Baptist pays Jews to teach Catholicism to atheists."

In the background the three producers of the Playwrights Theatre Club, 1953: (left to right) Eugene Troobnick, Paul Sills, and David Shepherd; in front of them, Zohra Lampert, who became their leading lady after one performance of The Caucasian Chalk Circle.

The Playwrights Theatre Club company on the set of Volpone *in 1953: (back row, left to right) Eugene Troobnick, David Shepherd, Paul Sills; (middle, left to right) Sheldon Patinkin, Edward Asner, Marvin Peisner, Heyward Ehrlich, Bill Alton, Bob Smith, Byrne Piven, Phil Morini; (front, left to right) Sandra MacDonald, Joy Grodzins (now Carlin), Helen Axelrood, Zohra Lampert, Joyce Hiller (now Piven), Ann Petry.*

PLAYWRIGHTS THEATRE CLUB

presents

Round Dance

by

Arthur Schnitzler

The Prostitute	Helen Axelrood
The Soldier	George Goritz
The Housemaid	Joy Grodzins

PLAYWRIGHTS THEATRE CLUB

presents

MOONY'S KID DON'T CRY

by Tennessee Williams

Moony	Byrne Piven
Jane	Norma Ransom
Directed by	Eugene Troobnick

WOZZEK

by

Georg Büchner

Wozzek	Edward Asner
The Captain	James Holland
The Doctor	Eugene Troobnick
Andres	Thomas Erhart

PLAYWRIGHTS THEATRE CLUB

presents

The Coming of Bildad

by

PAUL SILLS

1560 North LaSalle Street, 1953.

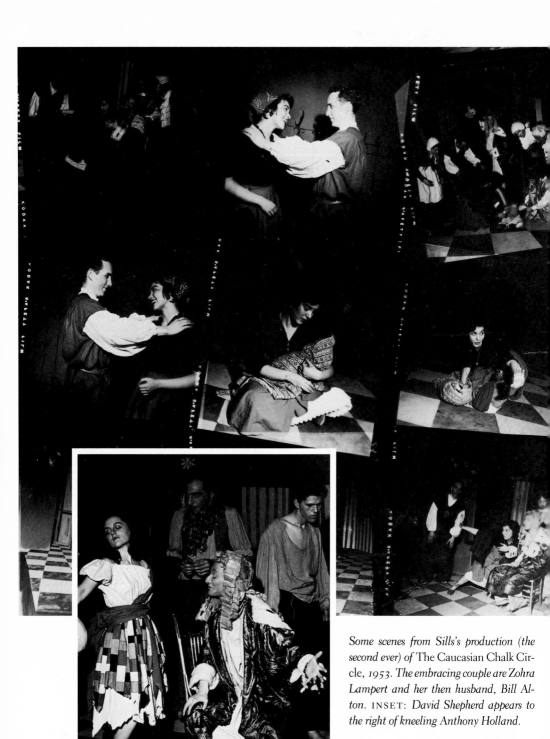

Some scenes from Sills's production (the second ever) of The Caucasian Chalk Circle, *1953. The embracing couple are Zohra Lampert and her then husband, Bill Alton.* INSET: *David Shepherd appears to the right of kneeling Anthony Holland.*

Paul Sills (right) making his acting debut at University Theatre with Jon Jackson in Elder Olsen's Faust: A Mask, *c. 1950.*

(Left to right) Edward Asner, Anthony Holland, and Eugene Troobnick rehearsing Wozzek, *summer 1953. Sills's direction, unlike his acting, was described as "sweaty, earthy, unorthodox."*

Elaine May playing Hippolyta to Byrne Piven's Theseus in Bill Alton's staging of A Midsummer Night's Dream, *the first production of the Playwrights Theatre Club Shakespeare Festival, 1954.*

Barbara Harris in her first speaking role at Playwrights Theatre Club. She was 19 years old. Her hair was deliberately cut to look like Ingrid Bergman's in Stromboli.

From Enterprise, *the first improvised scenario play. Roger Bowen, the scenarist, as Crazy Jake, (second from left); at his right, Larry Zerkel; at his left, Sid Lazard (who became a Compass Player), Ned Gaylin, and Leo Stodolsky, as the boys who buy a used car. Reynolds Club, May 1955.*

He thought of engaging workers to construct their own play. Failing to engage any, he sent out the first of a stream of "Compass Newsletters," requesting plays, one recipient remembers, of "fifty-five short scenes, to which the workers could beat the drums on their lunch tables."

He ran ads in England in *The Times Literary Supplement* and *The New Statesman and Nation*:

Wanted: Ten scripts for popular theatre opening Chicago, 1954. Prefer Brechtian fables and political satires, plays on famous modern events, cabaret material. Will correspond w. would-be playwrights.

When Omar Shapli returned from Korea, Shepherd asked him to coauthor an epic event about the Korean War.

At Playwrights Theatre Club, he staged a reading of a play by David Daniels, a member of John Ecks's workshop. Shepherd describes *Born Out of Hell* as "a Mafia play in forty-three scenes of one or two lines. It turned me on."

Shepherd had by now determined that a script that could survive the rowdy informality of a cabaret environment was one which was extremely fast-paced, with short scenes and rapid changes of setting, producible with a company of five or six actors doubling up very quickly so that in the course of the action one actor could play an assortment of parts. The presentation would be done with extremely simple lighting effects on an empty stage.

During the incubation of the Compass, searching, as his diaries say, for "new types of plays more efficient, theatrical, poetic and morally aware than the current product," Shepherd points out, "I wasn't aiming for improvisation. I couldn't find the plays."

From his earliest observations of the way Viola Spolin's exercises were played at Sills's Saturday morning workshops, however, Shepherd had sensed the potential for using these improvisational techniques as the basis for a full-scale production, as a means of expressing a complete theatrical idea, that is, as a writing tool.

Sills had grown up with improvisation. He considered it "the family business." But he did not now, nor would he ever, share Shepherd's obsession to create "new types of plays." "Paul was more interested in what he called 'little entertainments' that mixed together songs, blackouts, and psychological pieces," Shepherd recalls. "In other words, revues."

From the start of their collaboration, Shepherd's focus was on changing the content of theatre while Sills was preoccupied with its form. Addressing this difference between the two men, Heyward Ehrlich reflects that "Sills had an argument going with middle-class parlor culture. He belonged to the counterculture. He didn't have any of the experience that Shepherd did. Shepherd had experienced the Establishment, the real world. His travels were economic, political, historical. Sills's travels were in the world of imagination. He lived in a world of gesture and illusion. To Paul, a gesture was everything." The returning veteran Shapli surmised that "Sills wasn't interested in any cockamamie community theatre group. He was almost the toast of the town."

Sills was not part of the small group Shepherd summoned to discuss his theatre of the future. The only "professionals" among them were Barbara Harris and the young woman from California who was regarded as "fascinating but slightly bonkers," Elaine May.

At this gathering, "He kept talking about commedia dell'arte," Barbara Harris recalls. "He said it would be a theatre for the working class, with scenarios and characters that people could identify with because the theatre was too bourgeois. These scenarios would touch the core of people David felt were being ignored. He wanted them played by a mixture of actors and real-life people. By following the characters through the scenarios, the workers in the audience would see their lives on stage with heightened reality, in a more poetic form, so they would have an objective sense of their lives."

9

Enterprise

In the spring of 1954, the Reynolds Club, which housed the University of Chicago Student Union, was featuring low-key and amusing lunchtime debates on topics of the day. The debating club employed a style of argument David Shepherd remembers as the "British Style of Debating as Practiced at the University of Chicago," in which debating skills applied to random subjects resulted, for example, in a serious argument about grapefruits. Shepherd found the insane style of debating remarkable precisely because "the debators didn't care what they were saying. They were *playing* debators."

Roger Bowen, the man who launched the lunchtime amusements, was Colonel Henry Blake in the movie *M*A*S*H* and is often cast just right of slightly stuffy, or as a thoroughly respectable, intelligent, but somewhat dazed and sometimes even goofy management type. He is the author of *Enterprise*, the first improvised scenario play or "long form" produced by David Shepherd.

Bowen, an English major from Brown University in his hometown, Providence, Rhode Island, had applied to enter graduate school at the University of Chicago following new investigations of the House Un-American Activities Committee, when enrollment on campus had dropped by a half. He maintains that he was offered Brown's special scholarship to the University of Chicago Law School because "a guy who had even worse grades than I did was the only other Brown student to apply."

In Chicago, Bowen shared an apartment with Omar Shapli over Mitzi's

Flower Shop. "I'll never forget the smell of sweetness mixed with dead vegetation," he says. He wrote theatre reviews for the student newspaper, the Chicago *Maroon*, and was an enthusiastic supporter of the Playwrights Theatre Club.

After a year, he dropped out of the law school and had his scholarship switched back to the English Department, thinking he might enjoy that graduate program more. "I was a draft dodger," he explains. "I had no interest in law."

By the beginning of the spring semester, Bowen was supplanting the subsistence figures of his scholarship by running the debating club for Marvin Phillips, the new head of University Theatre. But he was losing it for English. Neither had he any interest whatever in the theatre as an actor. He intended to (and did) become a novelist.

Indeed, as a writer, Bowen was challenged by the idea of creating a prototypical scenario play for the theatre David Shepherd described over coffee as an improvisational workers' theatre presenting plays in the workers' own language that reflected their lives.

"How can I put it?" muses Bowen. "He asked everybody that he met to write a scenario play. In my ignorance and vanity, I assumed that he had chosen me for my special genius. I was flattered. So I said, 'What's a scenario play?' He said, 'We won't know until we've done it.' It sounded like fun."

Shepherd also wanted from Bowen a formula that would make it possible to create play after play after play. Bowen is still enthusiastic as he savors the problem that was put to him that bright and beautiful spring day. "You know," he says, "in the nineteenth century, plays were created from formulas. There's not so much of that now."

Walking down Fifty-second Street later that day, Bowen saw a flyer tucked into the windshield of an automobile that said, "I must have used cars." "This might be good for a scenario," Bowen said to himself. "Suppose some student bought a car . . ."

In seven scenes, Bowen outlined this scenario: One day, four teenage boys who own a junk heap of a car in common find a used car dealer's ad on their windshield offering to buy it.

At the car lot, for an added hundred dollars to be paid in weekly installments, Crazy Jake, the dealer, sales-talks them into swapping their car for one equally beat up and old.

As they are about to lose their car for nonpayment, they find an even more promising offer from another dealer.

On their way to Crazy Sam's lot, they smash up their car.

Finding themselves in debt with no car, they use the raw material from the smashed car and go into the handmade jewelry business.

Using Crazy Jake's methods, they are very successful selling junk jewelry, meet their car payments, and, at a special ceremony, are selected to receive a Junior Achievement Award. The head of the Junior Achievement Committee is Crazy Jake, the car dealer who sold them the lousy car.

Their prize is a new car. As they are about to ride off in it, they see in their windshield a new advertisement. As the four boys argue about whether to be satisfied with what they've got or try to make a better bargain with John the Madman, the play ends.

Besides a story synopsis, Bowen's text provided a detailed scene-by-scene sequence of actions for the actors. ("Four boys are warming up on a baseball field. They are waiting for a chance from the coach to call them into the game . . . The boys are talking about their car. A minor repair is needed. None of them has enough money to afford the repair.") As a group, he characterized the four boys as "unable to make a statement without provoking the others."

To motivate his characters, Bowen employed Stanislavsky's "internal action" technique, which, he says, "I guess I had heard about from David and Omar Shapli, since it was several years before I even read *An Actor Prepares*."

According to Stanislavsky, an actor must be prepared to render not only the external actions of his character (including such behavior as the accent, the carriage, the gestures, and the furrows on the brow) but to understand as well the character's internal actions, the inner circumstances, such as the goals, fears, ambitions, and wishes, from which all external actions spring. To grasp the internal action of the character, Stanislavsky observed, is to know what moves him through the play.

In *Enterprise*, Bowen supplied the whole group of boys with the same internal actions: "hypnotized by automobiles and having no other motive than getting a better car" and "regarding going to work as the greatest danger in life."

To individualize these actions, he borrowed an idea from Mark Kennedy's *The Pecking Order*, a book about group behavior that was popular on campus at the time. Thus, the leader of the boys was described as "the strong silent type . . . given to spasms of violent and unreasoning anger." The second was a "loudmouth . . . whom the others do not respect." The third was a "snob who praises and plays up to the first one." The fourth was "good-natured and shiftless . . . moderates the disputes . . . and effects compromises." The used car dealer was characterized as "a master of many roles . . . at once fatherly and avaricious . . . a perfect confidence man."

A conventional script provides an actor with his external action and his dialogue. In *Enterprise*, Bowen contributed both the external actions and the inner circumstances. The dialogue was left for the actor himself to improvise.

Shepherd had conceived of the scenario as a play with player-provided dialogue, composed of short scenes studded with set pieces, such as songs, jokes, orations, salestalks, or "any urban dynamic that would brighten it up." Like songs in a musical comedy, these set pieces would function as reliable pillars around which the not-so-reliable improvised material could ebb and flow.

The set pieces Bowen incorporated into *Enterprise* were the advertisements of Crazy Jake ("I must have two hundred used cars by Friday . . ."), Crazy Sam ("If I don't get three hundred used cars in the next five days, I will go broke . . . I have paid up to a thousand dollars for a car like this . . . Come and take the shirt off my back . . ."), John the Madman ("They say I'm crazy and they're right! I cannot stay in business if I do not get one thousand cars by next week. I might be in a mental institution in five days. Don't wait!"), and Crazy Jake's ceremonial speech ("It is boys like these who show us that . . . many a junk heap conceals a fortune . . . Who would believe that this piece of jewelry was really a hubcap? Or that this handsome paperweight was ever a radiator ornament? What we're honoring today is the American spirit of hustle. America is a nation of hustlers. Thank you.")

With *Enterprise*, Bowen succeeded in establishing not just a formal but a substantive prototype for subsequent Compass scenarios that filled Shepherd's bill. It pictured American society and its economic system from a Marxist angle, as an ineluctable force that shapes its members and conforms them to an image in which they remain fixed. *Enterprise* also focused on a group that had no image of its own reflected in the existing theatre. The high school students in Bowen's scenario are not from the middle class but just a peg below. They are not intellectuals. They are not critical of society. They do not hope to change the world. As Bowen conceived them, the boys "belonged to a class of society below the point where these middle-class ideas that we batted around had any significance. They didn't conceive of themselves in the big picture. They weren't concerned with idealism versus realism. They didn't care if Henry Wallace was a nice guy."

When Bowen heard that one of the features of the University Theatre's spring program was an evening of one-act plays at the Reynolds Club, he asked Marvin Phillips if he and Shepherd could tack a couple of scenario plays onto the evening, and Phillips agreed.

With Bowen's assistance, Shepherd directed *Enterprise*, as well as a second scenario, the unrecorded *An Exam Play*, which took place in a girls' dormitory and whose authorship was credited on the program to the cast.

The Reynolds Club was far from the working-class setting in which Shepherd had intended to sow the seeds for his theatre. Here were an elite group of students performing for another elite group, temporarily cloistered in the Hyde Park community and without real roots in its life. Yet these college students were amateurs, ordinary people taking the stage to improvise about a subject (cars) that was meaningful to their lives.

The two scenario plays appeared on May 14 and 15, 1955, on the same bill as O'Casey's *Bedtime Story* and Pirandello's *Chee-Chee*. *An Exam Play* did not go over, but *Enterprise* was received with enormous enthusiasm by the audience, which included Elaine May.

A student, Ted Gershuny, was so impressed by the production that he put up $2,000, thus becoming the principal investor of the nascent Compass.

"We had the whole improvisational theatre right there in that one show," says Bowen. "It was successful. It was fully blown. It sprang from the head of Zeus, so to speak. And without help from Paul Sills."

"We rehearsed *Enterprise* in a totally pragmatic way," says Bowen, "by 'brainstorming' the material. We did not use Viola's games. The only technique we used was the internal action—the thing that would get the actor through the scene."

During the course of rehearsal, Bowen observed that as the director worked with the actors to sharpen their motivations, the character differentiation within their pecking order became much more distinct and authentic teenage dialogue began to emerge.

Shepherd had been absorbing Sills's techniques for the preceding two years. In his renderings of narrative plays like *The Caucasian Chalk Circle*, *Rounddance*, *Wozzek*, *The Threepenny Opera*, and *Peer Gynt*, Sills had shown himself a master of the short scene. From his work with Sills, Shepherd had learned that by using a "where," a very strong space environment or setting, it was possible to give life to a short scene based upon a completed action or beat.

"In *Enterprise,* we worked with beats," Shepherd explains. "I also thought each beat should be accompanied by a very strong activity which would give the players a point of focus. I also learned that from my work with Paul."

During the brainstorming process, Bowen remembers that "David would say, 'Okay, you'll be waiting on the baseball field. What are you doing?' And the actors would answer, 'We could be throwing the ball back and forth.' Sid Lazard thought his character would be reading a comic book." Throwing a ball and reading a comic book are not actions but activities. There is nothing preconceived in an actor performing an activity.

Bowen himself still has a vivid memory of an invisible baseball rolling over to Sid Lazard, the snobby character, who was reading a comic book. Lazard had made his character so lazy that his fingers could barely pick up the space object tossed his way. The actor may have achieved Stanislavskian laziness, but he reached for Viola Spolin's kind of a ball.

At Bowen and Shapli's apartment, Sills listened to the crude recording of *Enterprise* that had been made on audio tape.

"The tape. That's what convinced Paul to join forces with us," says Shepherd, who supposes that "Paul felt I finally had a good directorial approach to scenarios: short scenes based on strong activities stimulated and enriched by the 'Where,' which would change from scene to scene."

"I don't know why they're laughing" is what Bowen remembers Sills remarked. "But they're laughing, so it must be good."

"Maybe I wasn't that interested at first," Sills reminisces. "But when we got heaved out of our theatre, that was the move. The only alternative was that.

"The Compass was a long time starting," continues Sills. "There were a couple of months of workshops, at least. I remember driving south each night, somehow getting south, and working at the university. We went back to the university to start this thing."

10

Viola's Workshop

The Renaissance troupes who performed commedia dell'arte were nothing if not all-around entertainers. The Italian improvisators were men and women learned in poetry, geography, foreign languages, and history. Besides composing their own scenarios, they sang, played musical instruments, and were expert at acrobatics and pantomime. While holding a glass of water, the great Vincentini would turn a somersault. Another Italian actor, famous for the way he played the sword-swinging bully Scaramouche, was reputedly so agile that at eighty-three he could still box the ear of a fellow actor with his foot.

But the virtuoso or solo skills of the players were not nearly so unusual as the skill they displayed in playing with each other. Actors who perform in scripted plays have the lines of the playwright on which to rely. The fate of an improvisation hangs on the response of another player. Fine tuning and an almost familial intimacy and trust are required onstage among actors who improvise. In Italy, where commedia dell'arte originated, the family was the bonding ingredient in most improvisational troupes. A sense of mutual purpose was necessary for a troupe's survival offstage too. The irreverent, shocking, and sometimes sexually explicit nature of their satires provoked frequent battles with civil authorities and the church, and the troupes and their horse-drawn carts and dogs and parrots were accustomed to being kicked out of town.

The sort of person David Shepherd invited to help create the Compass more than met the intellectual requirements for a practitioner of his new commedia dell'arte. Most of them had emerged from Hutchins's well-read and well-informed community of scholars. All of them were intrigued by Shepherd's idea of awakening society to change through the theatre and were supported in this exciting prospect by a burning desire to express their own views as well as by the collective spirit of irreverence that permeated Hyde Park.

Pivotal to this group were five people Bowen calls the "Compass Brain Trust," the conceptual and creative core of the theatre, who, since the production of *Enterprise*, had been busy writing scenarios and building a pool of material. Besides Shepherd himself, the Brain Trust included Sills, Bowen, Elaine May, and the late Robert ("Bob") Coughlan, a writer who was equally committed to his work as a counselor of industrial relations at the University of Chicago, a position that allowed him a summer leave. Bowen describes Coughlan as "a good decent guy with a pure heart," and Shepherd remembers a "diligent, loyal, and dedicated person" with an "incredible manic drive" to see his insights into American society materialize onstage. "He had more energy than any three of us," Bowen sighs.

The Brain Trust was backed by an unusual and enthusiastic group of people eager to execute their work. Prominent among them was Andrew ("Andy") Duncan, a graduate student from a working-class family in Detroit, an alumnus of the University of Michigan, whom Bowen had met in a class in Middle English and whom Sills and Shepherd had seen in a University Theatre production of Ibsen's *The Wild Duck*. Having directed *Bedtime Story* on the same bill, Duncan had seen both performances of *Enterprise*. Michael ("Mickey") LeGlaire had entered the University of Chicago at sixteen, when, he says, he was "past my prime," and at twenty-two was a newly defected Communist party organizer fresh from a disillusioning year in the steel mills. Haym Bernson was a psychology student, a suitor of Elaine's, with intense and brooding eyes. A senior at the university, Sidney ("Sid") Lazard, of the banking family Lazard Frères, had played one of the four boys in *Enterprise* and was about to embark on a career as a journalist. Robert ("Bob") Patton, the only black member of the Compass, lived in the neighborhood and went to Roosevelt University. Morris ("Mo") Hirsch, a graduate student, was a mathematical genius who played the guitar. There were a number of women too, described by Barbara Harris as "dark and mysterious U. of C. types, gorgeous-faced girls who never said anything or complained and who looked like they knew everything. They stayed for a while and disappeared."

If there were no riveters, ditch diggers, bricklayers, plumbers, hospital orderlies, glassblowers, or lumberjacks among the inaugural Compass Players, neither were there acrobats. In fact, except for Elaine May, Paul Sills, and Barbara Harris, who had come with Shepherd from the Playwrights Theatre Club, none of the group was committed professionally to the theatre. Almost none of them had any experience onstage whatever, much less any stage technique.

Brecht himself had observed the similarity between an acting ensemble and an athletic team. As in sports, teamwork onstage requires mobilizing energies not generated by the intellect or, as Sills and Spolin say, "the head."

The protégés of Robert Hutchins, however, were notoriously nonathletic. "You could ask them anything about instant egress or Bertrand Russell," says Barbara Harris, "but they couldn't tell you how to play baseball."

Thus, it was particularly fortuitous for the improvisational theatre when Paul Sills's mother, who knew more games than any eighteen-year-old in her Hull House Recreational Training School class, returned to Chicago to direct a production of *Juno and the Paycock*, among the last gasps of the Playwrights Theatre Club in the spring of 1955.

It was not nearly so fortuitous for O'Casey's play, nor for The Paycock, Ed Asner, whose performance was panned. Asner compares Viola as a director to Lee Strasberg, "who was revered as a god of sorts in the classroom but was totally ineffectual when it came to making a play successful on the stage." Elaine May, Viola's former workshop student, played the part of the Irish upstairs neighbor in a Jewish accent.

Vaguely, Spolin recalls that "Shepherd wanted a political theatre, but he had no way to put it on the stage." More vividly, she remembers that she had lost her theatre in Los Angeles behind the Women's Club on North La Brea and that her marriage to Ed Spolin was on the rocks. She was therefore persuaded by Shepherd to remain in Chicago after *Juno and the Paycock* closed to run workshops in her improvisational techniques that spring.

Ed Asner was not invited to attend. "They were not eager to perpetuate any of the star idea," he says. "They knew they were going into a new medium. They were on shaky ground. They wanted everyone to come in on equal turf, as willing subjects. They didn't want to bend over begging anyone to be part of the company." Asner instead made plans to star in Chicago summer stock productions of Sam and Bella Spewack's *My Three Angels* and "a pink sudsy soap opera," *Good-bye, My Fancy*. Meanwhile, according to various participants, between forty to seventy beginners showed up to improvise in the little theatre Shepherd rented in the battlement of Mandel Hall.

"I learned more from Viola Spolin," Andrew Duncan exclaims. "If she hadn't kicked their asses, they never would have gotten on with it. After they put on *Enterprise*, they were just hangin' around there in Chicago. It was all talk. It was Viola who really got them going. She was a real dynamo."

"I don't know if Viola was good as a director," says Mickey LeGlaire. "I was only in *Juno and the Paycock*, so I can't judge. But she was a wonderful teacher, I'll say that. The greatest. Those workshops she ran were terrific."

As a teacher, Sills has been described by one actress as "not famous. His vision was always fantastic, but his main instruction was, 'Do it.' " According to Andy Duncan, it was Viola who "instilled in everybody a sense that this is something you could do. Sills would just scream and yell at you. And David would be talking enigmatic mystification. But Viola was a realist. She was the one who dealt with the problems of improvisation that were moment-to-moment, which an actor needs."

At the Mandel Hall workshops, Viola ran exercises that helped train the novices to concentrate, to relax in the stage space, to develop an environment and a character, as well as to cooperate and to share stage space and *Focus* with the other players.

In Building a Where, each player in the group was required to add something to the space through pantomime to make the "where" more specific. "The aim is so simple: to fill the space," Barbara Harris explains. "It requires the concentration to remember where other people put things in the space, to walk around them not through them, and to go without props and things. And because one thing leads to the other to add up to the whole, you learn to work together. It's very equalizing."

In Contact, the players were not permitted to speak a line of dialogue without first making a connection with their partners in a physical way.

A favorite among the players was the "how-to-do-it" or teaching scene, in which one player teaches a partner to perform activities as disparate as asking the boss for a raise, behaving at a smorgasbord, and frying a fish.

"Viola helped us understand what it feels not to be attached to a script or to know what's coming next," says Barbara Harris. "The exercises gave you a point of concentration outside yourself. You didn't have to be brilliant. It wasn't competitive. They had one aim which anyone could accomplish, no matter how unsophisticated or unschooled. Say the game is that you can't leave the stage without touching ten objects. If that's all anybody cares about and looks for, then anybody can play and develop, without breaking their hearts in the process. Shy types can succeed as well as aggressive ones. In fact, the intent of the game is so clear that people trying to gain center stage can be spotted as getting in the way of the exercise. So long as they touch the ten objects, no one comes off being a schlub, no one comes off being a star."

Some seemed more attuned to the process than others. "Barbara was very good at improvising from the beginning," says Mickey LeGlaire.

"The reason I was able to do it was . . . I had so little information about failure. I had nothing to fail from," she explains. "I mean, you couldn't *grade* the games. You weren't getting an A or a pass. You didn't solve a logic problem. The people who had the most trouble were the ones trying to fit themselves into some space that made sense."

"Barbara and Elaine," says Mickey LeGlaire. "They were the main people. Elaine was terrific. A great, great improviser."

Bob Coughlan had never acted. "But he could improvise," says LeGlaire. "He made you nervous sometimes because he talked so fast."

The High Priestess of Improvisation would unfortunately not remain to help the budding Compass Players develop and advance their craft. Viola remembers waiting at the bus stop as the time came for her return to Los Angeles. Running toward her was Elaine, who called out, "We need you, Viola. Don't go!"

After Viola left, Sills took over the workshops, with the assistance of Shepherd and Elaine, and began trying to cull an acting company. Rehearsal spaces changed and workshoppers continued to come and go. When Annette Hankin heard there were free classes at the Y in Hyde Park, she was a sixteen-year-old high school girl from Lawndale, a working-class neighborhood on the West Side. She and her friend Roberta Gnippe went out of curiosity. "It was a great bonanza for a kid," Hankin recalls. "I was struck with awe at the glamour of it. It was the first time I'd heard about the theatre in a social context, about theatre having to do with things going on in real life. I remember being intoxicated by it all."

Improvisation workshops were held constantly. Saturday mornings. Sunday afternoons. At night. The workshoppers were all urged to study the newspapers and read David Riesman's best-seller, *The Lonely Crowd*. By the end of May, when Hankin and Gnippe weren't improvising at the Y, or in the park, or in someone's apartment, they were in the back room of the Compass Tavern painting chairs.

II

The Early Compass

Backed by a group of Ph.D. students looking for a capital investment, one of Jimmy's bartenders at the Woodlawn Tap, Fred Wranovics ('50), was taking over the Hi-Hat Lounge, a bankrupt after-hours club on Fifty-fifth Street, and the gypsy joint next door. After earning his college degree at the University of Chicago, Wranovics had run out of his GI Bill entitlement and, forced to postpone his graduate studies, had become a saloon man of great popularity, with a reputation among his large following as an "Aristotelian Catholic" with a passion for argument, ethics, and Ezra Pound.

"I don't know anyone who would classify Fred as a centrist," says Omar Shapli. "He'd go on about the liberal homosexual conspiracy. He'd say the right side had won the Spanish Civil War."

"I was not that much into left-wing criticisms of the government," says Wranovics. "I was an ex-paratrooper."

At Jimmy's, Wranovics had learned from his future partners that the people from Playwrights Theatre Club were regrouping. Wranovics had been on friendly terms with many of them since college. He had acted at University Theatre. He knew Sills. He knew Asner. As undergraduates, he and Mike Nichols had thrown mailbags together and stuffed envelopes for Sears. In the outdoor garden of the bierstube that adjoined the Sieben Brewing Company, he had listened to Sills and Shepherd's "notion of a storefront theatre with educational intentions" and agreed that they would renovate and rent as a theatre the long thin space adjoining his prospective tavern and that they would call the whole enterprise the Compass.

By the midfifties, Hyde Park was one of the top ten high-crime neigh-borhoods. The black population was "moving in from Washington Park" to settle uneasily in deteriorating pockets of Hyde Park, where they faced the open hostility of the neighborhood's poor working-class whites. At the University of Chicago, the board of trustees was alarmed, even considering a move to Lake Geneva, so seriously did the situation threaten the en-rollment of what Hutchins Plan veterans contemptuously called "the coun-try club crowd." Hutchins's successor, Chancellor Lawrence A. Kimpton, beseeched the federal government for assistance. As a former president of Columbia University, President Eisenhower was sympathetic: he had faced a similar situation in New York's Morningside Heights.

The South Side Urban Redevelopment Plan, the first one in the nation, was designed to get rid of blacks. The blocks to be leveled were very carefully gerrymandered. Urban redevelopment wove in and out of streets, with demolition focused on buildings that were occupied by blacks. By 1975, the University of Chicago would thus be a safe and respectable middle-class community, completely sealed off by a fortress of official structures from the unsavory poor.

In the meantime, racial tensions escalated. Students caught in the cross-fire of black-white warfare were constantly getting mugged. In Fran Gend-lin's dorm, there were always fresh flowers sent by Chancellor Kimpton as an apology to young women who had been attacked.

For a theatre that addressed the issues of this distressed community, the time was ripe.

Sills's former roommate, Charlie Jacobs, teamed up with Shepherd as the business manager of Compass. Throughout his law school term, Jacobs had remained active at Playwrights Theatre Club, where, on most pro-ductions, under his stage name Charles Mason, he was in charge of publicity and lights. With his strong background in German theatre (in-cluding the German cabaret), he was invaluable to Shepherd, balancing, as Shepherd puts it, "the cynicism of his business experience with the ideals of the liberal fringe." Before he entered the University of Chicago Law School, Jacobs had worked for a booking agent who supplied speakers and entertainers to ladies' clubs. Since graduation, he had been working at the law school as research assistant to Saul Mendlowitz, a young lawyer Shepherd had already asked, as a friend and fan of Playwrights Theatre Club, to do the legal work on Compass.

Besides making his energetic presence felt in the law school, "Charlie managed to get the Compass going when under all ordinary notions of business, it shouldn't have," says Mendlowitz. "The sonofabitch did everything. He raised the money. He bought the secondhand air conditioner. He knew who to schmeer. He knew which bills to pay. He became the business manager, and I was the lawyer. So quote he hired me. I should please incorporate them. I should negotiate, y'know. Jesus, the deals we made for those people. I don't think they paid me anything."

Mendlowitz negotiated a short-term summer rental agreement with Wranovics that spelled out the percentage of the bar that would belong to the theatre. By suggesting that the back-room patrons pay for their drinks in tokens, Jacobs devised a way to monitor it. "Freddy was a nice guy," says Jacobs. "But he was a bartender. His accounting was a mess."

It fell to Jacobs to secure the cabaret license and deal with all the other technicalities of this marriage between art and alcohol. "We've paid off the police and the fire department for safety violations. Now the new alderman wants three thousand dollars for a cabaret license and that's too much," Mendlowitz recalls that Jacobs finally confessed.

Mendlowitz was horrified. "If they'd had the three thousand dollars they'd have paid that too!" He called a friend for the proper connection to the Daley machine to get a license from the state liquor commission without a fix and then "to get the alderman off their back." The unimpeachable friend was Avner Mikvah ("Mr. Integrity, for crissake"), now a judge on the U.S. Court of Appeals, then a former editor in chief of the *University of Chicago Law Review* who had run for state representative against the Daley machine and won. The name he suggested was one of two Greek brothers, who, Mendlowitz says, "knew what was going on in town." The appropriate brother cleared a path to the man at the top.

Soliciting the mayor, Jacobs presented a squib on the Playwrights Theatre Club that had appeared in the culture section of *Time*. "These guys are culture," Daley told his boys. "Lay off."

The company of commedia dell'artisans began to volunteer their "support skills," such as carpentry and public relations to mobilize the action, a group dynamic Shepherd still deems philosophically essential to his notion (and his budget) for a people's cabaret.

To create an entrance to the theatre, Andy Duncan knocked a hole in the wall through the Hi-Hat Lounge. To keep the sound of the barflies from intruding on the theatre patrons, he built a sound baffle, "an L-shaped thing where you'd make a turn and come in." He and Sills built the stage. Duncan says, "It was pretty primitive, that stage."

To compensate for the length of the room, the stage was higher than usual, its underpinnings disguised by facing in the front and one of the sides. One side adjoined a wall. A sink, a gaping hole, and a staircase of planks on braces were all concealed backstage. By using the staircase, it was possible to crawl through the series of frames supporting the stage.

Having gained experience at Playwrights Theatre Club on such ambitiously lit entertainments as *Wozzek*, Charlie Jacobs took charge of wiring and lights. Andy Duncan recalls that "Charlie put up some pretty good lights. We had about eight: two big spots, two lekos, two baby spots for mood stuff, and a few regular lights. We were lit pretty good. Everyone looked wonderful under those lights."

Roger Bowen wrote the promotional material and took on the function of running the Compass on dark Mondays, booking and introducing amusing debates or folk music nights.

Although he was planning to leave for England in the fall, Sills this summer turned an unabated energy on the Compass and began directing the first week's show, as he would continue to do for the next ten weeks.

The curtain raiser, *Love Through the Ages: Three Kinds of Kissing*, was assigned to two workshoppers who performed vignettes of Courtly Love (knight and lady), Eighteenth-century Love (a couple dancing a minuet), and Love Today (teenagers, as Bowen recalls it, "doing some clutzy thing").

A week before opening, Bowen devised a format for the segment Shepherd had envisioned as the Living Newspaper, which was to be gleaned straight from the pages of the press each day. According to Shepherd, the technique (similar to one that later became the keystone of Paul Sills's Story Theatre) was much like a device he and Sills had admired at Robert Breen's Chamber Theatre at Northwestern, in which actors weave in and out of narrative and into character and dialogue. The title he knew had been used in the thirties in the theatrical revues of the WPA.

As Bowen recalls it, Shepherd shared only the latter bit of theatre exotica before asking if Bowen could create one.

"What *is* a Living Newspaper?" Bowen asked.

"I'll know it when I see it," his guru replied.

At the Compass, a narrator (Bowen) and three or four actors would enter with newspapers and proceed for twenty minutes to satirize selected news items and articles by interpolating pantomimed or spoken bits. The bits Bowen remembers from the first week's news were: men dueling with shotguns; soldiers learning to resist brainwashing; believers on a mountaintop waiting for the end of the world; Dulles lashing out at Gromyko at a summit conference; and French designers discussing the "X" look and the "Y" look (in between Bowen's reading of a preciously written article on Christian Dior).

The first scenario was Sills's own, *The Game of Hurt*, which he had adapted (he says "stolen") from the first chapter of Thomas Hardy's *The Mayor of Casterbridge*, about a man selling his wife. The game played by the cigar salesman, Herman Gruber, and his slovenly wife, Marian, was a popular one at the University of Chicago and predated a similar game played on the stage in a fancier vocabulary by a tonier couple, George and Martha, on the fictional college campus of Edward Albee's *Who's Afraid of Virginia Woolf?* It is an insult contest, the couple's special entertainment, in which the loser calls out to the winner, "Hurt!" The cigar salesman was played by David Shepherd. Marian Gruber was played by Elaine May. Loretta Chiljian and Barbara Harris alternated in the role of the Grubers' complaining daughter, Loretta.

A transcript of *The Game of Hurt* indicates that Herman Gruber proves himself the superior player in the first scene, as Marian informs him that "every time I see a man in the street, I start thinking that you wouldn't have to take me out in the street and sell me. If I had a chance to get away, I'd go for nothing." Herman doesn't flinch. "Oh, yeah?" he replies.

They go out to a bar, where Marian flirts with Joe, a naïve young factory worker (Bob Coughlan) out for the evening with Buddy (Sid Lazard), a more sophisticated friend. Joe is smitten by Marian. "I'd give all I have for her," he says. Herman auctions off his wife to the younger man for $350. Joe borrows most of it from his friend.

"Sold to the man in the white T-shirt!" cries Herman.

As Joe carries Marian off, Marian calls out to Herman, "Hurt!"

By the time Marian phones home, Herman has realized that he needs his wife and wants her back. Herman tells Marian to walk out on Joe. But Marian has discovered that Joe is a wonderful man who "loves me and has built his life around me." She is also appalled that Herman would try to welsh on his bet.

Buddy becomes envious of Marian for monopolizing his friend. He pays a special visit to the Gruber house to give Herman Joe's address. Herman takes off for Joe's house while Buddy remains with their daughter, Loretta, who falls for his phony—"I've spent a lot of time in Hollywood, baby"—line.

At Joe's apartment, warmed by Joe's adoration, Marian has sprung to life. Unlike Herman, Joe sees Marian as a wonderful housewife. He loves her pickle and raisin sandwiches. He is thrilled by her imaginative ideas for home decorating in white leather. He is mesmerized by her description of the latest plight of her favorite soap opera character. Joe has never been exposed to such cultural events as "The Romance of Helen Trent" on the assembly line.

As Marian Gruber, Elaine May's description of the plight of Helen Trent—over thirty-five and torn between the prominent attorney Anthony Brown, her fiancé of seven years, and Morgan Thomas, the slick young advertising executive she has chosen as her new flame—was a riveting seven-and-a-half-minute soliloquy. As Marian/Elaine describes Helen's current crisis, she is out for the evening with Morgan Thomas at the Tivoli Theatre. While Morgan is waiting in line at the candy counter to buy her a sweet, she spots Anthony Brown slouching in the lobby, looking thin and drawn. Marian's story comes to a crescendo as Morgan turns to see Helen eyeballing her old flame. Marian takes a dramatic pause. Joe asks, "Who got her? Who got her?" "I don't know yet," Marian replies.

The doorbell rings. It is Herman Gruber. Like Anthony Brown, Marian notes with pleasure, he is thin, drawn, and contrite. He tries to persuade Marian that it is futile for her to try to find a life with someone like Joe, who is too young and too low-class. "What am I going to say when people ask, 'Where's Marian?' That she's living with a cinder snapper down on Sixty-ninth Street? They won't understand." Herman defends marriage by exhorting Marian to leave, explaining, "People are made to stick together, like animals in the ark."

Marian starts to leave with Herman. No matter how strangling, real life is about to resume for the Grubers. "What did I do wrong?" asks Joe. "Nothing," Marian replies.

The secondhand air-conditioning system broke down on July 4, during one of Chicago's worst heat spells, and the first performance of The Compass Players was postponed to July 5.

To supplement their twenty-five-dollar-a-week starting salary as Compass Players, Andy Duncan and Mickey LeGlaire had taken jobs in the tavern as bartenders, making more money that way than as actors. Duncan, one of the strongest male actors, played no part in the opening scenario, as he was also still building the baffle and had no time to rehearse. Waiting for the air conditioner to be repaired, he heard Fred Wranovics repeatedly express what seemed to Duncan like apprehension of the theatre crowd and its left-wing political bent.

"I didn't approve of revolutionary politics," Wranovics recalls. "But what did I care? Around that neighborhood, you could carry on debates and arguments sixteen hours a day. There was nothing novel about it. Liberal attitudes were de rigueur. There were no right-wingers in Hyde Park." Wranovics measures the political inclinations of The Compass Players as "about the dimension of Mort Sahl."

The former Hi-Hat Lounge on Fifty-fifth Street now featured jazz and classical music played over a hi-fi system designed by an Australian chemist who was one of the investors, handmade tables and chairs, bartenders who recited poetry, a bookshelf lined with the eleventh edition of the *Encyclopaedia Britannica* to settle any scholarly disputes, Michelob on tap, and fifty (thirty imported) brands of bottled beer. Wranovics discovered his own taste for "big" music to be "sensationally crowd-pleasing." On weekends, it became a ritual to pack the tavern by playing at top volume a recording of Vivaldi's *Gloria* or the fourth movement of Beethoven's Ninth Symphony. (Conversely, one of the investors once emptied the place, recommending Verdi's *Requiem*, which was also music that could be classified as "big." The crowd was down to "about three people" when Wranovics put on the fourth movement of Beethoven's Ninth and "everyone came back. By two a.m., the place was jammed again.")

In the early summer of 1955, facing the onslaught of urban renewal, Fifty-fifth Street was "wonderful, full of shops and artisans," recalls Fran Gendlin, who at eighteen was finishing her third year at the University of Chicago, and, with her husband, Gene, was among the backers of the bar. Down the street from the Compass Tavern were the Cadillac Lounge, the Crown Propeller Lounge, the Cotton Club, and the Bee Hive, a jazz club where greats like Charlie Parker, Roy Eldridge, and Dizzy Gillespie played. Jimmy's also was a few doors down. The University Tavern was across the street. Around the corner, on Harper and Fifty-seventh, was a co-op grocery store. The Buddhist temple that served the small enclave of Hyde Park Japanese was on Dorchester and Fifty-first. On Woodlawn and Fifty-eighth, the Chicago Theological Seminary was serving students lunch and dinner at its headquarters, Robie House, the first of the horizontal Prairie Houses designed by Frank Lloyd Wright.

Five or six other bars catered to the students who crowded in and out of them all day. Only the Compass served Michelob. "You got Schlitz or Budweiser in the other bars. The basic beers," says Shepherd. "Michelob was totally exotic in those days." The tavern was instantly popular, filled to capacity day and night, Wranovics says, with "amazingly meritorious people from all walks of life."

Renovated, the gypsy joint next door had taken on "a kind of darkness, an old-fashioned atmosphere," says Andy Duncan. "It wasn't modern in the hi-tech sense. Physically, there was very little about the Compass that was seductive. It had a kind of Brechtian alienation about it."

It wasn't quite a theatre. It was a storefront with plaster walls and wooden floors. The ceiling was corrugated tin. Over the plywood stage was "some dark brown kind" of linoleum, which Duncan and Sills had laid in wide strips. "It wasn't carpeted or anything," says Duncan. "There was no comfort there."

Backstage, no construction had been done to cover up the treacherous gaping hole between the stairwell and the backstage sink.

Music was provided by an old-fashioned phonograph. All audio recording was to be preserved for posterity on a 1953 Wallensach set at low speed, a budgetary sacrifice of quality for more time on tape. The acoustics weren't the best. The sound system consisted of two microphones suspended over the stage. On crowded Saturday nights, the actors would have to project over the noise of the bar as well as the loud city sounds of the street.

In order to draw in Hyde Park pedestrians, the Compass, unlike most nightclubs, was never curtained or draped. From the storefront window, a bare platform with a backdrop of brightly colored louvers could be seen. They would catch people's eyes from the street. Inside, there was no cover charge. A beer cost fifty cents. People could park their bikes, pull up a chair, and sit around all night. "That was the idea," says Duncan. "We were really like dropouts from society, and this was our club."

Exiting the Compass, Sid Lazard's father, an elegant man with blue-white hair and the three-piece suit appropriate to a partner of Lazard Frères, gazed back at his son on the stage with an expression that said to Duncan, "What have I done wrong?"

Five nights a week, the Compass offered its audience a show that consisted of a curtain raiser, a Living Newspaper, a forty-five-minute-long scenario play, and, from audience suggestions, an improvised set. There were two shows on Friday, three shows on Saturday, and a new show each week.

Perhaps, in this frenetic schedule there was, as Sills reflects, "too much productivity."

Unlike commedia dell'arte and its high-tech counterpart, the television sitcom, Compass scenarios or stories did not use recurring characters and sets and fit them into a plot. They were not created to "service" the talents of the individual players, but to express a collective point of view about

American society. Moreover, they were not created in workshop, through audience suggestion, or chance. All of the successful Compass scenario structures were the fruit of a writer's disipline, insight, and ideas.

And, unlike the naturalistic experiments with improvisation that year at the Actors Studio, which resulted in a full-scale Broadway production of Michael V. Gazzo's A *Hatful of Rain*, the Compass scenarios were not worked and reworked to perfection. The lines, which the actors created, were never written out. Every night they changed.

Each week, one of the writers in the Brain Trust submitted a story skeleton involving six or seven characters in nine or ten scenes. Each character was provided with a very strong action that would keep him or her in conflict with the other characters, and a more specific scene-by-scene action, setting, and strong pantomimed activity. The actors found their way through the space settings by agreeing beforehand on a floor plan. Chairs were the only "real" stage furniture. The how-to-do-it or teaching scene learned in Viola's workshop was incorporated throughout the scenario as often as possible. (In *The Game of Hurt*, for example, the Grubers show their daughter, Loretta, how to play the game, Buddy shows Joe how to pick up a woman, and Buddy shows Loretta how to make a Texas omelette as a prelude to making a pass.)

In each performance, the actors created an assortment of spontaneously prepared scenes based on audience suggestions (for a subject, an object, a story, a location, a first line and a last line, a phrase or a word) that were recorded by one of the players, in crayon, for all to see, on a big flip pad.

"Weird types set the standard for Compass," says Andy Duncan. "It was a strange group from Mickey LeGlaire to Bob Coughlan to Elaine to Shepherd to Sid. There were very few 'pretty' boys and girls. Barbara probably came closest to the romantic thing, and I had hair in those days, so I looked kind of like a leading man. But even we were a little off. We just weren't stock."

Of all the actors, Elaine was the most experienced, and her commitment and confidence showed in her work. Duncan and Barbara Harris also took the stage with ease. By contrast, Bob Coughlan's brilliance and energy onstage emanated less from skill than from his sheer desire to express himself. "He was fun," says Duncan. "He looked like an owl, with no chin. He was a good character man who just couldn't shut up. There were some exercises he needed. On the other hand, he was so open, the stuff would just flow out of him. He came up with some wonderful stuff." As

Joe, the cinder snapper, Coughlan became so enthusiastic with Marian/ Elaine's home decorating, he said, "White leather? Oh, honey, you got a million ideas. How about goin' in the other room and lyin' down and restin' our eyes?"

For all his contempt for the breed, Shepherd was an outstanding actor at the Compass in its formative days. Bowen saw him do "brilliant and inventive things, playing aspects of his own character, a kind of slow-talking, deep-thinking person who would come out with wonderful satirical remarks."

Bowen himself had intended to participate in Compass only as a writer, but when Sills invited him to join the company, he accepted. Compass actors earned "twenty-five dollars a week, when we got it," while writing was paid for in gratitude. It fully satisfied Bowen to play minor parts: "I wasn't an actor and didn't do it very well. I could be a broad character and get up and give a speech. I was always okay for that. But any subtle interpretation—that was beyond me."

In the scenarios, all the actors tended to be cast in roles they could play as exaggerations of their own personality types. Thus, Elaine often played pushy mothers, Barbara played flaky teenaged daughters, Sid Lazard played cynical know-it-alls, Andrew Duncan played smooth-talking salesmen, David Shepherd played fuzzy Establishment types, Bob Coughlan played everything with manic energy, and Mo Hirsch played the guitar.

"There was a kind of sameness about the acting," says Duncan. "There was no character work at all. Bob Coughlan was always Bob Coughlan. And nobody knew how to handle the emotions. Sure, you might get into sentimentality. But you have to risk it. This was purely verbal."

"All our work was inconsistent, attenuated, and belabored," says Shepherd. Yet there was something happening onstage the audience found fascinating. To Shepherd, the late-night improvised sets were the most interesting "because they were the worst. People would sit out there for two or three hours trying to figure out what was happening onstage. And we'd be out there trying to learn how to do it. It would go on . . . interminably. But on Saturday nights you didn't want to go to bed. You just stayed around with whoever happened to be there and watched Elaine May and Barbara Harris improvise. There might be five people in the audience. *We* didn't care."

"We'd get onstage with sandals and no shirts," says Duncan. "There was no pretense or chichi. If the air conditioner broke down and we were sweating, we took off our clothes. Or we'd wear shorts!"

Once the theatre opened, Sills devoted himself to directing and Elaine took over the workshop and the role of acting coach. Elaine's workshop tended to reflect the Stanislavsky training she had received from Ouspenskaya whereas Sills was involved solely with Viola's games. In their points of view about improvisation, Annette Hankin observed that Shepherd and Elaine, unlike Sills, were much more inclined to let improvisations wander until the charged moment evolved and much more willing to take risks.

In Elaine's workshop, Hankin reports, "We did lots of sense memory exercises, stereotypical Method work, like playing a toaster, and lots of fairy tales." Elaine also borrowed exercises from Viola. In one improvisation, to great effect, Snow White and her reflection played Viola's Mirror exercise. But First Line/Last Line, often attributed to Spolin, was a game that Elaine introduced. In her set-up, the players were supplied with random opening and closing lines to a scene and were challenged to connect the two pieces of dialogue by improvising the stage action and dialogue in between.

Since acting demands emotional involvement and creating a scene requires detachment, Hankin "experienced conflict" over how to be simultaneously involved and detached: "Elaine, being a genius, was able to do both things at once. Her sense of truth was Zenlike. Everybody talked the word 'organic,' but she did it, although I think her head always informed her heart."

Her most consistent advice was "Never betray what you believe in at the moment" and "Maintain your sense of truth." Hankin says, "I don't remember hearing those words from anyone else."

For all the laissez-faire of the workshops, the actual performance process, which Roger Bowen describes as "brainstorming," was quite pragmatic: "We'd do what any person thrown into that situation would do—just make it up as you go along. You'd try out ideas that came to you, find out what worked, or just give up and do funny stuff." When Sills directed Compass, Bowen says, "He would start out with Viola's exercises, but when it came time for the show, he'd throw out all that stuff in favor of whatever worked."

Shortly after the Compass opened, John Ecks, their former colleague, returned with his own group from Cuautla, Mexico, where they had taken a working sojourn. Bob Patton first saw Ecks and his group when the door burst open in the middle of an exercise while Elaine was rehearsing a workshop in the gym at the Hyde Park Y. As Annette Hankin recalls, "This very scruffy group walked in—tattered and dirty and dark from the sun—while we were being trees." "They came in like gangsters and sort of cowed everybody," says Patton. "We were scared to death." Elaine let out a yell, dropped everything, and jumped into Ecks's arms.

"I'm sure his group thought we were impure," says Bowen, who remembers them sitting in the back room of the Compass "dressed in black, like crows on a fence," looking on with disapproval as they watched the Compass group rehearse. Ecks had "very strong ideas," says David Shepherd. "His group was into Gurdjieff. In the Gurdjieff Fourth Way, it's all about concentration and communal work. They felt that we were namby-pamby, that our show was too conventional, that we were not taking risks."

The audience felt otherwise. Young people who met or dated at the Compass tell David Shepherd now to his surprise that it was shocking. In the Compass scenarios about adultery, deceit, greed, and the initiation of unformed youth into the sculpturing hands of a corrupt society, an audience member remembers, they were "observing situational morality for the first time in their lives. Things were not described as black and white. Things were described as gray and gray."

In 1939, Viola Spolin had written that "the most dramatic material lies within our everyday lives." At the Compass, material on topics of the moment—urban renewal, academic pretensions, the middle-class identity crisis—now came pouring out. Because it was improvised, there was no language censorship. Compass actors, unlike revue performers, did not sweeten their satires by giving consumer products and political figures adorable names. The hypocrisy of sexual rituals was constantly scrutinized. And always the middle-class parent was under attack.

The first improvised marijuana-smoking scene occurred at the Compass in *The Minister's Daughter,* the featured scenario of the second week.

"I tried to write the corniest scenario I could," says Shepherd of his story of an aristocratic clergyman (Shepherd), who chooses to live in his lower-class parish and whose expectations for a beatific family life are disrupted by his two adopted children, one an incipient runaway (Barbara Harris) in love with a worthless beatnik (Sid Lazard), the other a college student (Roger Bowen) whose year at Cornell has turned him into a reactionary snob.

As the story progresses, the children discover their true origins and they relax into the roles of the social misfits they really are. The daughter's wayward ways lead her to invite a dope dealer to the family rumpus room, where he passes around pot. The role of the dope dealer was given to Bob Patton, the only black player in the group. Patton's reasons for joining the Compass were not those of a social critic or renegade. He had been working with a Roosevelt University theatre group for several years and knew himself still to be an amateur. "I wanted to grow," he says. He did not equate being a professional actor with being middle class.

"It was odd at that time in Chicago to have any kind of mixed company," says Patton. "There were very few opportunities for that." Chicago has always been a much more ethnically segregated city than New York. There was almost no cultural crossover between Chicago's Polish, Irish, Italian, German, and Jewish neighborhoods. In 1955, it was the most racially divided city in the world outside of Johannesburg. Patton lived in the neighborhood that was the strange and volatile exception, Hyde Park. Even so, "I didn't know any other black actors," Patton says. "Neither did Paul or David or Elaine. They weren't in University Theatre. I met very few blacks at all socially. And no actresses. No bright-eyed things looking for parts."

Patton did not then nor does he now feel that he was breaking any conventions by participating in the Compass. "I was aware that I was the only black member of the group. That was pretty obvious. But it really played no part. I took whatever roles came along."

To Patton, the scene where the dope dealer turns the daughter on to reefers was "my big scene. It was shocking, I suppose. But I didn't think about it. It was acting. I was just playing a part. We were supposed to 'go out' mentally each night while smoking these imaginary joints. I had to make up new jokes each night. Just freeform, you know. I didn't even smoke grass at the time. I had grown up in the middle-moral class. I knew what it was, but I wouldn't go near it. Dope was really proscribed."

At the end of one show, when some blacks in the audience complained to Shepherd about Patton playing this "dissolute role," Patton thought, "Those stupid assholes. They complain about my great role."

Watching Patton kiss a white girl onstage so agitated one of the bartenders that during rehearsals he climbed under the hollow stage and pounded on it. One night in a fury, he leaped on the stage.

If Patton and the company were oblivious to his color, it was symptomatic of their lack of connection to the one cultural issue the Compass never quite addressed. The Compass scenarios focused on the white underclass. Were it not for Elaine May, the focus would have settled on a white male underclass.

As she initially conceived *Homecoming*, her first scenario, a cynical and manipulative young man named Averill Schatz (Roger Bowen) insinuates himself into George Hasselman's (Andy Duncan's) conventional home during a college vacation and disrupts it by turning George into a rebel, provoking him to coldly have sex with his girlfriend, Elizabeth Fist (Barbara Harris), the daughter of George's father's business associate (Sid Lazard).

While sitting in a pizza joint on Fifty-fifth Street, the male members of the Brain Trust decided another mean character was needed to balance Averill Schatz. From his work as a counselor of industrial relations, Bob Coughlan knew it was currently fashionable for businessmen to take off for Aspen, Colorado, hire a guru, and meditate. The men proposed the introduction of a swami (David Shepherd), who would act as an adviser to Mr. Fist and as a foil to Averill.

In the amended version of *Homecoming*, the swami shows Fist how to achieve Nirvana in a how-to-do-it scene. When the adults discover Averill's poisonous influence on George, the swami orchestrates a showdown with Schatz. The showdown between Averill and the swami is an exchange of proverbs, which the swami, with his incantation to The Goat Maiden, wins. He implores Averill to "rethink the wisdom of his path" and, when no one is looking, bribes Averill to get lost.

"Elaine had a conception of Averill Schatz as a hypnotic guru type, capable of messing up people's lives, something like Lenny Cantrow, the character in the Neil Simon film she directed, *The Heartbreak Kid*.* I couldn't play that, so we threw in the swami," Roger Bowen admits. "Elaine felt we had made a travesty of her idea. There was a display of anger. And we, being men, just ignored her. Nothing new about that."

In fact, they had distorted and dulled the point of her story. While creating a showdown between the two male gurus resulted in uncovering the swami as an old charlatan even more skilled than young Averill Schatz, it also succeeded in diffusing the conspiracy against Elizabeth, who, in conclusion, is pushed by her parents into marrying George, her rapist, as if through marriage her violation would be redeemed.

In David Shepherd's *Five Dreams*, the last scenario performed in July, the five actors representing the Lonely Crowd wore paper bags on their heads. A bag would be removed as each actor in turn began to reenact his or her dream, which were nightmares of urban alienation, such as being caught in the rush hour or trapped in an office or factory.

---

*One life Cantrow messes up is his bride's. In the film, she was played by Elaine May's daughter, Jeannie Berlin.

Bob Coughlan's scenario *The Drifters* featured Coughlan and LeGlaire as Clint and Luke, two characters described as "cornballs." They are sold a phony map to the Inca treasure by two practical jokers they meet while unloading a UPS truck. En route to the Southwest, the alleged site of the buried treasure, the drifters take advantage of everyone they meet.

Hitchhiking on the highway, they encounter a salesman (David Shepherd) who hawks Saint Christopher medals and religious comic books. After fixing his flat tire, they rob him of his car and suit.

In a Robert Hall clothing store, a salesman (Andy Duncan) pushes a wardrobe of shoddy clothes on Luke, which he buys with a worthless check.

They meet Marv Solomon, a Hollywood press agent (Sid Lazard), and Kiki (Waldene Jacobson), who are on the road promoting their studio's new African film. They perceive the drifters in their middle-class suits as easy marks.

In a cow field, the drifters see a stranded cannibal, Uganda, who is really Hector de Vries, a black actor (Bob Patton) hired for publicity purposes by Solomon. The drifters assume he is an authentic African slave and set him free. To teach the "slaveholders" a lesson, they tie up Solomon and rape Kiki, feeling moral and self-righteous that they have given an "eye for an eye."

Like the other outcasts who pervade the first scenarios of Compass, Coughlan's drifters are seen again and again as bunko artists in a society that is constantly conning them.

At last, in Oklahoma, they pass themselves off as uranium prospectors to honest and illiterate Amos Barker, a farmer (also played by Shepherd) who discovers them trespassing in his cave. The drifters, secretly planning to dig for Inca treasure, are surprised when Barker welcomes them to "survey" his worthless land, arid since the Dust Bowl days. The farmer and his daughter (Elaine May) rejoice when the drifters dig into an underground spring, now gushing water and renewing the land. The farmer is deliriously happy. Impressed with his worldly ways, the daughter falls in love with Clint and invites him and Luke to stay. They all celebrate. But the sheriff has tracked down the drifters and arrives to arrest them. They are hauled away from this paradise of integrity.

If Elaine had sacrificed the hard-edged realism she intended in *Homecoming*, she did not make the same concessions with her next scenario, *Georgina's First Date*. Sills took charge of the rest of the evening, including a Living Newspaper version of *True Romance* magazine, but Elaine herself directed this story of a young woman's sexual initiation, one of several ruthlessly unsentimental studies (including her previous production of *Miss Julie* and her subsequent films *A New Leaf* and *The Heartbreak Kid*) of outrages perpetrated against vulnerable women by their mothers and men. With characteristic perfectionism, she trained her workshoppers in this project for weeks.

To get into a fraternity, Eddie (Haym Bernson), one of the sharpies at the high school, agrees to take Georgina, a fat girl (Annette Hankin), to the prom. Georgina's parents (May and Shepherd) are thrilled. In their eyes, their teenaged albatross has suddenly become a beautiful swan. While shopping for a prom dress, Georgina and her mother meet another mother and daughter. The mothers brag about their daughters in a game of vicarious one-upmanship. In further preparation for the prom, Georgina's older sister (Roberta Gnippe), in a sharp and funny how-to-do-it scene, teaches her to dance by pretending to be (and using all the standard come-ons of) a teenaged boy.

When Eddie comes to call, the parents fall all over themselves to interest the young man in Georgina, encouraging the young couple to stay out as late as they can.

At the dance, Eddie's pals goad Eddie into "scoring" with Georgina as a conclusion to their prank.

After the dance, Eddie parks his car and rapes Georgina in lovers' lane.

When Georgina returns home, her mother is ecstatic with curiosity. Georgina refuses to yield to her mother's relentless interrogation. She keeps insisting, "I had a wonderful time." With a glassy-eyed smile, she goes upstairs. Her mother says, "Thank God."

According to her student Annette Hankin, Elaine's intellect, curiosity, responsiveness, drive, and performance ability were all connected to the same overwhelmingly cool vision of truth and reality. "It was not a pretty vision," says Hankin. "I think she saw all things as tradeoffs, and love in a cruel light. It was a terrible, awesome vision, that of a person who has survived an emotional holocaust. That may have been why she was so distant. I saw her cry more than once. I'm not sure I know why. I thought it had something to do with the fact that her mother was raising her child."

Indeed, much of Elaine's energy, according to Hankin, was spent defending herself. "She was one of those women who perceives herself as very vulnerable. In fact, she was one of the toughest women I ever knew, a real tough cookie. It came from some perception that she had to defend herself in a world that would eat her alive. The heroines of her plays are always very vulnerable people who are eaten alive."

Throughout the summer, the Compass was a community theatre even more magnetic than David Shepherd had envisioned it would be. It had begun to attract not only a steady stream of students and faculty from the University of Chicago but locals from Hyde Park. In this down-sliding neighborhood, about to be ravaged by urban renewal, there was not much cultural nightlife.

"I think the neighborhood was starved for a theatre that would speak to Chicago issues, and the whole academic bullshit which had to do with expectations that parents had about children, and the whole Eisenhower ethos," reflects David Shepherd.

"When David came to the front of the stage to ask for contributions," says Mildred Goldberger, "it was clear what his notion was, and still is: the pleasures of community as embodied in the theatre."

The Socratic atmosphere of the University of Chicago, where doubt was a virtue and all assumptions were questioned, was extremely receptive to the uncertainties of improvisation. To Gene Gendlin, "The improvisation was really a living theatre. In American film and theatre, it was much more usual to hide the process. It added drama to the drama to see the drama made in front of you." "People would go in there and say, 'I don't know what's going to happen,' " says Barbara Harris. " 'It may be awful and it may be good, and it may not be anything. It may just be a transformation before my eyes. But I'm out on a hot summer night, and I don't want to study, and oh, wow, I can watch them in the back room satirizing David Riesman and listen to Vivaldi in the bar.' "

Hyde Park, in fact, turned up an audience uniquely disconnected from the Hula Hoop culture of the Eisenhower years. These "folks" were supersophisticated, politically savvy, and hungry to have their own suggestions dramatized and their own idiosyncratic attitudes expressed.

Psychiatry, for example, was very fashionable among these intellectuals of 1955. As a graduate student in psychology, James Sacks became a devoted patron. Like other shrinks, he was drawn to the Compass. Like other shrinks, he was drawn to Elaine, who possessed some key to her own unconscious and was able to convert these findings on the spot into dark and humorous art. (One audience regular, a psychopath who sometimes leaped on the stage to be near her, was also her adoring fan.)

Thus, when references were made to psychiatry in Vienna, there was usually a Viennese psychiatrist in the audience. "Anyone who was anyone in left-wing politics came to the Compass," says David Shepherd. And David Riesman, the author of *The Lonely Crowd*, dropped into the back room to see for himself how he was being ridiculed. In a period when Norman Vincent Peale's *The Power of Positive Thinking* was a best-seller and "I Believe" was an American anthem, this crowd—whose standard answer to "How are you?" was "Relative to what?"—responded wildly to a theatre that represented them.

"If there is such a thing as altruism," says Barbara Harris of the early Compass, "then it was altruistic, with a kind of generosity of energy and spirit. We were pursuing something that we didn't know would work. It wasn't very down-to-earth. It wasn't practical. It wasn't realistic. But it filled a need that made sense. I think the motivation of the people made it different. Everyone may have had his own motivations, but money and vanity weren't among them."

"None of us had any ambition or wanted to be a star," says Andy Duncan. "We really had no profession. We were cultural gangsters. I mean, who were we kidding?"

12

The Summer Ends

The Coast Guard describes a compass as "ambiguous" if it has demagnetized and gone off course. The ambiguous moves of the Compass were the responsibility of the navigator, David Shepherd.

He had envisioned Compass as a popular theatre. But within three months, a working-class person would have been prevented from participating in this venture if he or she tried. The amateur actors were replaced by professional ones. The strong ensemble form that had defined Compass, the scenario play, became less important to these actors and almost disappeared from the improvisational theatre's repertoire. The players began to freeze their shorter work, and what was frozen could be played anywhere.

In Italy, when a commedia dell'arte actor couldn't make it from Larderello to Pisa in time for the gig, by written contract he owed lire to his fellow players so they could hire a replacement for the missing Pantaloon or Columbine. As a shareholder in his company, he shared the responsibilities as well as the profits. There was no such financial stake for a Compass player. The prototypical socialist theatre was not organized so that the actors, who were also the writers, would participate in a royalty or profit-sharing plan.

There were these and more ambiguities of the Compass.

Compass became a vehicle for soloists—individuals concerned and fearful for their own approval and success. The spiritual machinery for creating theatrical surprise was surprisingly easy to convert into machinery for a comedy assembly line. The anticommercial art form Shepherd reinvented became so commercial as to strike one of its founding members, Barbara Harris, as "a total paradox." And Elaine May, a radical and remorselessly uncompromising artist of the form, became a show-business curiosity.

What happened to the Compass? What were the reasons for its disintegration in Chicago? What steps led to its demise?

The litany of off-course events exhausts David Shepherd. He sighs: "I hadn't been to theatre school. I hadn't been to the Harvard Business School. That first summer we were flooded, taking in thousands of dollars at the door, sucking up every possible resource. I was ignorant. I didn't expect it to happen so fast."

The early Compass had gained its strength from the points of view of people who brought to their improvisations the insights of an assortment of experiences and professions. It soon became apparent, however, that the people who worked elsewhere in the community had no time to rehearse. To participate in the rigorous and consuming schedule of the Compass at its going salary of twenty-five dollars a week required an independent income like Shepherd's, unusual free-lance skills like Duncan's, or a total indifference to personal comfort like Elaine's.

As the summer came to a close, most of The Compass Players were planning to go back to their studies or to work and Shepherd's Brain Trust was falling apart. Upon joining the Compass, Roger Bowen had given up graduate school, and without a student deferment, his number inevitably came up for the draft. He had already begun taking frequent trips to say good-by to his girlfriend in Providence. The theatre was also to lose the driving presence of Bob Coughlan, who had to resume his post as a counselor of industrial relations from which he had taken a leave. Sills's Fulbright term was about to begin in Bristol, and he and Barbara Harris were preparing for a year abroad. Soon the Compass would consist of a loose and uncommitted band of players backing David Shepherd, Charlie Jacobs, Andy Duncan, and Elaine May.

The last scenario in August, *How to Catch a Tax Evader*, or *The Mousetrap*, was written by David Shepherd in collaboration with Donald Dryfus, an accountant. The premise was inspired by a "brainstorm" Shepherd had after reading a study of how a used car salesman had evaded taxes. Shepherd played the tax evader, and Duncan played the IRS inspector who pins him to the wall. In a small part, Dryfus, Shepherd noticed, "did a creditable job for an amateur."

How to Catch a Tax Evader started an unfortunate precedent for a theatre that required immediacy: it was so popular it was held over and ran for two weeks. By the end of the second week, Duncan and Shepherd got so bored they decided to switch parts. "That's how impatient we were," sighs Shepherd. "We craved new material, new experiences, new productions. We were eating up material." In hindsight, he can see that "a show that good should have been revised and rehearsed again. It would have run for six months."

In a letter to Roger Bowen, Shepherd confessed his growing apprehensions. He was having difficulty finding not only new scenarios but a way to sustain the underrehearsed theatre pieces that became increasingly rigid and wooden after the spontaneous excitement of opening night. He was worried about replacing Paul Sills and Barbara Harris. He was overwhelmed by the prospect of writing, directing, acting, and running the Compass. He despaired of bringing "new blood" into the Compass, observing that at Playwrights Theatre Club, Rolf Forsberg had already combed Chicago's talent for *The Taming of the Shrew* and "come up with nothing but dregs."

In Shepherd's vulnerable condition, John Ecks now represented "strong competition." Ecks had settled into Chicago as a resident theatre guru, and his workshop was already beginning to attract would-be actresses frustrated by waitressing at the Compass and never getting parts. After attending Ecks's workshops, "They'd become very superior," Duncan observes. "His work was like the Becks'. He was doing wild stuff."

At Elaine's suggestion, Annette Hankin had attended Ecks's workshop during the development of *Georgina's First Date* and found it "very Stanislavskian and very intense. He was forever going to put on an early play by Brecht about a man and a man he bullied.* Rehearsals went on for centuries."

It mattered little to Shepherd if Ecks's work reached fruition. "These zealots may never put on a play," he wrote to Bowen, "but will criticize the dead rationalizations of our stage." More than the scorn of Ecks, however, he feared that in Sills's absence, "Elaine may very well be tempted to join Ecks's group at some future date." Annette Hankin viewed the relationship between Ecks and May as "the chess match of the century. Perhaps they shared the same vulnerability. And neither one was ever going to win."

As a backstage diversion at the Compass, chess was constantly played. Even now, Shepherd sees the maneuvers of a producer—"finding a new location, or dealing with the liquor commission, or staffing or training,

---

The Exception and the Rule, a short play.

or public relations, or building a corporation, or organizational development"—as "chess moves" for which he had poor skills. In the matches he next would enter, however, it was not just lack of skill but a failure of focus that made winning an impossibility. After the gloriously promising summer of 1955, the moves Shepherd made at the Compass were not simply challenged by stronger opponents. Indeed, following the conventional wisdom of show business ("Go for it. This show is good enough for New York"), he was playing against himself.

Paul Sills and Barbara Harris left for Bristol on September 11, the week *The Fuller Brush Man*, a play about the evolution of a huckster, was on the boards.

"With Sills gone, there was less pressure," says Andy Duncan. To Duncan, who was becoming a resourceful and adroit performer, the effect was "positive and negative at the same time. Sills was both a father figure and a child. He was capable of dominating and also of throwing tantrums. There was a constant contradiction between the demands of the work and the demands of the audience. Although Sills was always screaming in rehearsal that we had to do it right, if you went out there and did a 'Where' exercise, the audience would boo." It was not uncommon for Sills to grab an actor offstage and say, "We've got an audience out there, for crissake." "If we had been Equity—a director who grabbed you offstage—they'd have the place closed down in a minute. David, to his credit, would never do that. (He had the consideration to wait until after the show.) But when Sills left and he tried to fill the vacuum, well, he was just incapable of taking charge of this thing."

A less confident and seasoned player like Mickey LeGlaire felt that "when Paul left, something really went out of it. It just really went down."

Without Sills, who had been instrumental in transforming amateurs like Zohra Lampert, Barbara Harris, and Mike Nichols into serious actors, Shepherd discovered that he could not train or nurture a native amateur company.

In contrast to the painstaking and serious approach to teaching improvisation used in the Compass workshops, Shepherd set aside Tuesday nights as an open house for the audience, or Amateur Night, at which any eager member of the audience was welcome to get up and improvise. Like the regular cast, they used no props, and the only costumes were hats. Suggestions were also recorded on a big flip pad. The newcomers were given five or six minutes to prepare a scene or scenario, assign the parts, and decide which player would run the lights.

In theory, Amateur Night was closer in spirit to Shepherd's concept of a people's theatre than the other six nights. It featured the greatest degree of audience involvement and total spontaneity.

In reality, it was chaos, and assisting the amateurs was a task Shepherd soon assigned to the salaried members of his cast.

While interning as a psychologist at Mantino State Hospital, James Sacks was a frequent member of the audience workshop, where he felt "pleasantly accepted" by the regulars. In one scene he wore a wastebasket over his head and played a robot; Elaine May, wearing a twisted-hanger headdress, played a mad Venusian queen.

What Shepherd did not foresee, or chose to ignore in his eagerness to create an open stage for the community, was that improvisers begin to seek their own level of expertise. The amateurs would "get up there and they would stink," says Jim Sacks. "They were self-involved and narcissistic and not funny. And they would stay on stage too long."

"They were even worse than us," says Sid Lazard.

Still nothing had been done to fix the hole backstage between the stairwell and the sink. The regular players had learned to be careful. "You had to be," recalls Andy Duncan. "Suppose the lights black out. You're in the dark. You step off, elated from the crowd. And the next thing you know . . ."

Often, between improvisations on Amateur Nights, there were screams.

Sills shared Shepherd's commitment to the community, but, unlike Shepherd, his first commitment was to art. He was no more articulate about his improvisational theories than Shepherd was about his political ones. But he possessed the practical tools of stagecraft, the confidence, and the personal magnetism to make the performance process accessible to a company of amateurs. Whatever "professionalism" existed at the Compass was due to his practiced hand. Also, unlike Shepherd, he had a clear view of his calling. Sills was a director with an objectivity and detachment that was impossible for Shepherd, who without the chops of Lord Olivier or Charlie Chaplin, was constantly himself onstage. For the chance of becoming a trusted authority figure for actors already hired, Mickey LeGlaire says, "David didn't have a prayer."

When Shepherd took charge of the theatre, LeGlaire sensed he was in conflict with Elaine. "It wasn't a big deal, but I can remember it now. She was just stronger than he was. It wasn't like she threatened to leave. She was sort of low-down. She was living in basements and cellars. She wasn't ambitious in that area. She was a real—what you'd call a beatnik, you know?"

Elaine bought her clothes at Goodwill, and sometimes they matched. Once, after a visit from a male relative she described as a gangster who had made his mark during Prohibition (and as a model for *Mikey and Nicky,* her saga-in-progress of friendship and betrayal between two small-time Jewish criminals), her wardrobe was temporarily enhanced.

Onstage, she was transformed, "radiant," "gorgeous," "devastating." Watching Elaine May at the Compass, the audience never noticed or cared that she was safety-pinned together or that she used green thread to hem her black dress.

"We weren't as good as Elaine was. We weren't up to her," says LeGlaire. "I wasn't that good, and I used to do big parts. David wanted to get other people to save it, to attract an audience and hold them, you know? He went to New York to find them. And that's about it."

After finishing his fourth summer season at the Barter Theatre, in Abingdon, Virginia, Severn Darden ('52) drove his second Rolls-Royce through the Lincoln Tunnel and headed for his apartment on MacDougal Street. On foot in Greenwich Village, he ran into Jenny Lee Davis, a fellow Barter actor who had once played his Lady Macbeth. Davis mentioned that a producer from Chicago was in town auditioning actors, and Severn arranged to see David Shepherd that night.

At Severn's audition, Shepherd remembers, "He hardly did anything, two or three things. You know, to show that he could act."

"We met in an incredibly, uh, sordid apartment," recalls Severn, "and he gave me a somewhat confused idea of what was going on."

Shepherd demonstrated improvisation for Severn by performing a scene with him in which Shepherd played an irritable hunchback and Severn played his boss.

"The producer acted for the person who was being auditioned," snorts Shepherd. "It was true to Severn's form." When the demonstration was over, Severn chewed his handkerchief and said, "That was interesting. I'll come."

Some days later, in Sheridan Square, stopping for a drink at the Riviera Bar, Severn recognized a face he had often seen around campus at the University of Chicago during his student days. Without jubilation, Mike Nichols ('52) mentioned that he was on his way back to Chicago to join The Compass Players and had heard that Severn had been hired too.

"The guy had been highly touted," Shepherd reflects. "I was told that

Mike Nichols could talk his way out of anything. Paul said, 'He's brilliant at talking. We should get him to come.' I said, 'But that's not what we're about. We're not about talking.' And Paul said, 'Get him anyway. It'll work out. You'll see. He's good.'"

In New York, before shipping out for England on the *Queen Elizabeth II*, Paul Sills and Barbara Harris had paid a visit to Sills's old colleague, who was still studying acting with Lee Strasberg, supporting himself with an endless series of odd jobs and living the life of an unemployed New York actor, in a room, Barbara remembers, without any furniture, just a TV set (on which night after night he saw no roles for himself) and a mattress on the floor. In the ensuing hours, Nichols heard Sills argue quite persuasively how great it was in Chicago and how appropriate and right it seemed for Nichols to join in this cabaret.

Nichols would later remember how he "slunk back to Chicago," filled with discouragement, reflecting also that "if I'd stayed in New York with Lee Strasberg—who was very important to me—and just tried to be an actor, nothing would have happened to me."

Modestly, Sills refuses credit for luring Nichols from his classwork into the improvisational theatre, explaining, "Shepherd hired him."

Finding a woman who could hold the stage in place of Barbara Harris was a more difficult case. Women of the fifties shied away from the aggressive choices required of an improvisation. With scant access to most jobs and professions, they were also more role-bound than men, inclined to play mothers, daughters, secretaries, wives, and nurses rather than to exploit their distance from traditional male roles in order to satirize them.

Elaine May was the exception. "She broke through the psychological restrictions of playing comedy as a woman," Shepherd says. She was not an ingenue. In her improvisations, she rarely chose traditional female roles. She played challenging, sophisticated, worldly women. She was the doctor, the psychiatrist, the employer, the wicked witch.

"She was very mischievous," says Sid Lazard, "always amusing herself by putting everyone into the most difficult positions onstage." As a wicked witch, she once tucked Lazard's leg behind him and insisted that he hold it there.

After climbing into the backstage hole and opening the louvers, Andy Duncan would play a scene as Toulouse-Lautrec by placing a pair of shoes in front of his body, which was visible only above the waist. Elaine's joke as his fellow player, Duncan remembers, would always be to coax the little Lautrec onstage.

If she challenged the others into spontaneously dealing with comedic situations, she was also the one who saw the way to get them out of trouble, to provide a scene with an ending, to resolve an impasse with a funny line.

Following Viola's exercises and Elaine's example, Barbara Harris had also been capable of creating original and satirical characters, as Duncan describes them, "modern teenagers, sort of young women on the move." In contrast to dark, sultry, and aggressive Elaine, however, Barbara was blond, innocent, soft, and sweet. Fran Gendlin still pictures her with a bandana around her hair and "a beautiful open face."

It was her looks rather than her insights into the American female that the producers sought to replace. "It wasn't that they were sexist," says Duncan. "They really looked for women who could do it." Nevertheless, whatever her talent, it was also incumbent on the other Compass actress to decorate the stage.

Kenna Hunt had a B.A. in drama from Scripps College in Claremont, California. In her two years at the Omaha Playhouse, she had won the Dorothy McGuire and Henry Fonda awards. She had spent two years at the Royal Academy of Dramatic Art (RADA). Shakespeare was her strength.

Sills had auditioned Hunt for a production of *Hamlet* at the Playwrights Theatre Club. He was so impressed with her Gertrude that he invited her to understudy in Chicago with the understanding that she would come over to the Compass when she wasn't acting, and learn to improvise. Finding that Hunt had "a kind of very healthy buxom quality, and energy onstage," Shepherd agreed with Sills that she should come.

Shepherd was still in New York holding casting calls during the rehearsal slot given to Roger Bowen's scenario *The War Bride*. "He told me to direct it," says Bowen, "and I'm no director. I didn't know a thing." The lead was played by Lucy Minnerle, a Brazilian chosen for her accent, not her acting ability, and Bowen cast Mickey LeGlaire as the veteran who brings back the alien bride. Their performances were "terrible, terrible. They could do well in small parts, but that's it," Bowen says. "They couldn't play leads." By popping over the louvers, Elaine joined the cast as the nosy neighbor upstairs. Her performance could not sustain *The War Bride*, which Bowen maintains was "just a disaster, probably the worst thing we ever did."

In the audience watching *The War Bride* one night were three right-wing steeplejacks who had responded to one of Shepherd's periodic handbill

showerings of working-class neighborhoods. The scenario provoked one of
them into shouting. All of them were drunk. The bouncer for the evening
was Theodore W. ("Ted") Rosenak, previously the *University of Chicago
Law Review*'s editor in chief. He suggested that the steeplejacks remove
to the bar. They left the show room somewhat mollified. In the barroom,
the shouting resumed.

At the sound of the ruckus, Bowen recalls, the only actor willing to join
the fight was Elaine. "The rest of us didn't want to get involved. But she
was feisty. She said, 'I'm going out there,' while the rest of us cowered
backstage."

The bartender, of Irish extraction, was a Ph.D. candidate in educational
psychology who kept a shillelagh behind the bar. As the disturbance escalated, he pulled out the shillelagh and hit the loudest drunk over the
head, knocking him down and giving him a wound that would merit six
stitches.

"The bartender and the three guys were booked. The troublemaker was
a guy on probation after a six-year rap. The second guy also had a prior
record," recalls Saul Mendlowitz, who was hired by David Shepherd to
defend the three steeplejacks. "That was David's ideology," summarizes
Mendlowitz. "He wanted people off the street."

Coming back from Providence at the end of the summer, Roger Bowen
was confronted by "David's long face. He said, 'The bar can make more
money without us. Freddy wants us out.' "

Between the two units of the Compass, there had always been, as Wranovics describes it, "a friendly rivalry." The back room by and large attracted an out-for-the-evening Coca-Cola crowd, while the round-the-
clock barroom patrons in front relaxed with a beer and a shot. Wranovics
contends that balancing the finances was simply a matter of adjusting the
beverage prices gradually, so that by the end of the summer a Coca-Cola
in the back room cost as much as a rum and Coke at the bar.

Bowen maintains that Wranovics "made jokes so the audience would
hear him. He'd say derisive things about the show. 'If it weren't for the
show,' he'd say, 'we could have twice as many people in here.' That kind
of thing. Also the fight. Freddy blamed us for that. So he rode us out of
there."

Could Shepherd's own jumbled priorities have made it convenient for
him to divert the blame to Wranovics? With so few seats, it was, as Charlie
Jacobs says, "hard to bring in enough dough to pay the performers." He
recalls that he and Shepherd had already started wondering if it was possible

to get a bigger space when they ran across the owner of the Dock, George Schall.

Late in August, they commenced negotiations with Schall, whose family restaurant and show room, the Dock, was on South Lake Park Avenue. "If we are willing to invest another three thousand dollars," Shepherd wrote to Bowen, "we can double our net by moving into his room. It would seat fifty percent more." The Compass Players moved off the University of Chicago campus in the fall. The Compass Tavern was open for the next five years, until 1960, when it was torn down.

13

Enter the Actors

Severn Darden returned to Chicago in the impromptu spirit his new
job required, without a clue to what awaited him. He drove his
Phantom I Rolls-Royce. His fifty-five-dollar-a-week deal with David Shepherd did not include air fare. An actress friend, Diane Cilento, who later
married Sean Connery, lent him money to buy gas.

The first line he heard spoken onstage ("Adventure is a small town at
the mouth of the Essequibo") was quoted by David Shepherd from *National Geographic*. (By the summer's end, keeping up with the daily press
was already proving too much of a grind, and the Living Newspaper had
become, in fact if not in name, the Living Magazine.)

He received no other preparation, no statement of purpose, no expla-
nation of technique. His initiation into the improvisational theatre would
become the tradition for new players at the Compass: he was thrown out
on the stage.

In the sink-or-swim atmosphere that was to characterize the post-Sills
Compass, Severn Darden swam, and, as Shepherd calls it, "the Dada or
anarchist component" of Compass humor suddenly bubbled up.

Now, before the Living Newspaper and the scenario play, Severn in-
stituted a nonsense lead-in, a Dada warm-up time. "We had an old door
with missing panes. We'd bring it onstage and take the lights down," recalls
Andy Duncan. Severn did readings of Kurt Schwitters's one-letter poem,
"W" ("Wuh!"), inventing an upside-down reading of it: "M"
("Mmmmmm"). "We did 'Anny, Anny, thou art from the front as behind:
a-nay-a-nay-a-nay.' Crazy Dada poetry stuff. Or we'd have one guy reciting

a poem while another rang a bell so you couldn't hear the poem. All that stuff to infuriate the audience. They loved it."

Using a German accent, a huge vocabulary gleaned from *The Oxford English Dictionary*, a vast and obscure store of erudition, an insider's knowledge and experience of the peculiarities of the University of Chicago, an innocence to his guile, and a profound sense of the ridiculous, Severn created the character of the mad Professor Walter von der Vogelweide, named for a medieval minnesinger. In this character, "He could go on for an hour," says Kenna Hunt. "The audience went wild." Usually, The Professor would deliver a lecture on metaphysics ("the branch of philosophy that asks, 'What *is* everything, anyhow?' ") from which the following observation is an excerpt:

> For centuries, philosophers have told us that thought cannot be seen. It cannot be felt, read, cannot be tasted. It is not in the key of G. Or F. It is not blue. Nor is it mauve. It is not a pot of geraniums. It is not a white donkey against a blue sky. Or a blue donkey against a white sky. It is not a little girl singing an old song. Nor does it have aspirations to become archbishop. It is not a saffron-robed monk, pissing in the snow.
>
> In other words, philosophers can tell you millions of things that thought isn't, and they can't tell you what it is. And that bugs them.

Often, he would take questions from the audience. To the question "Do fish think?" he once replied:

> I had a fish once. Her name was Louise. A small, fat fish. And every day at the same time, I would go over to the edge of the pond and throw her a bunch of grapes. Every day at the same time, the fish would be there. After a few days, you see, it knew. At one forty-five: grapes. Bam! Fish! I began making it fifteen minutes later every day. You see? And then when I was there at two o'clock, she'd be there at one forty-five. She was fifteen minutes behind. And she starved to death. Yes, fish think, but not fast enough.

Frequently, The Professor would introduce a lecture on metaphysics and then proceed to "talk about anything." The development of Attic black-and-red figureware to red-and-black figureware from the third and second centuries to the second and third centuries—a period of 600 years. Egyptians with twelve stomachs ("conspicuous consumption"). Even- and odd-toed angulets. Prehistoric animals in the upper atmosphere. The condensation of pterodactyls into tractors. "When you talked archeological terms to an audience, it would become meaningless, and they would laugh," he says.

Occasionally, he played an invisible organ. Or, David Shepherd recalls, "He would make an elaborate diagram on this nonexistent blackboard, with a 'p' and an 'a,' and you'd put it together in your head. He would never actually say it. There was an 'a'-ness about the 'p.' Yeah, that was it. If you followed through this equation, you'd get the 'a'-ness on the 'p'-ness, or the 'p'-ness on the 'a'-ness. The laughs would come in after a few seconds, sometimes after ten seconds. And in twenty minutes, somebody else would figure it out."

To eighteen-year-old University of Chicago sophomore William A. ("Bill") Mathieu (now called Allaudin Mathieu), "Severn was the funniest person who lived." Mathieu had been dragged to the Compass by a fellow musician, a theatre buff, to audition as house pianist, a job that would need to be filled once the Compass moved to the Dock. Shepherd turned down the theatre buff, but Mathieu got the job: "I played three or four minutes and David said, 'Fine.' "

Mathieu's first view of the Compass was a workshop improvisation between Bowen and Shepherd on an invisible ocean liner. Bowen, as first mate, was demonstrating the smokestack. "What does a smokestack do?" asked Shepherd, playing a passenger. "It cleans up the smoke, just like the hairs in your nose," Bowen replied. "To make the connection between a smokestack and a nose," says Mathieu. "I thought that was the wittiest thing I had ever heard in my life." In the same mental picture (of "the moment I decided these people were okay"), Mathieu sees "a handkerchief, very clearly," and behind it, Severn. "He was like Charles Laughton. He had tremendous power. He was like a symbol of the old South, risen again. He was all dignity and extraordinary power. And at the same time, he was absolutely crazed. He would say and do things that left people truly paralyzed."

Once, he announced a lecture on "Some Positive Aspects of Anti-Semitism" by Bruno Bettelheim.

During late-night sets, Severn sometimes brought onstage his friend Conrad Yama, the Asian-American actor. Their "Fu Manchu" scene opened with them onstage, as Roger Bowen flew through the louvers crying, "Which one of you is Fu Manchu?"

With Elaine, he created "Doors," an allegory about two people in love trying to find each other. On the phone, Max would tell Emma he had a surprise for her. To see it, she would have to meet him by carefully following his directions: "You go down the street, turn right, go over the bridge, turn left, go up the flight of stairs, into the little green room, through the little brown door, into the big red room, turn right, go up the stairs, walk onto the roof, crawl over the ladder . . ." "I'd give her endless instructions," Severn recalls, "and then we'd endlessly carry them out, miming and climbing and crawling." Throughout, as they shouted out to each other ("Where are you? It's very big in here!") Max would carry a bass drum case. So numerous were the entrances and exits of Max and Emma, that after a while the audience would not notice that Max was no longer carrying the drum case. When the lovers finally meet, Emma would say, "What's your surprise?" "I lost it," Max would reply.

Two anecdotes remind the classics scholar Seth Benardete of his old friend Severn Darden. One is fictional: a gentleman is invited to a glittering costume ball and asked to dress to the nines. When he shows up wrapped in an old piece of canvas, the other guests are horrified. "What have you done?" they cry. "This is supposed to be a glittering costume ball." The gentleman throws open the old canvas wrap. Inside is a Raphael.

The other anecdote is oral history: Benno Landesberg, the esteemed authority on Assyriology, left Istanbul to join the department of Oriental studies at the University of Chicago. At 2:00 a.m. of his arrival day, he urinated in the bushes and was arrested by the campus police. Landesberg was furious. "In Istanbul, everybody urinates in the bushes," he shouted. "I have always urinated this way."

According to Benardete, Severn was the comic version of these gentlemen, "a man of station with perfect contempt. He was a noble funnyman. That's paradoxical to begin with and quite out of place in this country, where an extraordinary amount of comedy is really an expression of self-contempt."

If most American comedy is rooted in minority identification, Severn Darden's humor belonged to a pristinely Bohemian New Orleans gentleman, or, as Benardete puts it, "a minority of one."

With this solitary perspective, he was fearless.

In Benardete's telling, Severn was dressed in evening clothes when he and a black friend entered the Stork Club, an elite nightspot in New York, notorious for practicing Jim Crow. "Where can we piss?" he shouted at the maître d', and captured the attention of the room. Severn and his friend moved to the loo. No Stork Club employee was clever enough to top such a stunning entrance line.

Translating his irreverence to the stage was only a matter of getting on it. Almost immediately he discovered that there was no such thing as "talking up" to an audience. An obscure or erudite reference was as funny to them as a low one.

In a single improvisation, he once said "shit" 200 times. He was not afraid of being booed out of the theatre.

He was afraid of Elaine.

When Mike Nichols arrived, Annette Hankin recalls that "people were really writing him off: 'Oh, yeah, *him*,' somebody said. 'He can do a toothache really well. He studied with Strasberg.' "

According to Fred Wranovics's calendar, Nichols first appeared at the Compass on a Saturday afternoon. Peering into the back room, Wranovics observed that Nichols and Elaine were "sitting on these stools. It was like a summit meeting. It was a big deal. The two of them sat on those stools doing these routines, testing each other's ad-lib ability and spontaneity. Everyone was watching. It was like the Actors Studio versus the local fast gun. I'd come in every thirty minutes and they'd still be at it. I guess they hit it off."

Before an audience, however, as a newcomer to the Compass, Nichols, normally a wit and a "talker," found himself confused and plugged up. He had returned to Chicago a Method actor, with no sense of externalized characterization or the intuitive energies that flowed for an actor who succumbed to the space. From Strasberg, he had learned the theory of "true emotion" and the actor's obligation to allow only his own deepest feelings to move him onstage. While improvising, the feelings that apparently came up for Nichols were "hurting" and "revenge," and he expressed them either by crying or whining or by deploying hostile verbal attacks. Although it inhibited his physical imagination, onstage, to conceal his nervousness, he constantly smoked cigarettes.

Soon after he arrived, while he was playing a witch in an improvisation on *Hansel and Gretel*, the cast threw him into the "oven" by tossing him through the louvers. He landed in the backstage hole and broke his collarbone. Onstage, the scene continued, but backstage an ambulance was called. A few days later, Nichols returned to work in traction. Wearing a neck brace, he was now even further immobilized.

Once, alone on stage, Severn began to set an invisible table. It became clear through his pantomime that he was setting up for an elaborate dinner party. He laid all the invisible silverware and napkins and carefully lit invisible candles. Backstage, Nichols remarked, "It sounds kind of quiet out there." Fearing the silence, he entered the scene. The audience gasped. Nichols had erased the whole invisible set by walking through the table.

Characteristically, his breakthrough as a player occurred in his voice. As he tells it, he and Elaine were "fooling around" onstage one night, playing two English people riding horses on a bridle path, when one of the offstage actors rushed toward the others who were relaxing at the bar, crying, "Come quick! Mike has a character!" "I guess my character was that I was English," Nichols says.

Although outside of group scenes, Nichols had trouble improvising with everyone else, he had no trouble at all doing it with Elaine, who was so technically proficient and so accustomed to playing herself truthfully that she was always capable of challenging or disarming fellow players into responding from an equally truthful place.

When Nichols took the stage with her, she tapped into his core. Elaine's characters, previously portraits drawn from lower-middle-class life, now, in response to Nichols, moved adroitly up the social ladder. As foils to her domineering mothers, officious supervisors, seductive psychiatrists, and idiotic starlets, the characters he came up with were, as Heyward Ehrlich observes, "the Mike of a previous period. The Nebbish, The Schlemiel, The Snobby Sophisticate—all the types he played with such perfection— were Mike himself." Ehrlich saw that "tremendous self-revelation" fueled these sendups of emasculated males of the middle class.

Their first important scene, however, was based on a situation that transcended class: two teenagers making out in a car. The "wonderful poignant scene" Nichols and May developed reworked the same moment in the war between the sexes as the lovers' lane scene in *Georgina's First Date*. Here, too, a young man is trying to seduce an ambivalent young girl in a car.

Mike Nichols made a more captivating and vulnerable suitor than had Haym Bernson, and, in her performance as a susceptible virgin, Elaine, Annette Hankin noticed, was "more willing to be dazzled than Georgina." To a situation fraught with anxiety, the mere injections of their two personalities—fumbling, groping, smoking cigarettes—brought laughs. "Teenagers," which Nichols regards as one of the best scenes in their repertoire, was never recorded, and is relished even by him for these widely quoted lines:

"If I went any further, you wouldn't respect me."
"Oh, you have no *idea* how I'd respect you. I'd respect you like crazy."

Within a month of his arrival, Nichols and May were creating excitement as a performing team. People who witnessed their early theatrical encounters describe them as "brilliant" and "breathtaking," reporting that in one after another on-the-spot improvisation they displayed unflagging and amazing onstage rapport.

"Their stuff was really basic," says David Shepherd, "because although they played their characters with great detachment, they had a passionate need to present them in this way. And they did it with a lot of style. And taste. And brains."

Visiting the Compass during his period of "theatrical quietude,"* Eugene Troobnick saw that "Mike and Elaine were really something." Troobnick explains that civilians "think improvisation is getting up and saying funny lines. When you practice it, you learn that funny lines aren't it. The rule is to be truthful to the moment, and the funny stuff will flow from that. With Mike and Elaine, those rules did not apply. They could get up and say one funny line after another. Verbally, Mike Nichols was the fastest person I've ever known. He was a consummate wit."

According to Viola Spolin's theories, improvisation is nonverbal, its essence found not in the reserves of language but in that of empty space. In fact, where Paul Sills had been a pictorial director, Nichols and May were an audio phenomenon. Nichols was very much what Sills would call a "head person," intelligent, erudite, and "always intensely verbal," Nichols says. He also knew a great deal about music, and, as a radio disc jockey, had become very tuned in to the music of his own slightly nasal sounds. Elaine May was a playwright. Together, Nichols says, "We loved to listen, set up rhythms, catch their sparkle. We were in love with words."

According to Spolin, it is through the physical—the loss of mind—that we reach the white light of intuition, the pure improvisational state. As Nichols describes it, improvisation for him depended on "a certain con-

---

* Since Playwrights Theatre Club had shifted hands, Troobnick, the "young Fernandel," had remained an editor at Sears.

nection with Elaine, and a certain mad gleam in either her or my eyes when we knew something was starting." When a good scene took off, Nichols says, "By and large, I would shape them and Elaine would fill them." She was interested in character and the moment. He was interested in moving on. "I was always very concerned with beginning, middle, and end, and when it's time for the next point." He concedes also that he was "forced into" this editorial role since "she had endless capacity for invention. My invention was not endless," and because "she was a much better actor than I was. She could go on and on in a character. I could not. I had to move on to the next point because I was out. I couldn't do any more."

On the other elements of their chemistry, one must meditate. When he and Elaine met for the first time at the University of Chicago, during the Tonight at 8:30 days, Nichols notes that "we both had big reputations on campus for being dangerous-to-vicious, and so we were both interested in each other from that point of view." She had drawn the first sword, publicly cutting him down for enjoying his reviews in *Miss Julie*. In their first private encounter, two years later, a chance meeting on the platform of the Randolph Street Station of the Illinois Central, they had spontaneously begun, in whispered foreign accents, to speak to each other as spies. That evening, he had gone home with her and tasted "her specialty, which was a hamburger with cream cheese and ketchup," the only thing that she cooked. After that, they were "somehow safe from each other forever," he thought.

David Shepherd remembers the romantic interlude of Nichols and May at the Compass as "the three days that Mike lived with Elaine." During this time, Elaine borrowed Shepherd's copy of *The Kama Sutra*, and Shepherd noticed lines like "Let's do it like the Bending Lotus" cropping up when they were on the stage. When the three days were over, her interest waned. Now "Elaine's cruel drawings," a colleague noted, "were, strangely enough, of people without any hair."

Luckily, both of them had had extensive experience with psychoanalysis. The language, the subject matter, and the free-associational patterns of therapy were all improvisational tools they could share. Another comedian, Woody Allen, would find this aspect of their work inspirational. As a standup comic, however, even he could only make jokes about neurosis. As a team, Nichols and May dramatized it. Never have there been such intricate and hilarious examinations of the "transference" phenomenon as in their scenes about patients and shrinks, for example, the psychoanalyst who is devastated by her patient's decision to spend Christmas day with his wife and kids and the patient who must interrupt her free association to nurse her doctor out of his hiccups. Facing each other as equals, heavy hitter to heavy hitter, neurotic to neurotic, with all their hang-ups spread upon the (invisible) table, they were great.

Nichols has frequently attributed the dramaturgical advice "When in doubt, seduce" to Elaine. He also claims faith in the notion that improvised scenes must be based on a strong situation and conflict, the Stanislavskian approach. In fact, a hallmark of Nichols and May is their agreement. In Nichols and May dialogues, "Yes, yes" is often a motif.

Take this exchange in a postcoital scene in which a couple is listening to music, "Bach to Bach":

SHE: Too many people think of Adler as a man who made mice neurotic. He was more.
HE: Much more.

"Pirandello," never recorded, was perhaps their signature piece. At Compass, a third actor would announce it as "something we'd like to do in the style of Pirandello, which has to do with reality . . . holding a mirror to a mirror . . . well, we'll show you."

As the scene begins, Nichols and May are a young brother and sister, in the brother's room, where he is confined to bed with a cold. To keep him entertained, they play house, mimicking their mom and dad. Their imitation leads to insults and accusations, just like those of adults. As the fight gets angrier, the characters of the children slip away imperceptibly and they are simply grownups yelling. Just as imperceptibly, the game becomes real, and Mike and Elaine themselves are hurling slurs and put-downs at each other, with their "dangerous-to-vicious" wits, tearing at each other's psyches. Clever as they are, the audience gets nervous watching the actors fight. When she turns to leave the stage, he grabs her, ripping her blouse. She begins to cry. The third actor arrives to intercede. "What are you doing?" the third actor cries. "We're doing Pirandello," they reply, and bow.

Their humor was not that of noblemen. It was not without self-contempt. In the annals of American humor, they were, in this respect, mainstream. Yet like Severn Darden, they typified the ambiguities of the Compass. As Roger Bowen points out, "They weren't your average working-class guys."

As for Kenna Hunt, the males in the company took pleasure in inverting the initials of her name. Hunt was doing double duty, commuting between the Playwrights Theatre Club and the Compass. She was an excellent actress, but as an improviser, at the Compass, says Andy Duncan, "She was wrong from the beginning. She didn't look like the rest of us." In the photo cover of *Chicago* magazine, the camera caught Duncan peering at Hunt's bosom. "I look like something out of Brecht," says Duncan, "with this incredible schnozz and German face, and my hair was long and everything. She looked like she was in a Broadway musical. She just didn't look right."

No one knew better than Hunt that she had been miscast. From the outset, she had been disappointed to discover that she could not work with Sills, with whom she had experienced an instant rapport. In his place was David Shepherd. "I saw his heart was in it. I saw he was the driving force," Hunt says. "But he didn't know how to communicate with actors. For all his wonderful ideals, he was not a substitute for Sills."

Without a director, she observed herself and the other new cast members as "wallowing," "scrambling," "undercooks in the kitchen without a head chef," and "thrashing wildly about." Hearing the others rave about Paul Sills, she wished for structure, guidance, for someone at the helm. She enjoyed the scenarios, which "took all of us putting them together," because they were prepared in advance. She liked the Living Newspaper, since Roger Bowen helped put them together. "He was not a director," she says, "but he was very informed and very smart." She enjoyed the gibberish operas in which she played the unfaithful wife in a love triangle with Severn and Andy Duncan. A trained singer, she could handle looking wistfully out the invisible window without knowing what she was singing, garbling and jabbering lines.

But when it came to audience-suggested scenes, she became "glazed-eyed": "You were thrown out onstage without knowing whether you were the doctor or the patient" in front of an audience that was as rowdy and intoxicated as it was intelligent and sharp, and "You had to do it or die. The audience wanted to be stimulated. They wanted to laugh. You just died if you weren't funny. You had to capture them with mercurial wit. I didn't have mercurial wit."

Within a month, Severn had found his niche with The Professor and his "crazy shenanigans" and Mike had found Elaine. Hunt "had no crazy shenanigans to pull." Realizing that the improvisational theatre "wasn't my ball of wax," she asked to be released, but, reminding her that Barbara Harris had suffered similar stage fright, "They asked me to stay."

In mid-October, while Shepherd and Jacobs were preparing to move The Compass Players out of the Compass Tavern into the Dock on South Lake Park Avenue, two more professional actors were added to the cast. In New York, visiting Mark Gordon's Method acting class (in which John Ecks had briefly been a student), Shepherd had watched Gordon direct Elaine in a scene from *Miss Julie*. "I had the feeling," Gordon says, "that she was testing me." At the end of the class, Shepherd asked him to direct an upcoming production of *The Devil's Disciple* at the Playwrights Theatre Club.

Gordon was interested, but he had fallen in love with the leading lady of some one-act plays he had just directed in workshop (with two young actors, Martin Landau and Shelley Berman, also in the cast), and he was planning now to marry Barbara ("Bobbi") Glenn. Shepherd resolved Gordon's separation anxiety by inviting Bobbi to join the Compass. The Gordons were married on October 14 and, immediately after the ceremony, took off from New York.

They arrived at Chicago at midnight, exhausted from the drive. Shepherd dropped them at the theatre, where they waited with their bags. Since he had forgotten they were coming, he had not remembered to provide them with a place to stay.

In New York, Shepherd's description of the Compass as a "proletarian theatre" had sounded "really great" to Gordon, who was from a working-class family. His mother was a dressmaker, his father a Marxist Hebrew teacher. Gordon himself had been an actor at the Actors Lab in Hollywood. His teachers had been veterans of the Group Theatre. He had been blacklisted. "A proletarian theatre," Gordon muses. "That's all he had to say."

But waiting for a crash pad his first night in Chicago, he observed that the actors "were acting as if they were fully dressed in tuxedos. They were doing a quartet where one was gargling water and one making sounds like a violin."

When he saw what was happening at the proletarian theatre, Gordon was glad he had been hired to direct George Bernard Shaw.

That night David Shepherd vacated his own apartment so the Gordons could honeymoon.

Entering the Compass, Bobbi Gordon, who had been acting professionally since she was a child, felt she had "two strikes against me from the beginning. One, I wasn't funny. And two, I wasn't a writer. A strange aura pervaded the place. Elaine was off eating her apple cores. Severn was off eating his handkerchief. And David was in a stew from the day we got there."

Mark Gordon had been told that the production budget for *The Devil's Disciple* would come from the receipts of the *Hamlet* running at the Playwrights Theatre Club. At the theatre, Gordon counted a cast of thirty and an audience of two. With amazement, he noted that the actors "accepted that as normal. They didn't care if there was no audience. They were doing *Hamlet*. They were doing great plays." As it dawned on him that there was no way to finance another production at Playwrights, Gordon accepted Shepherd's suggestion that he move over to the Compass.

There, he joined Bobbi in noticing that rehearsals were chaos, that nothing ever struck the group as good, acceptable, or right, that Elaine's scenarios were savagely criticized, that Shepherd's suggestions were routinely ignored, and that, in fact, "What we used to call 'rehearsal' was a lot of fighting and arguing, full of anguish and angst."

The new actors had no reason to suppose their work process might be different. The strengths of the early Compass had been Shepherd's idea for an immediate and relevant theatre addressing subjects that were on people's minds, Bowen's techniques for executing a few of Shepherd's dreams, Viola's training, a group of selfless and committed actors, the scenarios of the Brain Trust, and Sills's direction and gift for creating excitement on the stage. Suddenly, "You had Mike Nichols and Severn Darden and Mark and Bobbi Gordon," reflects Roger Bowen, "who didn't know David's conception, who didn't have Sills's direction, who didn't use my techniques, and who didn't know Viola from a hole in the wall. They arrived, and there was nobody but me to welcome them. Outside of some cryptic instructions from David, they had no idea of what improvisational theatre was. They just went out and did it."

Thus, Nichols perceived the Compass as "a group of six or seven people thrown onstage with no idea at all behind it. There was no plan. There wasn't even exactly a positive aim. There was the negative aim of doing something without a playwright. There were no tools or methods or techniques."

Severn Darden was not informed that the Compass had a political point of view until he read about it in *Something Wonderful Right Away*, Jeffrey Sweet's 1978 collection of interviews with improvisational artists. "It was never a political theatre," he says. "We did social satire with a few political remarks for the benefit of the masses. Oh, once the FBI was supposed to be coming to see us, which made everyone frightened. And happy." And yet, "dim in my memory" is a picture of a scene he witnessed onstage the month he arrived. "A group of people were banded together. They were failing at something, and moaning. They were all dedicated to something in this very solemn and serious way, and because it was the McCarthy period, they couldn't say what it was. And as a matter of fact, a lot of them had no idea what it was. But they were all dedicated to it. The whole thing seemed corny and sentimental. It ended with someone playing Wobbly songs on a guitar."

The scene he refers to may be from *The Fifth Amendment*, Mickey Le-Glaire's maiden writing effort, and the songs (played by Alex Hasselef) from the Spanish Civil War. But, in fact, says Gordon, "*The Fifth Amendment* was about as political as we got. It was an honest attempt to do something about the blacklist, and the only thing we could do was sentimentalize it. We couldn't go deeper than that and make it say something to the neighborhood."

As Compass gained in notoriety, various community groups sought Compass variations on themselves. "The atomic scientists wanted to do something about them at the U. of C. We could do it in a day. Once the PTA wanted us to do something. That's how Mike and Elaine's PTA scene first occurred." The atomic scientists were from the liberal *Bulletin of the Atomic Scientists*. "They wanted a whole hour show. And they paid us," Severn recollects. A group of Compass Players was first taken on a tour of the Nuclear Physics Building. "They gave us all white coats and badges," says Bobbi Gordon. "We went to see the cyclotron. They told us all about it. Then we looked through it. And watched them split the atom."

Back in the theatre, the actors devised the show. "I don't know if it made any sense," says Bobbi Gordon. "We did it like a World War Two air force movie. You know, everyone is killed off and their ghosts come back. At the end, we all marched in place, singing, 'Off We Go into the Wild Blue Yonder.' It was silly. We just had no other way to deal with all that." Nevertheless, she noted, the atomic scientists "loved the show. After all, they really wore badges. They really wore white coats. It was about them. They had a wonderful time."

The direction of the Compass changed.

In the back room of The Compass Tavern, during a hopeless improvisation, Elaine's crazy admirer had once shouted, "The Compass is a fraud. You can do it in your kitchen," and backstage, someone panicked and blacked out the lights. Within three months, the crazy man's insight into the first improvisational theatre's rustic innocence no longer applied.

According to Andrew Duncan, Sills and Shepherd had always reinforced the notion among the original players that they were strictly amateurs and far from indispensable, since, according to Viola's theory, anyone could improvise. At the same time, "They promoted the idea that the crass and materialistic New York/Los Angeles professional actor was the enemy." Compass players were encouraged to find sustenance in their amateurish purity.

Most of them did. For Sid Lazard, "There was nothing serious about it. I never for a moment considered myself an actor. I was a reporter for UPI, working some odd shift. We were just playing. No one said, 'This is my career.' I don't remember anyone suffering stage fright." If an improvisation was horrible, the humiliated actors would run out the back door and down Fifty-fifth Street toward Lake Michigan and jump.

When the leading parts in the scenarios were taken over by the pros, Roger Bowen cannot remember "any kind of jealousy, or anything like that. Most of us were relieved." "But once the New York people came," says Annette Hankin, "things were different." People still jumped in the lake from embarrassment, but "There just seemed to be a different edge." The scenario plays, Hankin notes, had always tended to have moments when "They were drifting, where no one knew exactly where it was going—until something happened." The state of drifting, of not knowing, is the soul of improvisation and, as Hankin points out, "can also be its death."

In performance, the professionals had far more to protect than the amateurs. Among them, there was an urge to make the play more perfect, to get the action going, to sharpen up the scenes.

The same pressure to achieve "results" was brought to bear on the improvisations. As the company solidified, there was less tolerance for failure. "I loved improvisation," says Hankin. "But I became aware that I didn't have the point of view toward life and relationships that allows you to be distant. I'm not cool like that, and I wasn't cool like that onstage. If I had to think of a funny line or a sharp cap to a scene, I couldn't do it. I was much more geared to the script."

The amateurs drifted away. "I dreaded the increasing pressure to be funny," Hankin says. "The minute that became an issue, that was the end of it for me."

Mickey LeGlaire joined John Ecks's group, although it was "one of those heavy drama things, and it was awful. But I knew I couldn't be in the Compass. I couldn't handle the people. They just overwhelmed me."

"Take a look at Severn and Mike and Elaine," Mark Gordon reflects.

"They were people so out of the community. And so beyond it. And there was no kidding yourself about that. They were the strangest, brightest, most frightening bunch of people I've ever met."

David Shepherd nevertheless continued to see himself as head of "a group of socialists" who were "going on to create a popular theatre that could be replicated in all cities of the world."

Following the collapse of his production of *The Devil's Disciple*, Gordon's greatest disappointment in Chicago was in realizing that the direction Shepherd continued to claim for the Compass was one it would never take. "The one it did take was marvelous. These were unique and gifted people who had something to say and who had to be heard. The kind of give-and-take that would happen among us was great. Even the conflict that sometimes happened onstage was exciting to an audience." What was more, they wanted to be serious actors. "As innocent and naïve and as raw as they were, their aspiration was up there."

"There was no question that the work became better," says Andy Duncan. "With the exception of—well, I can't say anybody, even Elaine—until the New York actors came, it had been pretty raw work. It really improved. The artistic work, the acting, was worlds apart from the early stuff. It was more entertaining. The audience raction were much better. I know. I was there. I never heard such laughter in my life."

14

"Dump Us at the Cock"

The Dock, on South Lake Park Avenue, became the new home of Compass on November 1, 1955. Except for Morton's, the elegant restaurant next door, the street was an industrial no man's land. The canvas walls had been painted to look like the ocean, and the interior decoration, suggesting the deck of a ship, featured lifesavers, railings, and ropes.

Before the invisible curtain came down on the theatre on Fifty-fifth Street, the last words to the audience had belonged to Severn. "As of Tuesday, we'll be known as Dump Us at the Cock. I mean, Compass at the Dock," he said.

"The Dock was a dismal place," says Roger Bowen. "It was too far from the university, near Fifty-third Street, right up against the I.C. tracks, a little too far east. We missed the flow of traffic. All of a sudden, the university vitality that we were in daily contact with was gone. We were left trying to build an audience of young urban professionals."

George Schall and his son, the owners, were not Ph.D. candidates playing restaurateurs on the side. They were serious about business. If the improvisational theatre was to be compromised by its bourgeois new setting, the Schalls were taking a chance by presenting who-knew-what every week.

At the Dock, shows went on nightly, except Monday. Tuesday was Folk Music Night. There was never a cover charge, and the minimum was $1.25. Between the sets on weekends, musical accompaniment was provided by Allaudin Mathieu on a piano that was missing some keys. The actors, who now belonged to Actors' Equity, rehearsed from 2:00 p.m. to

4:30 p.m., then rushed home to change for the cocktail hour at 5:00 p.m., to socialize with the audience until their curtain time (weekdays at 8:30, weekends at 9:15). At the bar, they were entitled to "shake the dice" with the Schalls just like the paying customers, on the chance of winning a free drink.

At show time, the actors left the bar at the front of the restaurant, passed a smaller bar in the back, then turned to the left, climbed a few steps, walked through the louvers, which had been transported from Fifty-fifth Street, and entered the stage.

The show room, which had been known as The Deck at the Dock, featured a semithrust stage that created an apron surrounded by tables at which 150 crowded patrons could sit. It was a less intimate, certainly a less Brechtian atmosphere than the one on Fifty-fifth Street, where on a hot night the actors had felt free to perform in shorts. And although the Compass was still patronized by the neighborhood regulars, there were now sixty more tables available for the suit-and-tie crowd from the North Side.

In the new setting, all gaucheries were magnified.

Opening night featured Roger Bowen's *The Rainmerchant*, a scenario play about a confidence man who promises to relieve a drought and becomes the victim of rural guile and stupidity, running afoul of the local law. "It was the Pied Piper theme played against a satire of the bureaucracy," says Bowen. "It doesn't sound like much, and it wasn't much. During the flood scene, people would cower as if big drops were going to fall."

As the youngest member, "definitely the baby," of the group, the pianist, Allaudin Mathieu, felt his role in the proceedings to be unessential, that of "the mascot." He idolized the players, especially Nichols and May, as "sort of my heroes." For this grand opening, he was flattered when David Shepherd consulted him about hiring a drummer who could play a cymbal with a wire brush to approximate the sound of rain.

As a jazz pianist, Mathieu describes himself at eighteen as "a novice." He was otherwise, however, a musical prodigy. At the age of fifteen, while still in high school, he began arranging music for another idol, Stan Kenton, and had maintained his association with the Kenton band. Mathieu offered to play the cymbal himself, soon realizing that it was a poor effect. But Shepherd liked it, so it stayed. "It sounded like the piano player was playing a cymbal," Mathieu recalls. "It didn't sound like rain."

The Rainmerchant had been rehearsed on Fifty-fifth Street under the direction of Mark Gordon, with Method exercises he had used for years. Allaudin Mathieu noticed that Gordon's leading man was thoroughly confused by them: "Severn would throw up his hands." People remember him finally playing The Rainmerchant like W. C. Fields.

Gordon's staging was also "a disaster," Gordon says. Having seen the Dock only in daylight, he had arranged for the Townspeople to parade through the audience. But to pack the room on opening night, the Schalls jammed the tables together, eliminating the aisles. The actors climbed across the tabletops.

In a brochure called "Plans for a Popular Theatre," Shepherd had tried to set down guidelines for new or would-be playwrights and, at the same time, make the Compass seem inviting:

> . . . We accept material that would never be shown on Broadway, Hollywood or TV . . . In fact we prefer plots that fit no formula, characters that are neither black nor white, and stories that move outside the family circle to show America's history and place in the world today.
>
> . . . We think poetry is achieved not by saying vague things in an unreal manner but by economy and intensity . . . At the Compass, the playwright can dare to cut his script to the bone, face his actors to the audience and unleash those tricks of the imagination that keep the classics alive to us.
>
> . . . We need plays with a juggler, a hypnotist, an argument, a song, fight, game, impersonation—anything you can watch or listen to for itself, any strong activity . . .
>
> . . . If the writer prefers, he can bring his own form to the Compass: the animated newspaper, the illustrated lecture, the fable or parody.
>
> ALL WE ASK FOR IS A FORM THAT CAN BE RECOGNIZED BY THE MAN-IN-THE-STREET, AND THAT IS STRONG ENOUGH TO STAND UP IN A CABARET. Write to us.

For a script requiring no set "other than curtains and props," running "less than 75 minutes," with a cast of "less than 10, including the narrator," the producer of the Compass promised ". . . 10% of the gross—including profit from liquor sales. Any play that can hold our audience will earn you $150 a week, while a hit will make over $300."

Since most writers take up their awful pastime because it offers a unique opportunity to discharge internal energy through words, it might be guessed that even for 10 percent of the gross, very few would be seduced by the chance to cut their scripts "to the bone" or overjoyed to dispense with their most obsessive interests, such as exposition, character study, political discussion, local color, or psychoanalysis. The pool of scripts remained shallow.

A sendup of Dylan Thomas's rhymed play, *Under Milkwood*, was the first unsolicited manuscript to arrive over the Compass transom that Shepherd considered a "producible" play. *Under Deadwood* was the work of two former University of Chicago students still on the scene. Jane McCachan ('48) had become Jane Kome the housewife and one of Mike Nichols's "reliable" friends. Mildred Goldberger, who had worked on the Manhattan Project with her husband, Marvin ("Murph," now head of the Institute for Policy Studies at Princeton University), was retired from mathematics and raising a family. Around the Goldbergers' kitchen table, surrounded by the hubbub of children (one of them Penney Kome, the Canadian author and feminist), the women had contrived a scenario that would make use of Nichols's imitation of Dylan Thomas, one of his favorite party gags. "We had no idea what they wanted. Mike wasn't very helpful," Jane Kome Mather recalls. But she was such a Dylan Thomas fan herself she had named her son for him, and, with Nichols in mind as the narrator, she now unearthed her own facility for parodying Thomas's verse style. The "deadwood" in the version referred to the tree in front of the Woodworth Book Store, the neighborhood bulletin board. By 1955, as if embodying the decline of the neighborhood, the tree was so rotten that it had to be braced by a cage of wire fencing. Since it had become so central to neighborhood life, the neighborhood faithful had refused to allow the city to have it removed.

Like a series of burlesque skits, each scene of *Under Deadwood* took off on a want ad or notice that might have been posted on the tree. It was a charming idea that "resonated with the neighborhood," Mildred Goldberger says.

Kome and Goldberger wrote the prelude, or preface, as well as the signs introducing each skit. Nichols, playing the Dylan Thomas character, delivered the set material with a scarf around his neck. The other actors improvised the rest. Their thoughtfulness and ingenuity impressed the scenarists. Kome admired the way they "went for character and background. They never allowed themselves to go for the cheap laugh." They climbed invisible stairs to an attic room in "Wanted: Quiet Tenant for Elegant Room in Private Home with Bath." They tried on invisible tight clothes in "Complete Designer Wardrobe for Sale. Size 10." In this skit, the woman selling the clothes (Elaine May) has recently been to a reducing salon. The woman who comes to purchase the wardrobe (Kenna Hunt) is too fat. Elaine helped Hunt as she struggled into invisible tight clothing. "It was much funnier done without real clothes," Goldberger says. "Maybe you should take off your ring," Elaine said.

The piece Kome and Goldberger called "Cute Cat" was based on a sign that read, "I am an adorable nine-month-old kitten looking for a loving home." Her owners come home to find a couple being interviewed by their cat. "That's all there was to it," Goldberger says. "Elaine played the cat."

Meanwhile, traveling in Europe, Paul Sills and Barbara Harris went to the Theater am Schiffbauerdamm in East Berlin and saw Brecht and the Berliner Ensemble in action. Sills sent letters about them to the folks back home. The one to Byrne Piven referred to their old argument over detachment versus emotion. Brecht's acting company was, of course, required to follow the principles of epic acting and to "alienate" themselves from personal temperament in the service of a detached, detailed, and thoughtful exposition of the chain of events that constitute the play. But, Sills noted, the Berliner Ensemble also had the emotional power to make both themselves and the audience cry.

If Sills understood the wellsprings of this German company's post–Third Reich passion, according to Mark Gordon, it was not evident from his letter to the Compass. In fact, Gordon recalls that Sills's letter "made me laugh. He said their Communist philosophy gave Brecht's theatre a purpose. 'Everybody should work on being a Communist' is what it implied to me. Coming from a working-class background, I know you don't *become* a Communist. You're a worker. And there's a boss. And capitalists. And you feel oppressed. It's a gut reaction that happens from a way of life." Sills's exhortation was "an eyeopener" to Gordon: "There are intellectual Marxists. Sure." But it occurred to him that "this was just University of Chicago snobbery, pretending we could impose a left-wing philosophy on a theatre without any identification at all with the working class."

On South Lake Park Avenue, where there was no class consciousness, no ideology, no sacred texts, and no maestro, the company was simply using trial and error, eight shows a week, individually and collectively searching for a technique, an identity, a theatrical expression, and a truth of their own.

"We never looked to each other as a family or to love each other. Never for a minute," Mark Gordon says. As a Compass player, Gordon's life now consisted of "walking in every day early in the morning and spending three quarters of the day listening to people say, 'No, I won't do it.' Poor Elaine. Every time she brought in a scenario, people would shake their heads and say, 'What *is* this?' There was no director. We were on our own. There were six totally different minds to decide 'I don't know.' "

I n December 1955, Roger Bowen was inducted into the army. The adaptation of A *Christmas Carol* he prepared for the Compass was to be his swan song. The first architect of the improvised long form was gone. Based on his format for the Living Newspaper, the Compass continued to satirize such publications as *TV Guide, Look, Fortune, Playboy, Reader's Digest, Harper's Bazaar, The New Yorker, Bulletin of the Atomic Scientists, The New York Times Book Review, House and Garden* (in which Severn performed a gardening mime), and *Hot Rod* (featuring Andrew Duncan and Mike Nichols's underwater mime).

In Bowen's absence, David Shepherd's expectations for the scenario play would not work out so well. "You see, scenarios were hard," says Bowen. "And people weren't coming up with such good ones. I couldn't come up with any more. Shepherd couldn't. Coughlan couldn't. By the end of nineteen fifty-five, we'd all pretty much come to the end of our string."

As his own model of excellence, Bowen cites the comedies of the Italian cinema "because they have a very strong point of view. Take *Bread and Chocolate*. It's not just a lot of funny stuff. When it's all over, you see that it's political, that it's very serious stuff about who is going to run society and for whose benefit it's going to be run."

The scenario play had been the principal vehicle through which The Compass Players expressed both David Shepherd's vision of "new types of plays more efficient, theatrical, poetic, and morally aware than the current product" and their collective point of view. If these plays were not so efficient as to follow a formula, as Shepherd had initially wished, they did have a theme (that people are bent into the shape society dictates to them) that recurred again and again.

Thinking about Bob Coughlan's "marvelous" scenario, *The Drifters*, Bowen says, "I mean there was some sense to it, you know? Behind all the early stuff, there was a point of view, a very clear socialist point of view."

With the coming of the cosmopolitan outsiders, the social, political, and stylistic sensibility that had originally informed the scenario play was atomized. Although they each assumed writerly functions, none of the new players was a writer per se. Even if they had been inclined to devise Brechtian scenario structures, none of them had either the background or the desire to write about the lower middle class in Chicago, the hopes and dreams of South Side cinder snatchers, Fuller Brush Men, and high school punks.

Elaine May alone among them had both the talent and the mania for committing words to paper. And she remained astoundingly prolific, despite the fact that her scenarios were routinely savaged by the other members of the cast. Her own cosmology was full of drifters, people on the fringes. "Elaine came through Prohibition and the Depression and the Jewish family," reflects Mark Gordon, "and yes, she did know about that, and it was all in her work. The aspirations of people within her scenarios were beautiful. I mean, it was stuff you heard on the radio, about how to be a better person, about winning a dance contest. It was lovely, stuff like that."

"While you have the opportunity," Elaine once told Allaudin Mathieu, "grab the moment by its balls, its essence." In that spirit, while the Compass stage was hers for the grabbing, she did not bind herself to any ideological formula and created material of great variety.

For New Year's Eve she devised a short piece for herself and Bobbi Gordon; its theme of the insensitivity of men to women was reminiscent of *Georgina's First Date*. Dateless on New Year's Eve, the two women go to the YMCA, where they remain alone together as the clock strikes midnight, after fending off the advances of a group of louts who have stopped by to "raid" the place.

May the playwright was also a sophisticated practitioner of parody. As she ran down the plot of her version of *Ten Little Indians*, it seemed that all the characters would end up dead on the stage. "You can't do that!" shouted the cast. "But that's the whole point," she insisted. "In the last scene, everybody on the stage is dead."

"There was no point" to this restaging of Agatha Christie's classic locked-room murder mystery, Mark Gordon recalls. But the cast told Elaine, "We'll do you a favor. We'll try it tonight."

As in the book (and the movie and play), "Everybody played a weird, far-out character," Bobbi Gordon says. She played a stripper. Mark was a bookie. Elaine was a German psychiatrist. "We each get a message to come to this place. We take a ferry to an island. There's a lot of fog. One by one, we're all killed off. The lights would go out. You heard the ticking of a clock. Each time the lights came up, there was another body on the floor." In the last scene, two detectives (Darden and Duncan) explain what happened. Throughout their interpretations of the crime, the lights would black out and come up again as they were seen playing tennis, hiking, swimming, bicycling. "It went on and on and on," says Bobbi Gordon. "And the interpretations didn't mean anything. They were nonsense."

To the surprise of the company, *Ten Little Indians* turned out to be very funny, says Mark Gordon, "a wonderful parody. It was always a shock that her things would work. You'd get up and do them and they would work."

Elaine continued to create "some wonderful scenarios, like little one-act plays." *The Real You* was one she would actually develop as a one-act, *Adaptation*, which she directed herself off-Broadway in 1965. From a text Bob Coughlan submitted about self-improvement programs he had learned about as a counselor of industrial relations, Elaine devised a simple and well-structured scenario: separately overhearing a radio commercial for Success School, various aspirants to self-improvement (a factory fore-man who wants to impress his daughter's suitor, a man wishing to score with a female office worker, a newlywed who lacks the courage to ask his wife for plain fried eggs, two elderly sisters who fantasize their elderly gentleman caller will finally choose one of them for romance) sign up for a course strongly resembling such latter-day exercises in assertiveness train-ing as *est*.

Back in their own environments, each of the students "acts out" the training. They are confrontational and aggressive, demanding and bold. In each case, their new behavior turns off the people they seek to impress. They wind up worse than before.

Along with May's productive output of scenarios, Elaine went on de-veloping her work with Mike Nichols and, Mark Gordon notes, their pieces were also beginning to resemble "little plays."

At Compass, Elaine May's dedication to her inner truth may have been unnerving, but it was not regarded as it would be in the arenas of show business she soon would enter, as a punishable or self-defeating trait. It was simply a fact that she was "a perfectionist" who was not moved in the slightest by other people's praise. "Elaine didn't give a shit if the audience didn't like her work," Mark Gordon says. "When you talk about elitism, that's her snobbery. She worried when the audience liked it too much."

In this, she was in sharp contrast to Mike Nichols, who had no pre-disposition to taking a chance. "Michael's role was the commentator,"

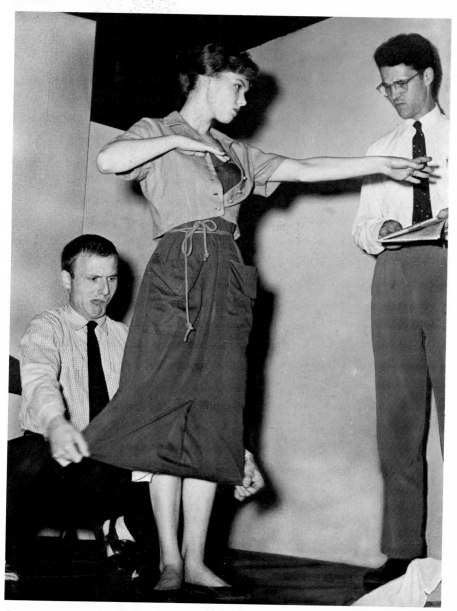

Opening night at the Compass. Andrew Duncan (left) is a French couturier, Barbara Harris is the model, and David Shepherd is Christian Dior in a Living Newspaper satire of the Chicago Daily News, *July 1955.*

(Left to right) Tammy Allen, Elaine May, and Lucy Minnerle improvise during a Compass Amateur Night, summer 1955.

(Left to right) Andrew Duncan, Omar Shapli, and Mickey LeGlaire in a Living Newspaper takeoff on the want ads, summer 1955.

RIGHT: *"Time for the workers' picnic!"* *(Left to right) Barbara Harris, Mickey LeGlaire, Andrew Duncan, Roger Bowen, and Elaine May in* The Stakhanovite Worker, *summer 1955.*

BELOW: *The air-conditioning was broken during this lampoon of the Soviet system with Roger Bowen (left) as The Boss and (left to right) Andrew Duncan, Mickey LeGlaire, Barbara Harris, and Elaine May as The Workers.*

The minister's adopted children, Roger Bowen and Barbara Harris, take a new look at each other upon learning their true identities in The Minister's Daughter, *summer 1955.*

Elaine May and Bobbi Gordon liked to play little girls. Here, one of them gets a chameleon for Christmas. They put it on assorted surfaces to watch it change colors. On a checkered tablecloth, it dies.

Each narrator brought his or her own style to the Living Newspaper. Mike Nichols liked to follow a pretentious bit of news with an ad for a remedy for piles.

ABOVE: *Mike Nichols and Elaine May performing "Teenagers" at the Dock in late 1955.*

LEFT: *Andrew Duncan and Kenna Hunt graced the December 31, 1955 cover of* Chicago Welcome: Your Guide to a Pleasant Visit. *David Shepherd's ad in the pamphlet promised "real offbeat excitement . . . lusty intimate theatre in the style of the strolling minstrel, Shakespeare—an invitation to drama and drinks." The same week, comedian Joe E. ("The Joker is Wild") Lewis was playing at the Chez Paree.*

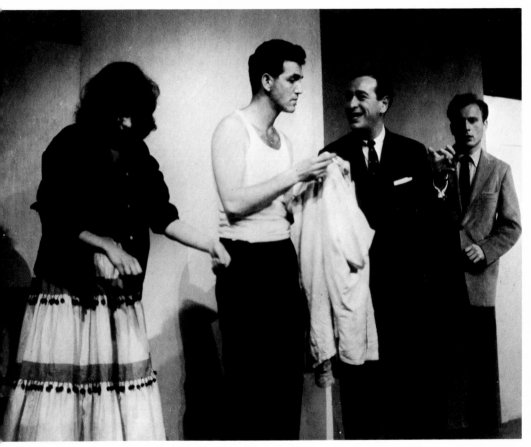

Shelley Berman in his first scenario play, The Fuller Brush Man: *(left to right) Bobbi Gordon, Mark Gordon,* Berman, Andrew Duncan.

At the Dock on New Years' Eve 1955, Severn Darden and Bobbi Gordon performed an improvisation at the bar.

The end is near for the company at the Argo Off-Beat Room in the late fall of 1956. (Left to right) Severn Darden, Larry Arrick, Elaine May, Shelley Berman, Mike Nichols, Rose Arrick, and Barbara Harris.

Gordon says. "He always stayed outside. He was keenly aware of the audience. Elaine thought of what the audience *should* want. She didn't give a damn."

Paul Sills describes the job of staging a scenario as "hack" directing. "You know, you get people up there, move 'em around, get 'em to do things, tell 'em what things to keep, and have 'em do it again the next night." Sills himself now prefers to "direct" for the performance that wll only last the night. Nonetheless, at the Compass he had been the man who understood the rhythm and dynamics of the narrative play. Without him, there was really no one to orchestrate them in the Brechtian style, no detached director's eye.

At the Compass the job fell to the actors themselves, who were all invariably required on the stage. (Curiously, as a Compass Player, Mike Nichols showed no more interest in directing scenarios than he did in writing them. "He performed," says Roger Bowen, "and that was it.") According to Severn, "The scenarios as they were written out were fine, but we couldn't put actions and words to them. They were the thing I wanted to do the most. They were the thing we were aiming for as a company. But getting them to work seemed too difficult at the time."

Difficult or not, David Shepherd was dead set on presenting them. Andy Duncan recalls that "he kept trying to force them down." And the more unfocused his demands for these ambitious theatrical offerings became, the more resistant the cast was to him. Unwittingly, Shepherd served to draw the group together, "out of a need to protect ourselves, so we could go on at night," according to Mark Gordon, who remembers that they would keep him busy writing during their rehearsal time. Even then, "We were afraid of what David was bringing in. He wasn't hitting the Chicago issues. Once he wanted to go after the cartels in South America. It was stuff that had no meaning for our audience. It had nothing to do with their lives."

The territories that persistently occupied Shepherd as a writer had always been global ones—India, Italy, John Foster Dulles's tariff agreements, Dien Bien Phu. The theme of the scenario he outlined in *The Coffee Brokers* was exploitation in the coffee industry. "The idea was good," Gordon recalls. "Politically, it was fine. But we couldn't grab it. It had nothing to do with people. I mean, what else are you going to put on a stage? His thinking wasn't theatrical. It was intellectual, Marxist, textbook. It wasn't human enough."

The odds favored the duds.

One was Mickey LeGlaire's *Fifth Amendment*. The author describes his scenario as "a disc jockey who ends up being questioned by The Committee. And it leads up to . . . you never know what he did. They messed around with it. Mike played the disc jockey who loses his job. He hated his part. Mike Nichols wasn't a natural actor," LeGlaire recalls of his leading man, "but he did have a very clever mind." Although Nichols himself had been a disc jockey, Andy Duncan points out that "Mike was an FM guy. You know how they are. Elitist snobs." The folksy populist LeGlaire intended, says Duncan, "wasn't really Mike's kind of role. It didn't allow for a lot of Mike Nicholsisms. I remember him complaining that the rest of us had better parts."

"I played Mike's lawyer in *The Fifth Amendment*," Severn says. "I'd come onstage to bring him some good news. I did everything to get him to cheer up. But he would just sit there. I attempted to be funny. He refused to be moved." After the first performance, Severn asked Nichols why he did not react to the good news. "I didn't believe you," Nichols replied. "So next time, I said, 'Hurrah!' and stood on my head. Yes, I kind of stood on my shoulders, with my feet straight up in the air, and told him the news. And right onstage he said, 'I still don't believe you.' "

The remaining performances were "full of the same kind of sentimental mush with which the Communists surrounded their folklore," says Roger Bowen. "Mickey didn't like it. It wasn't what he wanted. It wasn't the spirit in which he had written the piece." LeGlaire is a kind, guileless, and plainspoken man. One friend compares him to Saint Francis of Assisi. (For several years LeGlaire trained Seeing Eye dogs.) Bowen says, "He was the only one who really knew about the Communists. He had been a Party member. The others were just sentimental liberals. So he was disgusted. He was beside himself."

"They didn't do it the way I wrote it," explains LeGlaire.

The night he went to see his scenario performed was the same night Mike Nichols met his future wife. Pat Scot was a jazz singer, whom LeGlaire recalls as "a celebrity of sorts." She was a regular on a live late-night variety show on burgeoning Chicago television. Andy Duncan thought her "very attractive and glamorous. She had a very attractive apartment, very modern, with wall-to-wall carpeting and an Eames chair. We all lived in walkups with bare floors and roaches."

"We were anarchic and rebellious, but we were armchair Marxists. We weren't revolutionaries," says Duncan of the company that played the Compass at the Dock. "We weren't good at that New York school of left-

wing theatre. Compass was much more successful in the political area
when it was being crazy and surreal." But there would be considerable
experimentation with both the style and substance of the scenario play
until, as Roger Bowen puts it, "Comedy won out."

The scenario that launched the new year was Elaine May's *Concupiscence and Crucifixion,* promoted as "the story of a young writer who loses
a few illusions and all of a first novel in the script machines of Hollywood."
Mark Gordon played the naïve writer facing the Philistines. ("I like your
book. I liked it the moment it was read to me." "It's a wonderful book.
Who did the jacket?") Screaming his part in unintelligible gibberish, Severn played his agent, Max. In a German accent, Mike Nichols played the
imperious European director Vladimir Foocker, famous for his great film
Quietly ("I have made many great films. I have made many important
films. But I never made another *Quietly*"), who has optioned and will
mutilate the young writer's book. *Concupiscence and Crucifixion* plainly
reflected the concerns of the new cast members, not those of the community.

"Their first attempt at a historical play" was the way the Chicago *Maroon*
distinguished *Private Slovik,* Shepherd's adaptation of William Bradford
Huie's portrait of the only U.S. soldier to be shot for desertion since 1864
(for refusing to shoot his gun). Mark and Bobbi Gordon played Slovik and
his wife with "a realness one rarely sees in small theatre group productions,"
the *Maroon* reviewer said. It was a stunning performance, although missing
a satirical flavor and not in the usual Compass mode. Mark Gordon
remembers that the Schalls were unhappy with it: the audience was so
fascinated by *Private Slovik* that they forgot to order drinks.

Another successful interpretation of the long form was *PTA Open House
and Fun Night,* created at the request of a local Parent Teachers Association. After thanking a shamelessly long list of "the wonderful girls who
have made tonight's program possible," the chairman of Fun Night, Mrs.
Gordon Hall, an indefatigable clubwoman (Elaine May), introduces to
her audience of PTA mothers a series of guests, among them a bad eleven-
year-old tap dancer (Bobbi Gordon), accompanying a bad nine-year-old
violinist (Mark Gordon), and a distinguished Southern playwright, Tennessee Glass (Mike Nichols). Tennessee delivers a dense magnolia-scented
lecture on the Creative Flow ("a process at best tenuous, evanescent,
fleeting, shimmeringly mobile, like those strange creatures, all moss and
glitter, that we carry with us as our first tremendously exciting memories
of church or Mardi Gras. Mardi Gras—that wunnaful, vulgar, syncopated,

strangely shimmering symbol of sexuality so unavoidable in our present ambiguity").

Mrs. Hall follows with her own remarks about Art ("one of the best mediums for self-expression in the world—there is no day so full that we couldn't shove in a little more art") and turns the program over to Hartoon Basset (Andrew Duncan), a local artist who has been to New York and actually seen Willem de Kooning and Robert Motherwell on Fifty-seventh Street. After a long plug for the painting colony he runs at Fox Lake (where other members of his family teach clay modeling and leather crafts), Hartoon introduces "a German Expressionist left over from the war."

The Expressionist is none other than Severn's professor, Walter von der Vogelweide, who addresses himself to the question "What does a painter do?"

When a painter sees a landscape, does he paint every tree, every apple, every blade of grass, every cow, every swine? No. He eliminates what to him is uninteresting, what is unneeded, what is unwanted, what is unbeautiful. He gets rid of the uninteresting cow, the unwanted apple, the unnecessary pig. If he sees a color that he doesn't like, and he thinks another color would go better, he puts in the other color. The painter knows better than nature what the color should be. Nature is haphazard. Who painted nature?

Vogelweide brings with him a painting, presumably a masterpiece. Severn Darden describes the prop painting he chose as one on which "you couldn't see anything. It was almost cream-colored. It seemed to be a painting of a lemon." Vogelweide describes it as a painting that "should be seen from the front, but imagined from behind." He proceeds to explicate it. With each performance, the interpretation changed:

In this case, the Spanish fly refers to Manuel Roderiguez, a Spanish fly of the fourteenth century, the inventor of the famous building-climbing shoes, *zapatos de rojos locos*, or, freely translated, "crazy red shoes."

Even these quasi scenarios required immense energy from the actors. "We were rehearsing a new play every two weeks," says Duncan. At the Dock, it had become obvious that "no group could do it. It was killing. That's when those scenes really started coming in."

15

An Escalation of Scenes

Implicit in David Shepherd's call for scenarios that would "rework the classics" had been the Brechtian assumption that well-read, well-educated playwrights were necessary to lead the proletariat to properly reflective stage pictures of themselves. By contrast, the work process of the actors in the scenarios was Stanislavskian, a search in rehearsal for emotional truth. To fulfill the audience and its suggestions, however, an improvised scene at the Compass did not require either Stanislavskian reality or Brechtian strategy. For here, the requirements were strictly Violan: to respond to another person in the uncalculated, uncharted moment, not to acting theories, playwriting formulas, emotional expectations, or David Shepherd's idées fixes.

Improvised scenes, of course, are to the narrative play as the short story is to the novel or the song to the symphony. In a play, a character is not just observed by the playwright, his fate is changed by the events or action of the play. In an improvised scene, there is no such change. As Mark Gordon soon learned, "An improvisation is much too short for that. It's a one-event scene." An improvised scene turns on an epiphany, a moment of truth that is experienced by the audience. For the characters, life goes on as before.

Despite their aspirations to be "serious," the actors made note of these realities. "The individual things were easier. They worked better," Severn says.

Paul Sills has called improvisation "a kind of confrontation with an unknown. What's between you is unknown, unspoken, unsomething. Some silence is between you. Well, if what's between you is the need to go out the door and into the next scene, you always know where you're going. You're basically just using your intellect." Indeed, even on Fifty-fifth Street, Compass Tavern investor Gene Gendlin had observed it was the improvisations and the scenes that were born from them that the audience liked best.

By the time the Compass reached the Dock, the shank of the evening consisted of audience-suggested scenes. As Roger Bowen took off for the army, he noted that "all this stock of good scenes had been accumulated. It was all heading in the direction of the revue form."

According to Sills, the scenes gained precedence because they gave space to the improvisational impulse, unlike the scenarios, which were written out, a narrative blueprint without dialogue, an outline on a page. "In a scenario, where you have an outline to follow, you can make up a few lines," he says. "You damn well can't improvise."

As psychologist and backstage guest James Sacks recalls the actual scene-making process at the Compass, however, these "confrontations with the unknown" were not entirely without a blueprint, although they were un-rehearsed. "They would take suggestions and then sit around a table back-stage. There would be some discussion like 'No, that's stupid. Let's do it like this . . .' " or "Okay, let's go out and see what happens." As long as people had a starting idea, it would be resolved onstage.

Reflecting the shouted concerns of the audience, The Compass Players found themselves making fun of American culture night after night, and they left scarcely a satirical stone unturned. Among the scenes that emerged were TV parodies (of *Captain Video and His Video Rangers, Person to Person,* and *The $64,000 Question*) and TV satires (a Tennessee Williams play with commercials, Paddy Chayevsky's *Hamlet*). There were French, Italian, Japanese, Western, and epic movie parodies. There were scenes about sports, the theatre, dating, selling, hitchhiking, and suburbia. There were literary sendups of Sherwood Anderson, Ibsen, O'Neill, and Piran-dello.

And the energy for scene making did not stop when the flip pad was closed. These were people in a constant state of suggestibility, ready to improvise on any idea.

"The Message," a short scene that became a Compass staple, was a dramatization of an anecdote James Sacks told the cast about one of his psychotic patients at Mantino State. The scene that took shape looked like this: a man and a woman are seated in a living room when the doorbell rings. The man opens the door on a Western Union messenger. The messenger sings "The Happy Birthday Song." "Happy birthday, dear Emma," he sings. "Happy birthday to you." When the messenger has finished singing the entire song, the man turns to the woman. "Emma, it's for you," he says.

"People would drive twenty-five miles to see Mike and Elaine tear apart Jack Eigen," David Shepherd recollects. Their appearance on his radio show (on which visiting celebrities were encouraged to join him behind the microphone in the lounge of a nightclub, the Chez Paree) had precipitated the creation of a scene, "Disc Jockey," and "it was asked for again and again." As Jack Ego, Mike Nichols played the name-dropping Chicago broadcaster bragging about his great pal, "Bernie" Baruch. As Ego's compliant guest, Elaine May played dumb starlet Barbara Musk, adding her two cents about "Al" Schweitzer ("Personally, I've never dated him . . .") while in town to promote her "major motion pictures," including the musical extravaganza *Two Gals in Paris*, with Sal Mineo as Ernest Hemingway and herself as Gertrude Stein.

A news item provided another scenario. In an effort to add numbers to a student population that had been decimated by the black-white conflict in Hyde Park and the pressures of the McCarthy years, Chancellor Kimpton had made a startling proposal to his board of trustees: a trial balloon, at least on an intramural basis, that the University of Chicago football team be revived. Hutchins loyalists were horrified. A football team stood for everything that Hutchins thought a university should not provide.

The idea for "Football Comes to the University of Chicago" had come to Roger Bowen the same day he read the news in the Chicago *Maroon*. In the structure he devised, four intellectuals show up to greet the coach (a role subsequently taken by Andrew Duncan and others, but which Bowen played first). As the cast embellished it, one was a theology student, the second a historian of arithmetic, the third a foreign student, and the fourth a music student who has come to the class by mistake and remains, thinking it a rehearsal for a quartet.

The coach is shocked to find that no one understands football ("Morgenstern," he says, "tell Pim what a naked reverse is." "I imagine that would be turning around bare-assed," Morgenstern replies) and gradually discovers that it is impossible to communicate with his future team, even with blackboard diagrams. ("That's not a line, sir, that's a line segment." "That's not a circle, sir, it's an ellipsoid.")

They practice huddling, calling signals, and centering, but the activity doesn't work any better since the intellectuals can't even visualize the contest that will take place. ("The ellipsoids have the ball!")

The coach instructs them all to select uniforms and report for tackling and blocking practice. The intellectuals disappear, leaving the coach onstage alone, listening to a four-part Bach invention being whistled down the hallway.

To Bobbi Gordon's chagrin, Mark began appropriating material for the show straight out of their marital life. ("Gee, that was good. Let's do a scene about this fight.") "Candle" was inspired by a candle in a glass Mark lit and put on their fireplace. In bed, watching the candle, he remarked, "That candle will never go out." "How can you say that?" Bobbi asked. "The wax will melt back into the glass, so it will just keep burning," he explained. "That's impossible," she objected. "It has to go out." "What happens to the wax?" he demanded. "It melts," she said. "And where does it go?" "Back into the glass." "And where's the wick?" "In the glass." "Then it will last forever," he yelled.

In real life, it had been a terrible fight. Onstage it worked very well, a subtextual view of a couple's intimate domestic moments. Invariably, after they finished performing "Candle," the Gordons would continue the fight.

The company called such pieces, which glimpsed at the "unknown, unspoken unsomething" of relationships, "people scenes." To the players who created them, people scenes were a source of great professional pride. "But they happened rarely enough," Mark Gordon says. "The audience was a seducer. 'Cause they laughed, you know?"

Laughter—spontaneous bursts of approval—can be a dangerous intoxicant to the performer, a highly distracting and addictive drug. Of all the mysterious ingredients that produce it—timing, rhythm, gesture, the "rule of three" (three repetitions are funny, the fourth spoils the laugh), the sound of "k" ("duck," "kvetch," "schmuck"), or falling down—the serious improvisational actor knows that "trying to be funny" should not be one. His delicate and paradoxical mission is to move forward with his work, which is to keep allowing the unexpected. Theoretically, only by playing in the moment with his fellow players can an improviser maintain a true connection with the audience, their expression of pleasure, the flow of laughter, and, indeed, his own "fix." Making a joke is merely a mental calculation, a diversion, an escape from the uncertainty of facing the emptiness of the moment, the fear of giving up control, of "losing your head." In reality, if a joke is funny and amuses the audience, they laugh.

Thus, although the Compass audience "loved" the people scenes, Mark Gordon points out, "They loved jokes too."

The actors began to master certain verbal tricks that would produce those crowd-pleasing, ego-boosting laughs. They learned, as Bobbi Gordon describes it, that "you could turn something around in the middle—make a statement, make fun of the statement—and get a laugh. There were lots of word games and put-downs. Anything that was sacred, you attacked it, and you'd get a laugh. There were key words like 'Nietzsche' and 'Kierkegaard.' You just mentioned the right word and the kids would laugh."

The easy laughter that could be provoked in the improvisations proved quite divisive. "It made me a little angry," Mark Gordon says. "I had never felt secure in the skitty area. Wits do, comics do. People who write and think verbally do. But it wasn't my milieu. Spot improvs, which I regularly did with Elaine, were always a horror." Gordon preferred the structure of the scenario, "something you could sink your teeth into. My pleasure was that hour show." Bobbi felt the same. "When it became easier to go for the funny, that's when my terror struck. That's when I felt I didn't belong onstage. I didn't know how to handle it. I couldn't be witty off the top of my head. I couldn't be clever for clever's sake."

The more accommodating a performance was to the audience, the more that David Shepherd hated it. (He particularly disliked parodies.) At cast meetings, Andy Duncan remembers Shepherd complaining, "I'm so sick of jokes up there," and, in response, "everybody would get serious and want to be an intellectual." But onstage, Shepherd was as susceptible as any of them to taking the easy shot.

According to Duncan, Shepherd under pressure would "break up" onstage a lot. "He was one of the worst breakers. But he was big on pantomime. And he did love to get up there. He thought of himself as a kind of Jean Louis Barrault. I remember sessions where we would practice miming sewing and stuff with detail. And he would show us how to bring it out. You know, that resistance thing. Like walking in the wind. He kept talking about that. But we were terrible at it. I mean, we weren't mimes."

Like Sills, Shepherd was enamored of the physical, the kinetic. "As a matter of fact, they preferred that kind of thing to words," Duncan reflects. "He and Sills hated the word, and the fact that Severn or Roger or Mike or I were very good with words, and the kind of intellectualism that finds pleasure and sensuality in words. You know, puns and things. They always wanted us to get away from that."

Although language censorship had never been much of an issue at the

Compass Tavern, at the Dock Duncan now found himself under the surveillance both of Shepherd and the moralistic Schalls. "For all the talk about getting away from the bourgeois theatre, we were straitjacketed in a way." Duncan found that he was "constantly being sat on" in terms of "well, freedom." Elaine was even more explosive in her language than the men and blithely ignored any taboos about profanity or bad taste. "She also had a way of sitting, folding her legs, that could have been construed as flashing," Duncan adds. "I don't know if she did it on purpose, or didn't know, or didn't care. But it upset them. They didn't want that. I mean, they wanted to be respectable in a sense."

David Shepherd admits to being "such a prude in those days" that in a scene about a student wedding in *Under Deadwood*, he objected to the line Duncan used to present his gift, an egg poacher. "He liked to say it was a good place to put your diaphragm. I would tell him not to say it." ("Andrew," Duncan remembers he said, "I don't think you should say 'diaphragm' onstage.") "And he would say it anyway. It always got a laugh."

To amuse themselves, the cast regularly played name games, working into their dialogue the names of their friends. "Mo Hirsch" or "Ned Polsky" would pop up in scenes as scholarly authorities or authors of obscure works. Jane Kome Mather remembers a night she spent at the Compass when the actors worked the word "pig" into every single sketch. For example, playing a Connecticut suburbanite in search of an unusual gift for his wife, Nichols usually asked Duncan (playing a farmer) if he could sell him a cow. Some nights, to sit in the back seat of his convertible, he also wanted a cat. This night, when he asked for the cat, Duncan replied, "Well, wouldn't a pig do?" "At which point," says Mather, "they both broke up."

Earlier that week, Severn Darden had worn his cape to the Rockefeller Chapel for a Sunday service, Mather learned backstage. During the organ recital, he had leaned over the balcony and yelled, "Mike Nichols fucks pigs!"

Nichols was the company member most likely to break up onstage. (To milk a funny line, he would even simulate breaking up by turning his back to the audience and letting his shoulders shake.) After the Rockefeller Chapel incident, all that was required to crack him up was the mention of pigs. This night, continually, Mather observed, everyone else uncharacteristically broke up too. A furious David Shepherd dressed down the cast. "No one is ever to crack up onstage again," he announced, "and no one is ever to mention the word 'pig.' "

"It was a problem working onstage with someone you worked for, especially if you offended him," says Andy Duncan. Shepherd's desire to control the expressive content of the actors was for Duncan a constant irritant. It seemed to him a flaw in the Compass ideology that Shepherd wanted the work onstage to reflect the concerns of the community, when, in actuality, he insisted that this reflection be compatible with his own taste.

If Shepherd faulted Duncan's humor for being too knowing or risqué (as he never did Severn's, which was so far out it seemed innocent), neither was he a fan of Mike Nichols's sensibility, which Duncan thinks represented to Shepherd "a kind of decadent New York thing." As Duncan remembers the relationship, "There was always a friction between David and Mike."

Shepherd describes the kind of material produced and typified at Compass by Nichols as "laden with a kind of quick, satirical point of view. And his attitude was never to want to do a scene unless he knew what that point was." Had Nichols been given his choice of programming, Shepherd envisions sets composed of "scenes about French fashions or French and British styles of lovemaking compared to those of cowboys and Indians. And he would construct this stuff so that it was funny and pertinent. But I don't know whether Mike was interested in content like the other folks. He was very uncomfortable with people scenes. He was not interested in political scenes. He didn't like scenarios, that's for sure."

In short, none of Nichols's concerns concurred with the "Intention of Compass," as Shepherd had so plainly expressed it way back in September of 1954: "The Compass will try to find the fables that give substance to our fantasies so that we can see what our fantasies are."

But David Shepherd's conception of Compass was, and always would be, greater than its execution. "He was perpetually dissatisfied," Roger Bowen recalls. The improvisations on the stage would never match "what he had in his mind, and so he would always look kind of worried. Mike and Elaine were doing these wonderful things, and that was all irrelevant to him because if it didn't in some way carry forward his concept of popular theatre, then he couldn't really appreciate it."

As Andy Duncan points out, however, "The moment you release the freedom of the person and the individual, then obviously you can't control it." In the moment onstage, an improviser can only be true to himself.

But Shepherd did not bend easily to this Violan reality. To his distress, "The actors were pretty much running the show."

It is not in the nature of power that caught in a power struggle a socialist producer would choose to act as a producer second and a socialist first. For now, Shepherd was forced to suffer the knowledge that there really was no way for him to tangle with the actors. Without them, there was no show.

In a premonitory Compass scene about a British mountain-climbing party, however, Shepherd originated the role of Sir Edmund, the lead mountain climber joined to the other climbers by an imaginary rope. At the Northwest Wall, politely, with British calm, Sir Edmund announces to the second man that they will execute a "Rosenkrantz Busch." The second man (Duncan) calls down the order to the third man, Wilson (Nichols), who is heard but never seen. "Did you say a Rosenbusch Krantz?" Wilson yells. In response to Wilson's error, the second man vanishes from the stage.

When Shelley Berman inherited the part of Sir Edmund, he heard that in response to Duncan's fall, "David had a magnificent way of losing his footing and literally gliding across the stage as if he were being pulled. Obviously, the man knew how to move."

A somewhat static scene when first performed, with Shepherd distractedly heading his party toward the peak, "Mountain Climbing," Duncan recalls, had actually been set in motion by the offstage direction of Elaine, who had loudly whispered to Nichols, as the action waned, "Fall!"

Indeed, from then on, it would be revealed entirely through the pantomime of the onstage players that Wilson is a clumsy climber. Not only does he lose his footing, he requires frequent breaks for tea and cookies and weighs a hefty twenty stone. After Wilson loses his grip on a Leica, Sir Edmund quietly, finally, withdraws his knife and passes it to the second man, who cuts the invisible rope. As originated by Nichols, Wilson's last echoing words are "Aargh!" As originated by Shepherd, Sir Edmund calls out to the remaining climber, "Carry on."

"It was a gigantic task to turn that shit out every day," says Duncan. "The burnout was enormous." But not, it is worth noting, in him. "I never minded it. People asked me, 'How can you do it?' Like Picasso said, when you're young, you can do anything. I was young. And, in a way, the openness of the form allowed you to do it, as long as your energy was up. I always had the energy."

Both Shepherd and the actors simply took for granted Duncan's role as linchpin. At the Dock, Shepherd often began to withdraw from performance, taking frequent trips to New York or concerning himself in Chicago with scenario writing, plans for the future of Compass, business matters, and paperwork. The others began to take rotating vacations every six weeks. "It took us a long time, but we learned to do it," Mark Gordon says. "There was something about being on your toes every night. After a while, you got irritable. So it was necessary to be revitalized." It was surprising to Gordon that no matter how strong the absent player was, "The company would just close ranks. It was amazing. When anyone came back, they'd say, 'I can't do that.' They'd get stage fright all over again."

Piano player Allaudin Mathieu did not learn until the last weekend in March that Severn's spring vacation would last through the summer, five months, three in Virginia at the Barter Theatre and two in Mexico. Aggravated by his dilapidated piano, Mathieu decided one night to fix it himself by propping up the pedal with a Rube Goldberg rig that he undid after the show, telling Shepherd he refused to play anymore unless the piano was fixed. According to his diary, Mathieu was almost as upset with his own working conditions as he was by the impending change in the cast. He was such a fan that he "talked in 'Severn' " to his laundryman. ("Do you realize that OTTO spelled backwards and upside-down is TOOT?") "The Compass will lose its best actor," Mathieu glumly wrote.

It was still snowing in Chicago on April 6, 1956, the night Mathieu first saw Severn's replacement, Shelley Berman, on the Compass stage. "It is hard to compare him to Severn," he wrote. "He is just as good if not as delightful." As Mathieu's diary also took note, "He got a big round of applause."

"I brought in Shelley," recalls Mark Gordon. "I had directed him with Bobbi and Martin Landau in New York. Shelley wrote comedy material and after rehearsal would improvise or read us his material and we'd sit around and laugh. And Shelley was a fine actor too. So when it began to turn skitty, I said, 'Look, I've got somebody.' "

"I remember joke theatre really coming in with Shelley," says Bobbi Gordon. "I remember the first night he was there."

That night the company was playing Elaine's scenario *Rumplestiltskin*. Usually, in *Rumplestiltskin*, Severn played The King. On receiving the part, Berman was heard muttering over and over, "What can I do with this?"

"The man had literally never seen us do anything," says Bobbi. "And suddenly, the whole scenario was about The King. I mean, it was a running comedy monologue. I remember that night so vividly because everybody turned to everybody else and said, 'Uh, oh.' It was a moment when everybody knew. It was also the moment when choices could have been made very easily. By all of us. By sitting down together and saying, 'No, we're not going this route.' By sitting down and talking to Shelley. Instead, out of anger at Shelley and his facility, there was no dialogue about what was wrong with that night. And to Shelley, there was nothing wrong. He was getting laughs."

Shelley Berman's face, at once pugnacious and pained, resembles the comedy/tragedy masks. The *Christian Science Monitor* once described his voice as having "the battered elegance and mock rhetorical cadences of an elocution teacher, hair tonic salesman and prize fight announcer." In fact, as a young boy, growing up in a family of poor immigrant Jews on Chicago's West Side, Berman had studied to be a cantor, the singer in the temple, the voice, as it were, of the Jewish soul. In his teens, he says, he had become "disenchanted with the liturgical aspect" of Judaism and "grown away from my religion," along with "my parents' and grandparents' ambition for me."

"Pushing thirty" in 1956, Berman was still a struggling actor and losing his remaining faith. He lived in Greenwich Village with his wife, Sarah, who worked to support them by creating and demonstrating fancy bows for a ribbon company. At the time he got Mark Gordon's call, Berman was just beginning an adjunctive career as a comedy writer, selling free-lance material to Steve Allen's *Tonight* show, but "I decided to join them anyway, because it sounded right to me," he says. "First of all, Mark had recommended it. He said it was improvisation, and that was good. And he said a lot of it was comedy, and that was good. I knew I could be funny. I was entertaining at parties, you know. And I'd studied acting. I knew I could be amusing on a stage. But I was a straight actor. Classical, no less." After being dismissed from the navy as asthmatic, at seventeen he entered the Goodman Theatre drama school. He played in summer stock. In New York, he studied with Uta Hagen for two years. He had even appeared on a few live television shows in New York, like *Philco TV Playhouse* and *Goodyear TV Playhouse*, but in the spring of 1956, "I wasn't working anyplace. I was a displaced Chicagoan anyway. It was old stomping grounds for me. I was just in New York doing the struggle, the actor's struggle. I got the call from Mark Gordon. So I went."

Berman received no preparatory talks from Shepherd on the proletarian theatre, enjoyed no deep conceptual talks about the cabaret with Paul Sills, nor did he play "the boss and the hunchback" as a demonstration scene. With even less introduction to the Compass philosophy than anyone who preceded him, his initiation was startling: "They threw me out onstage. At first, I thought the whole idea was just to stand around there and be funny. I didn't know *how* to improvise. I knew how to improvise in class. But, ha, watching these people, I realized I didn't know the first thing about this. I suspected that I had a great deal of talent. I had something going for me. But I had no real savvy. And I had worked as an actor for a number of years. And here were these kids making me look like a monkey. They were *very* good. So I decided to learn how to do it. And I did, very quickly."

In teaching himself this mysterious art form, Berman learned "to pursue the action, to work the beats. And, the absolute top thing you did was not go out there to be funny. You went out there to respond as a character in a situation. And pursue your action. That was all. And that was basic. And when I tried to be funny I was terrible."

He also discerned that "the thing that will make one player better or more acceptable within this improvisational framework is simply a capacity for creating words. They must be there. They must be part of you. But while you're improvising, you mustn't think of creating them. If you start to playwright, it won't work. You just *go* with it. You improvise." Like most of the other Compass Players Shepherd hired to replace the amateurs, Berman improvised from a verbal center, with the writer's sensibility that was, ironically, always downgraded by Shepherd and Sills.

A revival of *The Fuller Brush Man* was the first long piece Berman felt he did with any success. In this excised version of the story of a shy and reluctant job applicant who is slowly converted into the sleazy salesman that his job requires, Berman played the boss and Nichols the prospective employee. "They told me I was supposed to inspire him to sell brushes. He wouldn't think he was good at it. He wouldn't think it was the job for him. That was all they told me. I knew I had to love the brush. I recall talking about a brush made of the quills of the porcupine." When Berman picked up the invisible brush, he remembers saying, " 'The porcupine, an animal who laid down his life to keep America clean.' And it got tremendous laughter. I had done nothing but attempt to persuade this young man to sell brushes. That's all my character wanted to do. And it turned into something humorous."

Berman grabbed up parts in other short scenes too, becoming the coach in "Football Comes to the University of Chicago" and Sir Edmund in "Mountain Climbing." He replaced Severn as the announcer in "Piran-dello," where the task was simply to introduce the piece and reappear at the end to intercept the fight between Nichols and May. "They asked me to do it, and I was delighted because I thought it was the best thing they did. I was thrilled to be part of it. At the beginning, at the end, it didn't matter to me." Within a month or two, performing nightly at the Compass, "Everything that Uta Hagen had been trying to teach me for two years suddenly became very clear. After all those years in acting, I finally was learning what acting was all about."

Offstage, he was more uncomfortable than he appeared on it. "I was a new guy, but I wasn't a kid like they were. They were younger than me. Not by much, but it was enough. Mark was a little older too, so I felt a kinship with him." Nor was it reassuring to Berman that "the nucleus—the solid part" of Compass was affiliated with the University of Chicago.

In fact, by the time Berman arrived, the only Compass players with an official connection to the university were Duncan, who had been a graduate student, and Nichols, who had been a dropout. But "It was part of my hang-up that I was not an academic. I did not regard myself as an intellectual. I wasn't a college kid. I was just a struggling actor who didn't know what the hell to do with his life. They weren't a clique, but I wasn't a part of the group. I always felt a little bit outside of it, although I did love to work with them. I think the greatest joy I ever had in my life was working with them."

Like so many others, Berman was enchanted by Elaine. His rapport with her was instant, but he entered into an ambivalent dynamic, a clash of egos, and a rivalry for her partnership with Mike Nichols from the first day.

Time would only exacerbate their "strained relationship. It was difficult for me to reconcile myself to the fact that I recognized in him a super-brilliance," Berman reflects. "I could never be as beautifully informed as Mike Nichols. I thought he was an exceptionally informed man. And there was no way to deny how much I admired him and how much I enjoyed working with him."

Berman's attraction to Nichols was complicated by the fact that, like many of the characters he played, Nichols—an aesthete, a gourmet, an equestrian, a doctor's son, a University of Chicago prodigy, a German Jew, a psychoanalysand—was a consummate snob. Berman observed himself to be "a bit more vulgar than Mike. As a matter of fact, a bit more vulgar than all the others. I mean, in choices, in selection. I found myself working less from my head than my gut." With the kind of familiar contempt that a German Jew might feel free to express to a Jew of Eastern

European origin, Nichols was capable of remarking to Berman as he came offstage, "That was the most tasteless thing you've ever done."

The French improvisateurs, who took pride in their style and finesse, as well as their reason and logic, disdained their Italian counterparts, whose cruder and more boisterous naturalism was doubtless regarded as pigs' feet to the foie gras of their own *comédie improvisée*.

Psychologically, the comedy of The Compass Players (consisting as it did of such aspirants to high culture as prep-school socialists, assimilated Jews, and college dropouts) really had less antecedent in the *commedia* of the Italians than the French. Until Shelley Berman arrived, Compass improvisers (with the exception of Bob Coughlan) had characteristically fitted Roger Bowen's profile of a "cool and cerebral individual, not the type you would meet at a Polish wedding."

You could meet Shelley Berman at a Polish wedding. Shelley Berman was hot.

It was "amazing" to Berman that others in the company were not driven to "take over, to be most loved by the audience, to be chief of the night. Me? I was hungry for recognition. I wanted to get somewhere. I was looking at thirty years old, and nothing was happening in my life. It was scaring the hell out of me. I was getting panicky. My energy was that of a man running. Sometimes it was a bother to the others. Sometimes it was a bother to me. I developed a facility for improvising, but I was always inclined to go for the laugh. I was very pushy about that. I always wanted to be onstage. I wanted to hog the evening. I wanted to get all the laughs. Here were these brilliant kids, and I was competing with them. I didn't feel competitive, but that's what was happening up there."

No one who shared the stage at Compass with Berman will disagree. If another player's line got a laugh one night, he would often hear it coming out of Berman's mouth the following night. In the course of a scene, he once upset Mark Gordon so badly that Gordon walked off the stage. Gordon had come to Berman with an idea for a people scene based on a real event in Gordon's life. Berman was to play a father to Gordon's son. The son wanted $10 to go to acting school. The father wouldn't pay. "It was a great idea," Berman recalls. "We'd do a whole generation gap." Offstage, he and Gordon "talked our beats out." Onstage, "I gave him nothing but static. I was just an impossible father with a very thick Jewish accent. And I was getting lots of laughs." As they got offstage, to Berman's surprise, "Mark was really pissed at me. Really pissed. He said, 'Why not go for where it's really at? You're just going for the laughs.'" Even so, according to Bobbi, the scene was "thrilling beyond thrilling," with long silences that were "beautiful and real."

A few nights later, the men tried the scene again. "The father and son. I'm doing similar things," says Berman. "And I'm still getting laughs." Bobbi recalls the second performance as "Shelley's monologue." This time, according to Berman, Gordon didn't wait to discuss it: "He stops pursuing the scene. He gets up and walks out. Well, I knew what he meant by that. He gave up on the character. But it was Mark giving up on me." As Gordon recalls it, "He gave me the money. He made himself the hero. It was a mushy, sentimental ending. I threw the money back." Says Berman, "The routine, after two attempts, died right there." Says Gordon, "It wasn't a Compass scene anymore."

When Berman similarly upset Elaine, Shepherd recalls she informed him that "the next time you fuck me up onstage, I will pull down your zipper and pull out your dick."

If he and the others were birds of a different feather, however, no one could say that Shelley Berman's weren't bright. In fact, if he had been less brilliant, his compulsive energy might not have been so threatening. Instead, it was contagious.

Mark Gordon recalls that "people began to harbor resentments. They tried to outdo each other. In the pairing up before the spot improvisations, people began to think funny things up. It became a contest of who could be funnier. That's when things really began to fall apart."

The Gordons had already sensed a change in the work. There had been, first of all, the shift to skits. "We were already doing a lot of old stuff," says Mark Gordon. "We were already doing a lot of things that worked."

In the pursuit of new forms of expression, there had been great supportiveness. "Nobody competed. Nobody thought, 'Why aren't I doing that?' It had been obvious what each of us could do." "And everybody appreciated everyone else's riches," Bobbi Gordon adds. "Until Shelley came. Then it became, 'I can do that!' Then, 'I can do that better!' And that to me was real sad. Because nobody really knew what was good about what they did."

Arguments had previously occurred, in Andy Duncan's description, as "fighting friends." In all these disagreements, Bobbi Gordon felt there had remained "an appreciating, a reaching out for each other. Shelley really broke that chain. It became 'Me.' And once that 'me'—and a very powerful 'me'—began to take over, then it was, 'I've got to protect myself.' And everybody began to withdraw."

In late April, David Shepherd told Allaudin Mathieu his sad story: Compass had been losing $100 to $150 every week since November, and since he had been paying the actors' salaries from funds for their withholding tax, he was $1,500 in debt to the government. He had four options: (1) buy the building from the Schalls as of May 1, (2) move the theatre to a new location downtown or north, (3) have the company travel, or (4) play in country clubs and resorts. "We work the next few weeks on credit," Mathieu was forewarned.

The first week in May, after a Saturday night show that Mathieu described in his diary as "a nightmare . . . the actors were particularly unamusing," the pianist watched Shepherd, Charlie Jacobs, and the actors —all but Mike Nichols, he noticed—depart to discuss the future of Compass at a meeting at Gladys's Restaurant.

Mathieu himself had just been told that the Compass would soon be settling on the North Side and that he and his bassist would not be invited to move. Shepherd wanted musicians on a caliber with the actors, he explained. At the new location, Eddie Baker would be playing piano with his trio six nights a week.

Two weeks later, Mathieu was among those Friends of Compass who received a card in the mail: "Dear Friend: You are invited to a preview performance of *The Real You* and *The Living Newspaper* at the Argo Off-Beat Room, 6400 North Broadway at Devon, 9:00 p.m. Thursday, May 17. No cover or minimum on this night. Grand opening Friday night."

The creation of a permanent stage came late—200 years—in the development of the commedia dell'arte. For generations, the masked troupes had lugged their costumes, stage equipment, babies, roadies, pets, and books of scenarios and notated *lazzi* (bits of stage business and pantomime shticks) in carts across the Italian provinces and Europe, drawing crowds and filling up the strongbox (sometimes by overcharging on the ceiling price the government allowed). A roof over his head—a theatre— gave the improvising actor of the Renaissance a dignity unknown to his former fellow performers, the wandering minstrels, funambulists, and charletans.

Security was won at the expense of spontaneity. As the comedy troupes gained upward mobility, they acquired a literate following. In order to please this critical audience, they exchanged extemporaneous performance for rehearsed, sure-fire plays. Following Goldoni's example, the wordsmiths among them began to write things down. But the *commedia* tradition was honored throughout Europe, its extravagant satirical characters and plots absorbed into the literary theatre, most notably in the comedies of Molière. It took centuries for commedia dell'arte to die.

Remembering amphetamine nights at a later improvisational theatre, The Second City, Tony Holland, a playwright as well as an actor, said, "Goldoni probably got exhausted making up a play every night. He said, 'I can be a writer and take it easy. Why don't I write this down?' "

In David Shepherd's version, "The Duke of Padua said, 'The royalty wants to be comfortable. I want you to come indoors.' " Some courts even provided the troupes with custom-designed stages to suit their plots, their entrances and exits, their chases, their intrigues. "When they moved indoors, then forget it. First of all, they had to please the monarchs. They lost contact with the people and started to work for the court."

"The Argo Room was bigger," Mark Gordon recalls. "It was really a step up. We got a raise immediately. I think the salaries went up to seventy-five dollars. Plus the owner gave us food. They had a kitchen and stuff. And they got places for us to live. And a space to park our car. The show room had a little balcony. There was a jazz trio. We did shows and then ate and got drinks in between. There were a lot of advantages there. It had a canopy. It had a nightclub atmosphere." The Argo Off-Beat Room had been a Prohibition nightclub. As Mark Gordon heard it, there was even supposed to be a swimming pool under the floor.

"We wore suits at the Argo Room. And ties," Andy Duncan says. "The owner, what's-his-name, McCloskey, insisted on it. Shelley wanted it too. At the Dock we were still Bohemians with a kind of scholarly academic University of Chicago veneer. In the winter, Mark and I wore turtlenecks and Mike would wear a jacket over a shirt with a crew neck. In the summer, we'd wear chinos and T-shirts. Severn was always elegant, with a foulard tie and a handkerchief in his mouth."

In the original version of *The Fuller Brush Man*, the job applicant was asked, "Do you have a tie?" and Duncan in his T-shirt had answered, "My brother has one" and gotten "a long laugh." In the Argo Room revival, the job applicant wore a real tie and a seersucker suit. Says Duncan, "We got very formal up there."

The limos started coming and the interviews with *Playboy*. "Once that stuff starts happening," says Duncan, "you stop experimenting. You can't take chances anymore."

Spontaneity and flexibility had been the hallmark of the Compass shows. Since the only thing "set" about a scene was its "beats," the actors would fill in for each other in group scenes quite indiscriminately. In "Football Comes to the University of Chicago," Elaine was likely to appear as one of the applicants for the team. Returning to the Dock after a vacation, Nichols remembers sitting at the bar with Severn, admiring Duncan's performance in *The Real You.* "I was supposed to have that part," said Severn, "but I went out for a cup of coffee."

As for "freezing" the lines, says Bobbi Gordon, "We all got guilty about it." Says Mark Gordon, "It was traitorous." "It was amazing," continues Bobbi, "how people really did not go out to repeat what was done. On the North Side, there was much more of 'Let's do that scene that was so funny the other night.' "

"What began to happen," says Mark Gordon, "the jokes would remain and the scene would go away. The magic of repeating scenes was something that had never been learned. Except by Mike and Elaine."

It is Elaine to whom their colleagues attribute the continued freshness of their work. "Mike had the capacity to remember everything he said the night before, and block it, and redo it, and go for the same point," says David Shepherd. "Elaine was interested in playing to the drunken sailor in the audience. Or nun. She always knew that last night is not tonight."

"She was very pure. She had a commitment to improvisation," says Mark Gordon, "and she was not going to let it go. Whenever he would go for a joke, she would do something unexpected, throw him off balance, side-skirt him. She was truly remarkable. And Mike loved working with her. He enjoyed the head game going on between them. It also made it fun for us, 'cause it would always be a little different from the way it was before."

Outside work for the actors started coming in. "Now there was an awareness of commercial possibilities," says Mark Gordon, "and that was another part of the downfall. As long as the naïveté was there, it remained pure. As soon as people began to realize the commercial possibilities, the competition became fierce. It was known. It was visible. You could feel the competition. It was tangible, for god's sakes."

16

Out of Step at the Argo
Off-Beat Room

When Barbara Harris returned from England with Paul Sills, she found that "everything" about the Compass had changed. "It was in a completely different neighborhood: It was in a bourgeois uptown neighborhood where nobody ever heard of the University of Chicago. People sat down, you know, in suits and ties. It was in a nightclub. It called critics in. And it had grown in such a way that . . . I couldn't do it. It had grown and it had re-formed. In the beginning it was very much David's. David may have thought the new neighborhood would lend itself, but as soon as there's a club owner who wants people coming in there, and doesn't want to disappoint the audience, it's like . . . life. It transforms. I mean, people had to come in there and clap, to pay the bills, and buy the drinks, and get the critics in. David was out. He couldn't work on the things he wanted to work on. The scenario idea was having trouble. They were still doing them, but they were much slicker. They weren't rustic and commedia dell'arte. And the scenarios weren't as strong as the one and two people scenes.

"What I found was that the strength of it was in the actor. And they were using their creativity irrespective of the original idea. It was really because of the change of location. They weren't at the University of Chicago. They weren't doing *The Lonely Crowd* for David Riesman, if you can believe it. The circumstances had changed. David Shepherd had become a producer instead of an inventor. He no longer had the ideas that fit the circumstances. I mean, the actors said, 'Well, we're the ones standing here with egg on our faces, not you.' Or 'That died. Let's get Shelley to do a telephone. We know that works.' And Mike and Elaine were very inventive on their own. They didn't need an inventor."

"When we went to the North Side, to Broadway and Devon, it was somewhere in there that David Shepherd ceased being an active part of Compass and eventually left it," Shelley Berman recalls. "I didn't quite *know* this less and less of David. I never got to know him that well. I didn't know about a man who punished himself for making wrong decisions. What I knew of him was all on the good side. I knew that he had created an atmosphere for me to ply some kind of trade. And it had been years since I could say, 'I'm working tomorrow.' I had been struggling a long time. So I think of him with a great deal of appreciation. If it weren't for David, the opportunity wouldn't have existed for any of us. One could say David fulfilled his need. He created this thing, and now he was no longer essential to me. I do know that I got there, and I could do what I was doing, and it had nothing to do with David after that."

In July, consumed with depression and exhausted by his own sense of dissatisfaction, impotence, and overwork, Shepherd asked Sills to take over for him at the Compass until a suitable replacement was found. To Shepherd's relief, Sills agreed.

Settling back in Chicago, Sills had begun teaching classes in the apartment he shared with Barbara and feeling out the local scene. Bernie Sahlins, Sills's and Shepherd's former business partner at Playwrights Theatre Club, was refurbishing a 1,200-seat behemoth, the Studebaker Theatre, for a fall opening. In creating the Studebaker, Sahlins intended to follow the Playwrights Theatre Club model, running subscription productions of classics and other high-quality plays but on a grander scale, with guest stars like Geraldine Page and E. G. Marshall heading local casts. Sahlins's project promised work not just for Sills but for the whole Playwrights and Compass community. In the meantime, Sills welcomed Shepherd's salary.

Off the Compass payroll as of the first of August, Shepherd spent a week revising his "coffee scenario" and, postponing his study of Chicago until the fall (when he was scheduled at the Studebaker Theatre to teach a playwriting course), he took off for the East. In Washington, D.C., he wrote nine pages about the Compass for a treatise on popular theatre he wanted to sell as a book. He read about Einstein and the Panama Canal and transcribed his scenario *The Minister's Daughter* in hopes of entering it in a Studebaker Theatre playwriting contest. After almost four years in the Chicago theatre trenches, at thirty, unable to see that he had already made it, he was getting desperate to accomplish something that would make his mark in life.

Meanwhile, at the Argo Off-Beat Room, Shelley Berman remembers that "we were doing all right, but the place itself was not a known place. Come Fridays and Saturdays, gosh, it was marvelous, but during the week, it was tough." As Andy Duncan perceived the mood of the company, they were "all living for Saturday nights and fighting to work with Elaine."

Into this fitful atmosphere, he recalls, "Sills came back, throwing his weight around. He came in and saw the mess. We were in trouble up there. The show was falling apart. It had no unity. Lights would come up and there would be a scene, and then the next scene would have nothing to do with anything. And there were no new scenes being produced. We were stagnant. Something had to be done. But Sills came in, obviously recharged, and The Terror started again."

Paul Sills was not being complimentary when he described the Compass he returned to at the Argo Off-Beat Room as "brilliantly entertaining." On the upside, "They could do four or five hours of material—start at nine and go on until two in the morning. They could do anything. They could do scenes and scenarios and they could improvise. They did 'em very well, real quick. They had all these people at the peak of their performance. They were marvelous. I couldn't get over it."

Sills remembers a talk show takeoff and a Gian Carlo Menotti parody in which Shelley Berman was "trying to get a job in corporate life where he brought with him his lunch which was a banana. I remember him crying out, 'God! I've squashed my bah-nah-nah.' That was very, very good. Mike and Elaine and Shelley did Hamlet set in a delicatessen." Elaine was Gertrude, the delicatessen owner. Shelley was Uncle Claude. Mike was Hamlet, "sitting around smoking and grousing." Sills approximates Elaine's New York Jewish accent saying to Hamlet, " 'Listen, Mrs. Rosencrantz and Mrs. Guildenstern, *their* sons don't act like this.' That kind of thing. It seemed to fit perfectly."

When faced with the chaotic interludes of rehearsal, Sills, from early in his career, had intimidated actors with his tantrums. "He was always a troublemaker that way," says Duncan. "When we started Compass, he would be very demanding, then get angry and leave. He would flounce out the door, and, for a while, we'd all be happy. 'Hey, the old man's gone, let's have some fun.' Then he'd come back, see we were doing fine without him, and start pushing in again. I mean, it was partly his club.

We couldn't do anything about that. Then he left for England. We could push David around, and the owner was on our side. McCloskey was a nice enough guy. And David was a marshmallow. You could get angry with him and he'd respect you. So it was really an actors' theatre, kind of an ideal place to be. I would say the classic period of Compass was when Sills was gone. It was the most fun. He was always an inhibitor."

It must be noted that Sills, who was aloof to Shepherd's preproduction plans, had no financial interest in the Compass. Charlie Jacobs (looking forward to basic training at Fort Dix) was Shepherd's only partner, although that information was apparently not known to the cast. It is part of the naïve and enthusiastic nature of theatre fledglings not to read (in the case of the Compass, not even to know there was) fine print. Even Sills seems to have been unaware that from its inception the Compass was a legal entity in which he had no share: "Ownership? The place took in five hundred dollars a week. We just shared the income. There was no owner. That's not how groups form." As for Shepherd's role, Sills adds, "We'd say, he's the producer, 'cause he's active in that direction, he's the guy that does that. I directed all the first shows. That didn't make me somebody's hired hand."

The right of the director, to select the players, to hire and fire, Sills explains as "hidden into any theatre," presumably even a cooperative one. In fact, he enjoyed proprietary privileges only because Shepherd gladly and respectfully conferred them on him. (Doubtless, Sills would have quit the Compass otherwise.) It was Shepherd, however, who retained all subsidiary rights to the Compass name, to future franchises, and to all the material created on the Compass stage.

Shepherd claims that "I had these lawyers in New York who kept saying, 'You're The Compass Play Corporation. And it owns everything. This is your show. This is your material. Everybody that improvises anything, it belongs automatically to The Compass Play Corporation.' There was always the idea of using improvisation to generate material that had value and that could then be sold to somebody else. That was the concept." Whose concept? "The lawyers' concept. They would say, 'You're too loose, David, you're a socialist. And you're not concerned with the fact that these properties have value, and that nobody's going to invest in your little corporation unless you can show them that you're gonna generate some property that has value.'"

Unfortunately for thinkers, dreamers, and producers of plays without playwrights, the laws of copyright do not protect a format, concept, or scenario. A written work cannot be copyrighted without its full supply of words. According to Shepherd, his New York lawyers told him, "You can only copyright the words, so please put the words on audiotape and copyright them, and they will belong to you forever."*

As a convert to socialism, raised to regret his grandmother's frivolous sale of family timberland, Shepherd lacked perhaps the perspicacity or horsesense to apprise his lawyers of the elementary Marxist precept that "property is theft."

In the unwitting service of the capitalist legal strategy that governed Shepherd's proletarian theatre, the actors, who had never demanded, or ever been offered, the rights and powers that traditionally accrue to playwrights, could, if he chose to harass them, easily be cowed by a man with the "hidden" right to hire and fire: Sills. Protected only by the least demanding of contracts applicable through Actors' Equity, the actors, who night after night provided the words to fulfill a producer's "concept," were viewed scornfully by their management as "bourgeois." Economically, they were more vulnerable than nut tighteners on a Detroit assembly line. Therefore, whatever power he lacked on paper, Sills, who would be looked at in the Marxist landscape as just another wage slave, made up for by his influence on Shepherd and by his own imperious attitude.

No less an actress than Geraldine Page was floored to find herself the butt of Sills's contempt. Page had arrived in Chicago to star for three months at the Studebaker Theatre in a series of plays. She had been informed of the doings of Compass through her old classmate at the Goodman Theatre, Shelley Berman, and found the players "so clever, so funny, so pungent" that during her extended stay in Chicago, she became a fixture in the audience. "After our show, the cast got in a car and, in the middle of the night, we'd go over there," she recalled in a conversation only weeks before her death. "We used to go regularly. I remember sitting up in a little balcony."

Page recalled Sills mentioning that he and Barbara were planning to start a repertory company and that Alfred Ryder (then married to the

---

*Only later was it discovered, when the tapes were transcribed, that among the many blowholes in this ownership arrangement, the written products weren't salable anyway because, as Shepherd says, "In print, they were boring. A lot of what was coming across the footlights was nonverbal stuff. It had to do with inflection. It had to do with timing. It had to do with body language, or facial mannerisms, or the position of two bodies, or hands. It had nothing, or very little, to do with words."

legendary Method actress Kim Stanley) had agreed to direct. Sills asked Page to join.

As Mike Nichols perceived him ("Paul doesn't stratify people. He'd get pissed off, but he'd get pissed off at anybody"), Sills was democratic. He gave Geraldine Page evidence that an air of condescension was an equally inviolate—almost an absent-minded—facet of his personality.

Page remembered, "I said, 'If Alfred's going to direct, why don't you get Kim Stanley?' 'Oh, she's too busy,' Sills replied." Page's face replayed her stupefaction. "This little shit," she said.

As for his absorption in Brecht at this time, Page suspected that "he was enchanted by the alienation theory, probably." Assured that Sills's homespun or Violan version of the alienation theory was perhaps the backbone of his work, Page observed that in her experience of the theatre, "People hold on to some little thing like this and make a big deal about it to avoid the problem of what it's all really about. It makes me so outraged."

"We had been working for a year without a director, and we loved it," recalls Mark Gordon. "When Paul came back, he did something that we didn't like, which was scenarios they'd done the year before."

"A director was always interested in a scenario," Sills explains, "and they were always interested in the short scenes because they worked. I got 'em back into doing scenarios. (I remember sitting down and talking about Brecht.) I don't think they were *very* antagonistic. They were glad to try. I went back to *The Game of Hurt—The Game of Hurt* all over again with the gang—and a couple of other things."

Mark Gordon remembers that Sills also directed *The Stakhanovite Worker* and a new incarnation of David Shepherd's *Five Dreams*, the scenario in which the actors wore paper bags on their heads. "It was a director's kind of thing," Gordon says. In this staging, Andy Duncan recalls, "Shelley had two bags over his head. When he pulled one off, he had one bag over his head. It got a 'Ha . . . Ha . . . Ha.' You know, one of those reluctant laughs."

Backstage, Elaine particularly balked at doing old scenarios, says Gordon, "because that was safe ground. And it was no longer the place for that kind of work. We were in a nightclub situation, not a theatre. So going back and capturing the stuff that had worked at the University of Chicago wasn't appropriate."

One Compass player completely neutral to the shift in power to Paul Sills was Shelley Berman. "I never knew anything about the politics of

Compass," he says. "I did not know about the leadership. And I frankly didn't care. All I wanted to do was get up onstage."

Geraldine Page described the young Shelley Berman as "just a wonderful, brilliant actor. Particularly in the Shakespeare. But he also used to do all these funny skits at the parties—the embryo of the kind of thing he did later. One-man pieces, yes. And pieces on the telephone." Page picked up an invisible telephone, the signature device that Berman himself cannot remember using until he began writing for *Tonight*.

The associate producer, a friend from summer stock, suggested that Berman write a comedy routine for himself, as a *Tonight* show audition piece. Berman recalls, "I was an actor. I didn't know beans about being a comedian. There was no way I could be funny directly to the audience. So I wrote this little monologue where I wouldn't have to talk directly to anyone."

Berman talked into a telephone about the woman hanging out the window of a department store. He auditioned with the piece and was booked on the show, where, ironically, "I was introduced as a budding young comedian." The bud didn't blossom. "I just got myself on the show, and that was that. I didn't do the routine anymore."

But from his earliest days at the Compass, Andy Duncan recalls that Berman would allow himself to be "interrupted" by an onstage telephone call. "He had a sense, if a scene was dying, to pick up the telephone," says Duncan. "Like in *The Fuller Brush Man*, when he was giving me the lecture, he'd suddenly turn and pick it up." Duncan's voice begins to resonate like a hair-tonic salesman as he sings, "Yallo? Uh, huh. You're where? You lost your brushes?" And then, Duncan remembers, "He'd make jokes on the brushes. He always did phone bits. It was part of his repertoire."

It was not until Paul Sills returned to the Compass, however, that Berman picked up the invisible telephone "in one" again. Applying himself to the tasks of a monologist, Berman really began to thrive.

To stimulate new material, Sills would provide a theme for the actors, who were to come back the next day with a piece on which to improvise. One week "selling" was the theme. While the others teamed up in their "selling" scenes, Berman worked on his alone. His idea was "Selling Yourself to Yourself," in a scene in which "I would first find out that nobody cares for me and then look into the mirror and sell myself to myself. I didn't have any lines written. We were improvisationalists. But my beats were nicely structured. I did this short thing on the phone where I found out my friend wasn't really my friend, there was a party I wasn't invited to, that a girl had stood me up. Then I'd put the phone down, go to the bathroom, wash myself, and start my monologue into the mirror." In the audience watching that early two-part version, Geraldine Page was among those who were convulsed to hear Berman wail into his mirror, "Doesn't the world know how much I am like Howard Rourke?" Berman remembers, "I heard Gerry screaming. She almost fell over the balcony."

Since the selling routine had "turned out to be a pretty good thing," Berman kept repeating it, and every time he did—five or six times— the phone call got "a little more elaborate and fun." One night as he hung up the phone, the audience burst into applause. "I thought it over. At the phone. It's over. Paul agreed. He said, 'It's finished *there.*' "

Sills doesn't think he had much influence on Shelley Berman's oeuvre. "Not really," he says. "His one-man pieces occurred because he was really a one-man big band. It was easier for him that way. But I also saw him improvise with the others for hours. He was great."

I n New York, David Shepherd found a good candidate for a director to replace the uncommitted Sills. Larry Arrick was a struggling young director, married to an actress, Rose. On summer hiatus from a teaching job at Bennington College in Vermont, he was holding classes at the Herbert Berghof Studio in Greenwich Village, where anyone could audit for a dollar. Strangers often came to the class. As Arrick tells it, Shepherd shook hands with him after class and announced himself as the producer of Compass. Arrick said, "What's that?"

"I didn't know anything about improvisation, cabaret, or Chicago," remembers Arrick. "He tried to explain it to me, and that's not David's strength." Interested, nevertheless, in pursuing their amiable connection, he invited Shepherd to see his work in Chestertown, New York, where he was directing a number of veteran actors, including Luther Adler, Morris Carnovsky, and Jack Gilford, and a young one, Alan Arkin, one of his Bennington students, in a summer troupe at Crystal Lake.

In late August, Shepherd visited Chestertown and was sufficiently buoyed by their meeting to enter its upshot into his diary. "Succeeded in getting L.A. to come to Chicago," he wrote.

It was, perhaps, a symptom of Shepherd's Jonah complex that the failure he felt over the Chicago Compass did not deter him—in fact it seemed to spur him on to the pursuit of his greater global mission. While the first company of Compass Players were foundering at the Argo Off-Beat Room, he saw a chance for a branch of Compass International to take root in the soil of another great university campus, the University of Wisconsin in Madison. On his many side trips from Chicago, he had sown the seeds of enthusiasm for a community theatre among a group of people there.

That summer, Andy Duncan recalls Shepherd taking him aside one night. "He said, 'I want you to drive up to Madison with me. There's a possibility of our starting a Compass up there.' So we drove up. There was nothing happening on campus. The university was on summer vacation. But we met all these excited people who had heard about this thing. At that time, they sold beer in a beer garden on the university premises. The theatre was right there in the beer garden. Driving back to Chicago, Shepherd asked me what I thought of the setup. 'It looks fine,' I said. 'The theatre is nice and the people are interesting. But there's no group. You'd need a group.'

" 'Well, that's what Paul and I want you to do,' he said. 'We want you to go up there and start one. You pretty much know Viola's exercises. And we'll oversee it. Paul will come up and help you out.' "

Duncan weighed the offer. "On the one hand, they would be giving me the responsibility, and, on the other, they'd be looking over my shoulder, as if I were a baby. And furthermore, they had no money."

"Would I stay on the same salary?" Duncan asked.

"Oh, no," Shepherd answered. "You'd have to do it on your own. You can get a job as a carpenter or waiter. You know, the way you did it before."

Duncan gasps at the memory. "Can you imagine? They wanted me to go up there—to get a group together, teach them Viola's exercises, cast the company, oversee the theatre, build a set, put up lights—for no money, for some future kind of thing!" Duncan demurred.

In a gloomy tone, Shepherd told his diary that he had "laid the groundwork for Madison Compass, but failed to get Duncan to represent us there."

Back in Chicago, business had fallen off badly, and McCloskey was pressing for less theatre and a stronger nightclub act. Like Duncan, Shelley Berman remembers Burr McCloskey as the most cooperative of club owners. "He was very sincere, a very good man. He loved the artistic end." In fact, until Sills arrived, McCloskey had so much more daily involvement with the show than the peripatetic David Shepherd that Berman says he "didn't know who I was working for. I thought I was working for Burr

McCloskey. He was running that room. He was trying to get a pianist. He had dancers over there. He tried everything he could to make it work." But McCloskey was no substitute for a producer. As dazzling as the talents of these Compass Players were, the audience stayed away.

In September, Severn Darden rejoined the company. Over the years, he has shared a stage with countless configurations of improvisational artists. This one at the Argo Off-Beat Room he refers to as "a higher-wattage group." In its new surroundings, he also found that Compass was "a bit more uptight. There was more pressure. It was harder to fill, both with people and improvisations. And it was much more difficult to play due to the size and shape of the room, the balcony, and the two band-stands."

He was introduced to Shelley Berman with whom he quickly established a strong onstage rapport. Severn was impressed with Berman's intensity and dedication to the work. After rehearsal, while everyone else went out for dinner, "He'd go home and work some more, and by the time he came back for the show that night, he'd added forty new good ideas."

"Some of the best things I ever did I did with Sevvie," says Berman, who thinks their scene "The Panhandler's Apprentice" would have been "one of the classic scenes of burlesque theatre." In it, Severn played the apprentice panhandler to Berman's old pro. The form, which had become as traditional to Compass as it was to burlesque, was that of a teaching scene. As the old pro, Berman would deliver a few pointers on how to approach passers-by for "carfare" and then stand back to watch the way his student worked the invisible crowd. "Severn was so surprising on all occasions," says Berman. Once he tipped his hat and said, "Excuse me, Sisters . . . ," and Berman, horrified, yanked him away. "Then he went after a midget, the tiniest little man in the world," and solicited half a dollar. "He doesn't have room in his pocket," Berman would scold.

"He was absolutely great to work with," says Severn of Berman. "You could work on a really thin wire with Shelley and know that you wouldn't fall down." "He had an enormously wonderful mind, just a fantastic mind, filled with information and an ability to articulate that was so wacked out," says Berman of Severn. "He was a true improvisationalist."

Watching raptly from the balcony was Geraldine Page, whom Severn still can picture in a brown tweed skirt with her hair piled haphazardly on her head. Unaware of the tension backstage, Page simply regarded Compass as one of the most exciting theatrical offerings she had ever seen. "It sure was magnificent," she said. One improvisation she remembered as "hilarious" was about two starving poets trying to sell poems to Mike Nichols, who played the editor of a magazine called *Doom*, which bought poetry "by the yard." Of Nichols and May, Page observed, "They clanked together with great efficiency. Like a juggernaut, you know. They were terribly professional. They'd take over when they got onstage."

Several Compass players have transformed Page's position in the balcony to one on the stage, where, they swear, they saw her join in and improvise. "Never, never, never," Page insisted. "I don't even recall them nudging me to do it. Of course, I would have been too scared." Once, however, after a lecture Severn was giving on Gothic art, she admitted, "He was taking questions from the audience, so I raised my hand and said, 'Professor, you've told us about Gothic art, can you tell us anything about Visigothic art?' And without batting an eye, he started this long thing where he took different strains of art history and interwove them together so that they canceled each other out. Then he said, 'And that's Visigothic art.'

"I know the answer was on the spur of the moment," said Page, "because I made up the question, and I know nobody knew I was going to ask it. I asked one question. And that's the only thing I can remember contributing in any way. But there's no use stemming the tide of what people like to think. When we were doing *Clothes for a Summer Hotel*, José Quintero kept telling the press, 'It's so wonderful for Tennessee, Geraldine, and me to be working together again.' " Quintero had directed Page and himself to sudden fame in Williams's *Summer and Smoke* at an obscure little Greenwich Village theatre, the Circle in the Square. "Well, Tennessee didn't work with us at all on that. He never heard of us. It wasn't till we got good reviews that he came downtown." Page kept trying to correct the press. "But they didn't like the real story. They liked the romantic version."

In the unromantic version of the Compass story, Geraldine Page did not get up on stage. And Paul Sills did not return to save the day. As before, his tenure was not meant to be long-lived. For a director whose great strength was in "throwing out all assumptions and starting from scratch," it was not the best use of his talent to corral back into a Platonic ensemble of amateurs a company whose muscle now resided in professional and Aristotelian soloists. Thus, Sills says he soon gave up trying to help Shepherd realize "David's dream of the 'long form,' as he calls it."

Sills's own powerful scenario, *The Game of Hurt*, would survive, but only in a macerated version, played in one scene. Andy Duncan recalls the abbreviated *Game* as a verbal insult contest in which the players scored by saying "something sociable that was actually insulting, like 'How nice. You bathed today,' or 'Secretly, you enjoy television.' Mike used to play *Hurt* very well. He was excellent at it. He was developing an approach that was anti-Viola. (He always rebelled against the Viola stuff.) In Viola's thing, you stay within the reality of the character. Mike would always step outside it. He was always for the wisecrack, the brilliant remark."

At first, Sills had suggested bolstering the company's social point of view by inserting real newspaper clippings, jokes, quotes, and moral precepts into the scenarios. When the company showed no particular social point of view to be bolstered, and no enthusiasm for scenarios, he recommended setting up an alternative group on the South Side, where highly prepared and polished scenario work could be performed for a more sympathetic audience. For Sills, it was obviously too late to implement theatrical ideas in the spirit of the original Compass at the Argo Off-Beat Room. The only choice seemed to make the existing company more commercial. He told Shepherd to make some changes in the cast. And then, as Sills puts it, "I think I disappeared."

"After that trip to Madison, well, it was obvious" to Andy Duncan. "The handwriting was on the wall." Now, his worst suspicions were confirmed. "I was out. They fired me."

The uselessness of professional actors had always been David Shepherd's theme. "There's something about the psyche of the actor," says Duncan, "that David just can't stand. He feels they're selfish, privileged, you know. He ignores the fact that actors don't work, they suffer when they're not wanted; they're the pariahs of our culture."

In fact, in the weeks before Duncan was dismissed, he recalls that "Mike in his paranoia thought it would be him. David was taking him aside every night. As Michael put it, 'David is very disappointed in my work.' Mike was sort of a sit-down comedian. And David didn't want wisecracking. He wanted the Viola stuff, the 'Where.' "

But Nichols's fears were real, not paranoid. The week before Sills returned, Shepherd had seriously considered firing him. Sills backed his old friend Nichols all the way. Indeed, Nichols claims that Sills's encouragement made it possible for him to continue at the Compass. Under Shepherd, his confidence had been greatly undermined. As Nichols recalls it, "I kept saying, 'I want to go home. I'm terrible.' " And Sills would say, "Stay. It's all right. You'll be fine."

"It was ironic that he fired me," says Duncan. "You know, I was a carpenter, an electrician. I could do sets and lights. I was a laborer. I had come out of a factory background. I was everything he purported to be in favor of, in Marxist-Brechtian terms. And my work was good there. At first, I wasn't unhappy about leaving. I was a little depressed. But I didn't want to go through that shit with Sills again."

Of Andrew Duncan, Mark Gordon observes, "He had been a forest ranger, had worked on a boat. He could do practical things with his hands. It was the same kind of thing with his work. He was always there and able to do things. He was always there for the scene." Onstage with Duncan, Bobbi Gordon says, "I always felt very safe. I knew in the middle of a scene he wasn't going to turn around and say, 'Oh, by the way, do you realize that the porthole just broke and this ship is flooding?' when you've been doing the scene as if you were in a living room. The others did this kind of thing constantly—pulling these things out from left field."

Denying the invisible reality through words, however amusing, is known to improvisers as a "negation," a no-no, a scene-killer, an act of desperation. "We all knew that kind of thing was wrong," Mark Gordon says, "but some of us did it anyway."

The only act of scene-stopping either of the Gordons can remember Duncan ever committing was delivering the line about using an egg poacher to store a diaphragm.

The comic plays off the reality created by the straight man, points out Roger Bowen, an excellent straight man. "The more reality the straight man creates, the bigger the balloon gets blown up so the greater the pop when the comic sticks the pin into it." "Straight men have to know what you're going to say, more or less," says Severn Darden. "They have to psych you out. They have to know where the joke is. Andrew Duncan, among other things, I think, was the best straight man ever, which is extremely difficult improvising." Onstage with Duncan, "He would make you look very good, like you were making all the jokes."

After Duncan was fired, Mark and Bobbi Gordon soon gave notice. "We thought if Andy could be let go, then we knew where Compass was headed," says Mark. "Andy wasn't one of the funnymen. He held everybody together. He was our glue."

"With the scenario gone," remembers Bobbi, "I felt my usefulness in the company was so limited that I wanted out."

Shepherd, with his ear to Sills (who thought the Gordons "unimaginative"), did nothing to stop the domino effect of these two company members who lent the scenario play so much support, a sacrifice play he would later describe as a "goof."

By October, a year after joining Compass, around the time of their first wedding anniversary, the Gordons would be gone.

It was surely one of the outstanding features of commedia dell'arte that the company of actors was more important than the play. This x factor, the chemistry of the ensemble, would remain of uppermost importance in the American transplant. At the Argo Off-Beat Room, "They had a great company and they destroyed it," Andrew Duncan submits.

Larry Arrick was flown to Chicago to see what might await him at the Compass should he agree to direct it. "The first time I ever saw it," Arrick noticed that "Geraldine Page was in it. Yes, she was. She was in it. She *was* pretty nervous," and that there were others, "these strange-looking people on the stage doing things I could not believe they were doing. The company consisted of the Gordons, Shelley, Severn, and Nichols and May. It was a fantastic evening, but I had no idea how they did any of it." Arrick explained to Shepherd that he wanted the job, but he was married, his wife, Rose, was pregnant, and he could not leave her in New York. "Oh, fine," Shepherd answered. "Bobbi Gordon is leaving. Rose can be in the company too." Beyond the impressions of the Compass Arrick gathered from his several nights in the audience, "I knew nothing else about it," except that "Rose and I would be getting sixty-five dollars a week."

Arrick returned with Rose a few weeks later and Sills was gone. Mark and Bobbi had returned to New York, and Barbara Harris had been added to the cast. Having her rejoin the company had been Sills's idea. "I didn't take the job because I wanted it," she says. "They were paying seventy-five dollars a week. Paul said, 'God, take it.' I watched it for about a month, met Severn, and went in it. I wasn't prepared. Shelley and Mike and Elaine? I mean, come *on*. I was like a fish out of water." Easing back into Chicago life after her year in England, she was "feeling very quiet and private and not in a performing mood. I wasn't highly ambitious then. I didn't have the need to be there, except via Paul. Mike and Elaine and Shelley were very *evolved*. I mean, they were an *act* by that time. And nobody was talking to each other. And nobody could goof off. They were, you know, *artistes*. They had no use for me at all. I was on lights mostly. They'd throw me in, and I'd get stuck out there."

Thus, Bobbi Gordon encountered "this beautiful quiet little dandelion puff child who didn't open her mouth" when Barbara first reappeared.

For the Arricks' arrival, Shepherd had secured an "incredible" apartment for them, which "we had to leave immediately," Larry Arrick says, forgetting why. But Rose Arrick remembers that the apartment was across from an old folks' home and that "the sounds there were not to be believed. We could hear people dying all night." "David always wanted everyone else to participate in his rejection of comfort and wealth," Larry remarks.

Elaine recommended an apartment to the Arricks in her walkup building, several landings higher than her own. Carrying up the groceries, or the coal that Arrick nightly shoveled into the coal stove, the Arricks would often stop off at Elaine's to catch their breath, noting that between performances she wrote voluminously, on a typewriter, in bed.

Shepherd, meanwhile, spent one day a week at the Compass. He was teaching a playwriting course three days a week at the Studebaker Theatre and, with his own writing endeavors, experiencing some blocks. Lack of concentration, interruptions, and insufficient gusto for the job plagued him as he nevertheless entered all writing stretches in his diary ("Wrote from 1:30–5:30. Made all mistakes") and continued thus to ride himself. One week each month he spent in New York, where he now saw a chance to open a branch of Compass International, this one in partnership with Theodore J. ("Ted") Flicker, an old friend of Severn's from Bard. The same week Severn auditioned for Shepherd, he had introduced them, observing their bond.

Flicker, surely, had been as much as Shepherd a maverick in his own social setting. He hailed from Freehold, a small farm town in New Jersey, a state that featured a tenure system in its public schools. As a high school sophomore, Flicker was elected to the state student council. At his inaugural meeting, Councilman Flicker rose to suggest that the tenure system be thrown out and teachers be made to return to training school every two years. To back up the demand, he proposed a statewide student strike.

Soon after this meeting, Flicker's high school principal called his father and said, "I think it would be a good idea if Teddy went to private school."

Flicker's parents had in mind a good Ivy League prep school, where, he imagined, "I would wear tweed coats with patches on the elbows. All I could think of was how nice it would be to wear a uniform." When their son chose the Admiral Farragut Academy at Pine Beach ("because I loved boats and the lure of fascism"), his parents were appalled. ("What Jewish kid goes to military school?")

Cadet Flicker spent "two years of blind terror" performing his military duties, until one day, while he was out sailing, the recall flag went up on his boat. "Cadet Flicker," the cadet officer said at the shore, "get into dress blues and report to Captain Dodge." Flicker put on dress blues, slipped on white gloves, strapped on his saber, and snapped his commander a smart salute. Captain Dodge, the headmaster, smoked a pipe and was missing an arm. He said to young Flicker, "I've been thinking about you. There's a little college in upstate New York. The people up there wear sandals. I think you belong there." And he handed Flicker the entrance form to Bard.

"I guess they accepted me because I was so weird," muses Flicker. He had shown up for his college interview in his cadet uniform.

At Bard, besides Severn Darden, Flicker discovered art and his desire to act. After two years, he took off for London and a Victorian theatre education at the Royal Academy of Dramatic Art. His horizons quickly expanded. "As soon as I heard about Henry Irving, I wanted to be an actor-manager."

The rigorous discipline of RADA and his military lessons now hugged Flicker's Bard education like a pair of parentheses. He returned from London to discover "with horror that the Broadway theatre I had been trained for had ceased to exist. It wasn't the temple I had planned to serve. It was in the hands of the charlatans."

Like Shepherd, Ted Flicker at twenty-five already had a long-standing ambition to produce a popular theatre. Flicker's initial concept for bringing theatre to the masses was "a really elegant, comfortable theatre that would fold up into six trucks and move from town to town." He had shelved the Rolling Theatre upon finding that it would cost a million and a half dollars to build. "And even then the engineers couldn't guarantee that the wind wouldn't knock it down." (For The Rolling Stage, the bus and truck show David Shepherd produced following his return from India, Shepherd found a truck for $765, only $15 over his estimated budget.) Flicker's new dream was of a New York company that would sell tickets to repertory plays at minimal cost ($2.50 for orchestra seats and 50¢ for the balcony). While Severn kept him apprised of the action in Chicago, Flicker found a grind movie theatre on Third Avenue and Thirtieth Street, occupying New York's oldest legit house. Flicker had raised $38,000 in promises to buy it but needed salary concessions from Actors' Equity and the craft unions, which the latter refused to give. Flicker now had thirty-eight grand in promises and a bank of information from Severn and Shepherd on the progress of the Compass and improvisation, which to Flicker sounded great. "The more I thought about improvisational theatre, the more I thought this was the route to go. So I called Shepherd," Flicker says, "and made a proposition. I said, 'Look, I've got this money. Maybe we can use it to start an improvisational theatre in New York." He had been able to persuade his backers to divert their money into this new project, "so I was going to bring the Compass to New York."

It was a relief to Shepherd to have in Flicker such an energetic, smart, and solvent business partner. He got busy preparing lists of all the Compass material that might, with sufficient organization and revision, hold up in New York. He made plans to write a definition of a Compass scenario, a statement of intention, and a two-page report on the lessons as Compass playwrights he and Elaine had learned. For this future Compass, he envisioned no more than six people (two of them women) in the cast.

Despite what seems to have been considerable, if not incontrovertible, evidence to the contrary, Shepherd continued to believe that "in order for Compass to assert itself in American theatre, about one hundred sixty-minute plays need to be written for it. I want to write the first ten." Of all the "chess moves" he saw open to him, he gave this one, writing ten plays, top priority.

With Shepherd so occupied, as Andy Duncan heard with pleasure over lunch with Burr McCloskey, the Compass in Chicago was rapidly "going downhill."

On leave from the army, Roger Bowen returned to the Compass as the cold weather crept into Chicago in the fall of 1956. From the audience of the Argo Off-Beat Room, he saw a very small cast ("All I remember is Mike and Shelley and Elaine. I think there were a couple of others, but they were kind of pushed into the background") perform an evening of sketches in the format of a nightclub revue. "It was a hodgepodge, really," says Bowen. "I think Paul was back then. Nevertheless, it didn't have the kind of good structure he usually gives a show. I seem to remember Shelley doing a monologue and some of the older scenes." An entrapment scene that was new to him featured Shelley and Mike and Elaine. In it, Elaine is the young woman sitting at an invisible bar. The two men enter and "come on very strong. She's modestly resisting them and trying to turn them away." The men persist. Finally, the young woman succumbs to their invitation to accompany them for a drink, whereupon the men pull out their handcuffs, revealing themselves as cops. They accuse the woman of soliciting.

Bowen had no sense of disappointment with the show. "I thought it was very funny. What I saw I liked. I laughed and enjoyed it. I wasn't carrying the flag for scenario plays. My feeling had always been to put on whatever was good, whatever was fun, whether it was written or improvised, whether it was sketches or scenario plays. At the time, I thought it was an entertaining show, and there were some relevant things in it, so I was satisfied. But later, I felt unhappy that the experiment had failed."

17

Another Enterprise

The new director of the Compass at the Argo Off-Beat Room, Larry Arrick, gamely took on the never resolved task of accommodating the actors, the club owner, and the audience by sharpening the show while simultaneously trying to satisfy the greater goal of the producer to "move toward longer pieces. It was always an ambition of David's to move toward scenarios and away from the scenes."

Without any prior vision of Compass, no disappointment over what it might have been or illusions of what it might become, Arrick was not burdened by the same pressures that seem to have stymied the improvisational impulses of Shepherd and Sills. Arrick did not resist the wind.

Ironically, even as it was losing money, Compass was acquiring elements of chic. Among the audience were seen such Chicago luminaries as the novelist Nelson Algren, the radio personality Studs Terkel, and the young comedian who was making such a splash at Mr. Kelly's, Mort Sahl. In the business of standup comedy, Sahl had already been famous for several years as a pioneer. Sauntering onstage in a sweater, carrying only a newspaper (to which all his material would refer), he had single-handedly brought his profession into the modern age simply by speaking his own impudently liberal thoughts to the audience, in real conversational time, about a forbidden subject: politics. Sahl was much more than a novelty: he was an alternative press. His remarks were followed closely by the brighter politicians. The former governor of Illinois, for example, Adlai E. Stevenson himself, came in often to Mr. Kelly's and became Sahl's friend and fan.

Sahl had made his mark among the students and intellectuals of San Francisco's North Beach, but, like the Compass, he had gained, and would flirt for, a wider appeal. While the Compass was spinning wildly from its own lack of direction, David Shepherd observed that Sahl was "doing fine, holding court for a couple of hundred businessmen who loved to be mocked." Like any satirist, Sahl's success in show business depended on the good will of a paying audience of people he made fun of: the rich, the powerful, the educated—not the working class.

Another celebrity visitor (a sandwich had been named for her at a North Side delicatessen) was Pat Scot, Mike Nichols's fiancée, who is remembered as a "generous," "warm," "tremendously nice" woman, who would come into the Compass after her own better-attended singing engagements to catch the late-night sets.

The rest of the audience, "what there was of it," Larry Arrick observes, had "graduated from tweed jackets with patches on the elbows to Brooks Brothers and Guccis and Puccis." Whatever David Shepherd's aspirations, Compass was becoming a theatre "for the rich kids in Evanston to drive down in their Mustangs to Chicago on Friday or Saturday night to hear dirty words."

Arriving at rehearsals in a still smoke-scented room, Rose Arrick remembers "trying to get lost backstage, hoping no one would ask me to do a scene," and watching the others go through their preshow rituals. Shelley Berman would be "sort of grumpy," while Severn would "walk fast in a circle with his arms stretched out, chewing his handkerchief, trying to levitate," often while carrying on conversations with Elaine in the adorable voices of the Smalls, a dear sweet couple that they played onstage who were crazy about each other. Barbara Harris, with her "beautiful legs, tiny nose, doe eyes, little pursed mouth," reminded Arrick of "a bisque doll." And Mike Nichols "would come in late with a carton of orange juice, his loafers flapping." (While living with Pat Scot in her fancier apartment, Nichols would sometimes spend his whole week's salary on pâté and caviar and invite the company to eat it there.)

Even Elaine spruced up for the gig, setting her hair with the aid of a cigar box full of hair rollers and a jar of Jo-Cur, a bright green hair-setting goo. Taking account of this new vanity, there was still more "elbowing for the mirror," Rose Arrick noticed, among the men.

Like the other actresses who entered into Compass, Arrick accepted her impossible mission with professional grit, as "taking your life in your hands." Onstage with Elaine, however, "I always felt safe. I can't say how much she helped me." She remembers a scene in which they played two

Jewish sisters who shared an apartment where they were visited by their nephew (Berman). "Everybody loved the laughs except Elaine. She was a delight to act with. I don't think she ever knew it, but she was *the* presence, a powerhouse there."

In the nightclub environment, even Barbara Harris found it "scary to be in front of the audience" and "scary to improvise." Like Mark and Bobbi Gordon, she had preferred the scenarios because "I had a form I could work in. I didn't have the background Mike and Elaine did for the improvisations. I remember the feeling of their heftiness. I mean, they were thinking *all* the time. And I wasn't. I think Elaine was much more definite and purposeful than I was. She was much more independent. And much more assertive. I felt I was just the boss's wife really. I kept wondering why I couldn't stay home and bake cookies."

"Barbara Harris was brilliant, *brilliant*," Shelley Berman shouts. "Ask her about the Menotti opera. Oh, my god, she was fantastic. We sang duets." Berman remembers her playing a waitress in a scene with Mike Nichols and Severn, in which Severn kept asking her for more and more sugar, which he stirred into his invisible tea. When he had stirred in a tremendous amount of sugar, he asked her for a lemon. "A whole one?" she asked. "Honey," Berman says, "Barbara Harris was great."

"Barbara could sit on a couch and imitate every actress in the world," says David Shepherd. "Boss's wife?"

"I'm sure she thought that if she said so," says Larry Arrick. "But I never saw her that way at all. I saw her as very much trying to make a contribution, and very much a part of it. In fact, she was making more of a contribution than Paul."

Arrick himself had very little contact with Sills. When Sills not infrequently dropped in to see the show, "he seemed uneasy" to Arrick, "as if he had outgrown this."

Without access either to Sills's greater knowledge of improvisation, or reference to Viola's work, Arrick nevertheless managed to contribute to the improvisational process some important techniques of his own for including the audience, developing new material, and getting away from jokes.

Arrick was the first to confront a paradoxical problem: "The company had gotten so good that the audience didn't believe they were improvising." Mike and Elaine displayed such virtuosity that Arrick himself was often nonplused. He observed they were especially wonderful at parodies. After a particularly good improvised parody, he said to Elaine, "That's the best essence of Faulkner I've ever seen. How did you do that?" "I don't know. I've never read Faulkner," she replied. From his own reactions, Arrick realized that "I've got to think of some way to start the show which tells them right from the top that we really do make it up." He realized that the excitement of improvisational theatre depends on the audience's belief that the players may fail.

Arrick invented a game that involved the audience and produced unguarded moments in the players infallibly, right from the start of the show. Story-Story was to become a performance staple of improvisational theatre, an invaluable group formation device, and a classic theater game.

As Arrick first devised it, a story title would be solicited from the audience. Arrick then would point to one company member to begin a narration, and "off we went." Intermittently, at crucial points in the storytelling, Arrick would interrupt the speaker and point to another player, who was obliged to pick up the story, without pause, where the previous player left off. As the story concluded, Arrick would call out, "And the moral of the story is . . ." and point to one of the players for a summary.

Sills and Spolin were later to devise variations on Story-Story, as did "eighty-two other people," Arrick says. (It even provided the basis for *You Don't Say*, a TV game show.) In one variation, the narrative passes from player to player as the group tosses an invisible ball. Some players begin to tell a collective story by each contributing only one word, progressing to sentences, interrupted sentences, interrupted syllables, and so forth. Played skillfully, such variations always produce amusing results, even if the story itself does not.

"At the time," says Arrick, "I was less interested in virtuosity than in storytelling." As he perceived it, "We were all going to share these stories and there would be something Jungian in the way we revealed our collective unconscious. It was a more innocent time."

The pressure on the company to excel in the opening piece actually made Story-Story at the Argo Off-Beat Room less than the Garden of Eden–like pastime Arrick describes. By November 1956, virtuosity had become the improvisational theatre's middle name. According to Mike Nichols, it was through this game that after weeks of silence Barbara Harris finally broke through her fear and, warming everyone's heart, opened her mouth for the first time. As she recalls it, "Larry hurt my feelings *so* bad because he wouldn't point to me. Or he'd point to me and grimace when I spoke. He'd say, 'And the moral of the story is . . .' and I'd raise my hand, and he'd point to me and I'd say, 'Uhhh,' and he'd say, 'Waghh!'

And everybody would say, 'Waghh!' I finally came up with the one Mike thought was so funny: 'The moral of the story is: Love is the key that opens every door.' I don't know what was so funny about that."

Arrick also introduced what he describes as "pretentious literary things," devoting half an evening, for example, to an improvised dramatization of *Before the Law*, the parable in Kafka's *The Trial*. He suggested expanding the teaching scene into the teaching scenario, instituting long how-to pieces like *How to Break an Engagement, How to Escape the Draft*, and *How to Exist in a Complicated World*. "They were extremely sophisticated and cynical, kind of New Yorky," David Shepherd recalls. "They turned on the folks from the North Side."

During his first visit to Chicago, Arrick had noticed that Compass had been problematical for the Gordons, as they struggled to do "the right Stanislavskian thing. Surrounded by all these fancy talkers, it was like they were doing *Bury the Dead*. They worked in a totally different style." Nevertheless, they were deeply engaged in learning the harmonies of ensemble performance. Arrick also read strength in the fact that "the Gordons hadn't been glib."

Arrick now brought into the company an actor-director named Walter Beakel, whom he had known in New York at the Herbert Berghof Studio. Shelley Berman had also previously worked with Beakel, first as a fellow student at the Goodman Theatre, and later, when Beakel directed Berman and Geraldine Page in a reading of *Hedda Gabler* in New York at The New School.

Beakel was far from what Andy Duncan would describe as "an authentic improviser." As Beakel himself explains it, "I never ever felt a real part of it. My master's thesis was in Greek drama. Improvisation was not my cup of tea. I could do it, but I used it to further my understanding of the written drama. Getting up and doing the gags and the ha-ha was not my first choice in life. I hated nightclubs. But I was out of work, and I needed a job."

Nevertheless, by adding Beakel to the cast, Arrick hoped to replace the unfrivolous quality he thought had been missing in Compass acting since the Gordons left. "I thought he'd be good in his mumbling, stumbling way. He wasn't glib."

David Shepherd was still not happy with the results. "Failed to provide Larry with material," he told his diary. "Larry failed to reform company (which addicted to yocks) and to get material from sources other than myself."

"David was always disappointed when things were successful, as well as devastated when they were unsuccessful," says Arrick. "It was reflexive. It was very hard for him. I felt he was getting almost no satisfaction from our successes. He was desperately unhappy. The company's attitude toward him ranged from patronizing to rude. They were asking him to be what he wasn't meant to be—a businessman."

"I don't know how to take a ten-dollar bill and put it into the theatre and pull out a twenty-dollar bill," Shepherd says. "I can take a ten-dollar bill and put it into the theatre and pull out a five-dollar bill. I never had any commercial sense. Mike Nichols has a commercial sense."

Nichols had begun pressuring Shepherd to disband the company of seven and reconstitute it with "just him and Elaine and Barbara and Shelley or Severn," a tighter company. "He wanted a company of soloists and stars who could come up with their own revue material. He wanted hip people who were verbal and who could figure out the point of a scene. And he wanted to cut down the size of the company so that he himself could make more money." Shepherd resisted. A larger cast than four or five, he maintained, was needed for the execution of a scenario play.

Nichols, of course, had never put stock in scenario plays. For one thing, he was a sit-down comedian, not a sit-down writer, and thus could not enjoy re-creating the form the way the founding Compass Players had, as an exercise in semiclassical commedia dell'arte, a vehicle for thoughtful and poetic social-political comedy. For another, he was not a physical or moving actor the way the others were, and he preferred the surer sailing of his work with Elaine, in which he could spotlight his great gift for repartee. Nor, as promoted by David Shepherd, did the scenario seem in any other way a form to suit his personality. To Larry Arrick, it was plain that "Mike hated the whole idea of the scenarios. He hated the politics of them, which he didn't really believe in. Mike's politics were the politics of J. D. Salinger. He found the form constricting, pretentious, and boring. He would rather do style. He would rather do how hard it is to get a ticket at the airline. He would rather do that New Yorkeresque thing that Michael did so well. And David was always ready to fight the revolution."

To Shepherd, Nichols seemed to be insisting that "this is an intellectual theatre, and it doesn't have to do with behavior, or stories, or sentiment. It has to do with a panoply of finely sharpened barbs. You present these barbs to the audience. And you pop balloons as big as you can."

It was not as great or as deep a conception of a modern commedia dell'arte as Shepherd had in mind. It had nothing to do with bringing theatre to the masses and mirroring their lives. But for Mike Nichols, time was wasting. For Actors' Equity minimum, why should he indulge David Shepherd's impossible dream? He was performing brilliant short, smart pieces with Elaine, as Sills says, at the peak of his performance. When would he ever have this chance again? His vision of the Compass, unlike Shepherd's, was not in the slightest clouded by ambivalence. "He was saying, 'You have to do it my way. You have to do it the Mike Nichols way.' "

As the audiences at the Argo Off-Beat Room seemed to prove, the theatregoing middle class loved to be satirized, to see the popping of balloons filled with their own hot air. Clearly, the Mike Nichols way was on the money, the smoother way to go.

"He was right about several things, you know," David Shepherd reflects. "After all, he did become a director and a producer making millions of dollars. But he wasn't interested in producing popular theatre. He was interested in producing *Annie.*"

"Mike was always very trendy," an old friend says.

Onstage, in the "Mountain Climbing" sketch, the lead climber, Sir Edmund, bound for the peaks, cuts off the support rope to the bottom man, Wilson, who has damaged the equipment, threatened group safety, and whose personal needs prevail. In life, the incessant glare of Mike Nichols's headlights on success proved so distracting to the head man, Shepherd, that he was actually ready to cut Nichols himself off the invisible rope. "He refused to go along with a scenario Elaine was working on," Shepherd recalls. "That's why I fired him."

Larry Arrick remembers the scenario-in-progress as *The String Quartet,* in which a revolution is occurring outside a hotel room while, inside, a string quartet plays on. (The string quartet was an old Compass bit, the one Mark Gordon was so distressed to see onstage at Fifty-fifth Street on his arrival night.) Arrick himself was no great fan of scenario plays but remembers liking this one a lot. The theme of shutting the world out reminded Arrick all at once of Ionesco's plays, Herman Melville's story *Bartleby the Scrivener,* and Ivan Goncharov's novel *Oblomov.*

"It was longer than most of Elaine's scenarios," Shepherd recalls, "and it was not completely finished. It needed to be developed as we rehearsed it." When the assaulted playwright sought action against the renegade actor Mike Nichols, Shepherd stepped in to protect Elaine. "I said, 'Well, you're disrupting rehearsals and whatnot. Why don't you quit?' And he and Elaine stayed up all night arguing, and he came back chastened the next day."

Shepherd and Nichols would continue to coexist thereafter in a less affable state of ideological stalemate.

Of course, in the improvisational theatre, as in the greater culture, ideology is determined by economics, not the other way around.

David Shepherd concedes that in 1956 he and Mike Nichols had very different financial balance sheets. As Shepherd puts it, "I was not forced to do schlock in order to get a hundred people to come in on a Friday night." Indeed, he was now pouring his own money into the show without a profit in sight, but unlike the actors (who were investing other assets), if and when Compass closed in Chicago, he would not be destitute.

Andy Duncan has remarked that "Compass was a classic case of any group where power is the problem and who has the power." The actors had the power of creating material, holding the audience, and the power to quit. The producer (or his surrogate) had the power to hire and fire. The producer's other power was that of ownership.

The fact that Compass never made a profit in Chicago, was, in reality, a losing proposition, while Mike Nichols and other Compass Players eventually got rich, has persuaded David Shepherd that their powers were always equally matched.

But were they? According to the contract Shepherd's New York lawyers devised, in exchange for paying their salaries as actors, The Compass Play Corporation owned all the material the players created on its stage. "The principle," says Duncan, "was the General Motors thing: if you develop a generator under contract to them, they own it." To Shepherd, who was losing money on a supply of material of dubious or ephemeral worth, hiring improvisers the way that General Motors did seemed fair. Under these terms, actors who were no longer part of Compass would have no rights to material they had created there except by paying royalties to lease it back. The other way, not contemplated by Shepherd (although he had used it himself in presenting *The Caucasian Chalk Circle* at the Playwrights Theatre Club) was the Brechtian way: steal it.

As any playwright, screenwriter, or television scribe knows, written material is collateral. To them, the Compass royalty arrangement would seem unthinkable. Actors, who only have their flesh to sell, take work when and where they get it. In 1956, there was no other "where" to improvise. How else but as a Compass Player could an improviser display this uncategorizable skill that was "so much fun we'd do it for nothing," as Duncan says. "And they took advantage of that."

The nonrecognition of the players as profit-sharing partners in the company they created, which was built into the Compass contract, established a reverse precedent that would subtly infantilize the players of the commedia dell'arte's modern American counterpart and neutralize their powers. A paternalistic producer of an improvisational theatre, like Bernie Sahlins was soon to become, could (and did) assure his actors that even though he owned their material, they would come away from a stint in the company they created, The Second City, with "a good credit," a special entrée to auditions. Recalling this notion, Andy Duncan observes, "That's like knowing how to pick cotton so well you can get into the best plantation." From Duncan's point of view, "The producers had the copyrights to the name and whatever accrues. When the actors were fired, we had nothing." Without the matrix of a company or a body of material, instead of a "cultural gangster," an unemployed improviser was a stray cat, as vulnerable as any hungry actor to the vagaries of ordinary show business.

Shepherd, meanwhile, was preparing a repertoire for the projected New York Compass of scenarios and scenes created by a group of individuals who had no contract and no promise that they would be chosen to participate in it. Nevertheless, as Shepherd sees it, by "using Compass as a training ground to perfect an act he had in mind that would be very commercial," Mike Nichols was violating a trust.

Clearly, Shepherd and Nichols had very different visions of the way to appropriate the bounty of improvisation—neither one unselfish, neither unambitious, and therefore, by Violan standards, neither of them pure. But there is no hard evidence to suggest that Nichols yet "had in mind" the canny strategy Shepherd implies. In December 1956, when the Compass was close to collapse in Chicago, Shepherd was an absentee landlord, making plans with Ted Flicker for Compass International's debut in New York, which he had not cast. And Mike Nichols was not aware that he was accepting a salary from Shepherd's proletarian theatre to accumulate material (on which he and his partner would pay no royalties) for a fabulously successful comedy act.

With his future so uncertain at the Compass, Nichols discovered a little bar on the North Side that was hiring entertainers on the Compass's off nights. He and Elaine could as easily play their duet material there. "They invited me to work with them," says Shelley Berman. "We were forming a trio and I was thrilled."

Thus inspired, Berman suggested several scenes that he had previously improvised with Elaine. One was "The Driving Lesson," in which he taught Elaine how to drive. The other was "The Lost Dime," in which Elaine played a telephone operator and Berman a desperate caller, stranded in a phone booth miles from nowhere with a stalled car, who has dialed a wrong number and is trying to retrieve—in coin, not the usual postage stamps—his last, his only, dime. As their improvisation explored the helplessness of man against bureaucracy, Berman recalls, "I plead with her. I have to spell things out for her. I'm going crazy. And she won't give me back my dime."

Berman's part of the act now consisted of these two pieces and the "Selling Yourself to Yourself" routine. Mike and Elaine had accumulated an extensive repertoire together, and Berman had "three things that I'm doing, but I want to do more. I wanted to work with Mike, but we always fought. (Mike and Elaine fought too. But Mike didn't like working with me.) I said, 'Can't we do something together, the three of us? Can't I do something with you, Mike?' " Nichols ignored him. Even as they continued to meet for rehearsals, Berman began to sense that something was amiss. He would bring in lists of names for the act—"*lists* of names"— and one by one Nichols would discard them by simply saying, "No."

"Finally, I said, 'There's something wrong here. Why can't we work on more things together? After all, we're a trio.'

" 'What trio?' Nichols said.

"It ended right there. I was dismissed. The trio stopped being. I was devastated. I was so hurt. All I could say was 'Oh.' We used to rehearse at a friend's place. I was blinded when I left there. I couldn't even see my way." And Elaine? "She didn't say anything. She just sat there. She didn't say a word."

Yet Elaine had some ideas of her own for naming the trio that conveyed her perception of this chapter in her career. Larry Arrick remembers her trying out on him "Two Wigs and a Wag." Severn remembers hearing her call it "Two Cocksuckers and Elaine."

She was, after all, not entirely a stranger to playing a gangster's moll. She was no neurasthenic aristocrat like Miss Julie. She was a survivor. And like most women at war with their mothers, she was not averse— despite the price—to accepting the protection of men.

So charged with negativity and ego, so devoid of the altruism of the early days, the atmosphere at the Compass had become unbearable for Barbara Harris. She had watched Shepherd fire Nichols. She had seen "Mike sitting in a state of catatonia, wondering why." She had witnessed the displays of ego, the power jockeying. She asked herself, "Is this my life?" And then, "I fired myself. I stopped. I quit." As for the work, Sills's most attentive student "didn't like it any more than David did."

It should be restated that the Violan ideal of improvisation is the state of not knowing. According to Barbara Harris, at the Argo Off-Beat Room, there was no longer an openness to the mysteries of the moment, the uncertainties of theatrical chance. "They seemed to know what they were doing. They just *knew* everything. If someone walked through an invisible wall, they'd say, 'You're walking through my Noguchi' and know they'd get a laugh. They made Bruno Bettelheim jokes. Laugh. 'Nietzsche.' Roar. Then they'd frame that stuff with something everyone could identify with: a make-out scene. It was a different kind of standup comic routine. You had to be real competitive. I mean, it wasn't an opera that came out of nowhere, from a bunch of people humming dum, dum, dum."

Larry Arrick's tenure "lasted a while," and then he gave notice too. Sills, supposedly, was coming back. "And Rose didn't like doing it at all. She began to feel the obligation to be funny as a heavy weight." Before leaving Compass in the directorial hands of Walter Beakel, Arrick cast as a replacement for the two exiting women an ingenue from Knoxville, Tennessee. Collin Wilcox had trained at the Goodman Theatre and had begun an affair with Beakel earlier that year, in Rhinelander, Wisconsin (working home of the Lunts), where they were both in summer stock.

"I was never one of your more brilliant improvisational artists," says Wilcox, with the faintest Southern drawl. "I can only imagine I got in because they didn't have anyone else, because I was the director's girlfriend, and because I was cute. I didn't have much else to recommend me." She was only twenty-two, "a classically trained baby" and "way out of my element." Watching Barbara Harris, whom she was soon to replace, Wilcox was "overwhelmed by her brilliance. She was exceedingly funny and out there."

Wilcox remembers the Argo Off-Beat Room as "a stinky, awful place" that reeked of old whiskey sours and featured a raccoon in the basement who ate the maraschino cherries. For an actress accustomed to the polite hush of anticipation customarily granted to performers by a theatre audience, the typical alcoholic distractions of a nightclub made it even more of "a horrible place to work." Even the Compass veterans had never really gotten used to an atmosphere where people routinely chatted through their performance and glasses clanked. Shelley Berman's response, Wilcox noticed, was to "get onstage and start to slam down these pretend windows because the waiters made so much noise." Wilcox also remembers that in the same spirit of trying to make himself heard, Severn once sang the chorus of "Goodnight, Irene" "at least seventy-five times."

Offstage, an air of impatience pervaded the company. "It was a time of transition," says Wilcox, "I think for everybody there. Everybody was doin' what they were doin', but everybody was goin' somewheres else. They were older than I was. I hadn't been through the scenes they had. I was a protected little Southern flower. To me it was a new color, but they'd been wearing black turtlenecks and black hose and black black black clothes for a long time."

Among the others, there was a growing sense that money was due. When the paychecks were late or not forthcoming, as was now the rule, Wilcox shared none of their financial stress. "I was getting auditions and modeling for pictures on the back of soap boxes. And I had parents who sent me some money. I was havin' a wonderful time."

Her future husband's task was more difficult. Besides acting himself, it had fallen to Beakel to piece together into an ensemble what had become a deeply divided cast. Beakel recalls the rift between Shelley Berman and Nichols and May becoming "more and more apparent as we went along. Mike and Elaine were a pair. They were more cerebral than Shelley. Mike didn't want to work with him. It got to the point where I was more a psychological traffic manager than a director. It was all about how to keep people from cutting each other's throat. Everybody wanted the first spot. 'Well, you gave it to Shelley.' Or 'You gave it to Mike and Elaine.' The ego! One time I appealed to Mike. I said, 'I'm not your father. Please, lay off me.'

"With Severn, it didn't make any difference," recalls Beakel. "Severn just floated. He never got into any personality conflicts. He would work with Shelley in a shot."

Occasionally still slipping in to join the cast was their producer, David Shepherd, usually to re-create the role of Sir Edmund in the "Mountain Climbing" sketch. Beakel admired the piece as skillful, and, like many others who saw him in it, found Shepherd's performance excellent. In return for the financial power he exercised over them, as well as their exasperation with his failings as a producer, the others appear to have become more and more unnurturing of Shepherd's creative capabilities. Yet Beakel sensed in Shepherd "an underlying desire to be an actor. But it frightened him. He didn't like the pressure or the heat. He wouldn't put himself on the line. It takes a certain amount of guts to be an actor. I don't think he had the guts."

Although Beakel discerned in Nichols and May "such a wonderful team . . . a marvelous pair," he was one of the few males in her purview not bowled over by Elaine: "Obviously, she was a very resourceful, creative, bright, inventive human being. As Bill Shakespeare said, 'the mirror up to nature.' Not that it's bad, but Elaine held the mirror up to Elaine."

As the chill of its final winter fell on the Chicago Compass, Elaine and her director maintained "a sort of distant respect, I guess, for each other," he recalls. "We learned how to stay out of each other's territory." Thus, Elaine did not submit her scenarios to Beakel, and Beakel's most important contribution to the Compass had nothing to do with Elaine.

As a "straight theatre" person, Walter Beakel was most interested in staging a long form. Searching through the Compass "library" ("a collection of ideas for improvs, these things that they'd throw at you"), he dug out a scenario called *The Liars*, based on a short story originally published in *Harper's* magazine as "The Boys," prepared for the Compass (months before it opened) by its author, the prematurely deceased Chicago writer and intellectual Isaac Rosenfeld. Shepherd had never tried to produce *The Liars* "for the same reason I didn't put on *Waiting for Godot*. I didn't like it," he says.

In the three years since Shepherd had passed on the opportunity to stage Beckett's play at the Playwrights Theatre Club, it had become an international sensation, receiving critically acclaimed productions in Zurich, Paris, and London and an English-language publication by Grove Press.

In *Waiting for Godot*, two tramps in bowler hats (Vladimir and Estragon) kill time with each other and three more characters (a landowner, Pozzo; his servant, Lucky; and Godot's messenger, a boy) while waiting on a desolate landscape (a bare tree on an empty country road) for a sixth character (Godot), who never appears. From this startling and contrary piece of dramaturgy the Theatre of the Absurd had been born. With a poetry as spare as its construction, *Waiting for Godot* featured riffs of vaudeville humor and long pauses in counterpoint. In these stipulated silences, Beckett dared to focus on the stillness of the moment. There he found that life was cruel and meaningless, salvation futile, all reasons for existence vain, faith unrewarded, and "nothing to be done." Jean Anouilh had called the Paris debut "as important as the premiere of Pirandello in 1923." Tennessee Williams called it "one of the greatest plays of our time."

A more entrepreneurial producer than Shepherd, Michael Meyerberg, had acquired the American rights. In the spring of 1956, the play Beckett called "a tragicomedy" opened on Broadway, following a disastrous trial run for the winter tourists in Miami Beach. On Broadway, the new director,

Herbert Berghof, drew a stunning performance from the great clown who played Estragon, Bert Lahr.

Being stuck in Chicago and missing *Godot* became Mike Nichols's frequent lament. Although all the intelligentsia flocked to see it, it played only fifty-nine times.

Other social critics of the left (including Norman Mailer, reviewing for *The Village Voice*) shared David Shepherd's aversion to the moral inertia of the Theatre of the Absurd. Over the theatrical consciousness of the decade, Samuel Beckett's vision, with its minimalism and mordant humor, would nevertheless prevail.

Within the year, Walter Beakel would be directing Mike Nichols in a Studebaker Theatre production of *Waiting for Godot*. Meanwhile, says Beakel, "When I saw *The Liars*, I said, 'Yeah, I'd like to do this.' " He reoutlined the scenario and "threw it out to the actors and said, 'Let's go at it.' I blocked it and did the whole megillah in one afternoon."

The four principal (male) characters in *The Liars*, Fox, Baer, Wolf, and Lieberman,* are a car pool of suburban high school teachers who travel in each other's company from Chicago to Gary, Indiana, and back each day.

Rosenfeld conceived Fox, Baer, and Wolf as old friends in their middle thirties, "somewhat pockmarked by . . . the various economic and social obligations that their position in life has imposed on them." Lieberman is the odd man out, a refugee with a thick accent, "quite unpleasant in manner . . . he asks for the treatment he gets."

Irritated by Lieberman's pushiness, and fed up with his company, the three friends each take a turn at putting Lieberman on, at first rather harmlessly (Fox convinces him that he was once a Trappist monk) but gradually becoming more aggressive (Wolf pretends to have a homosexual passion for Lieberman).

Fox and Wolf help prepare Baer's put-on with great secrecy, begging Lieberman to meet them at a seedy nightclub, where Baer will claim he needs the men to help him dispose of the body of a gangster, Six-Fingers Malone. Lieberman is scared but is shamed into the car. All but Lieberman know that the packages of "body parts" they are about to pick up are chicken gizzards. The packages are thrown at Lieberman's feet.

---

* There were five characters in Rosenfeld's story and his original scenario draft. Because there were only four men in the company, the version Beakel directed at the Compass omitted the fifth man, Katz.

Abruptly, at the lake, Fox cuts off the road. Baer instructs Lieberman to dump the parts in the lake while the others stand guard. Left alone, Lieberman disposes of five packages but is too frightened to touch the last—the "head." The others rush back, convulsed with laughter. They reveal the actual contents of the package to Lieberman, who tries to share in the joke. Instead of accepting a drink at Baer's house, however, he walks off, saying he will take the train. Realizing that they have gone too far, the three liars call after Lieberman.

In the school lunchroom the next day, Baer confesses that he has complicated his apology to Lieberman by claiming his wife has been institutionalized with a schizophrenic breakdown, moving Lieberman to such sympathy that he now asks for the hospital's visiting hours to go see her. Disgusted with himself for the mess he has made, Baer pleads with the others for help. Fox and Wolf burst out laughing.

The piece was performed without blackouts, the scenes broken only by the movement of the actors rearranging their chairs. Mike Nichols played Fox, Severn Darden was Baer, Walter Beakel was Wolf, Barbara Harris was a waitress, and Shelley Berman played Lieberman, the obnoxious refugee.

According to Beakel, the piece was "boffo" from the first night. "It worked like a charm. The four chairs, the setting up. It was just a dream. Then it became defined and refined. It became our second act. Whenever we didn't know what to do, we'd do *The Liars*. It was our pièce de résistance, always good for a Friday or Saturday night. The wit of the people and Shelley's personality made it work: his aggressiveness, his abrasiveness, his desire to belong." Like Geraldine Page, Beakel recognized in Berman a superb classical player, "a wonderful Iago, a truly wonderful actor," whose only flaw was a tendency, as Berman puts it, "to overdo." Directing him in *Hedda Gabler*, Beakel had found that "you almost had to go in there with a riding crop to keep him in line, or he'd go too far. He would get angry with me, but I think he always trusted me."

A director of a scripted play can guarantee an actor that he won't be allowed to look like a fool. Making lines up fresh every night, an improviser has no one to monitor him but himself. "One of our principles was that we were not to go for Semitic jokes. We were not to indulge in that particular area," says Beakel. Using a thick Yiddish accent, Berman nevertheless "played Lieberman like an Israeli you just can't deal with. He was sort of the goat. And we were unmerciful. He absolutely hated doing his part."

Berman took small comfort in the glowing notices he received for his tour de force, finding both in the play and in the excess of his performance a Jewish self-hatred of which time has not made him more proud. Even aside from its sensationalism and its anti-Semitic reverberations, it is easy to see why Shepherd disliked *The Liars*. It was as far from the early Compass scenarios as S. Ansky, the author of *The Dybbuk*, was from Brecht.

Like *The Dybbuk*, however, *The Liars* was a great success, so compelling, in fact, that it attracted an audience of 900 at the Studebaker Theatre, where it was booked by Bernie Sahlins to play for a night.

U nable to woo Elaine from Mike Nichols to help him execute the New Year's Eve audience's suggestion for "The Morning After the Night Before," Shelley Berman decided to try a new phone monologue. Through the haze of a terrible hangover, Berman's character hears from his host on the phone all the heinous acts he committed as a guest the previous night. The piece was a winner. The next night, Severn Darden would provide what became the most memorable line in the piece when he whispered to Berman on his way from the wings, "Throw the cat out the window, Shelley, not the lamp."

U pon entering into his partnership with David Shepherd to produce the New York Compass, Ted Flicker made plans to spend some time in Chicago at the Argo Off-Beat Room "to see what it was that they were doing and learn what it was all about." His partner was not around for Flicker's first few introductory weeks: "I don't know where he was, but he wasn't there." Settling in as an observer, Flicker discovered a group in terrible conflict in which his friend, "Poor Severn, always tried to make peace. He was distressed by all the Sturm und Drang. I mean, Walter was jealous and hated me, the invader from New York. Then Shelley was such a divisive force. He was angry, anxious, desperate. Elaine has an absolutely flawless bullshit detector when it comes to art. So she was always angry because nothing worked. And one of the reasons it didn't work was Shepherd. I think chaos was his idea of order. And Mike was interested in only one thing: getting ahead."

Two and a half years after it opened, Ted Flicker perceived the Compass as "just a mishmosh. Nothing was holding them together. There was no cohesiveness, no unified idea, except to improvise. And everybody had a different idea of what improvisation was."

As the new producer, Flicker also did not fail to notice that Compass was in deep financial trouble. The salaries of those actors who had agreed to Shepherd's request for salary postponements were cut from fifteen dollars a week to ten. "I also thought it was a lousy show," he says. "I mean, the only thing it had was a lot of brilliant people trying to figure out how to improvise in public. So sometimes it was staggeringly brilliant, and other times it was *painful* how boring it was." Flicker, of course, had never seen Compass in its early days on Fifty-fifth Street, "when it was supposed to have been so wonderful," but "They did a couple of scenarios while I was there. I thought they were appalling. I felt if you're gonna write, write, and if you're gonna improvise, improvise. I never understood this half improvising a story." It particularly bothered his sense of theatrical propriety that the actors wore street clothes and smoked onstage.

While the new producer watched the prototypical Compass and pondered the assets and liabilities that seemed to inhere in the improvisational theatre, an offer came from Fred Landesman in St. Louis to start a Compass in the Crystal Palace, a club he had started for the avant-garde crowd.

Nightlife was gaining an uncharacteristic intensity in St. Louis. Unfortunately for Landesman, the eye of the storm was heading (along with his star bartender) for Gaslight Square, a restored turn-of-the-century section of the city, previously known as Bed Bug Row. Thus, business had been falling off at his own establishment (once a gay bar called Dante's Inferno) on Olive Street.

Landesman had seen the Compass on what David Shepherd suspects was "one good weekend" at the Argo Off-Beat Room and on the strength of those performances was ready to propose a deal. There was room in the Crystal Palace budget—and on various floors of Landesman's own family mansion—for an improvisational acting company of four.

"I wasn't interested in St. Louis any more than David was," recalls Ted Flicker. "Because we had thirty grand, baby, and we were goin' to New York." With Shepherd's consent, Flicker promptly offered the St. Louis enterprise to Walter Beakel: "I said, 'You go to St. Louis and open a Compass. I'll open this one in New York, and we'll rotate companies. And Walter told me to go fuck myself. I wasn't losing *him* in St. Louis."

Upon reflection, it occurred to Flicker that *he* should take a new company to St. Louis and learn how to run an improvisational theatre there. After studying the Chicago Compass, Flicker had already come to the conclusion that he would run it very differently. "I thought I spotted why it wasn't working. The way improvisation works is that nobody can be a star. The reason it didn't work properly in Chicago was they never understood the basic concept of unselfishness."

Closing night of Compass at the Argo Off-Beat Room, a Sunday in mid-January, the temperature was 10° below. To Shelley Berman, it was "just another night. I think we were very busy forgetting it and moving on."

Missing that night was Elaine May. She had a new suitor, the film editor, Howard Alk. And, in Walter Beakel's opinion, with the ascendance and repetition of *The Liars*, she had become "really bored."

David Shepherd also wasn't there. Three days earlier, he seemed again to be "chasing tomorrow," writing Roger Bowen that he was happy it was shutting down, "Happy because for the first time I don't care. I am doing what I should do—compiling 13 programs out of the 18 months of performance."

The newcomer, Beakel, had the distance to observe that "it was a horrendously pressured situation to keep up the level of performance. It was too much: to be creative yourself, to deal with other people and all their personal problems, to deal with the audience, especially Saturday night audiences who were usually drunk." As the only Gentile in the group of Liars, Beakel had often been teased by the others as "withholding." To him, Compass was "like any family. Like all families, it had complexities. But there was respect for each other. Deep down, there was respect. And admiration for each other's talents too."

There was too much snow to drive, so old fans Murph and Mildred Goldberger and Jane Kome took a cab to the El on closing night and "damn near froze" making the long, rarely taken trip to the North Side. At the Argo Off-Beat Room, they joined some physicist friends from the University of Chicago, and all enjoyed Shelley Berman teaching Severn Darden how to beg. *The Liars*, featuring Berman, Darden, Nichols, and Beakel, comprised the second act, with Barbara Harris's part as the waitress played by Collin Wilcox.

In fact, not one of the players on stage that night had been present when the Compass opened, not one who could remember that it had been one of Chicago's hottest nights.

For the final production, David Shepherd had tried to revive the very first, the prototypical, improvised scenario, *Enterprise*. Shepherd had always supposed that the wellspring of Compass energy was in the play.

Hence, the revival of *Enterprise*. But, as he wrote the author, Roger Bowen, "Neither our new director (who liked it), nor the cast (which didn't) had any insight into it at all."

It may be recalled that *Enterprise* is the story of four high school boys who are slowly ensnared into the arms of capitalism by trading up used cars. The boys are en route to the used car lot of Crazy Jake to trade in a car they are already about to lose for nonpayment when they smash up their car. In debt, with no car, they make junk jewelry out of the remains of the car and become so successful as junk jewelers they receive a Junior Achievement Award.

More comfortable as back-stabbing high school teachers in *The Liars*, none of the men in the Compass company at the Argo could much identify with the needs (a shared car) and dreams (a better shared car) of adolescent boys. The time had long passed at the Compass for exploring the social-political issues that had been presented with such rude vitality in the original version of *Enterprise* at the University of Chicago Reynolds Club.

Time, in fact, had made *Enterprise* a parable for Compass, whose remaining players were about to win a Junior Achievement Award themselves for the brilliant and unusual baubles they would fashion out of the improvisational theatre's own demolished Ford.

18

The Atomic Compass

Shelley Berman stayed on at the Argo Off-Beat Room for another six weeks, headlining for The Commedia Players, a group that consisted of "just me, a girl, and another guy," whom he directed, supplied with ideas and material, and taught to improvise. He realized there was a chance that something soon would start up with the Compass in St. Louis, but "I didn't want to do that. I was getting old." At thirty-one, after a nonstop ride on the roller coaster of the improvisational theatre, his craving (similar to David Shepherd's "chase for tomorrow") still gnawed at him: he still wanted "to *do* something with my life." Now, however, he was determined to incorporate into it what he'd learned from improvising at the Compass. "There was no question. I was going to make use of it." On his solitary journey, he would take "some of the things I'd created there, some of the ideas I had, and some of the facilities that I developed there and put it all to use. I knew I had to do this. There was no other way to go."

Berman's little group worked well, he thought (among other pieces, even trying out the father-and-son routine Berman had first performed with Mark Gordon), but their act "wasn't drawing at all." In show-business terms, the beauty of having played under the equitably anonymous billing of an ensemble translated into the big liability of being a nobody. "People would call up to reserve for The Compass Players, and they'd say, 'We have The Commedia Players with Shelley Berman.' What good was that? I had no name."

As plans firmed up for the move to St. Louis, Walter Beakel was upset to learn that "David wanted to copyright everything. 'You're about four hundred years too late,' " Beakel protested. " 'You have no exclusivities on improvising. Check your history book and you'll find out.' He even tried to copyright the set. We had a number of boxes that varied in size—two feet square, two-and-a-half feet square—they were his contribution. He had them built. Even the doors of the nightclub—the revolving doors with different colors—those were his too! The early Italian theatre used those for entrances and exits. There was nothing new in this particular thing." As for himself, Beakel says, "I wasn't in the business to get rights until I got sophisticated and thought I'd better protect myself. I didn't think of myself as Molière. The performers always made the contribution. They were the ones with their butts hanging out up there." But he imagined future Compass productions of the play he had fathered. Beakel drew up a script of *The Liars*, and, with the permission of the players and the Isaac Rosenfeld Estate, he copyrighted it. Then he and Collin Wilcox left for New York.

Since his dismissal from the Compass, Andy Duncan had endured "an emptiness. I remember going into a retreat kind of thing," he says. He lived in a small room on the South Side and "just withdrew socially. I read and became very morose and unhappy. Totally distraught. It was as though a meaning had gone out of my life. Like a divorce." He took a job as a social worker. A counselor. He worked with the prisoners in the Cook County Jail. When Bernie Sahlins asked him to stage-manage at the Studebaker Theatre, Duncan grabbed the opportunity to be back in the theatre, feeling himself sentenced to civilian life and suddenly reprieved.

For a production of *Lysistrata*, Sahlins had imported Vicki Cummings, a second-string Broadway comedy light, to star in Aristophanes' comedy about a sex strike by the women of Athens. Cummings's supporting cast included Duncan (doubling and tripling in parts that included a precurtain satyr, dressed in a diaper and ringlets and horns) and Eugene Troobnick, lured back for a whole subscription season of acting from his editorial job at Sears. Also invited into the production were two local actresses, Barbara Harris and Elaine May, whom Sahlins knew to be unemployed. Mike Nichols, also at large, was chosen as Leader of the Chorus of Old Men, and, in a strange casting stroke, Severn Darden was picked as Leader of the Chorus of Old Women.

The play was not long into rehearsal when the director, George Keathley, approached Troobnick with a red face. "Miss Cummings would like you not to be so funny," he said. When she saw how many laughs Elaine May was getting as Lysistrata's cohort, Myrrhiné, Cummings wanted to switch parts. They tried it once. Elaine played Lysistrata like Carrie Nation, an interpretation Andy Duncan found most startling, a feminist coup. The change of casting might have been Elaine's big break as a legitimate actress, but Vicki Cummings asked for her part back. Elaine was funny no matter what she played.

A week or so before opening, Paul Sills was called in to take over for George Keathley, who could no longer cope. Sills did his best. "I'm a big hulking man playing the Leader of the Old Women's Chorus, and nobody's given me a single direction. Tell me something!" Severn implored. "Do it like Dylan Thomas," Sills said.

Reviewing for the Chicago *Tribune*, Claudia Cassidy described Vicki Cummings's performance as "a Gibraltar of ineptitude in a sea of incompetence" and the production as the worst *Lysistrata* in 2,000 years. For their work in the famous mattress or cockteasing scene, Sydney J. Harris in the *Daily News* singled out Elaine May and Troobnick (as her husband, Cinesias) as "very funny, but as Greek as bagels and lox."

Paul Sills and Barbara Harris went west. In Hollywood, Barbara got a part in an episode of a hit TV show, *The Defenders*, and Sills wrote a screenplay about a working-class guy in a Civilian Conservation Corps camp who gets mixed up with a local girl. He sold *The Treehouse* to two old friends, the wealthy Chicago brothers Yale and Haskell Wexler, who had once before performed as producer and cinematographer on a low-budget film they had personally financed. A director, Irvin Kershner, was hired. A cast was rounded up, including Michael Landon, Edward Asner, Barnard Hughes, and Barbara Harris. A woodsy location was found in Saint Joseph Island, Ontario, Canada, and principal photography commenced.

In Chicago, a local nightclub made Mike and Elaine an offer, and, based on their renewed connection in *Lysistrata*, Nichols invited Eugene Troobnick to join them as a threesome. Nichols said he felt his own work lacked sufficient physicality to sustain a whole act. (Shelley Berman had never received such a confession from his archrival. For Nichols to have considered that unlikely collaboration, a similar appraisal of Nichols's weakness might have been one Elaine advanced.) As a trio, Nichols explained that they would each get sixty dollars a week. Troobnick lived in an interracial housing project with his wife and child and had payments to make on an English car. As an editor at Sears, he was making $150 a week. He turned the idea of Nichols and May and Troobnick down.

T he Compass in Chicago had left David Shepherd with a mountain ($15,000 worth) of debts, including $500 to the State of Illinois and $3,000 to the Feds. These would be paid off by the proceeds from the new company in St. Louis, he hoped.

Shepherd's financial obligations would loom larger to him as the result of a serious new romantic entanglement.

At Larry Arrick's acting class in New York, he had been introduced to one of Arrick's former Bennington students, Suzanne ("Honey") Stern, as "the first honest man I've ever met." Shepherd gave the tall young actress a copy of his latest version of *Five Dreams*. In February, they had their first date. In March, Suzanne, who was a bright and very witty young woman as well as a good actress, was invited to audition for the St. Louis Compass, but, she says, "I did something wrong. They had this invisible element which at the time I didn't understand," and she failed. Nancy Ponder and Jo Henderson were chosen to join a cast that already included Ted Flicker and Del Close, a twenty-two-year-old actor from Manhattan, Kansas, whom Severn had befriended at the Barter Theatre and who could swallow fire, among many other surprising things. Even Severn was surprised that Close's favorite novel, like his own, was *Titus Groan* by Mervyn Peake.

Within a month or two, David Shepherd and Suzanne Stern would be planning their honeymoon.

S ince his early teens, Del Close had been looking for action in farther out destinations than his own (and Damon Runyon's) inappropriately named hometown. (In 1946, Manhattan, Kansas, had been displayed in *Life*'s Picture of the Week as "the typical American town." It was forty miles from the Great Plains and nine miles from Fort Riley, the home of some million army personnel and POWs and the world's largest infantry base. Close's grandfather had owned a 3.2 beer bar on Eisenhower turf in nearby Abilene.) Close served his apprenticeship as a fire-eater assisting Dr. Dracula, who toured the Midwestern movie theatre circuit with a print of *The Bride of Frankenstein* and twenty-five minutes of live entertainment called the Magic Horror Show. Entering to music from Ketèlbey's *In a Persian Market* and dressed in bulbol trousers, it was Close who carried out the master's edibles, flaming in a bowl. In one of the show's many scary blackouts, Dr. Dracula swooped down to the footlights. His words "A plague of worms will descend on you" were Close's cue to throw cooked spaghetti on the crowd.

Once, in response to his efforts, an audience member (perhaps a member of the cavalry) shouted out, "You call this entertainment? I just shit in my pants." Reflecting on this early impact on an audience, Close says, "I started at the top."

Close's adolescent attraction to horror and magic is not uncommon in the profiles of small-town WASP comedians. Perhaps their low-key or unexpressed emotional life is not easily exploded like those of urban and/or ethnic origins into more intense renderings of reality but made endurable by more intense illusions. In the same vein, Close voluminously read and wrote science fiction and was in constant communication with other sci-fi buffs. When he was fourteen, he turned out "the world's first science fiction poetry magazine" with a pen pal he'd met in the pages of *Startling Stories*. (He also wrote items for *Starbeams*, Bill Vaughan's comedy column in the Kansas City *Star*, and comic books.) Reading Theodore Sturgeon's *More Than Human*, about a five-brain psychic pathway, he became interested in the interconnections between human beings, the gestalt intelligence.

After his junior year in high school, he briefly accepted a music scholarship as a bass drummer at the Kansas State College of Agriculture and Applied Science, where one of the English faculty was Fran Striker, the retired radio writer of "The Lone Ranger." (The president was Ike's brother and Close's cousin's cousin, Milton Eisenhower.) Close worked in lots of school productions and on college radio. He learned his first lines of Schiller ("Ich weiss nicht was soll es bedeuten. Soll, das ich so traurig bin") from a campus visitor from Fort Riley, a high-ranking German prisoner of war, perhaps, Close thought, a former member of Hitler's High Command. Close summered at the University of South Dakota and moved on the next semester to the University of Iowa's drama and speech program on fellowship.

Then, following a precept he had seen advanced by Robert Hutchins
in a University of Chicago catalogue ("You don't have to go to college to
get an education"), Close dropped out of school. He had so far created
his own feverishly experiential study program, traveling with carnivals,
learning Dianetics from L. Ron Hubbard, hitchhiking to Kansas City to
see Martha Graham or to Lincoln, Nebraska, for The Royal Ballet. Now
he was acting all over the country in summer and winter stock. Hitchhiking
to Chicago after a straw-hat season in Wisconsin, he was already looking
for an actor's agent when he took in a production of *Volpone* at the
Playwrights Theatre Club.

When he arrived in the Big Apple at twenty, with three years behind
him as a working actor, Close had nothing but contempt for the notion
of unraveling his subconscious for Lee Strasberg or any other Method
acting teacher. Instead, he got some jobs off-Broadway and resumed his
practice of the drums. (One of the five drummers in his class—who did
happen to be Strasberg's student—was James Dean.) For a recital at Juil-
liard, Close was good enough to fill in for John Cage's sick percussionist.
He played Lucky in a reading of an obscure translation of an unproduced
play by Samuel Beckett called *Waiting for Goodie*, staged at the loft of an
artist acquaintance from the University of Iowa, Jasper Johns. Just before
joining the Barter, he reinvented himself as Azrad the Incombustible, a
human torch.

On Severn's recommendation, Close had already once auditioned for
the Compass at the Argo Off-Beat Room (he improvised a seduction scene
with Elaine) but, because of contractual obligations to the Barter, had
been unable to join. During that visit, Andy Duncan remembers Close
eating fire onstage to puzzlement and small applause.

For the virgin St. Louis company, Severn had suggested that Flicker
check again on Close, who had since been touring a show he and his
roommate, Jerry Hardin, had originated at the Barter, a capsule history
of the theatre in nine scenes. One of the scenes, an improvisation from
the work of Flaminio Scala (a commedia dell'arte scenarist), moved Flicker
to hire Close and Hardin on the spot. Close suggests that "we were the
only English-speaking humans available who had any experience at all
with this stuff."

After reviewing his St. Louis budget, Flicker withdrew the offer to
Hardin, deciding to fill the fourth acting slot himself.

RIGHT: *A gallows (here used by Del Close as Ted Flicker looks on) was one of the stage props at the Compass at the Crystal Palace. Ted Flicker (right) plays a malicious mechanical clown, St. Louis, spring 1957.*

BELOW: *"An island of affluent hipness" in blighted St. Louis. Jo Henderson and Del Close are the players onstage.*

LEFT: *Nancy Ponder and Ted Flicker play Mr. and Mrs. Centaur as Noah's ark takes off.* RIGHT: *Audiences often began the Compass's Presidential press conferences with frivolous questions like "Hey, Jack, what color are Jackie's new drapes?" but invariably ended by asking, "Mr. President, how can we achieve world peace?" Alan Alda is JFK at the Hyannisport Compass, summer 1963.*

(Left to right) Jerry Stiller, Nancy Ponder, and Alan Arkin spoof a science-fiction movie at the Compass at the new Crystal Palace on Gaslight Square, 1960.

ABOVE: *The Catskill Compass, (left to right) Leslie J. Stark, David Dozer, Louise Lasser, was a hit on the Yiddish-speaking circuit a week after Lasser's husband-to-be, Woody Allen, had bombed.*

RIGHT: *The final company of Compass appeared in New York at the Upstairs at the Downstairs in the fall of 1963. (Left to right) MacIntyre Dixon, Paul Dooley (both of whom later joined The Second City), and Jane Alexander.*

The original Second City company did not expect the show to run for thirty years. (Top, left to right): Andrew Duncan; Eugene Troobnick and Mina Kolb; Andrew Duncan, Roger Bowen, Barbara Harris, Eugene Troobnick, Mina Kolb, Severn Darden. (Third row, left to right): Roger Bowen; Barbara Harris and Severn Darden; Howard Alk and Paul Sills.

ABOVE: *At The Second City in Chicago, 1960, Severn Darden presented a midget to Andrew Duncan when they played a Mirror exercise on a receiving line.*

RIGHT: *"Where else but in a small room, late at night, before an audience more notable for its mind than its money, can the true satirist practice his art and polish his weapons?" wrote Kenneth Tynan in 1960, the year before this show opened on Broadway.*

John Golden Theatre

PLAYBILL
a weekly magazine for theatregoers

AN EVENING WITH
MIKE NICHOLS AND ELAINE MAY

Some descendants of THE COMPASS

Dan Aykroyd and his partner Valri Bromfield were performing on a radio show in Toronto when The Second City came to town. Both of them joined the company.

The most fearless comedienne since Elaine May, Lily Tomlin's great gallery of characters are mined from the dark side of life.

Since Nichols and May performed original material only, their manager, Jack Rollins, persuaded comedy writer Woody Allen to get onstage himself. He was terrified.

Steve Martin remembers listening to Nichols and May records "over and over and over" and can still hear Nichols's phrasing in his own delivery.

Whoopi Goldberg improvised characters she knew from the street. Mike Nichols brought the Goldberg variations to Broadway.

Gilda Radner's Emily Litella was born onstage at the Toronto Second City.

When Rob Reiner directed Stand By Me, *he rehearsed his 12-year-old stars by playing Viola Spolin's theater games.*

In 1961 Paul Mazursky, then a struggling actor and a member of The Second City Workshop, was hired by Paul Sills to be in the Los Angeles Second City when the original company moved to Broadway.

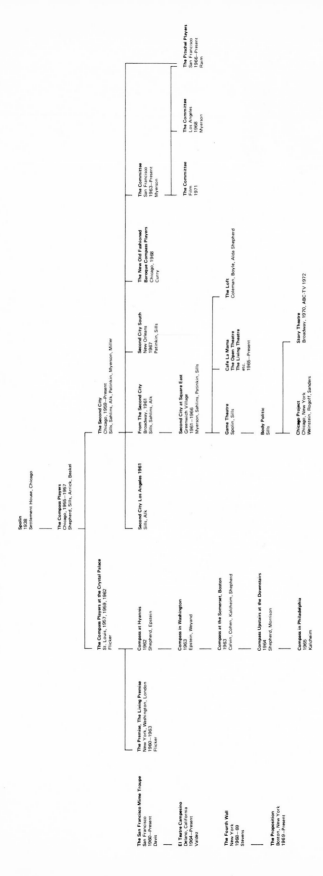

The state of the art of improvisation as seen in 1974 in Yale/Theatre magazine. Today there are dozens more branches on the improvisational tree.

"Attractive, magnetic, artistic, crazy people" is the way that Shepherd recalls the wealthy Jewish family of Fred Landesman, who owned the Crystal Palace. The Landesmans in fact had subtly figured in advancing St. Louis's cultural life for half a century, ever since Fred's father, Ben, emigrated from Berlin on commission from the German government to paint their pavilion at the 1904 World's Fair. During the Depression, he became a part-time antiques dealer, until he was hired by the Public Works Administration as a muralist, specializing in Teutonic cherubs and nymphs. Then Ben turned over the antiques business to his wife, tiny, cross-eyed Cutie, a canny nickel-and-dime shopowner who preferred pages of the *Jewish Daily Forward* to gift wrap. Under Cutie, profits soared.

Requiring a more artful modus operandi than that of his wife, Ben set up a second branch of B. Landesman Antiques in Houston, Texas, while their daughter, Gertrude, fled to New York and psychoanalysis. The three Landesman sons remained.

Alfred (Fred) was the eldest, like his father a painter with cultivated and original taste. By trailing the demolition crews through St. Louis's decaying inner city, he accumulated a warehouse full of urban archeology: architectural ornaments, bathroom fixtures, church pews, stained-glass windows, obsolete office furniture, and amusing Victoriana and objets d'art.

Eugene, called Gene, the number-two son, was an inventor, a mechanical genius. Long before he settled into manufacturing machinery for silk-screen presses, Gene had invented a means of fusing glass under extreme heat that rendered cracks invisible. On buying trips, the Landesmans actually sought out items that were chipped, flawed, or scarred, and people came to their shop from all over the country to have valuable broken objects fixed.

Upon reading *The Great Gatsby*, the youngest Landesman brother, Jay, had changed his name from Irving Ned. By all reports (including his own), he was the family gadfly, always in search of a special identity, which he easily gained as an epicure and spectacular party giver, and as a stud.

In exchange for their services during World War II, the Landesman brothers—all 4F—persuaded their mother to turn the business over to them, correctly sensing a postwar boom for antiques. As partners, they transformed the shop into the Landesman Galleries, "a show place," in Jay's words, and Cutie was given "a promissory note for her equity . . . and a lifetime job without pay." From Cutie's huge stock of nineteenth-century utilitarian cut-glass objects (vases, water tumblers, finger bowls, carafes), Fred began designing the wartime model of the Landesmans' most lucrative item: one-of-a-kind lighting fixtures that passed for antique crystal chandeliers.

In 1949, longing for a glory greater than the family business, Jay founded a quality quarterly of cultural criticism for the antibourgeois. The poetry of Marshall McLuhan, John Clellon Holmes, Allen Ginsberg, Judith Malina, and Leonard Bernstein made its debut in the publication that defined the intellectual contours of the beat generation, Jay's brain child, *Neurotica* magazine.

Neurotica's growing underground fame buttressed Jay's big move to New York, where he immersed himself in literary life: drinking with Jack Kerouac, inviting the street musician Moondog home for pastrami sandwiches, and falling for an Upper West Side groupie named Peaches at a Greenwich Village beatnik party hosted by Anatole Broyard. The smell of beeswax in her parents' penthouse at the Kenilworth reminded Jay of the Landesman Galleries, and he married Peaches, whose real name was Fran Dietz. When *Neurotica* folded in 1951, after a censorship battle with the U.S. Post Office, Jay panicked for security and returned to St. Louis and the family fold with his unenthusiastic wife.

Fred now was married to Paula and raising three sons, Rocco, Wyatt, and Knight, in a sprawling old mansion across the street from T. S. Eliot's birthplace. Conceived for a nouveau riche steel magnate, the "yawning whale" Del Close saw at 4411 Westminster Place that would house The Compass Players featured a tower, a ballroom, a three-car garage, and a wood-paneled rathskeller (which Fred had partitioned into two studio rooms), tiled with episodes from *Don Quixote*. A St. Louis architectural society called it a perfect example of Richardson Romanesque, or Victorian bad taste.

Jay moved Fran into a house only two doors away. She took up the life of a playboy antique dealer's wife and hated it.

It was to keep his sister-in-law in St. Louis that Fred built the Crystal Palace, a ninety-seat cabaret that he filled with his collection of drugstore chairs, marble busts, elevator grilles, doors of etched glass, a pair of life-size brass monkeys, and dozens of Landesman chandeliers. "There was something about all the darkness mixed with gold, crystal, whiskey and the tinkling of the piano that people found irresistible," wrote Jay in his autobiography, *Rebel Without Applause*. As Fred's son Rocco describes his family's contribution to pub décor, "They invented 'the fern bar.' "

Rocco Landesman is the Yale professor, stock market wizard, and horse breeder who at thirty-eight became, along with his wife, Heidi, a major Broadway producer with the opening of *Big River* in 1975, their first show, a hit. (Their second entry, a Tony winner, was *Into the Woods*, the musical by Stephen Sondheim and James Lapine.) Rocco's characterization of the original Crystal Palace as "a neat place for hip people in St. Louis to hang out" avoids hyperbole. "It was the hippest place in America," swears one habitué.

In this atmosphere, Fran Landesman entered into a period of unanticipated creativity, writing wry and sophisticated lyrics set to music by the Crystal Palace piano player, Tommy Wolf. The Landesman-Wolf songbook is an oeuvre of some twenty-five songs, among them "Ballad of the Sad Young Men," "How Do You Like Your Love?," "You Smell So Good" (inspired by a marijuana smoker), and "Spring Can Really Hang You Up the Most," which became a jazz classic, in 1955, the year after it was written, as recorded by Ella Fitzgerald, Jackie Cain, Chris Connor, and Sarah Vaughan.

Jay had turned to writing a novel about his Greenwich Village days. Even with a character based on Jack Kerouac, Landesman could not find a publisher for his tragic love story about overreaching middle-class beatniks, *The Nervous Set*.

In the war against sexual repression, however, the founder of *Neurotica* was still leading a vanguard crusade. After the nine-to-fivers had concluded their revels at the Crystal Palace, an even hipper crowd of couples "seeking absolution," in Jay's words, came out to hear jazz and swap mates.

Into this baroque spectacle of haute bourgeois recreation came former cadet Ted Flicker and (as they are remembered by Del Close) his company of improvisational androids. In early March 1957, they moved into their quarters at Fred Landesman's mansion and settled down to rehearse.

"We went out to St. Louis with a page and a half of scene breakdowns and instructions from David Shepherd," recalls Del Close. "Our task was to re-create the Chicago Compass without any of the people involved, without two of us ever having seen it, without any experience of Viola Spolin, or any knowledge of how to improvise. We basically had to invent our own way."

When Dr. Dracula refused to share his fire-swallowing secrets, Close had managed to teach himself, by dipping a torch in an automobile gas tank and consuming the flame. (He had stuck an iron rod down his gullet preparing to swallow swords.) He was not unaccustomed to taking risks. Yet to Close, who remembered the "horror and dismay" he experienced before improvising in the Barter Theatre project, the prospect of improvising a whole show seemed terrifying. For all his exotic activities, he had remained, he says, "a rigidly trained classical actor, very repressed and uptight." Back home in Manhattan, Kansas, his father had committed suicide. "Improvisation was the last form such a person as I would get involved in. I had a suave exterior, but I was screaming with neurosis inside." It was "because of my terror" that he says he connected so strongly to Ted Flicker in seeking a system through which to improvise. "I never could have done it without the sheer force of Ted's will and discipline," he says. Flicker's rehearsals in Story-Story, First Line/Last Line, setups, punch lines, and improvised poetry resembled military drills, not kindergarten games.

David Shepherd flew into St. Louis at the end of the month, looking forward, he advised his diary, to a quick getaway. His fantasy of including a scenario in the St. Louis show was interrupted by responsibilities attendant on Compass's April 2 opening: he had to get three panels built. A bulk mailing to get out. Publicity. Interviews. A sign to design and duplicate: the Compass Theatre logo would give the effect of light bulbs when it was spelled out, as he envisioned it, in dots.

Shepherd found such producer's chores, as usual, unfulfilling. He was in a hurry to get back to scenario rewriting and Suzanne. He did not bear in mind Grotowski's precept: the theatre belongs to whoever is making it. He left town before opening night.

Among left-wingers, Del Close has always felt "a little out of place, considering my position as a monarchist. I want to overthrow the government in order to get a royal title, not socialist justice." As a young man, he recalls that he was relieved by Shepherd's departure. "I'd had enough of his bullshit about 'You're an upper-middle-class housewife in love with a middle-class white-collar worker with lower-class parents.' He conceived of the whole thing as some kind of social therapy. As soon as he left, things began to work." Teaching themselves how to fabricate a show without a script, "We came up with a more circus-oriented approach. Onstage, Ted would play The Ringmaster, and we were the big cats."

"No one in the audience for the first night of the Compass at the Palace was likely to forget its impact," Jay Landesman's autobiography says. "The stage was dark. Two of the players were planted at a table in the audience. They began to argue, until the audience was hollering for them to shut up. As the couple made their way to the stage, Flicker, a small volatile man with a Mephistopheles beard, hopped onto the stage and shouted, 'Freeze!' The lights went up on the performers. 'What happens next?' he asked the audience. 'You tell us.'"

"Ted's idea was to present improvisation as an intellectual feat, as an unusual human ability," Del Close reflects. "Of course, at the time, we didn't know how usual it could be."

If David Shepherd had seized upon improvisation as a tool for developing new plays that reflected the lives of the audience, it was indeed Ted Flicker's un-Violan contribution to present improvisation as "an unusual feat," a cross between a cocktail party and a carnival act. Flicker's gimmick would become so successful and so widely imitated as to obscure his more significant innovation in St. Louis in finally throwing the spotlight on improvisation as process by escalating the degree of audience involvement and framing the show around each evening's audience-suggested scenes.

As they had been in Chicago, the bulk of these scenes at the Crystal Palace were planned backstage. Previously, however, the improvisations had depended on the audience's forbearance in watching works in progress. But Flicker was interested in presenting accomplished pieces of instant theatre, not in charging an audience for rough drafts.

Early in their association, Close recalls that Flicker had impressed on him the need to structure and drive a scene, to keep it moving seamlessly from its setup to its resolution, preferably one that blacked out on a laugh. If the spot improvisations in St. Louis lacked the same tight structure and coherence as the planned ones—and they usually did—the rule of blacking out on a laugh still applied. Nancy Ponder recalls as very theatrical the way the company performed "a collective swoon when we fell on our face." "We could always save ourselves with something crazy," says Del Close. Close had seen the Compass only once at the Argo Off-Beat Room, but found it "flaccid by comparison. I saw Shelley and Elaine do twenty-five-minute scenes that didn't earn their time." Particularly in the unplanned spot improvisations, Close felt that the meandering Chicago style tended to work less often to sustain the show than Flicker's "louder, faster, funnier" approach. "They'd go on and on until the audience would leave."

Trimming the fat from an improvisation does not guarantee that the rest will be meat. Because the burden on the performer in an improvised circus is more than ever presentational rather than exploratory, the well-trained Method actor of the day might find his or her usual habit of drawing upon interior feelings frustrated or undermined.

Nancy Ponder and Jo Henderson were actors of serious purpose. Henderson (who was killed in a car crash in 1988) was one of Uta Hagen's protégés. Ponder had also studied with Uta Hagen (in the same class as Shelley Berman and Geraldine Page), switched to Mira Rostova, Zohra Lampert and Montgomery Clift's coach, and practiced improvisation in

Tony Manino's class. Improvising on the job in St. Louis had had extra appeal because it was her hometown and her mother still lived there. But she regarded the work at the Crystal Palace as "heavy-handed and unsubtle. It didn't have much depth. It was too much like parlor games."

Del Close recalls with excitement the staging of his *Two by Four*, a modern Punch and Judy show (borrowed from his Barter Theatre repertoire), in which the players stood behind a waist-high curtain like giant hand puppets, satirizing suburbia in huge papier-mâché masks.* "It sounds exciting, but it wasn't," Ponder says. "Jay Landesman asked us not to do it again."

The experience of the women was of being dominated by the men. It was Close's penchant to improvise on plots from written works. He remembers with pleasure taking off on *Seven Types of Ambiguity* by William Empson, creating new dialogue for stories in *The New Yorker*, like those of Shirley Jackson and Roald Dahl, and adapting James Thurber's story "The Catbird Seat." Ponder remembers coming across these stories later and "the shock Mary Jo and I felt realizing they'd been stolen. We'd both assumed they were creations of the moment." She also recalls the men would steal the women's funny lines.

She cannot recall the night, in search of a more meaningful stage report, that she and Henderson harked back to their classwork and asked Flicker for time to do "a real improv" onstage. Close remembers them picking "the most conflictual situation: two sisters in love with the same guy. It lasted about twenty minutes. It didn't do any of the things they wanted it to do. The situation didn't really lend itself to disagreement. They forced themselves into red-faced emotion. The audience was bored. Ted and I looked at each other and said, 'Mmmm.' It was a great lesson: that conflict is boring and agreement is less boring and that we were into a new era of improvisation. Everything the Actors Studio did no longer applied."† Reconsidering the women's beleaguered feelings, Close asks, "What funny lines?"

---

*The masks were created by Brandy Johnson, an ex–union organizer and artist who lived across the street from the Landesmans in the T. S. Eliot house. He and his wife also made the Christmas displays for a St. Louis department store.

†Close uses the phrase "Actors Studio" loosely. In 1957, there were many American interpreters of Stanislavsky teaching the Method, it seemed, to every actor in New York. Only outstanding practitioners, however, were admitted to the Actors Studio after auditioning before its directors, Elia Kazan, Cheryl Crawford, and Lee Strasberg. None of The Compass Players (nor any of the actors from the Playwrights Theatre Club) were members of the Actors Studio at this time, although many had learned the Method and several had studied in Strasberg's private class.

Although their adoring St. Louis audience seemed thrilled by whatever The Compass Players produced extemporaneously, as they did four to six sets a night, both Flicker and Close realized that new techniques were clearly needed if improvisation was to transform from an acting exercise or rehearsal tool into an art form. When he came across a discussion of John Von Neumann's game theory in Norbert Wiener's book on cybernetics, *The Human Use of Human Beings,* Close naturally had never heard the term "theater games." Yet he became impressed by Von Neumann's strategy for game playing, which seemed to him to apply also to succeeding at the Compass: "Seek to fail less often rather than to succeed all the time. That sounds like playing it safe," says Close, "but it also is a way of staying in the game."

D el Close had persuaded Severn Darden to buy a motorcycle, a BMW double twin-cylinder 650cc, the Rolls-Royce of bikes. After visiting the company in St. Louis, he had borrowed Close's crash helmet for his traveling companion, and they took off for Ohio and the Antioch College Shakespeare Festival in Yellow Springs. In Xenia, Ohio, Severn ran a stop sign. He was hit at about sixty mph by a car that crushed his leg from ankle to hip. The girl in the crash helmet "came out okay," as Close puts it. Severn's leg was put together with pins. From the hospital he sent tapes of himself rhapsodizing on painkillers to his friends at the Crystal Palace, who listened to them while sampling the bar's obscure apéritifs. He sent a telegram to some of his Compass friends in Chicago who were opening in a Studebaker Theatre production of *Waiting for Godot.* It said, "Break a leg."

19

Meet Me in St. Louis

When The Commedia Players failed to ignite, Shelley Berman decided to break into the Rush Street nightclub circuit as a solo. An audition was arranged for him at Mr. Kelly's, the little room where Mort Sahl (whom Berman had frequently watched) had made such a success. "They loved what I did, and hired me at three hundred fifty dollars a week, which seemed to me like a million," Berman remembers.

In the meantime, he had a booking at a funkier cabaret called the Gate of Horn, which had been opened by an ex–city planner from Chicago's Roosevelt University. Albert Grossman was one of several barometric entrepreneurs throughout the country with a feel for booking timely folk-singing acts like Odetta and for creating an inviting bohemian space. Mort Sahl, who had made his reputation in San Francisco at the hungry i, the prototype of such spaces, remembers Grossman as a self-styled "man of the people" who would so solicit help and sympathy from performers when the club went bankrupt. He would gain more fame in the 1960s as a Benjamin Franklin lookalike and for the fortune he made as the reclusive manager of such stars as Bob Dylan and Janis Joplin. In the spring of 1957, Albert Grossman said he didn't think Shelley Berman was funny, and fired him.

The same spring, Mike Nichols married Pat Scot during the run of *Waiting for Godot*, the last play of the Studebaker Theatre. In spite of the reverberations that had followed the failed New York production, Walter Beakel's staging of Beckett for a 1,200-seat subscription theatre in Chicago was a daring choice. Beakel and the stage manager, Andrew Duncan (who also played the small part of "a boy"), designed and built the set, which Duncan recalls as "scenery the way *we* liked it—a rock and a bare light bulb for the moon." Mike Nichols's Lucky, recalls Eugene Troobnick, was "the best thing I've ever seen him do. Oh, he was good."

Beckett's Lucky is a man on a leash, driven by his master, Pozzo, on and off and around the stage. Tugged at and beaten into an animal insensibility, his only spoken words are a three-page nonsense monologue. On Broadway, the role had been played by Alvin Epstein, an accomplished mime. "I've never seen Mike so physical," remembers Duncan of his view from backstage. "He played it like a dog. Slavering. He would sit up and pant. He really threw himself into it. I was amazed."

"All Mike did was stand on stage and be whipped" was the way it looked to Troobnick from his harder-to-see seat in the audience. "But the way he rattled off that speech—it seemed with one breath—was sensational." "Mike did a really good job," concurs Fritzi Sahlins, Bernie's former wife. "But I guess people didn't understand Beckett. They walked out in droves."

Thus, despite his long stretch as an actor, Nichols made no notch in his career from this, his first connection to Beckett's (or, as he would one day come to call it, "Sam's") play.

At the wedding breakfast that followed the ceremony, Elaine flirted with Harvey Korman, who was also in the *Godot* cast. "Isn't it a beautiful first wedding?" Elaine remarked.

David Shepherd and Ted Flicker had pressed forward with their St. Louis plans, although even in the blush of their earliest partnership transactions, they had displayed very little artistic rapport. "Our aims were the same. Popular theatre," says Flicker. "But I always felt that he was a touch too visionary, and he always felt that I was a touch too crass." In the right mood, a Harvard man might defer to a University of Chicago dropout, but certainly not to one from Bard. "I think David's feeling at the time was that I had no business interfering in the art of it, that I was a financier." Still, no one else had been game or gamester enough to take on the St. Louis Compass. And Shepherd was counting on Flicker's backers from New York. Gentlemanly arguments had taken place between the two partners but no fireworks.

Flicker's company had been performing for about a month before Shepherd appeared in St. Louis again, "traveling with a knapsack and a big tape recorder," Nancy Ponder recalls, "and reminding us that he owned whatever we did."

The Flicker Compass began with an opening gambit like the "argument." (In one of Del Close's favorite constructions, the company wore pith helmets, carried flashlights, and examined the audience as if they were fungi or stalactites.) Story-Story (now adorned with flash cards suggesting an assortment of literary storytelling styles) led off a brisk twenty-minute set, after which the actors solicited suggestions from the audience. When they returned from a ten-minute intermission, Flicker had made it a requirement that every suggestion be rewarded with an improvised scene. (Observing later improv groups picking and choosing from a sea of suggestions, "I always saw it as immoral, as cheating," says Close. "We took it as a holy obligation to take every one.") There was a new show every night. The Saturday show featured a rerun of the best improvised scenes of the week.

As befitted their own preoccupations, the St. Louis audience, with much more frequency than the one in Chicago, solicited scenes about marriage. One such was *The Last of the Centaurs*, in which Flicker and Ponder played the heads and Close and Henderson the tail ends of a pair of these beasts, anticipating a heavy flood. Noah is preparing to evacuate all the animal couples in town in a specially built ark. Despite her husband's entreaties to hurry, Mrs. Centaur is detained by endless household chores. Anxious as he is to join the others, he cannot leave without her. They both miss the boat.

There was no denying that former cadet Flicker had got the improvisational theatre into shipshape. And among the middle-class citizens of St. Louis, the Compass at the Crystal Palace was not regarded as a subterranean experimental theatre. On the contrary, it had become *the* big entertainment in town, a roaring success, of which Flicker was most proud.

Assessing the directorial refinements of his partner and would-be co-mogul, David Shepherd watched the audience enthuse (along with Jay Landesman) over the pithy skits (of "sharp, biting satirical commentary on contemporary manners and morals") based upon their own deftly solicited suggestions ("on topical issues or experiences of the most embarrassing kind"). He noticed the actors dressed in black slacks and yellow button-down shirts, saw the actresses in black tights and belted thigh-length blouses, and observed an absence of cigarette butts on the floor of the stage. When the show was over, he turned to Flicker and said, "You've turned it into entertainment. You've ruined my dream."

" 'An entertainment.' That's like calling somebody in the Soviet Union 'an individual,' " Flicker reflects. "It was the first time in his life he had a steady income from the improvisational theatre. And he says, 'You've ruined my dream.' "

Shepherd had applied for and was offered a Fulbright scholarship to Paris. He would probably accept it, he wrote to Roger Bowen, "if only to start a Compass there."

Shelley Berman got a booking in Milwaukee on the strength of his Mr. Kelly's date. He borrowed some money to buy a train ticket and a suit. He arrived at the club, performed his first set, and got the heave-ho. For this, he didn't get a cent.

Mort Sahl had watched Berman's act at the Gate of Horn and made a few suggestions, which Berman recalls as "very generous and nice." For, by his own assessment, Berman was not a good comedian: "My god. I *wasn't* a comedian. I was an actor who had improvised a half-dozen routines. Nobody in nightclubs was doing anything like this."

Among the routines he had added to his repertoire was a solo version of the father-and-son scene he had first performed with Mark Gordon. In the new rendition, the father communicated by phone, from the apartment over the family delicatessen, in a Yiddish accent, to an unseen son, the eighteen-year-old Sheldon ("Let's face it, that's my name"), the only one of his circle of friends without the one hundred dollars needed for New York and acting school. This time around, Berman allowed the father to become a more sympathetic and three-dimensional figure, capable of finally yielding to his son's burning desire to become an actor and gruffly agreeing to fork over the money for acting school:

> All right, here's what I do with you, actor. You'll come downstairs by me in the store this Saturday coming and the next Saturday coming from this Saturday coming, you know what I'm talking? This Saturday coming and the next Saturday coming from this Saturday coming. You know what I'm talking. Don't say "yeah" if you mean "no." Because I know you, you don't understand English altogether. I'm talking two Saturdays coming. Coming, not going, gonif. You go downstairs. And you work downstairs. And you *work* downstairs. Not a half a Saturday. Not a quarter a Saturday. A *full* working day like everybody else in the whole world, fourteen hours. You understand what I'm saying to you? I'll give you . . . I'll give you . . . all right, I'll give you . . . a hundred dollars a Saturday. All right, don't scream in my ear, dumbbell. A hundred dollars we will send right away to New York with the gangsters. A hundred dollars is by you in the

pocket so you could take an airplane to New York, so you wouldn't
have to fly with your own hands. You'll have a hotel, a few meals,
a few dollars. If you do downstairs for me a good job—you'll put the
money in the register—I'll give you a Christmas bonus, fifty dollars.
A Christmas bonus. Don't tell your mother I said "Christmas."

The piece became Berman's favorite and greatest routine.

As meticulously as he worked out his monologues, Berman had yet to
discover what a nightclub comedian must do: "I had to talk to the audience.
I had to find ways." In the course of this search, he would become a star
among standups, although he was not really interested in learning their
skill. He had yet to develop "routines that had nothing to do with what I
do. And it took me years."

On Saint Joseph Island, the Wexler brothers panicked over their investment and pulled the plug on Paul Sills's film. Sills and Barbara
Harris drifted back to Chicago, not Hollywood. When a friend in Milwaukee offered facilities to make a pilot television show, Sills assembled
a group to drive up with him to tape "The Milwaukee Revue." Sills directed
Playwrights Theatre Club alums Eugene Troobnick and Vernon Schwartz
in a pantomime, Shelley Berman on the telephone, Nichols and May in
"Teenagers," and Barbara Harris as a weathergirl in sequins and net stock-
ings, all to no avail. Despite the array of talent, no sponsor for the show
was found.

Late in May, Ted Flicker was waiting for David Shepherd at the St. Louis
airport in a 1936 Cadillac convertible town car, a vehicle provided by
the Landesmans that transported the company everywhere. At 4411 Westminster Place, Shepherd found two of the rejects from "The Milwaukee
Revue," Nichols and May, sitting in the backyard, just arrived themselves
from Chicago by train. They all argued the fine points of improvisational
theatre until show time, when Mike and Elaine and Shepherd all joined
in the performance and were feted by the management of the Crystal
Palace with a round of drinks. In the wee hours of the morning, over steak
and eggs at the Rex Café, Mike and Elaine indicated they might like to
come out to St. Louis to work, beginning July 1.

Mike and Elaine would be a particularly attractive summer asset, since

Flicker's frequent absences were anticipated in connection with the big fall opening of the Compass in New York.

The one weak link in the company, in Elaine's opinion, Jo Henderson, would be fired to make room for them.

One June night, the members of the Crystal Palace audience gave as First Line/Last Line suggestions, "No, George, don't" and "No, George, don't." Backstage, a few days before her termination notice, Jo Henderson came up with a construction about a man leaving his wife. It began with Del Close packing an invisible suitcase. She doesn't want him to go: "No, George, don't." She begs and pleads and finally persuades him to stay. They embrace. He moves to stroke her hair. She recoils: "No, George, don't."

"No, George, Don't" would endure as one of the improvisational theatre's most frequently repeated little scenes.

The impact of Nichols and May on the St. Louis company was bound to be intense. As Del Close saw it, the confluence of their University of Chicago cum Stanislavskian style of improvisation ("their high references and psychological background and Jewish intellectual thing") made at first for "an uneasy blend" with Flicker's circus approach ("all our flashy tricks"). Mike and Elaine used improvisation to create set material while "We were attempting to mount a new show every night, to develop new forms, to create a circus atmosphere. It was difficult for them to adjust. They couldn't appreciate the honor involved in taking every suggestion. It was too fast and furious for them."

Mike and Elaine coolly dug into their own bag of tricks and their huge cache of previously played scenes and bits. In addition to playing such set scenes as "Teenagers," "Disc Jockey," and "Pirandello," they invited Del Close to be the third player in the one-scene version of *The Game of Hurt*. Nancy Ponder remembers Nichols leading the "class" in his specialty, "How to Appear Cultured," and Elaine once again twisting a wire hanger around her head to play a mad Venusian queen.

If the common frame of reference in Chicago had been Jewish family life, psychoanalysis, and books, connections now were based on books. "I haven't seen anybody operate on the literary level we did," Nancy Ponder says. They were all equally well acquainted with English literature, as well as with Proust, Beckett, Hemingway, Dostoevski, the Dadas and Surrealists. Thus, the improvisations "in a literary style" were "very detailed and ironic. But we were entertaining too. You didn't have to be familiar with Restoration comedy to get it."

Taking plots from works of literature was a practice Del Close continued to advance. In response, Mike Nichols discussed his desire to stage some parables from Kafka, inclined even at the prospect of literary lifting to repeat what had already been tried.

Despite such appearances of agreeableness, it was Close's impression that the only reason Nichols had come to this minor-league arena in St. Louis was to keep performing with Elaine, but she soon appeared to have other priorities than working alone with him.

If Nichols continued to experience Flicker's theatre as "an entirely alien operation," Close noticed that Elaine adapted. "She didn't like wearing tights, but she did it." Close compares the Compass to "a live wire" from which she could not let go. She loved improvisation. Ted Flicker was keeping a stage bare for it. He hadn't ruined *her* dream.

Nancy Ponder remembers that they all took great leaps as actors with the coming of Mike and Elaine, and especially Elaine, who was as always capable of giving less experienced improvisers on-the-job training, yielding to their personalities and enhancing their gifts, and, in Ponder's opinion, discharging the desperation and selfishness she felt had characterized the work of the men.

Del Close, for example, could be verbally dazzling, Ponder recalls, "But he wasn't a trained actor as I knew them." Method actors stress relaxation, classical actors move into bravura acting instead. Often Close's onstage posture froze with "one arm across his chest and one hand over his mouth, so things couldn't go in and things couldn't go out. He wasn't sure of himself. And Elaine did wonderful things for Del. She really did. She brought him out and gave him confidence."

Using the character of The Ringmaster, Ted Flicker had previously worked "in paintbrush strokes. He tended to act everything like a cartoon." Sometimes his violent impulses got out of control, he was so wound up with nerves. Ponder remembers once being pinned to the floor during an improvisation while Flicker pounded it with her head. Now, with Elaine's encouragement, as a piece of popcorn popping, "the lovable side of Ted opened up."

Ponder, whose own inhibitions took the form of speaking too softly, also grew more confident as an improviser through her work with Elaine. The improvisations of Ponder and May were mostly relegated to the late-night sets, where they developed the twosome of Doris and Dorothy, two

middle-class ladies with flat Midwestern accents. They played evil little
girls. They ripped up scientific theories together in a piece called "Scientists' Wives." They played the two elderly sisters from *The Real You*
who have been entertaining the same old gentleman (Del Close) for thirty
years. This is the evening they tell him, "You've been sittin' on our porch
and drinkin' our Schweppes all this time. You've got to make up your
mind which one of us you like best." As in the original, the old gentleman
does not choose either one of the sisters. In response to the self-assertion
of the women, Ponder recalls that "he just left."

Ponder had been the first woman to appear with Close in the adaptation
of Thurber's short story "The Catbird Seat," in which an abstemious clerk
succeeds in his plot to make the obnoxiously aggressive new woman su-
pervisor in his office seem insane. Improvising as the awful Mrs. Ulgine
Barrows, Ponder felt too soft, that she was miscast. A winning victim could
turn one of Thurber's most misogynistic tales into a feminist tract. Taking
on the same part, Elaine "played it like a ball-buster. The audience was
on my side at the end," says Close, who played Mr. Martin, the clerk. "I
thought of Elaine as an androgyne. I never got the sense that she was a
feminist."

"She was the strongest woman I ever met," says Nancy Ponder, "and
we made a good team."

When Elaine May settled down in St. Louis, she devoted some thought
to turning spot improvisation into a legitimate dramaturgical exercise instead of a stunt that probably would—and usually did—fail. Although
they were dedicated to doing them, the St. Louis company was still in the
dark about how to present these off-the-cuff improvisations consistently.
"We were very successful in St. Louis without knowing what we were
doing," says Del Close. "No one had ever really figured out how to
improvise in public," says Ted Flicker. "We were working off our energy,
not our minds."

The kitchen at the Landesmans' was on the third floor. Every day for
two weeks in this kitchen, Flicker recalls that he and Elaine articulated
"The Rules" for publicly performed improvisation in intense and private
sessions.* They reiterated some principles known (but not always followed)
by the Chicago company: (1) whatever verbal or pantomimed reality that

---

*Nancy Ponder remembers spending hours in the back seat of the Cadillac town car
with Elaine—perhaps in the same two-week period—"trying to solve the problem of spots
and why they worked or not. She and I were obsessed by it."

is brought to the stage by one player may not be negated or denied by the other; (2) while improvising, a player has infinite opportunities for choice, and it is better to take an active than a passive choice, ("take the unlikely choice," Del Close recalls as a phrase of Elaine's); and (3) in an improvisation, where there are no lines, or given actions, or dramaturgical "spine" to set a character in motion, *you* are your character, although not one called by your name. All characterization or "acting" comes from an exaggerated or intensified rendition of yourself called by another name.

Still, none of these acting guidelines guaranteed the creation of a coherent or well-structured scene. Flicker and May dissected the dramaturgical elements of the improvised scene and came up with more rules: all improvisations require the discovery and development of three elements; place ("Where"), character ("Who"), and a circumstance ("What") wherein a need for each other between the players is expressed. Missing any of these ingredients, an improvisational scene would become unintelligible and hit the skids. Since neither doing business (buying and selling) nor arguing are dramatic transactions, they were to be avoided as improvisational dead ends. Every day Flicker and May got together and invented exercises that excluded doing business and arguing and that would strengthen the players' grasp of circumstance, character, and place. Flicker says, "We came up with a teachable formula for performing improvisation in public in two weeks."*

In Las Vegas, where he had his next big job, Shelley Berman was the opening act for the singer Johnny Desmond at the Thunderbird. On the first night of the run, he was told by the owner, "Get out there and give 'em your best ten minutes, and get off." Berman explained that some of his routines ran about eight minutes and he would have to do at least two. The owner saw no problems. "Just cut 'em down," he said. Berman tried again: "But see, I do these phone calls, and they're pretty hard to cut down. They have a beginning, middle, end. This material isn't written, but I have to do my beats. See, I'm an improvisationalist." He was ex-

---

*The Westminster Place Kitchen Rules will not be found in Viola Spolin's *Improvisation for the Theater.* Spolin does not address the pitfalls in the public performance of improvisation because her book is a manual for teachers, not players. She is, as she says, less interested in improvisation for its entertainment values than as a teaching system, a path to creativity that *is* entirely intuitive. As a nonperformer, unlike Elaine May or Ted Flicker, Spolin was never pressed to find out how not to improvise in front of a paying audience and fail.

plaining his Arcadian comedic craft to a Las Vegas club owner. "And the guy looked at me like I was crazy."

Shelley Berman has since played the lounges and starred in the big rooms of Las Vegas. "When you're finished with a job in Las Vegas, you feel like they should give you a suit of clothes and take you to the station, and the governor should hand you a written reprieve." From his portfolio of assignments there, he has learned that "you go to Las Vegas to work, and you throw out everything. You throw away the book. You do a routine or two for those who come to see you. Then you stand up there with buzz words, trigger words that make people laugh. You can say shit. You can say fuck. You can make people laugh very easily."

Using his Compass material opening night at the Thunderbird on his virginal night in Las Vegas, Shelley Berman had beginner's luck and got some laughs. For the next four weeks, working seven nights a week, "I never heard a titter. For twenty-seven days, I didn't hear a laugh."

He left convinced that he was in the wrong business.

In St. Louis, Del Close noticed that Mike Nichols was "attempting to bring Actors Studio techniques like conflict and sense memory—handling real objects—into our work, where they had no place whatsoever. I felt he had a kind of half-baked understanding of what the Actors Studio work was," adds Close, "and also a rather primitive appreciation of what our own work might be."

Close himself had persisted in his belief that new, perhaps even quite complex, theatrical events could be built on strategies like those suggested by Von Neumann's game theory. "Mike had the idea that *Waiting for Godot* was the beginning of experimental theatre. I thought we were." Close thought the possibilities for improvisational theatre were limitless.

Nichols, by contrast, had grown to rely on Elaine to guide him through what Paul Sills calls the improvisational "deeps." His interest in the techniques of improvisation seem otherwise to have remained arrested in Lee Strasberg's class. (Lecturing at Yale in 1986, he still put forth these two contradictory formulas: "Improvisation is based on conflict" and "When in doubt, seduce.")

In fact, Nichols's dedication to improvisation had always been less than his colleagues'. His impulse had always been to scale down its use. If they were interested in improvising plays, he was interested in setting scenes. If they thrived in the context of an ensemble, he thrived in a team.

And now Elaine seemed to be intrigued by the work advanced by these novices in St. Louis, who thought improvisationalists could take off together without any advance agenda, into other reaches of experience than neurotic Jewish family scenes. The others in the company, captured by her commitment to a process that consumed them too, were, as usual, her big fans.

Nichols coveted Elaine's attention. In the backstage huddles of the small ensemble, pairings were less frequent. In St. Louis, the team of Nichols and May developed no new scenes.

20

A Harder Game of Hurt

In the St. Louis rendition of *The Game of Hurt*, Del and Mike are two college roommates. Mike is waiting for the arrival of his girl (Elaine), who has been away for a Christmas vacation or semester break. During that time, Mike has cheated on her.

Del is on the verge of leaving for the library to give the couple time alone, but the girl arrives early. Out of politeness, she urges him to stay. His sense of civility forces him to comply, although in so doing he fouls up his roommate's plans. Forced by good manners to conceal his irritation, Mike proposes an activity they can all do together, such as a game. He suggests the game of Hurt.*

It must be remembered that Mike Nichols was a master of the insulting one-liner, of one-upmanship. Elaine was his only equal at the game of Hurt.

At twenty-three, Del Close is recalled by Dave Moon, the set designer of the Crystal Palace and a pioneer television designer at twenty-six, as "a complete original" with "an outlandish mind. His whole persona was from left field." Close also felt himself to be "mentally unstable in those days" as a result of his father's suicide. In the presence of Nichols and May, moreover, he perceived himself in heady company, "a WASP among these

---

*Cruel party games were as popular in St. Louis at the time as they had been in Chicago. The local game was called Troika, in which various status deficiencies could bump a player from the safety of the troika (a three-horse vehicle) and cast him out upon the Russian steppes.

intelligent Jews, a kid from Kansas fresh off the farm, who didn't share their Freudian sensibility."

Although Nichols always professed friendship for Ted Flicker ("He acted like he was my best friend"), he did not pretend to hit if off with Close. Close was indifferent to Lee Strasberg. He was brilliant but not worldly wise. He drove a motorcycle. And he had never been psychoanalyzed.

Whatever his emotional armor, Nichols couldn't penetrate it. According to Close, "Mike didn't understand the WASP dynamic. It made him furious." Nichols's assaults ("Your motorcycle is a penis extension") only caused Close to laugh.

As the game progressed with this emotional undercurrent, the dynamics of the scene, as Close describes it, were "really Virginia Woolf" and "psychodrama." For Close it seemed revelatory of new pathways to group consciousness, "a fine blending of Mike and Elaine's serious Actors Studio approach" with Flicker's circus stunts.

Mike is getting hurt the most, by both his roommate and his girlfriend. Since they aren't hurting each other, it begins to look as though they are conspiring against him. When Del reveals that Mike has been unfaithful in Elaine's absence, Mike storms out of the apartment. In a long silence, Elaine and Del realize that they really do like each other. They embrace.

"It was very successful," Close recalls, "a powerful piece of work. The game unwound with the inevitability of a Greek tragedy. And that was how our relationship did indeed develop. They could hurt each other. I could hurt Mike. I couldn't hurt Elaine. Neither one of them could hurt me."

Offstage, although Howard Alk, an occasional visitor from Chicago, was still her official suitor, Elaine and Del Close were now seen to be romantically engaged. And Elaine had a sorcerer under her spell.

U pon his release from the hospital, Severn directed *Anastasia* at the Barter Theatre, and turned up again in St. Louis with his leg in a brace that Del Close describes as "an engineering marvel." Severn asked Flicker for a job at the Compass, looking, according to Close, "like a bionic man." Flicker gave him the job.

Close reflects that despite their differences, the company had "managed to create a gestalt, a group mind," when Severn arrived: "We didn't know how to use it, and we also didn't know how to get out of it. We had to spend all our time together, whether we liked it or not. We were like a swarm of gnats that formed an intelligence. Out of it, we'd be at a loss." The evenings of performance were exhausting and long, yet when they went to a restaurant after the show, they would cram themselves into one booth. That way, besides living together, driving together, rehearsing to-gether, performing together, and avoiding the advances of the wife swappers together, they could eat together and continue obsessing together about improvisation and how to do it "right."

"When I left, you were four neurotics. Now you're one psychotic," Severn said.

The others simply scrunched in a little tighter in the restaurant booth to make room for him.

The Compass in St. Louis now had Severn to pose a threat to all the rules and any formula or theories on how to improvise.

After he joined the company, he began to ask Flicker if he could perform a Dada sketch. "No, Severn, you may *not* do the Dada sketch," Flicker would always reply.

During one week, when Flicker was required in New York, "on one of my many trips to see if I could bring the Compass there, I came back without telling anybody. And I came back on a Saturday night. There was a silence in the Crystal Palace. I heard Severn shouting in German. I said, 'Omigod, he's doing the Dada sketch.' I slipped in back—nobody saw me—and sure enough, he was out there with Elaine and Nancy Ponder wrapping the audience in toilet paper. Then he got back up on the stage and said, 'You stupid swine, why are you sitting there taking this shit?' And they almost killed him. There was hollering and shouting. People got up and left."

Recalling the Dada scene in St. Louis, Severn says, "Yes, I emptied the house. It worked perfectly."

"The entire history of improvisational theatre was balanced on a pinpoint there in St. Louis," Del Close thinks. "It was one of the most amazing things that ever happened in world theatre, a creative experience un-matched perhaps on the planet. There's never been anything like it."

"No one has done what we did, or gone to the levels we went," Nancy Ponder agrees.

Dave Moon's memory of this St. Louis company is captured by a scene in which Mike and Elaine and Del and Nancy spent "ten minutes estab-lishing a vast invisible IBM computer all over the stage. Severn walked on with his hands held two inches apart" and gazed at their creation. "And here's the new model," he said.

In Nancy Ponder's opinion, the company was primed and ready for New York. "We worked like meshed gears."

That was why she was so puzzled when Elaine said to her with such sympathy, "You're like the child in a marriage that's breaking up."

Before he settled down at *The New Yorker* as a resident critic of American Theatre, Kenneth Tynan, reviewing for the London *Observer*, once described the onstage rapport of Nichols and May as "an unnerving display of mutual empathy."

According to most witnesses, their onstage empathy had always remained, in fact had grown, in inverse proportion to their offstage war. As David Shepherd describes it, "Mike's attitude was that you want to know on top what the point is. And Elaine always wanted to explore and find new points. That's why it was amazing that their partnership was as successful as it was. They were from such different bags."

As Ted Flicker analyzed their personality clash, "Mike is a superficial man of great taste and wit. Elaine is a passionate artist and an archetypical slob. Mike likes to dominate and control everyone around him. Elaine needs to dominate and control men. She trusts nobody." Although she disliked and resented editorial interference in her process, it was Flicker's opinion that "she's always needed someone to say, 'Stop, that's the point.'"

Elaine, it should be recalled, put no stock in "getting ahead." To her, knowing the point and coming to the point was a violation of truth. "In life, you don't decide for yourself what you'll do. It just happens," she once said. "It's all Kafkaesque." Perhaps it was a result of an early childhood in Nazi Germany, or simply his fill of incorrectly prepared White Castle hamburgers, but except for the rather outstanding exception of working with her, Mike Nichols had a very limited tolerance for the "Kafkaesque."

Exercising their various needs to control, either through chaos or order, Ted Flicker remembers that Mike and Elaine "routinely manipulated the hell out of each other."

As if seeking to tap into their deeper springs, Severn conceived a twenty-three-scene scenario for the Compass based on Hermann Hesse's *Steppenwolf*. This philosophical novel is a fictional rendering of the madness and spiritual awakening of Harry Haller, an intellectual in decadent post–World War I Germany, notable for his pessimistic outlook, his lack of animal vitality, his self-contempt, and his "boundless and frightful capacity for pain."

In Severn's dramatization, Mike Nichols would be Harry Haller, the Steppenwolf.

It is Hesse's Nietzschean proposition that "true humor begins when one ceases to take himself seriously." Harry Haller must experience his deepest dreams and desires before he can even hope to laugh. Until then, he is the Steppenwolf, a divided man, sick for want of resolution between his warring poles: man and wolf, Apollo and Dionysus, left and right brain.

Hesse describes the ambisexual Herman/Hermine as "like life itself, one moment succeeding to the next and not one to be foreseen." Before he kills her, it is Hermine who teaches the Teutonic Harry to open the personalities within himself, to dance to American music, to expose the infinite souls of the Steppenwolf. That part belonged to Elaine May. Del Close would play the sensualist Pablo, the drug dispenser, the jazz musician. Nancy Ponder would be Maria, the innocent whore recruited to help the Steppenwolf regain his sexuality. Severn was to play the bust of Mozart, the image of the true artist, in Hesse's view, a genius who can laugh.

The scenario was never performed. "Mike and Elaine refused to do it," Severn recalls. "Mike said it was childish. 'Adolescent' was the word I think he used. And Elaine went along with him. 'Adolescent.' She couldn't one-up him on that."

Indeed, it was the cunning of their psychological wiles that gave Mike and Elaine's scientist and his mother, their spies, their psychiatrists and patients, their teenagers in a car—and especially their "Pirandello"—such an incredible charge.

Comedy is other people's pain. "Pirandello" gave evidence that the very spectacle of their genius for mutual torture gave Nichols and May their theatrical click. Thus, not alone among comedy teams (*viz.*, Abbott and Costello, Martin and Lewis, and Neil Simon's Sunshine Boys), they were, as Flicker points out, "locked into their relationship because they were wonderful on stage together, and they knew it and we knew it." In fact, the great ensemble work at the Crystal Palace that so moved Del Close and Nancy Ponder is judged by Severn as "nothing" compared to the improvisations performed in Chicago by Mike and Elaine.

There are several romantic versions of how Nichols and May branched off from the Compass to become a separate performing unit. In one, Flicker fires Nichols for sabotaging group spirit, strips him of his invisible epaulettes, and bounces him off the stage. In response, Elaine announces to her producer, "You fire him, and I'll quit." Broke and jobless, but undaunted, Nichols and May set off for New York, get a job at the Blue Angel, a chic East Side nightclub, and overnight become stars.

According to the story that Nichols and May themselves disseminated, and finally perfected for their Broadway *Playbill*, they are already in New York when the producer of Compass finds himself without the means to recapitalize, "leaving the company stranded in Manhattan." Thus abandoned, "with $40 between them and financial ruin," on the suggestion of a friend they invest a dime to call Jack Rollins, an influential artists' manager, to see if he will manage them.

In yet a third version, another financial mission in mid-August 1957 took Ted Flicker to New York, this time for several weeks. The company sent him off with a celebration, good wishes, and a cake. Before leaving, he advised the company that although a director was always needed, the players should rotate in the role each week. "I thought everybody in the group should get a chance to shape the show," he says. Once he was gone, Mike and Elaine shared the assignment since none of the other players possessed a directorial dream.

The drama Nichols and May devised took place off the stage. To the best recollections of the supporting cast, the plot was motivated by Mike and Elaine's reservations about the way Flicker was directing the show as well as by their suspicions that the gig in New York was not guaranteed.

Following their scenario, Ponder and Close and Nichols and May would sidestep Flicker's entrepreneurship and form their own four-man team. In fact, Nichols already had an "in" to Jack Rollins through Rollins's old friend, Charles Pratt, an independently wealthy (Pratt Institute in Brooklyn was named for his family) photographer and theatre fan. Pratt's young wife, Julie, was an actress, one of Nichols's pals from Lee Strasberg's class. The St. Louis group could audition for Rollins forthwith, in Flicker's absence, by taking a quick trip to New York. Severn would be kept outside the undertaking since his good friend Flicker was about to be stabbed in the back by a betrayal of which the perpetrators were not unashamed.

On a flatcar at the St. Louis railroad, they took publicity shots of themselves as a foursome for their upcoming act. Their budget did not cover four plane tickets to New York.

Mike and Elaine suggested that they purchase two plane tickets. Nichols and May would represent all four of them. Del Close and Nancy Ponder each kicked in fifty dollars. It was just an overnight trip.

Mike and Elaine were back the next day in time for the show. Close picked them up at the airport to learn that the results of the meeting with Rollins had been ambiguous but encouraging. To his knowledge, no deal had been set.

A letter was delivered to Mr. Kelly's, where Shelley Berman was performing a routine about name dropping, informing him that he was being sued for improper use of material belonging to Mike Nichols and Elaine May. In Berman's version, the name dropper was "the most important booking agent in the world," who manically fields phone calls to "names so big you haven't even heard of them." ("Eleanor, sweetheart," he says to his secretary, "who's on the other line? Honey, you know how many people I'm handling here. Don't just say Picasso. Tell me who he is. Oh, yeah. Hello, Pablo! *Buenos días*, kiddo!") Berman's words had all been freshly improvised. His behind-the-show-biz-scenes character was driven and aggressive, not unctuous, as was the on-the-air Jack Ego, the name-dropping character Mike Nichols had not really invented, after all, but parodied. In fact, Albert Schweitzer and the pope were the only dropped names the two pieces had in common. Berman couldn't understand the fuss. Neither could his lawyer. He continued doing it.

U pon their return from New York, the relationship deteriorated between Mike and Elaine. A dispute Del Close describes as "artistic and interpersonal" erupted between him and Nichols during a rehearsal of a surrealistic five-scene Hitchcock parody called *The Wide Man*, which Close had constructed to include a Nichols and May scene, "Spies on a Train." Close had already deferred to Elaine as "my director." Elaine took Close's side.

All through the night of August 23, both Flicker and David Shepherd were besieged by long-distance calls, Flicker recalls, "from Severn, from Mike, from Elaine—such political intrigue!" Flicker was astonished to learn from Elaine that "Mike had tried to mount a coup to become the director and eliminate me. I flew back to St. Louis, at her insistence, heartsick at what was going on." He arrived on the site of the former Dante's Inferno to find that the iron discipline he had maintained at the Compass had "all fallen apart. The show was just a mess. That wonderful show we had going was now this chaotic, old-time Compass: disorganized, everybody distrusting everybody, everybody fighting and squabbling." Privately, Elaine told Flicker that she was leaving the company unless he fired Mike. "I talked with Shepherd," Flicker recalls. "I talked with Mike. Then I went back and talked with Elaine. And Elaine was adamant. So I fired Mike. He was utterly devastated. And I was too. I really liked Mike. I really didn't want to fire him. But Elaine said, 'You fire him, or I'll quit.' "

Once Nichols was fired, Close was no longer obliged to betray Ted Flicker or to commit himself to a four-man team. He was relieved.

Otherwise, "all kinds of people" prevailed upon Flicker to reinstate Nichols, including the Landesmans.

Nancy Ponder was stunned. "Without Michael, how can we do Story-Story with Style?" she thought. "How can you separate the warp from the woof?"

In the many long-distance entreaties to David Shepherd on Nichols's behalf, Ponder does not remember that the telephone receiver was ever lifted by Elaine. "I just assumed she wanted him back. But actually she just sat there. She didn't say a word."

Flicker felt himself to be persona non grata in St. Louis when he left to resume his Compass business dealings in New York. For him, the final upshot of the incident Shepherd recorded in his diary as "Mike and Elaine crisis all day and all night" on August 25 was that "for years, Mike Nichols hated me."

For Nancy Ponder, it was a huge phone bill.

During his stunning run at Mr. Kelly's, Shelley Berman was invited to appear on *The Jack Paar Show*, whose star prided himself on discovering unknown off-beat comedians. The national exposure helped open up another stage for Berman at the hungry i, Mort Sahl's home base in San Francisco. He did so well there that the management reoptioned him at almost twice his price. Soon there would be a booking at the Blue Angel in New York. He would enter the nightclub circuit in Los Angeles at the Avant-Garde. He did not encourage his wife, Sarah, to give up her job.

Ted Flicker's backer decided to withdraw the promised $38,000 that would launch the Compass in New York. According to Shepherd, when the devastating news was learned, Flicker "gave me the option to break up our partnership. He'd thought it would be easy to get his backers to pay up." According to Flicker, there was no such option. As he re-members it, "David Shepherd ceased to interest me on that day when he told me that my work embarrassed him and that since I didn't have the thirty-eight thousand dollars, I couldn't be part of Compass anymore." Neither man disputes that September 1957 marked the end of their part-nership. At least two of the remaining Compass Players, preparing to leave for New York, were not so advised.

Shepherd decided to postpone his Fulbright in order to devote himself to recasting the St. Louis company and to organizing his own "fund raising" for the New York branch. To this, he would invite agents, bookers and bankers, influential parties like José Quintero, and Suzanne's family. He would rent an appropriate space and provide material and expertise. Larry Arrick would assemble, rehearse, and direct the acting company.

S ince being sacked by the Compass, Mike Nichols had been crying on the shoulders of the various actor friends he camped out with in New York. From one of these pads, he tied up the phone with a series of long-distance entreaties to Elaine in St. Louis to follow him. It seemed like an appearance at the Blue Angel was waiting for them.

The outgoing Compass Players packed a bottle of champagne in an antique silver bucket and drove the Cadillac town car to the airport to meet the new players in an official changing of the guard.

Severn stayed behind to direct the new group. Nancy Ponder took off for New York in a plane; a Volkswagen bug transported Del Close and Elaine. What with the condition of the car and the amount of luggage, their trip took three days. In New York, they heard that Flicker's money deal had collapsed. And that Mike Nichols had a management contract with Jack Rollins for two, not four, people, as well as a Sunday night booking at the Blue Angel for Nichols and May.

Close looked upon the disappointing turn of events as "immediate karmic payback. We were conned into betraying Ted, and we were in turn be-trayed. So I didn't feel so bad." He understood then that "the goddess was more evident in Elaine than in most people—in all her aspects—the beautiful one and the wrathful one."

Only when Ponder and Close filed for unemployment insurance did they discover that for technical reasons they were ineligible to collect it. Ponder contested the ruling and pushed Actors' Equity to follow the case all the way to the Missouri court. The unemployment money was recovered. The fifty dollars she had paid to fly Nichols and May to New York was not.

Nancy Ponder had spent hours with Elaine, sharing confidences and buttoning the backs of each other's blouses backstage. "I loved her, and I thought she loved me," she says. For thirty years she never knew that Mike was fired by Elaine. "The heart of another is a dark forest," she reflects. "Maybe she didn't want to be the one responsible for our breaking up."

Del Close had never been told the story of the ending of the first *Game of Hurt*. In it, Marian Gruber gives up a fulfilling new life with an adoring young boyfriend and goes back to her hypercritical husband and their game of Hurt.

It was apparently upon the dissolution of the plans to start the New York Compass that Elaine was willing to go the road she had so far avoided, to give up the vagaries of the improvisational theatre and cast her lot with the partner she so recently had had fired, as one half of a comedy team.

Or had she been playing all along the Pirandello game?

Years after the Compass was gone from St. Louis, Ben Bagley's *Littlest Revue* was playing at the Crystal Palace and one of its players, Barbara Anson, was offered Elaine's room at 4411 Westminster Place. Proudly, it was pointed out to Anson that in this room, en route to New York, in the abstracted daze of her genius, Elaine had left on the mantel a decomposing watermelon rind and, in her clothes closet, a bag of rotting chopped meat.

21

Explosions

Along the Broadway of 1957, in show-business enclaves like the Brill Building, Lindy's, the William Morris Agency, and the Stage Delicatessen, Jack Rollins was even then a legend: a City College man, an intellectual, a chess player, a poker buff, a bilingual punster, a night owl, an appreciator of fine wine, cigars, and humor, and an excellent handicapper who only bet two dollars on a horse. The biggest *machers* in the entertainment industry now defer to Rollins as "The Dean," "The Guru," "The Poet of Managers," "a man of good will out there among the savages," and "Gentleman Jack." Searching for an appraisal of Rollins that excludes accolades for his decency and lack of guile, one finds only Groucho ornery enough to describe him, in a letter to Dick Cavett, as "that hoodlum who handles you."

"No one pretends to fully understand Jack," one associate observes. The comedians who have experienced Rollins's "unmistakable laugh" don't care. "Jack has vast reserves of subterranean mirth," an old friend says. "It's there, like offshore oil. You have to drill for it. He loves to laugh."

Rollins has been Woody Allen's manager and producer for over thirty years. He and his partners are also or have also been behind the scenes of David Letterman, Robin Williams, Louise Lasser, Robert Klein, Billy Crystal, and Martin Short.

"Jack's a gambler," says the old friend, the writer David Vern, who has known Rollins since the eighth grade at P.S. 149 in Brooklyn, more than sixty years. "He gambles on his projections like bankers do. I've seen a lot of acts with him. He can predict a person's future value. Other people can't."

At the time Mike Nichols and Elaine May flew in from St. Louis to see him, Rollins had already earned his reputation as a connoisseur of off-beat talent, for fashioning a career as a Calypso star for a beautiful singer cum short-order cook named Harry Belafonte.

Rollins grew up in the political cauldron of Jewish immigrants in Brooklyn called East New York. In the 1940s, he worked in the Windy City as a social worker and, like his chum Vern, as a writer for Ziff-Davis, which published *Amazing Stories* and other pulp magazines. During World War II, he was stationed in India as a sergeant in the Signal Corps.

In Calcutta, he and a Sergeant Hesselberg shared an apartment and a seventy-year-old bearer named Parak. They bought Parak a white coat with two boxing gloves embroidered on the back. The front said, "Rollins and Hesselberg, Sahibs." In downtown Calcutta, a major stopped them. The major was the actor Melvyn Douglas. He stared at Parak and said, "*My* name is Hesselberg."

Douglas was the new Special Services officer in charge of entertainment. He appointed the late gambler Abraham ("Van") Mitchell station manager of radio VUZ-ZU-Calcutta. Mitchell put his friend Rollins in charge of programming. After the war, Mitchell looked up Melvyn Douglas, who was producing the army review, *Call Me Mister*, and, with winnings from a racehorse Mitchell had owned in India, decided to invest in it. "It was a good gamble," says David Vern. Mitchell and Rollins reteamed, only to produce a flop in London that Rollins prefers to forget. By the late forties, working in New York as readers for Max Gordon (the producer, not the nightclub owner), they had office space in the Lyceum Theatre and aspirations to produce another play. Rollins became a manager by "sheer accident," he says.

"I was strolling in the Village, courting my wife. Jane was a singer with a quartet at the time. On Sheridan Square, we peered into the window of a tiny restaurant. And there was Harry Belafonte, flipping hamburgers."

The struggling singer Jane recognized from the road was planning a switch from pop to folk music, and in short order Belafonte invited his customer to help him build his new career. Rollins offered instead to help Belafonte find and shape a repertoire. "I had no other interest in it. That never crossed my mind. I happened to know something about folk music. It was building the act that interested me."

Friends have described Jack Rollins's dedication to the young Belafonte as "like a mother's." In the WPA archives at the now extinct Liederkrantz Hall, they plowed through thousands of reels of authentic folk songs with fifty choruses sung by singers from various backwoods. They worked ten-hour days with a guitarist. The Calypso angle and the open shirt were Rollins's ideas. When he felt Belafonte's act needed "one little comedy piece," Rollins, whom his partners describe as "a man with no rhythm," even wrote lyrics to "Man Piaba" ("That's *right*, de woman is smartah!") from a Carribbean children's tune.

After three years, Rollins deemed the act "brilliant." Nevertheless, because of his color, "pleading and begging" were required to get Belafonte a stage. At last, Max Gordon (the nightclub owner, not the producer) gave him time for three songs at the Village Vanguard. "Harry did the three songs, and there was instant pandemonium. And that's how I became a manager," Rollins says.

As Belafonte became an international celebrity, he took on a psychiatrist, who prescribed a new manager, her husband. For Rollins, who made deals with a handshake, it was not a flush time. He was about to recuperate from his "disbelief and disarray" over Belafonte's drop-dead dismissal by turning his considerable and pent-up energies to this pair of actors who had scored with their improvised scenes about urban anxiety in Chicago and, in October 1957, were starving in New York.

Nichols and May would recall themselves offhandedly auditioning for Rollins at the Russian Tea Room, "over beef stroganoff and cold schav." But it had been in Rollins's office, without benefit of an audience, that they demonstrated their wares. "I was stunned by how really good they were, actually as impressed by their acting technique as by their comedy," says Rollins. "They were remarkable immediately." He also saw that at the Compass, they had enjoyed the luxury of "no concessions. If they took twelve minutes with a sketch that could only live seven minutes commercially, they lived with it for twelve because that was their process." A nightclub act requires economy. "It was a question of lopping and polishing what they already had. But that was the only thing. Their work was so startling, so new, as fresh as could be."

Once they had decided to be managed, Rollins forthwith asked his friend Max Gordon, the club owner, who then coowned the uptown Blue Angel, as well as the downtown Village Vanguard,* to give his new team a spot

---

* The Village Vanguard flourishes still. The Blue Angel, Max Gordon, and his partner are gone.

on the Blue Angel's Sunday audition night. Nichols and May went on after the regular show, following the Smothers Brothers (in matching red jackets) and Eartha Kitt.

Legend goes that when the applause died down, Gordon offered them a job on the spot, to begin in ten days. In the interim, to allay Mike Nichols's fear of starving, Gordon suggested that they perform at the Village Vanguard as the opening night.

But Gordon was not present at the Blue Angel that Sunday night. The performance was for Rollins's eyes, and on his say-so Nichols and May played for Gordon at the Village Vanguard, positioned this time on a bill with Mort Sahl.

David Vern gave Mike Nichols a ride home from the Vanguard to the Lower East Side that night, where he was camping out in the tenement apartment of two young directors, George Morrison (U. of C. '49) and Ulu Grosbard. Nichols was nervous. He and Elaine had performed three pieces. The middle piece had laid an egg. Nichols asked Vern what he thought the price for that egg would be. Vern guessed: "Max will say, 'Don't do the middle piece.' "

When you called Jack Rollins during the time he managed Harry Belafonte, David Vern remembers that "Jane would say, 'Harry's in Detroit.' And that's where Jack would be." Beginning at the Village Vanguard, he took a front seat for his new team's lying-in.

Rollins got Nichols and May a booking on *The Jack Paar Show*, where they were given barely enough time to get their improvisation going before Paar, excited by his staff about the hilarious new team, got impatient for the customary volley of jokes and laughs and cut them off. They bombed.

On November 11, a Compass "preview" was presented for financially interested parties in a rather dingy banquet room at the Wellington Hotel. Although they were already performing at the Village Vanguard, Nichols and May were in the show. Nancy Ponder performed as well. Del Close was not asked. With Walter Beakel's permission, Larry Arrick directed his own version of *The Liars*, inviting Tom Aldredge to fill in for Severn Darden and Jerry Stiller to take on Lieberman, the Shelley Berman part. Nichols and Beakel were the only Liars from the original cast.

In preparation for his part, Stiller remembers he had been shown "this script that was hangin' on the wall." During the performance, he was amazed that just by speaking dialogue extemporaneously he experienced "tremendous freedom" and was rewarded with "tremendous laughs." "They did handstands out front," he says.

Peering from the wings when his own part was over, Stiller watched Nichols and May perform "Pirandello." He observed that "something completely new was happening out there. Their stuff was unreal, fantastic. I couldn't believe my eyes."

When the show was over, Stiller was yet again surprised to learn from David Shepherd that the potential backers in the audience hadn't put up a cent.

In the wake of the performance, visitors from MCA, the big talent agency, explained to Shepherd that among the several areas of entertainment where money could be made, Compass fell into the category of "variety." As a variety act, it would be a hard sell for agents, too problematical to book: the performance was unpredictable and the improvised acting seemed to range from subtle to amateurish. The comedy was unpredictable too, with too much space between the laughs. Television was out of the question: Compass simply broke too many taboos. The buyer of an improvised entertainment for television could obviously be sued for libel. There was no denying that.

David Shepherd decided to go forward with his Fulbright alternative, to Paris, where there were clearer vistas than the funny business, higher goals than *The Ed Sullivan Show*, and a more empathetic environment for a producer-inventor-author of un- and anti-commercial cabaret plays.

"I think the reason I left it behind was that the future seemed to belong to Mike and Elaine," he would later reflect. "And they didn't *do* scenarios. They did individual skits, hunks of comedy that could be screwed together in different sequences for various shows and television appearances, whatever they had to do, wherever they had to play. Whereas a scenario would require five, six, seven people, plus sound effects, lights, the whole thing. But that's what the theatre's about: not putting together hunks of stuff for television but telling stories about the audience, it always seemed to me."

A few days after the backer's audition for the New York Compass failed, he and Suzanne set sail.

Ten November days after they opened with the clarinetist Jimmy Giuffre, Nichols and May were replaced at the Village Vanguard by Mort Sahl and moved to the more prominent and sophisticated Blue Angel uptown. The week before Christmas, in his "Tables for Two" column in *The New Yorker*, Douglas Watt brought national attention to them in print, comparing their intimate overlapping conversations with those of the Lunts.

Although his bookings were widely spaced, Shelley Berman was now headlining in strategic nightspots in four big cities, but "if people didn't laugh, I got surly," he says. "I didn't know how to deal with an unreceptive audience, or a heckler, or someone who didn't like me. I didn't know how to address the audience. I didn't have any jokes. I could only do these little playlets on the phone by myself."

One night in Montreal, where he was appearing as the opening act for Billy Eckstein, the singer took him aside. "Shelley," he said, "tonight, I'd like you to try something just once. I'd like you to smile at the audience and say, 'Good evening' before you go to work." "I can't do that. I don't know *how* to do that," Berman replied. "I thought I was different. I wasn't different. I just wasn't a comedian. I became a comedian along the way. But it was not a willing or a happy thing. It was terrifying."

On December 29, Nichols and May appeared on *The Steve Allen Show*. Their name-dropping skit attracted the interest of *Omnibus*, a popular and tony Sunday "magazine" show about American culture, hosted by a charming and cultivated Englishman, Alistair Cooke. For an appearance on the *Omnibus* episode "Suburban Revue" (featuring Cooke in a straw boater), Jack Rollins this time insisted that a full fifteen minutes be allotted to the wayward rhythms of Nichols and May. In return, they would brilliantly perform "The Dawn of Love or The Moon Also Rises in an Automobile," a.k.a. "Teenagers" ("Isn't the lake suicidally beautiful tonight?"). *And* the scene Elaine May had previously developed and performed with Shelley Berman about a desperate pay-phone caller and (what was now not just one, but) a series of indifferent operators, now called "Telephone," formerly, "The Lost Dime."

The critics were floored.

The first week of the New Year 1958, Mike Nichols and Elaine May were catapulted from *Omnibus* to celebrity, just three months after they hit New York. Five thousand dollars per appearance was their new asking price. They would be seen in Hollywood at the Mocambo, in Chicago at Mr. Kelly's, and back in New York (where Pat Scot was singing at the Blue Angel) at Down in the Depths, the clubroom at the (now defunct) Hotel Duane. Mike Nichols took to driving himself and his wife to work in a Mercedes convertible. Also in the offing were *The Dinah*

Shore Chevy Show, The Perry Como Show, a television special, and other
deals.

B y his own diagnosis, Del Close "went mad" around this time. He
entered therapy on scholarship as a patient of Dr. Theodor Reik.

T errified or not, Shelley Berman kept hammering away at his "in one"
box and came up with a sparkling assortment of setups and segues to
adorn his telephone monologues. Such pieces as "The Department Store,"
"The Morning After the Night Before," "Franz Kafka on the Telephone"
(Berman's version of "The Lost Dime"), and "Father and Son" were now
highlighted by precisely observed and brilliantly vocalized harangues about
life's irritations and annoyances, like buttermilk ("It's not the buttermilk
that bothers me. It's the way the glass looks afterward") or tiny embar-
rassments ("You're talking to someone intimately, and all of a sudden you
spit on them").

Scores (if not hundreds) of comedians have squeezed juice from Berman's archetypal essay on the terrors of airplane travel:

Incidentally, if you do buy one of these life insurance policies, for
god's sakes, don't read it. Pay for it, sign it, send it off to someone
you want to worry, but if you read it, you'll *never* fly. What it does
is, it itemizes everything that can happen to you on that plane. And
there is one word that should be stricken from the English language
anyway. The word is *maimed*. It's a horrible word.

"Observational comedy" is the term by which such writing gambits are
nowadays glorified in the backstage areas of Laff Stores and Comedy Shops,
where they are often served up at the microphone as a comic's main dish.
Berman's piece on flying segued into a divertissement on "the incongruities
of the English plural":

. . . Before departing from this subject, I want to say just a few words
about stewardi. Stewardi is plural for stewardess . . . It seems to me
that the plural for yo-yo should be yo-yi. How about one sheriff,
several sheriffim? One goof . . . a group of geef. One Kleenex . . .
several Kleeneces. One blouse . . . two blice. Two jackeye.

And then segued back again to a hilariously acted (and perfectly written) dialogue between himself (the frightened passenger) and his target (the robotic stewardess):

"Care for a pillow?"
"Oh, miss, the wing is on fire out there."
"Oh, really?"
"Yes, really. Take a look out there. The wing is a sheet of flame.
   Take a look."
"Coffee, tea, or milk?"
"We don't have time for coffee, tea, or milk. We're doomed!"
"Well, then, how about a martini?"

Audiences were now responding to Shelley Berman fervidly. At the Blue Angel, he broke attendance records. He was signed for six appearances on *The Ed Sullivan Show*. There were articles about him in *Newsweek* and *Time*. As a baptismal into the big time, Albert Grossman, who had fired Berman at the Gate of Horn, now exercised his cannily conceived contractual option to rehire a very successful comedian at his original unsuccessful comedian's price.

The founder of The San Francisco Mime Troupe, R. D. Davis, ran into David Shepherd in a Parisian café one spring day when *Life* magazine was on all the newsstands and Nichols and May were featured in a big spread. Davis observed that their former producer was "very mad about the whole thing." Shepherd was hard at work on a play about the Badlands murderer Charles Starkweather and writing for journals like *Encore* and *Théâtre Populaire*. He was so set back by the *Life* article that he trashed his writing schedule to escort his parents-in-law around Europe. Watching the repertory companies of St. Etienne, Milan, and Mannheim, his enthusiasm for the theatre was somewhat refreshed.

That very month, as news of their latest achievements splashed across the Atlantic, Nichols and May suffered their first separate but equal critical lumps after appearing in public for the first time without their own material, as actors in the television version of *The Red Mill*, an old war-horse.

Although all avenues of show business were open now to them, on the few occasions that Nichols and May tried a departure from their Compass material, they did not enjoy satisfactory results. In April 1959, they were engaged as panelists on *Laugh Line*, a TV game show requiring each player to end the other's scene with a witty last line.

"If you hit the TV jackpot, you can make millions," TV newsman Mike Wallace observed while interviewing Nichols and May for his column in the New York *Post*. "That idea doesn't fascinate you?" "Oh, I'm used to living on twelve dollars a week," replied Elaine. "Elaine just doesn't have an acquisitive instinct," observed Mike. "I do. I really do. I enjoy the idea of having a Mercedes. I really do like wearing new suits."

Del Close's therapy was a success, apparently giving him the strength to endure two years of "absolutely humiliating defeat" as a nightclub comic. Typing jobs and Elaine helped pay his business expenses. "The sleazier the joint, the fancier they wanted the comics to dress," he recalls. "Like Mort Sahl could wear a T-shirt in Mr. Kelly's. In a toilet in New Jersey, I had to wear a tux."

Due to artistic differences with the show's management, and horrified by their first taste of network aesthetics, Nichols and May ended up quitting *Laugh Line* after only a month. "We were so spoiled," Nichols would later reflect, "we just assumed we would do what we wanted and everybody would say it was great." The same month, a devoted New York audience flocked to their brilliant concert of old Compass scenes at Town Hall.

"The more we became the talk of the town, the more I was afraid to try something new, when we had so many things that worked so well," Nichols would recall. "After all, other performers repeated their act. Why the hell should we have a new one every night?"

Ted Flicker had returned to the Crystal Palace for the winter stock season and electrified the cognoscenti with his production of *Waiting for Godot*, starring Tom Aldredge as Vladimir, Severn Darden as Estragon, Peter Bosche as Lucky, and Flicker himself as Pozzo, the man with the whip. For eight weeks, the house was SRO. Flicker asked the Landesmans for a producer's cut and heard it had been paid for in artistic satisfaction, since the show was a success. In response, he came up with an idea and an itemized budget for how the profits he had earned should be dispersed: by expanding the whole operation into a 300-seat theatre in which he could direct plays, Jay Landesman could produce revues and the audience could order drinks. Flicker's plan required a move to a hotter spot than Olive Street.

In Chicago, Paul Sills and Barbara Harris had divorced. The stresses of

marriage, however, had not pulled their artistic esteem for each other nor
their destinies apart. Barbara was acting at the Tenthouse Theatre for the
straw hat season. Sills got a job as house manager at the Gate of Horn.
Elaine's erstwhile boyfriend Howard Alk had a job there too, running the
lights. The new-style nightspot, featuring a casual dress code, reasonable
prices, young intellectual audiences, and hip entertainment, was redefining
Rush Street. The two former University of Chicago men soaked up the
vibrant atmosphere.

Back in St. Louis, Fred Landesman's opulent design for the new Crystal
Palace on Gaslight Square is described by his brother Jay as "a cross between
a church and a movie palace." Besides chandeliers, it featured fifty-foot
murals of cathedral stained glass. The walls and ceilings were painted
bright red. The first time Lenny Bruce played the room, he described it
as "a church that went bad."

The father of it all, Mort Sahl, had recorded his act on a long-playing
album, *Mort Sahl, Iconoclast*, and he talked his recording company and
Shelley Berman into immortalizing Berman's act too. With no expecta-
tions, Berman signed a long-term contract with Verve. Suddenly, "before
I knew what was happening," a live recording of his nightclub routines,
Inside Shelley Berman, was taking off.

At the Interlude in Los Angeles, where Berman was appearing with
Bobby Short, a line was waiting to get in every night, including "movie
actors I had admired all my life." At the big room downstairs, the Crescendo, Don Rickles was playing to a half-full house. One night, when
Berman popped in, Rickles cracked, "The guy's got one suit, and he's a
star." In nightclubs, costume changes are a measure of success. And
Berman was still taking off his only suit between shows, hoping that before
the second show "the wrinkles would fall off."

Shelley Berman has said that "the times call forth the comedian." Now
they called for him. All over the country, the "silent generation" were
retreating to their rec rooms and dormitories, listening to the "Method
Comedian" on their new hi-fi's. *Inside Shelley Berman* continued to rise
on the *Billboard* charts. Shelley Berman had indeed become a star. He
got a manager, a lawyer, an advance man, a valet, two secretaries, an East
Side apartment, a toy poodle, and a dozen suits ("all bent at the elbow,"
reported *Time*). And he was now stuck with the choice he had made
between "being a comedian or being unemployed."

22

Aftershocks

Far from the ragtag and radical community cabaret on the South Side of Chicago, where the shibboleths and icons of American society were nightly torn apart, Shelley Berman and Nichols and May had finally gained recognition and national followings on television, after honing their material into "hunks" of repeatable perfection in the most sophisticated and trendy boîtes of the day.

Like Mort Sahl, they were different in style and sensibility from the commercial comedians of the Eisenhower years, the joke-tellers who dressed up in tuxedos and paid their dues on the road, machine-gunning boozed-up audiences with shopworn patter and rerun routines in second-rate supper clubs, Mafia hangouts, Borscht Belt resorts, and strip joints. They shared with Sahl a connection to an underground network of students, beatniks, and intellectuals, a socially disenfranchised elite (Sahl liked to call them "my people"), aspiring to community and recognition, who heard the language they spoke—with all its psychosociological jargon and mocking highbrow references—as their own.* Like Sahl, their predecessor, and like Lenny Bruce, who flew in on their tails, these three young and serious actors had brought a new music to American comedy, a counterpart in its wandering melodies and off-beat rhythms to modern jazz. They were all similarly informed, articulate, low-key, and hip, that

---

*As a high-reference name dropper, Shelley Berman, who had joined the navy after high school, was, after his stint at the Compass, on the A team.

is, utterly unsentimental and unshuffling in their relationship to the audience and to their roles as entertainers. And they were no less rooted in
the Jewish comedy tradition than bop musicians were rooted in the black
tradition of the blues:

Mike Nichols is the apologetic Vanguard scientist who tells Elaine May,
who is playing his mother, that he feels terrible for having neglected to
call her:

> SHE: Oh, honey, if I could believe that, I'd be the happiest mother
> in the world.

Shelley Berman is playing his father:

> . . . All right, Sheldon, so forget about it. I'll forget about it. You'll
> forget about it. But I'll remember, Sheldon, and don't you forget it.

Thought patterns, riffs like these, were not picked up from Brecht.

Although they were even then received as a cultural phenomenon, the
"sick comics," as they were dubbed by the press, were friendly competitors,
not otherwise a group. Artistically, for instance, the former Compass players were much more complex and sophisticated than Mort Sahl was or
would ever be. Sahl was a talker, not an actor. What he said was all you
got. His technique was to deliver topical observations inspired by the
absurdities that he daily discovered in the news. Because he was at least
as informed as the newspaper, and because his choice of political targets
was so unflinching and courageous (Sahl had begun his career by putting
down the House Un-American Activities Committee, in 1953, the year
before the actors of the Playwrights Theatre Club decided not to risk their
careers by sponsoring a screening of Salt of the Earth), he was regarded
with some awe as an "intellectual." Kenneth Tynan once described him
just as inaccurately as "a liberal nihilist." Sahl was a fashionable performer
who tremendously enjoyed the perks of his celebrity. He called himself a
"social democrat." As an older, more calloused man, he became an antisocial conservative, arguing his right-to-life as a dinner guest at Ronald
Reagan's White House. What nihilism he endorsed in his heyday so scared
and threatened the political figures with whom he hobnobbed that they
regularly invited him on their payrolls to write their zingers. And it was
only then that they discovered he was really a moralist and couldn't be
bought.

As a comedian, however, Sahl was neither complicated nor deep. Other than that of a know-it-all, he had no comedy persona. Sahl made fun of people and events in the news. He never made fun of himself. He used the bullying aspect of his personality to defend his insides. In fact, his sheer bluff and nerviness often concealed scattershot material empty of revelation or laughs. ("I write my own material," Shelley Berman once jibed. "Mort's is written by William Randolph Hearst, Jr.") He did not delve into the "unknown, unspoken, unsomething" of the human condition. He could ad-lib; he could not improvise.

From improvising, from so much practice "letting go," Berman and Nichols and May produced more original and personal reports of life, specifically of their own eccentric inner workings: Elaine May's English character worries that her lover, the dentist, will "hate me for having a cavity." Into its most obscure recesses, they explored all the loose hinges of the human ego and made it clear that neurotic insecurities could be suffered even (or especially) by the most intelligent and witty persons: "Do you have moments in your life when you ask yourself, 'Why did I do that?' " Shelley Berman asked his audience. "I have *thousands* of them."

It had always bugged David Shepherd that the prime rib of Compass material was the tyranny of middle-class Jewish family values, not, as he wished, the spectrum of American life and politics. By the standards Shepherd raised, it must be said that as comedians the Compass improvisers still fell short. They were far less daring in their inquiries into the workings of society than Mort Sahl, although they had superior theatrical skills. Nor did they investigate other controversial areas of morality as did the rhapsode-junkie Lenny Bruce, whose essays on sex, religion, racism, and freedom of speech and expression profoundly changed America's comedy frontiers. The Compass comedians never really did hold up a mirror to society that could jolt awareness and so inspire change. Through the characters they created, they offered only unguarded, unvarnished glimpses of themselves. And did so with humor of such marksmanship and finesse that it would remain a hallmark to their audiences, an inspiration to their peers, and a beacon for a generation of comedy artists to come.

Indeed, the cachet the stars bestowed upon the Compass, improvisation, and Chicago gave a new direction to the others. By the time David Shepherd returned from his Fulbright term in Paris, the agents were standing on the bandwagon with bookings that roughly followed the footsteps of Shelley Berman and Nichols and May. Shepherd jumped on it, although the booking agents' Compass would never be accepted on its own merits but rather as the nebulous theatrical organism through which famous funny people had been—and still might be—produced. But Suzanne was pregnant, and for the first time in his career, instead of inventing a life in the theatre, Shepherd was feeling the heat to make a living in show business like everyone else.

He formed a new company with Nancy Ponder, Jerry Stiller, and Alan Arkin, Suzanne's schoolmate and Larry Arrick's Bennington protégé. He would have welcomed Severn in this cast of actors new to unscripted performance, but Severn said he preferred to stay in Chicago, trying out his own one-man turn at the Gate of Horn. His act included such unlikely nightclub routines as the Walter von der Vogelweide lectures on metaphysics, the Dada poetry, and his translations from the German of Christian Morgenstern.

The road company Compass was itself conceived as a nightclub act, not a theatre ensemble, and played disastrously in Cleveland at the Alpine Village on a bill with a baton twirler, with great success as always in St. Louis at the new Crystal Palace (where they were joined by Stiller's wife, Anne Meara), and very unevenly in New York at a mob nightspot, the Quadrille.

Ironically, while the Compass was on the road back to St. Louis, Shepherd's old partner, Ted Flicker, was moving on from his long sojourn there to Broadway. Flicker had directed an avant-garde musical at the Crystal Palace called *The Nervous Set*, using material from the Landesman-Wolf songbook and his own adaptation of Jay Landesman's unpublished book about his Greenwich Village days. Del Close played the editor of *Nerves* magazine.

Close had lately been supporting his comedy career by participating in REM sleep experiments under acid in a Brooklyn dream lab run for the Mercury 12 space program by the air force. When Flicker offered him the part, he took off for St. Louis on a motorcycle, with a suitcase of peyote on the back. A letter was forwarded to him from the military. It said: "Dear Mr. Close: You still owe the United States Air Force one dream."

The Nervous Set was a producer's dream, a "minimalist" production with almost no props, no choreographer, and no orchestra—just a jazz quartet on the stage. The costumes were sneakers and jeans. The set, copied from Dave Moon's St. Louis original, was a series of flat panels that accomplished a change of locale at a touch, without reimbursement to Moon. Jules Feiffer, the cartoonist who satirized neurosis, was brought in for the minimalist poster design. The new producer, Robert Lantz, had raised the tiny $35,000 budget in two days, merely appending to "Broadway's first wholly locally created musical" a new lead singer and a happy end.

Nichols and May and Jack Kerouac (upon whom the lead character had been based) were in the house with Leonard Bernstein and Richard Rodgers on opening night. Kerouac cheered when he saw his own caricature, then fell asleep. He left before the second act.

Kenneth Tynan thought the weakness of the production was "no point of view." Others opined that it belonged off-Broadway. Still others compared its mood and method to Brecht. "It was better in St. Louis," Cutie Landesman said.

The author of *Enterprise*, Roger Bowen, spent his last year in the army assigned to New York City. He enjoyed *The Nervous Set* with Paul Sills and Howard Alk (on a leave from the Gate of Horn). That summer, Bowen was discharged. Preparing for civilian life, he sent a résumé to the Associated Press, went through an interview, and was then ignored for months. In the interim, he decided to take Sills up on his suggestion to "come out to Chicago and do something."

Andrew Duncan had also been in touch with Sills, meeting him sometimes for coffee in Hyde Park or running into him on the Near North Side. Sills was contemplating a new project that conjured a renewed community. He described it to Duncan in his own unique fashion as "Barbara's around, and I talked to Gene Troobnick. Are you interested?" Duncan said he was.

That same summer, Sills drove down to St. Louis with Howard Alk to check out the show at the Crystal Palace. Sills said the new show was the best Compass yet. He told Shepherd that he and Alk and Bernie Sahlins were thinking of starting a Compass-type operation in Chicago—in this case, a coffeehouse and a show—which they hoped would attract a cultural cross section of would-be hipsters and the *Playboy* crowd. He also told Alan Arkin that if Arkin ever wanted a job in Chicago, he should look up Sills.

Arkin had abundant gifts. Formerly one of a successful folk-singing quartet called the Tarriers, he sang and wrote lyrics and played the guitar. He spoke in numerous dialects. He was poker-faced yet intense. Besides these credentials, Arkin, at eleven, had spent six months in Los Angeles at the Young Actors Company, training with Viola, a friend of Arkin's aunt.

This new Compass was not meant to last. Nightclubs, as Jerry Stiller noticed, "were not the right environment for social satirists, or at least not the nightclubs we were playing. Each place we were booked into emphasized this." At the Quadrille, the owners even had opinions about casting. "You got one guy that don't do nothin'," they informed Stiller. "That kid there, Alan, he don't talk. You gotta have people who talk up, like your wife."

"Tummling," or jousting with the audience, is a Borscht Belt term. Nightclubs like the Quadrille, which serve a well-heeled but not necessarily well-educated clientele of mostly urban ethnics, observe an etiquette that is foreign to the theatre, in which the audience enjoys its right to heckle the tummler if he is not "killing," "murdering," "wiping them out," or "destroying" them. The tummler must be tough. With his arsenal of "comebacks" and "toppers" and "zingers," he or she (most frequently he) is more like a lion tamer than an actor, skilled at controlling ("Look, if you want to lay an egg, lady, don't do it here") and appeasing ("Don't mind me, folks, it's all in fun") potentially angry beasts ("Is that your nose or are you eating a banana?").

A love of the forbidden is just a fact of human nature. Left to their own devices, most people find sexual inadequacy, perversions, and bathroom topics a sure thing to make them laugh. To hear them joked about in public is a thrill. Asked to contribute their scenic suggestions, most audiences try to be funny themselves, which is why their ideas for improvisations about sexual inadequacy or perversion are so often set in a bathroom.

As the first Compass woman clear of the shadow of Elaine May, Anne Meara was one actress/company wife to take on the challenges of dealing with audiences unshyly, with two guns. She quickly sized up the reality that others of the improvisational theatre adjusted to recalcitrantly: "In a nightclub," she observed, "your first objective is to get their attention. Your second is to keep it. And there's an obligatory response demanded throughout, namely laughter. Unless you're singing the Lord's Prayer."

For those reasons, Jack Rollins, a maven of nightclubs, was so careful in his choice of sympathetic bookings for Nichols and May. The Blue Angel and Town Hall were not the sort of venues, as *Variety* would say, where the audience might carry on licentiously or boo. Their dignity was never challenged by working the crowd at places like the Quadrille, or

Strip City (one of Lenny Bruce's training grounds), or a showroom at the Thunderbird. It was their rare good fortune (as it would be Woody Allen's) to be managed as a class act.

Between the scenes at the Compass, tummling with the audience became Anne Meara's task. What Shelley Berman did with difficulty, she did with ease. When the reviews came in, Meara rather than the material was singled out for praise.*

It was during this run of Compass that David Shepherd decided he was not good at writing nightclub comedy with jokes and punch lines. Or interested in nursing actors' egos. Or skilled at directing them to achieve the level of improvisational craftsmanship, intelligence, taste, and style he had previously seen attained. Or inclined to spend so much time on the road, in the boondocks, outside New York. In the summer of 1959, while he felt supportive, he had no eyes to team up with Paul Sills and his partners, Alk and Sahlins, in putting on a new Chicago cabaret. Indeed, he was enveloped by a deep depression as his friends moved forward with The Second City.

The name came up that summer on the very threshold of Bohemia, on the site of what is now an empty Crazy Eddie, the Greenwich Village Howard Johnson's—the same branch in which the customer had asked the waiter to name the ice cream flavor-of-the-month and the waiter, Mike Nichols, had answered, "Chicken." It was there, at this uncompromisingly corny landmark for out-of-towners that the visiting Sills and Alk joined Roger Bowen for a refreshment and began to write down a list of nightclub names.

The Second City was a title borrowed from A. J. Liebling's profile of Chicago, which he had characterized in a series of *New Yorker* essays as eternally shamed that it wasn't New York. To the group at Howard Johnson's, it also conveyed their conspiratorial sense of themselves as a cultural underground. As soon as Alk mentioned it, the men stopped making the list.

The Associated Press finally offered Roger Bowen a correspondent's job that would commence in San Francisco and move on to Japan. Bowen passed on the glamorous offer, proceeding instead to move into Paul Sills's dining room in a Louis Sullivan rooming house on Belden Street, in a

---

*Several years after their experience at Compass, Stiller and Meara decided to perform their own nightclub act. They tailored their work along traditional lines, developing a very successful team persona that had implicit physical comedy (she was taller), and which was unabashedly ethnic (he was the schnooky Jewish guy, she the brassy Irish-Catholic girl). They were likable and appealing, if not stratospheric like Nichols and May.

then rundown neighborhood on the Near North Side called Old Town, near Lincoln Park, a short walk to the defunct Chinese laundry and adjoining hat shop that Sills and his partners had leased.

Selling his tape recorder business had given Bernie Sahlins enough money to sustain his own temporary retirement and to lend Alk and Sills each a third of the $6,000 with which their coffeehouse cabaret would be capitalized. After Labor Day, the first improvisational theatre to display Paul Sills's version of communal sensibility became a "go." Still, Eugene Troobnick did not give up his latest day job as an editor of *Playboy*. Before there was so much as a rehearsal of The Second City, there were three months of workshops.

It was thus that Howard Alk, who had only been onstage occasionally at the Compass, where he came often with Elaine, would undergo his sole stage training before becoming a paid member of the cast.

As a single woman between acting engagements, Barbara Harris had been working at a hospital, sharing an apartment with another nurse, and living on eggs. With few expectations for theatrical success, she accepted Sills's offer to join the new company because "They were paying forty dollars a week. It was a respectable job."

Right up through rehearsals, Severn continued performing at the Gate of Horn. It has been shown that he was very comfortable in the farther reaches of performance art. But he did not like working alone as a standup comedian, perfecting a "set." As Shelley Berman explains it, "Put Severn into the acceptable, the prescribed format, and you've tied his hands. You've taken away exactly what allows Severn to do what he does. Say, 'Severn, get up and do what you want,' and you will have something to remember." Once, in Hollywood, Jane Fonda was speaking at a political meeting, propounding her newly acquired Maoist view of the Vietnam War. To register his opinion of her rhetoric, Severn left the auditorium as if he were having a heart attack. Once, in New York, into the pretentious lobby of Trump Tower, he carried a long-stemmed bouquet of balloons. A security guard was soon upon him. "What are those for?" snapped the guard. Severn threw up his hands in surprise. The balloons rose to the top of Trump's atrium, too high for the janitor's broom, and stuck.

"There are no formats for Severn," says Berman. "He never even thought of himself as a standup comedian. The word is inadequate. He's something else."

Severn was glad to be back in an improvisational ensemble, the medium for which a talent for "something else" could be most generously expressed.

He nonetheless continued to practice his act at the Gate of Horn, "to see if there was anything I could do after The Second City failed."

A lot of women passed through the Chinese laundry before Sills filled the second woman's spot (as the number had come to be fixed) with Mina Kolb. Mina was raised as a proper lawyer's daughter in a large Catholic family from suburban Wilmette, Illinois. After a five-year stint on Chicago television, miming to records on *Rain or Shine with Ray Raynor*, a teenage dance show, she had become a familiar face. She was new to University of Chicago humor and to improvisation, although she had been to the Compass at the Argo Off-Beat Room on her very first date with Bill MacMurray, her husband-to-be. Of that night, she mainly remembered losing her contact lens on the dance floor (which had to be cleared for a painstaking search) and the scenes of Nichols and May. "I thought I'd never be able to do that," she muses. "And of course, I never did."

Others say that from the start Mina Kolb had her own great comic sensibility and a profoundly complicated, almost mathematically illogical brain. Improvising in her variations on a bourgeois clubwoman, dotty as a laser beam, "She was the funniest person I ever saw," Andy Duncan says. "And she didn't know it, which was nice."

"My mother wasn't a clubwoman, and I wasn't a clubwoman," Mina says. "I had no conscious idea what that kind of woman really thought of. I only had sort of an idea what it was to be one. I thought it was having a kind of snobby dumbness. A haughty arrogance."

It was a mistake to confuse her with her character. If she could not name-drop with the rest of the cast, she could usually top them with her gift for the near non sequitur. Once she was pressed onstage by Duncan for an opinion of some modish sculptor's work. "Well, I really haven't seen it. I've been out of town," she said.

When it came time for the pilot Second City company to sign their complicated contracts, it was Mina, the attorney's daughter, who quickly calculated "what's collectible and what's not collectible" and correctly predicted that once they agreed to waive royalties for material performed in the city of Chicago by all subsequent casts, "We'll never see a dime."

In October, The Second City still looked like a laundry and Roger Bowen ran into Allaudin Mathieu at a University of Chicago campus concert at Mandel Hall. After touring with the Stan Kenton band (featuring June Christy and the Four Freshmen), Mathieu was back in Chicago, disillusioned by the discovery that "the band of my dreams had turned into a road dance band," and looking for a job. Bowen invited him to a rehearsal of The Second City, where he was reunited with his other old Compass buddies and introduced to Eugene Troobnick, Barbara Harris, and Mina Kolb.

Sills gave Mathieu a lyric to set as an opening song, which he composed on the spot. From then on he was no longer merely the between-the-sets piano player but responsible for the show's entire soundtrack, as it were, including the impromptu musical content of their improvisations and the witty accompaniment to their scenes—the Second City sound.

Ironically, it was David Shepherd who had written the lyrics to the song that Mathieu had been asked to compose. As an accompaniment to popular theatre, the piano had never appealed to Shepherd, who much preferred the folksy sound of the guitar.

But a great deal about The Second City was incompatible with Shepherd's taste.

The set and setting for The Second City, Sills said wryly, was based "on our profounder knowledge of the nightclub business and modern décor" and its appeal on Chicago's "backlog of guilt for not having supported these saints when they were originally there." Compared to the Compass, The Second City was slick. "We were even required to wear suits, like a uniform," Andy Duncan says. "That deteriorated, but I think the corduroy suits were three-piece or something." The women wore little black dresses with pearls. There was even a carpet on the stage.

Right up until the last few weeks, Sills was considering a thematic line to organize the accumulation of sketches, parodies, blackouts, written pieces (by Roger Bowen, David Shepherd, and the poet John Brent), and "people" scenes. According to Bernie Sahlins, because of Sills's indecisiveness about this move, Mike Nichols himself ("he and Elaine had already made it") was flown out to Chicago to study the Second City rehearsals for a couple of days.

As the only person to make millions from the improvisational theatre, it would become increasingly commonplace for Sahlins to exaggerate his creative contributions to its development and his almost nonexistent role in its birth. In Sahlins's memory, all three producers and Nichols sat down and "agonized over the whole thing. We finally came to the conclusion that we'd just do scenes." None of the actors remembers any such study of their work by Nichols. Sills remembers that Nichols was in town anyway, for a return engagement at Mr. Kelly's with Elaine, and that without Sahlins in their company, Sills and Howard Alk hung out with him one night.

As a director, Sills had supported Nichols in making some decisive artistic turns. Now Nichols returned the favor. It was in line with his previous vision of improvisational theatre, as an arena for satiric barbs and popped balloons, that Nichols encouraged Sills that night to forget about a thematic line for Second City and to stick to unconnected scenes.

Just as he seemed to have a special touch for assembling and developing a higher consciousness among a group of disparate personalities, Sills proved a master jeweler at polishing their disparate moments and stringing them into a theatrical strand. "Sills planned every second," Andy Duncan recalls, "from the minute the lights dimmed to the applause and bows."

The 120-seat house was packed with one-dollar ticket holders, who were enchanted by the charming, witty, and stylish revue they saw on opening night, December 16, 1959. As a spectator of The Second City (he later performed in it), Omar Shapli observed that it was well behind the Compass in taking risks: "There was much less improvisation there. Scruffy people came to Compass—university students in battle fatigues. Thin ties were worn by men in suits at Second City. Women dressed up for their dates. It was a red and gold atmosphere. It was meant to succeed."

It did succeed. Right from the beginning, The Second City caught on.

In the Midwest that fall, the handsome young senator from Massachusetts, John F. ("Jack") Kennedy, a Harvard man, was pounding the stumps in his campaign for president of the United States against Eisenhower's designated hitter with the five o'clock shadow, the immensely unpopular Richard M. Nixon, in the 1960 national election. Following the most optimistic projections of its producers, The Second City company in Chicago grew in this exciting climate and soon would multiply. If collisions over art and ego had vanquished the Compass, The Second City, performing night after night on the site of the old Chinese laundry, had meshed into a family of delightful and brilliant eccentrics, an incomparable cast.

At twenty-five Barbara Harris had begun to emerge as a most riveting performer, exuding beauty, charm, sexuality, vulnerability, humor, and brains, the rare improvisational actor who could hit emotional peaks at the same time she could improvise. Just as Elaine had forged new ground at the Compass as a woman in authority, Barbara etched her own bell-like and sometimes stammering voice (which could zigzag into different octaves) into the improvisational theatre, along with a persona somewhat confused by or because of her own powers, one that would become an inspiration and a guidepost for several generations of "kookie" comedi-ennes.

At the Compass, Andrew Duncan's thought processes were so fast, and his wit so quick, that his words emerged in a peppy, rapid-fire delivery. With his leading man looks that were slightly askew, he brought a per-cussive city energy and a sense of danger to the stage. As the m.c. of The Second City, it was Duncan who set the smart and sardonic tone of the show and gave it the flavor of a real cabaret.

Severn was Severn, and then some, whenever he improvised. At Com-pass, he had always liked to be paired with Barbara Harris. With her at Second City, he did his best scenes, in particular a teaching scene in which an overprotective sister prepares her socially backward brother for a blind date:

SHE: I told her you look like somebody.
HE: Who?
SHE: Guess.
HE: Toulouse-Lautrec?
SHE: No. Don't be silly, Malcolm. Jack Kennedy.
HE: It is amazing how I look like him, isn't it? We look just like
      twins.

As the author of The Second City's opening night parody, "Business-man" (the Ivy League savior of free enterprise, ready to do battle with Collective Man anywhere in the world, dressed in Bermuda shorts), it was the conservative looking Roger Bowen who continued to remind the more middle-of-the-road Second City of the Compass point of view. But unlike the other former Compass Players in the company, he did not feel himself evolving as an actor under the duress of Sills's direction and still considered himself a writer first and an acting amateur.

When Bowen took off for a writing sabbatical, Sills added to the cast Paul Sand, who had been Viola's student when he was eleven years old. In her production of The Clown That Ran Away, he had played the clown. At eighteen, after high school, he had gone directly to Paris to study mime with Marcel Marceau, only to find out that "I didn't want to be a mime." Back in the States, he had toured with Judy Garland as one of her "Couple of Swells" and, after experiencing life on the road as horrendous, quit show business.

As a child, Sills had watched his mother encourage the personalities of other children to emerge on the stage. As an adult, the director of his own professional theatre company, he trusted her process enough to hire them. When Sills sent Sand an invitation to Chicago, it was Viola herself who urged him to go.

Intimidated at first by the verbal brightness and educational background of the University of Chicago crowd, Sand remembers that "I wouldn't open my mouth" for a year, becoming, in his words, "The mime." In fact, by Sills's lights, Sand was the most Spolinesque of his actors, bringing to The Second City a strong sense of the stage as a play space and a distinctive, somewhat dreamy and childlike physicality, epitomized by his famous renditions of floppy dogs.

Some of Sand's physical fluency must have seeped into the company. While visiting his former protégé at The Second City, Marcel Marceau was asked after the performance, "Monsieur Marceau, what did you think of our pantomime?" "Oh," said Marceau, "it did not bother me."

In the spring, Severn requested a leave of absence to perform with his old classmate, Fritz Weaver, in an out-of-town *Hamlet*. Sills invited Tony Holland, his Aunt Pinky's former student, to replace Mr. Dada for a couple of months. Since last seen here—in Sills's production of *The Sea Gull*, as the doomed Treplev—Holland had returned only briefly to Chicago for a Studebaker Theatre run of *Androcles and the Lion*, directed by Sir Cedric Hardwicke. During that time, he had seen the Compass at the Argo Off-Beat Room and found it "terribly pedestrian . . . It didn't work for me." He retained his former University of Chicago art historian's sense of erudition and snobbery, possessed an extravagantly witty sense of comedy that Susan Sontag (U. of C. '52) had yet to call "camp," and integrated perfectly into the improvisational theatre, even in this brief stint, embroidering on Severn's parts.

After *The Nervous Set* closed, Del Close had stepped back on the standup route. He had worked his way up from the toilets to the class rooms like the Blue Angel, the Village Vanguard, and the Bon Soir. He had put out his own comedy record, one of the first interactive comedy discs, with Elaine's assistance on script. *The Do-It-Yourself Psychoanalysis Kit*, on which Close was the doctor and the audience was the patient, parodied his treatment with Theodor Reik. During the summer of 1960, he was working in Hollywood at the Club Renaissance, when he got a call from Howard Alk. The Republicans were in Chicago nominating Nixon, and Paul Sills was throwing a tantrum. Someone in charge was needed, and Alk asked Close to fill in. Close agreed to run workshops for the company during their first "communications breakdown" with Sills.

For the first time since the Compass workshops at Mandel Hall, the liaison between the improvisational theatre and Viola Spolin had resumed. At fifty-four, the High Priestess had embarked on her first work for a professional acting troupe. She had locked up her house in the Hollywood Hills, checked into a furnished room at the Lincoln Hotel, and begun training reinforcements for The Second City by running amateur and children's workshops in her exercises, which she still did not call games.

Then, six years after he had quit the Playwrights Theatre Club in exhaustion, when The Second City had been running a year, Sheldon Patinkin came back into the picture as its business manager, also again assuming the role of factotum to Paul Sills. Sills had steered the "family business" to prosperity and distinction. Yet he was observed as "crazier" than he seemed to Patinkin at eighteen. He had a violent temper, and he was already getting bored.

It took Ted Flicker six months to interview all 3,000 actors who responded to his casting call for the improvisational theatre he was planning to call The Premise, which would open in the heart of the action in Greenwich Village on November 22, 1960, on the corner of Bleecker and Thompson streets. In the spirit of St. Louis, Dave Moon covered the walls with old doors. Flicker could not renew the liquor license that had always been forthcoming for the premises of the former Port o' Call: it was against the old naval cadet's principles to hand out the expected bribes. The Premise would thus forgo the cushy profits made from liquor, serving instead the traditional menu of Greenwich Village cafés: pastries and coffee, espresso, tea, orzata, tamarindo, and other Italian syrup drinks. The entertainment was covered by the same city license as that of a circus: The Premise was registered as an "exhibition of mental agility."

The chaos and betrayal Flicker had experienced at the Compasses in Chicago and St. Louis had only committed him further to the notion that "improvisation is sharing" and that the most important factor in forming an improvisational theatre company was discovering improvisers capable of enduring "family bonding" and compatible enough to survive a long run. Before selecting Tom Aldredge, George Segal, and Joan Darling to join him in a permanent company, Flicker invited 1,500 actors to return for a second call.

Although Paul Sills was a nonplayer himself, he was paradoxically the expert and arbiter of Viola Spolin's supposedly nonjudgmental work. (Since he and Viola had been absent for most of the Compass activity, no one else knew or remembered exactly what Spolin's work was about.) As such, he exercised a unique and brilliant but nevertheless paternalistic power over the material created from the improvisations of The Second City. If he goaded players to a higher state of performance, they also grew dependent on his unpredictable approval and his greater authority to construct and edit their show.

Flicker and his cast shared the stage. Although Del Close would catch him reverting to the ringmaster's role he had played before meeting Mike and Elaine, he relinquished a great deal of control simply by putting himself on the line. Trained by the Westminster Place Kitchen Rules, a more writerly and self-reliant set of tools than the Spolin games, The Premise Players enjoyed more autonomy. Once, when they decided among themselves that Flicker's onstage activities had become too controlling and overbearing (he loved to play The Boss), they told him he was interfering with the higher intuition of their work and "fired" him.

Although Bernie Sahlins would later boast that Second City actors always remained "members of its growing family," except for cachet and theatrical status (or, as Andy Duncan views it, an entrée "to pick cotton in the best plantations"), no membership benefits or royalties from belonging to this clan were ever to accrue. But Flicker was determined that his theatre have financial as well as creative harmony. To this end, he created The Premise's unimitated profit-sharing plan. If improvisation was about sharing, he says, "it seemed natural" for the producer-director to share the bread.

A Premise Permanent Company Player was eligible automatically for a percentage of net profits, as well as eight weeks' paid vacation, "so people wouldn't get stale." If absent for longer, say, to act in an out-of-town *Hamlet*, their profit percentages were diminished but not to less than 5 percent. And the longer the show ran, the larger the profit. Flicker remembers how Joan Darling cried when she first saw "The Chess Game," a piece she created with George Segal (about a paranoid and overanalyzed woman who intimidates her mild-mannered opponent while seeing herself as the victim) performed by other actors (Barbara Anson and Francis Dux).

"And when she got her first profit-sharing check for it, she laughed with glee."*

Flicker reflects on his unique arrangement as "hardly altruism on my part. I was a serious capitalist. I wanted to be sure that the cast had a real rooting interest in The Premise. If somebody has a real incentive and a sense of ownership, you get the highest degree of productivity. That's just good old common sense."

The Premise tended to satirize cultural pretensions less than The Second City (or any of the previous Compass companies) and politics more. "The audience in each city shapes the show," Flicker observed. "Whatever preconceived idea we went in with was ultimately changed by them. In New York, they weren't hungry for culture with a capital K. They wanted political satire." Critics of the respective companies might also note that The Premise featured a slicker, faster-paced production and relied more heavily on gimmicks and formulas for getting laughs (each player brought to Story-Story—which opened the show—an invisible weapon, such as a noose, a poisoned ring, or a dry cleaner's plastic bag with which to commit hara-kiri if he or she bombed). Or that The Second City, being Spolin-esque, lacked a technique for solid scenic structure and restricted live improvisation to the late-night sets, where, without Sills to guide them, they would usually flounder for an ending and let their scenes go on and on. Under Sills, the performances were also more ineffable, the acting more effortless, and the set scenes more beautifully choreographed. Still, neither was so different from the other that it might have been mistaken for the Living Theatre, or the Julius Monk Revue.

The same month The Premise opened, the senator from Massachusetts, JFK, was elected by less than two thirds of a percent over his opponent and became the president of the United States.

Many idealists, intellectuals, Stevensonians, and cynics had harbored reservations as to whether Kennedy would be the perfect man. It was said that the election was bought in Chicago's Cook County, where Mayor Daley did business with Kennedy's rich and power-hungry dad, and that there was ballot stuffing in the city's numerous ethnic wards. It was still

---

*Only two more players, Buck Henry and James Frawley, were ever elevated to Permanent Company status by the head man. Subsequent Premise players—including Anson, Dux, Sandy Baron, David Dozer, Al Mancini, Garry Goodrow, Gene Hackman, George Furth, Cynthia Harris, Kip Curry, Peter Bonerz, Gail Coffin, and Barbara Quaney—earned only a salary. The Premise Permanent Company owned all the material they created on its stage in perpetuity.

a very close call. By law in Cook County, it would take a year and a half for a recount, but, in the interest of the continuation of the Republic, even Richard Nixon did not press the State of Illinois for evidence of fraud. "Let the word go forth . . . that the torch has been passed to a new generation of Americans," said the youngest man ever elected to his office, and it seemed that the world had transformed.

That winter, on a freezing-cold snowy day in January, he would inaugurate the short reign of Camelot. Most people saw on television the way he was not wearing a coat or hat. The great American poet, Robert Frost, had composed a verse for the occasion, but the sun glared on his notepaper, and he struggled with the words to his poem.

23

Fallout

The amazing and pristine success of Nichols and May had earned Jack Rollins his funny bones. His unpaid apprentice, Charles ("Charlie") Joffe, became his partner, and the comedy contingent began to seek their audience in droves, including Woody Allen, who first approached the Rollins and Joffe office as a writer for the team.

But Nichols and May did not use writers, although the autonomy they had thrived on and grown used to had stopped being either a creative or a financial advantage. Improvising on the Compass stage, they had been endlessly prolific. Now, when the demand for their work was most tremendous, their supply was down. "The bigger the nightclub we were in, the bigger the television show we were on, the more pressure there was to have the sketches we did be the best we had," Mike Nichols recalls. They couldn't produce their own material fast enough, and their work process did not make room for other writers. "And we found ourselves doing the same material over and over. This took a great toll on Elaine."

From their earliest interviews, it was apparent that the effect of their triumph had not been unpredictable: Nichols continued to experience a great deal of gratification from the role of "Monsieur Succès" (as a *Paris Match* writer once called him), while neither the trappings nor the compromises attendant on stardom were of any interest to Elaine. (Friends remember a Ping-Pong table as the only object in her living room.) Without the same at stake for her in show business, Elaine held on to her rebel values: the highest, the only performing achievement is to be in the moment, to improvise. "She was always brave," says Nichols. "But I became more and more afraid."

Their conflicting values became a source of uncreative friction. "I nagged the hell out of her. I was always saying, 'Can't you do that any faster?' and 'You're taking too long over this.' " During a performance of "Pirandello," they actually lost control during the staged fight and came to real and bloody blows.

The bookings and business dealings of Nichols and May had always been most carefully chosen and negotiated in accordance with Jack Rollins's interpretation of the two artists' desires and supremely good taste. Yet, after two years in the big time, their artistic horizons, instead of expanding, had actually shrunk. Frequent appearances on television, the medium with the most artistic interference (and the most money), seemed out of the question. (Radio, where their regular Sunday segment on NBC's network show *Monitor* was extremely popular, gave them and their improvisations a much freer rein.) They hated the false intimacy of nightclubs. Their first record album, *Improvisations to Music*, ad-libbed in a studio, is all style and vamping, and except for the scene about the insecure couple in bed, "Bach to Bach," is, by their standards, weak.

In an unprecedented managerial move, Rollins began making plans to return America's hottest comedy team to the financially conservative terrain of the stage. "They were, first of all, actors," explains Rollins. "It seemed appropriate to give them the stature of Broadway once they had the eligibility of fame."

Nichols likes to remember himself and Elaine as such snobs that right up until their audition at the Blue Angel they regarded their own activities in show business as "just something to make a living" until they "grew up and started our real lives," . . . "a big joke." If so, like the four boys in *Enterprise*, the joke was on them.

An Evening with Mike Nichols and Elaine May was simply and elegantly staged (with smoking accessories by Dunhill) by the esteemed Arthur Penn. When it premiered on Broadway on October 8, 1960, at the Golden Theatre for a select group (which had first been conveyed by the producer, Alexander H. Cohen, in a fleet of Rolls-Royces to a pretheatre buffet at Sardi's East), the two stars found their last and, by now, their true audience. When the curtain came down, these fans danced in a cordoned-off Shubert Alley while the world's greatest comedy team lost touch with the people, as David Shepherd might say, and started playing for the court.

Outside of one improvisation per show (based on a first line, a last line, and a style in which to play the scene—all suggested by the audience), not one piece that had not first been performed at the Compass appeared on their Broadway program. "We finally found that the safest thing was to stick with the set pieces, which changed a little bit anyway, do the improvisation, and then get off with some set thing we had prepared," Nichols says.

Even so, under what would seem terrific pressure, Elaine had her ways of tricking her less daring partner into the "not knowing" state and freaking him out. George Morrison remembers nights at the Golden Theatre when she would stretch her bit as Mrs. Gordon Hall, the chairman of PTA Fun Night, into a forty-five-minute routine.

A backstage alley connected the Golden to the Majestic Theatre, where *Camelot* (Lerner and Loewe's musical, not the government) was the resident hit. While playing King Arthur, Richard Burton turned his dressing room into a veritable saloon. Burton's wife, Sybil, his costar, Julie Andrews, and other theatrical luminaries, among them Robert Preston, Lauren Bacall, Tammy Grimes, and Mike Nichols, were regular celebrants there. If he was becoming unsettled in his relationship with Elaine, Nichols was acquiring rare Broadway friendships.

Nineteen sixty-one marked a year from the time the Food and Drug Administration had approved a birth-control pill called Enovid. And, as if it were part of the sexual celebration, there was a new kind of First Lady in the White House, a couturier beauty who invited Pablo Casals in to play the cello after a dinner of French food and wines. In the arms race, the United States was way ahead of the Russians, but as Kennedy had explained in a campaign speech, "I want to be ahead of them in rocket thrust."

The liberal left found it alarming, of course, that in the first dizzy days of his office, Kennedy had agreed to finance the despotic regime of Ngo Dinh Diem in South Vietnam, then to arm a group of Cuban contras, assembled under the Eisenhower administration by the CIA, who were planning to overthrow Fidel Castro by establishing a guerrilla beachhead on a swampy Cuban marshland off the Bay of Pigs.

Still, the stress on the free and inquiring or "egghead" spirit incurred by the Eisenhower era had been tremendous. Suddenly, Eisenhower rejects were Kennedy's advisers, the best and the brightest, the professors and intellectuals, the Ph.D.'s and the Phi Beta Kappas. Never had a chief executive looked so glamorous, knocking himself out like a kid at touch football while his suits were hand-tailored on Savile Row. JFK was a devotee of the arts, a defender of minorities, an activist for civil rights. And once every two weeks, without notes or rehearsal, he held a press conference, tossing the ball back and forth with a sea of reporters with amazing ease and wit. The president—and both his brothers—laughed at hearing imitations of their Boston accents. In fact, there wasn't much else to belittle in the society they commanded, the New Frontier.

When off-Broadway minimum was $35 a week, a Premise Permanent Player had a $200-a-week salary plus the money from the profit-sharing plan. As the replacements and the touring companies multiplied, "They all got rich," Ted Flicker says. "It's a wonderful thing, success. Sharing with them didn't affect the way I lived. I remained boss. We remained friends. I still had a penthouse and a Rolls-Royce."

Upon receiving a book, *The Authentic Arabian Horse,* as a gift from his friend Richard Avedon, Mike Nichols flew immediately to the Crabbet Park Stud Farm, Sussex, England, the stable of the author, Lady Wentworth. He bought a colt and shipped it back for weekend riding in Central Park. In Arabic, the horse's name was Maheyl, which means "Take it easy." Nichols called him Max.

Inside Shelley Berman continued to be purchased not just by the chic sophisticates who were the mainstays of the Nichols and May audience but throughout the American heartland. ("Everymanic Depressive," he was called by *Time.*) *Billboard'*s statistics are the irrefutable proof of Shelley Berman's huge popularity and fame. After hitting the charts in April 1959, the record rose to the number-one best-selling album in America and stayed in the Top 40 for two and a half years, in *Billboard* terms, an incredible 134 weeks. It was the first best-seller in record history to feature the spoken word.

Seven months later, *Outside Shelley Berman* was released. It rose to number six and remained on the charts for seventy-six weeks. In another seven months, *The Edge of Shelley Berman* climbed to number four on the charts and reappeared there for fifty-two weeks.

In the span of only a year, he had three gold comedy albums in the bins simultaneously.

By contrast, *Improvisations to Music,* which Nichols and May released on the Mercury label two months after Berman's first album for Verve, came in at number thirty-nine in the Top 40 and lingered there for seven weeks. Their Broadway show album attracted more fans. *An Evening with*

Mike Nichols and Elaine May rose to number ten in 1961 and held a place on the charts for thirty-two weeks.

Also by contrast, Berman's sponsor at Verve, Mort Sahl, waited until 1960 for a hit. *Mort Sahl at the hungry i* rose to number twenty-two, remained on the charts for four weeks, and fell off. (Said Sahl once, smoothing his feathers, "His records sold like magazines, and mine sold more like books.")

And the comedy albums of Lenny Bruce, modern comedy's patron saint, never hit the charts until 1975, almost a decade after he died.

Reminded that "the times call forth the comedian" is his remark, Shelley Berman nods. "But I'd rather not have made my contribution whether the times needed me or not. Being a comedian wasn't a blessing. I think it was a very bad idea, the worst thing I ever did."

Shelley Berman assumed that fame and recognition would bring him "all I ever wanted and all I wanted then, a part in a play." But the merchants of entertainment had other plans for him. Berman's agents "had their hands on a million-dollar comic, and they were not going to sell me my way." "They wanted to turn him into Red Skelton," remembers Mort Sahl.

As a student actor, Berman had been a great Iago. One Goodman Theatre classmate, William Harahan (now Gwyllum Evans), remembers him as "the greatest Iago I've ever seen," and "a Petruchio to conjure with," too. Their fellow classmate, Geraldine Page, has been described as "the greatest actress in the English-speaking language." When it came to Shelley Berman, Evans still recalls the way that "Gerry worshipped him." "He wasn't Red Skelton," says Mort Sahl.

"I was very naïve," Berman says now. "There came a time when I should have had the balls to stop, but I didn't." The balls to stop when? "At the height. At the absolute height. Quit." An inner voice told him, "Now you've got some money. Stop signing autographs. Get a cheaper apartment. Stop being a big shot. Get a part in a play." Geraldine Page remembered visiting his mansion in Beverly Hills and urging him to cut down on the $300 suits. He didn't listen. "It was too bad. The others—Mike Nichols and Elaine May—stopped at a certain point. I didn't stop. I stayed. The seduction was total and complete."

Actually, as Mike Nichols recalls it, he did not end his career as a comedian willingly. *An Evening with Mike Nichols and Elaine May* lasted a little more than a season, "and then we stopped because Elaine couldn't stand it anymore." She said her patience gave out during the PTA piece, when she saw Nichols giving her directions—actually snapping his fingers at her to speed up—from the wings.

When the show closed, she was hired to write a screenplay of *The Loved One*, Evelyn Waugh's sendup of Hollywood's luxury cemetery, Forest Lawn. She married Sheldon Harnick, a lyricist, whose work with Jerry Bock on the musical *Fiorello!* would be awarded a Pulitzer Prize. The marriage was so brief the joke went out that "she got custody of the cake." She also got custody of her analyst, David Rubenfine, who became husband three.

Terry Southern inherited her job on *The Loved One*. ("There's too much death in it," the studio said of her draft.) It did not deflate her ambition to write.

Nichols and Rose Arrick were the stars of her play A *Matter of Position*, about a man who will not get out of bed, like *Oblomov*, and reminiscent also of her aborted Compass scenario *The String Quartet*. Not only had she written the part of the man who stays in bed especially for Nichols, "It was also *about* me, which made part of the problem," he says.

"The play needed work," a colleague who saw its tryout in Philadelphia attests. "It had a brilliant second act, a third act that fell apart, and a confusing first act with all kinds of exposition that needed to be trimmed." As a prospective director, Arthur Penn had asked the playwright for changes and cuts. She hired Fred Coe (who had not).

During rehearsals, the playwright was much more critical of the leading man than the play. Nichols outdid the director in insisting on changes and cuts, which Elaine refused to make.

Fred Coe had been confident she would see it their way. In Philadelphia, she took out an injunction to keep him from changing a comma, effectively closing the play.

Nichols and May broke up, each feeling betrayed. The shift in their roles had created a disastrous imbalance. Nichols thinks that "we were so disoriented by no longer being together against everyone else. It divided us in some terrible way."

To avoid playing favorites, Rollins and Joffe elected to manage neither as a solo. But "Mike and Elaine, they were it for me," Rollins says. "They were the most original, distinctive, warm, incisive, hilarious comedians. They were true geniuses, I think. They simply were not destined to work together forever," Rollins continues, not without regret. "They were such different personalities. They could drive each other up the wall." Woody Allen's manager speaks with equal affection of "Michael" ("highly, highly intelligent—the world is his oyster") and Elaine ("completely disconnected from the practical world—surely one of the most gifted artists with whom I have ever worked").

When the team broke up, Nichols felt his life had reached its nadir, and indeed, among their contemporaries all bets for success were on Elaine. Walking down Park Avenue with Nichols, Leonard Bernstein threw an arm around his shoulder. "Oh, Mikey, you're so *good*," said Bernstein. "I don't know at *what*."

Shelley Berman, Mike Nichols, and Elaine May, the three composers of "The Lost Dime," a seminal tune on the phone company and human communications, did not improvise into maturity, unlike the masters of Italian comedy or great jazz musicians. On becoming stars, each member of the trio once referred to as "Two Cocksuckers and Elaine" had unwittingly pulled some plugs from the main currents of ordinary life that had charged their improvisations with humanity. They had been almost instantly isolated from the ensemble work of their peers, the extraordinary improvisational foot soldiers. Thus, their passage into celebrity did not return to the political comedy of the improvisational theatre any insights into the issues of status and money, or hard looks into the workings of power in the arts and society, or revelations about the entertainment industry. Without the focus and urgency of the improvisational theatre, they were atomized from their most integrated and revealing work. Substituting for commonality and spontaneity the narcissism and obsessions of show business, they grew silent in the society they once had satirized.

Some twenty-five years after their split, Nichols and May were reunited on the stage of the Shubert Theatre in *Comic Relief*, a one-hundred-dollar-a-head presentation to benefit AIDS for which 1,500 people got all dressed up. Not unlike the Compass, the benefit had been convened to reflect the concerns of a devastated theatrical community. Joan Rivers wept between her gay jokes, Gregory Hines tapped an improvisation for a dead friend, and Steve Martin dared to tap-dance with Gregory Hines. In the star spot, for which the audience was primed and waiting, Mike Nichols pointed out with some embarrassment that he and his former partner would perform "The Lost Dime," as always, even though pay phones had cost a quarter for a long time. They declined to improvise.

24

Radiation

Tony Holland had been traveling in Europe and was running out of funds. He wrote to Bernie Sahlins, the only person he knew with available cash. Sahlins generously sent $500 and an invitation to rejoin The Second City in May. After a trial run at the Ivar Theatre in Hollywood, the original company would open in New York, on Broadway. Two former Compass Players, Del Close and Alan Arkin, were already set for the replacement cast.

Zohra Lampert had made good on the expectations the Chicago drama critics had for her at the Playwrights Theatre Club and was stirring up interest on both coasts after appearing on Broadway in a comedy *Maybe Tuesday* and with Ernest Borgnine in a turn-of-the-century Mafia movie, *Pay or Die*. When Holland finished seeing the spring in Greece, he showed up at The Second City and found her there, adding to Barbara's parts her own philosophical personality and the corresponding vocal habit the *Herald-Tribune* drama critic Walter Kerr found so enchanting: "of inflecting questions downward and statements up."

After returning to Chicago to run University Theatre, Bill Alton, Zohra's former husband, had taken on the role in Second City that Andrew Duncan played—as Alton describes it, "the guy the audience identifies with, the guy in the suit, sort of the maître d' "—and provided the Chicago cast with another fine straight man when the original cast took off.

With this last infusion from Robert Hutchins's community of scholars, the improvisations of The Second City got one more booster shot of high purpose and regard for the Great Books, a whole new group whose roots were in the theatre, who could recite poetry, parody literary styles, sing mock fugues and madrigals, drop Kierkegaard jokes and satirize psychoanalysis. The newcomers were more than equal to the intellectual demands of The Second City, where even the waitresses were smart. (One of them was Carol Bleackley, a beautiful painter from Montreal who married Paul Sills.)

It should also be noticed how limited the second cast's contribution to the growth and development of the improvisational theatre was set up to be. Bill Alton was himself a director of considerable talent and skill. At the Playwrights Theatre Club, he had staged A *Midsummer Night's Dream* and a distinguished production of Tennessee Williams's *The Glass Menagerie*. Zohra Lampert had acquired more formal training and professional experience in the theatre than Sills.

At The Second City, Tony Holland often expressed outrageous opinions, as Severn did, through the character of a professional "expert." (Holland's was Dr. Herman Pisk, a Viennese.) On the suggestion "bull dike," he began laying the groundwork for his hilarious and shocking drag character, Rhoda Schapiroe (long i), "thinker, author, diplomat, wife, and mother," and lesbian. He improvised long ballads on the Russian Revolution. But he was also interested in improvising longer works on the American labor movement, for example, and on Emma Goldman, the anarchist. "Tony always had the mind of a writer," Alton says.*

But all three had been hired to meet high standards of performance, not to be theatrical innovators or architects. If Compass featured both the virtues and deficiencies of creative anarchy, The Second City had a power structure even more patriarchal than was traditional to the commercial theatre. In the purported absence of a playwright, the director was the main man.

But Sills had concerns on his mind other than the artistic evolution of his players, and two of them were at odds.

His first concern was to keep The Second City alive within the context that had made it successful: a bright and witty satirical revue. At the same time, his directorial attention was now diverted by a higher authority, that is, Viola, to the realm beyond the verbal and to her methods of achieving the improvisational state. Working for the first time with professional actors, Viola seemed to be achieving innovative results out of thin air in

---

*When Holland died in 1988, he left behind three plays, written in collaboration with William H. Hoffman, including *The Cherry Orchard, Part Two*.

those mystery areas of improvisation in which she was the expert, such as space substance, invisible objects, and transformations of character and place.

The intellectuals in the company found aspects of her work baffling. When Roger Bowen returned to the company in April 1961, he appeared in her children's production of *Rumplestiltskin* and found it "very workshoppy and amateurish." Del Close tried to share his thoughts on game theory with her, but Viola wasn't interested in his ideas. She was certain of hers. Viola walked through rehearsals, Tony Holland remembered, saying, "People, remember your 'Where.' "

Only Sills was fully able to tune in. He would say to the players from the University of Chicago crowd, "I've had enough fucking *wit*."

"Like a woman asked to marry a rich man," Zohra Lampert's teacher, Mira Rostova explained, "she likes the money, but she can't marry the man." When she left The Second City, her place was filled by a Larchmont doctor's daughter, Joan Rivers, a Barnard graduate.

Joan Rivers was the first woman recruited into the improvisational theatre who wanted to marry the man. She had a writer's interest in making her scenes work, a comic's addiction to getting her laughs, and very little curiosity about the mysteries of improvisational acting. In her work, the ease of an uncalculated self would never be seen: "I couldn't bear passing space objects and having them change. Who cares? I used to say, 'Come the day I'm in a Broadway show, I won't have to improvise holding a teacup because they'll hand me a real teacup.' " She regarded Viola's workshops with contempt, as "pantomime once a week . . . a children's theatre troupe, which you were in if you couldn't get in the adults' group," and refused to attend.

Alan Arkin, with his gallery of characters and accents, fit in so well with the original cast that they sent a message from the Ivar Theatre, asking to forward Arkin there. Thus, Arkin joined Andrew Duncan, Barbara Harris, Severn Darden, Mina Kolb, Paul Sand, Eugene Troobnick, Howard Alk, and Allaudin Mathieu in the illustrious first company of The Second City that would open in New York on September 26, 1961, at the Royale Theatre to mixed reviews that did not assure a long run.

In formal surroundings, with so much at stake, the New York producer, Max Liebman, did not wish to leave the material of an evening to chance. When he heard Liebman and Bernie Sahlins announce two days before opening that they were freezing the show, Severn says, "My blood froze too."

As a director, Paul Sills has the ability to see in an actor's resistant or rigid behavior toward written material the signals of a more elemental self, reporting, "I hate this" or "No." He calls it "the artistic conscience."

It was too late to consider such signals at the penultimate rehearsal, the day before *From The Second City* was to open on the Great White Way. Instead, Sills stormed out of rehearsal after telling the actors they were all incapable of doing the show and were all full of shit.

The next day, following the pep talk at the last rehearsal, Andrew Duncan went out for a sandwich with Bernie Sahlins and a subdued Paul Sills. They discussed the running order of the set pieces and returned to the theatre for the half-hour call. It was still summer, so the sun had not yet set as Duncan walked with Sills and Sahlins along Broadway. Passing the statue of George M. Cohan, Duncan was surprised to see a big grin light up and spread all over Sahlins's face. "Do you guys realize that if we succeed," he said, "we can own this street?"

The critics never even saw the Kennedy-Khrushchev "debate," with its impromptu translations of Russian-sounding gibberish. Three old Compass scenes, "Football Comes to the University of Chicago," "The Last of the Centaurs," and "The Message" (renamed "Emma") were on the program. Severn and Barbara played "Blind Date." Severn and Howard Alk donned top hats for the song spoof that was so funny in Chicago ("Broadway, Broadway / It might be hot and dirty / But that's the way I like it Gertie"). But no one improvised.

At the start of the New Year 1962, after only ten weeks on Broadway, the New York group was moved to Square East, a more appropriate cabaret space in Greenwich Village (now the Bottom Line). Deals would shortly be made for yet another company of Second City to appear in London, exchanging stages with an English satirical company, The Establishment.

That January, at The Star Club in Hamburg, Germany, the drummer for the Beatles was still Pete Best.

Viola Spolin describes her concept of No Motion as "not a freeze" but "a resting or nonthinking area between people precisely when they are busy with onstage dialogue and activity."

Posed with Paul Sills in the photo on their Broadway *Playbill*, the players of the first company of The Second City appear to be in this state of No Motion, separately contemplative and yet connected, fluid, and yet very still.

They will testify that upon leaving Chicago, a certain esprit de corps had been destroyed. As had happened before, when the focus was not on the improvisation but on the box office, the players were not perceived as an ensemble but singled out for special praise and rewards as well as outside jobs. Mina Kolb had already shot several episodes of a new fall TV series, *Pete and Gladys*, in which she played a running part. Now, Jerome Robbins cast Barbara Harris as the nymphomaniacal baby-sitter in Arthur Kopit's comedy, *Oh Dad, Poor Dad, Mamma's Hung You in the Closet and I'm Feelin' So Sad*. She began shuttling between The Second City and rehearsals of *Oh Dad*.

Paranoia set in in both companies, aggravated (some players think even fomented) by the critical Sills. Burned once already by the Compass firing, Andrew Duncan, one of the improvisational theatre's masterminds, always felt an impending apprehension about being replaced. In Chicago, there was so much competition among the replacement players for time on the stage that Joan Rivers wrote in her diary, "I'm so sick of the constant pushing needed in this business, maybe I'm not right for it." "You can be replaced by the bartender," she overheard Bernie Sahlins tell players who asked for a raise.

Rivers would also recall that her fellow players "made me ashamed that I wanted to move forward, that I wanted to be a star . . . their high calling was . . . so pure and elevated it was separated from show business."

In fact, as urbane as this attitude seemed in Chicago, in the fast lane of the New York theatre, the Second City actors were hicks. When he and Barbara were nominated for a Tony for their work on Broadway in *From The Second City*, Severn says, "I didn't know what a Tony was."

Joan Rivers quit the Chicago Second City on North Wells Street in frustration, and Zohra Lampert took over for Barbara Harris at Square East. Mina Kolb rejoined the group in Chicago. And Barbara, performing a hilarious character transformation from an innocent preteen in a pinafore into a rapacious nymphet in *Oh Dad*, tore the house down at the Phoenix Theatre and, after practicing hundreds of character transformations in the improvisational theatre, became an overnight star.

That month also, the astronaut John Glenn emerged from the Atlantic Ocean, after surviving the fiery crash of the Friendship 7 and the first American orbital flight. While more men prepared for the moon, a banner was hoisted at Cape Canaveral that said, "Welcome to Earth."

25

Radiation Burns

One image of Barbara Harris has always remained engraved in George Morrison's memory: she is singing Brecht and Weill's "Pirate Jenny" in Paul Sills's production of *The Threepenny Opera* at the Playwrights Theatre Club. It is a whore's bitter and ominous song of revenge. "She didn't do *anything*. She just stood there, looking like a doll, while those words came rolling out." Morrison's voice lets out a shiver. "God, she was great."

In the spring of 1962, Barbara signed a contract with Richard Rodgers and Alan Jay Lerner to play the lead in a Broadway musical they had not written yet. (Both men liked to have an inspirational leading lady for whom to create, and they knew they had found one after seeing Barbara in *Oh Dad*.) Barbara started taking voice lessons. "That funny little face—you laugh at it, and at the same time you want to pat it," Rodgers explained when the unusual deal was announced.

Barbara won the 1962 Vernon Rice Drama Desk award and an Obie for Outstanding Achievement in the Off-Broadway Theatre for her role in *Oh Dad*. She did not wish to smile for her post-Obie photograph. The reporter from *The Village Voice* wondered what occasioned her seriousness. "Since my reviews in *Oh Dad*, everything I say makes people laugh twice as loud," she said.

For many years, Viola had been assembling notes in hope of expressing her theories and collecting her exercises definitively. Now, having watched the results the actors were achieving with them onstage at Second City, she found an appropriate publisher, Northwestern University Press, and, as of May 1962, when the contract was drawn, her opus, tentatively called *Toward an Improvisational Theater,** was in the works. How much The Second City had borrowed from the pragmatic discoveries of The Compass Players the text would not reveal, and, in fact, Viola, who had never seen them, did not know. The author only acknowledged the contribution of her son, Paul Sills, who, through several revisions, had stood by her writing it.

As the Second City groups proliferated, and endless new shows needed to be produced, the pressures to keep them true to his and/or Viola's vision of what was spontaneous grew on Paul Sills. At least two actors in the Chicago company had been her protégés. One was Avery Schreiber, an endearing and brilliant West Side Chicagoan with street smarts, a working-class background, Goodman Theatre training, and a handlebar mustache. The other was the wizard of space objects, Dick Schaal. Andrew Duncan noticed that Sills would play the groups off against each other, demanding, for example, that a scene he brought with him from Chicago be played with equal dispatch and to equal applause in New York, even if, as Duncan says, "They weren't right for us."

Under Viola's influence, the improvisations of The Second City were much less witty and verbal than before. Sills wanted all improvisations to emerge this way. As the disparity grew between what he wanted to see and what he actually saw on the stage, he became more insistent that his and/or Viola's was the only way to improvise. Between Sills and his employees (including the replacement directors, Larry Arrick and Alan Myerson), there were fights, ideological disputes, and firings. "Even though he couldn't do it physically," Andy Duncan muses on Sills, "he wanted to be in charge of it all."

Alan Myerson's left-wing political attitudes had always been too "simplistic," as Bernie Sahlins says, for either himself or Sills. When differences within the Chicago company exploded into a fight between Myerson and

---

*This more speculative and interesting title was changed to *Improvisation for the Theater* before publication.

the royalist, Del Close, Sills sent Myerson to New York, where he found himself still battling for artistic autonomy.

During the Cuban missile crisis, in the fall of 1962, the New York company, under Myerson, took an anti-Kennedy line.

Stranded in London, the touring company of The Second City panicked. Before deciding to take a favorable position toward the American government, they tossed Del Close's *I Ching*. As Andy Duncan says, "There was no way we could have this vast universe of Second Cities all over the world operating from the brain in Chicago or wherever Sills was."

In January 1963, in his televised State of the Union address, President Kennedy reported that "the spearhead of aggression has been blunted in Vietnam," and *Camelot* ended its Broadway run.

Jerome Robbins was bringing Brecht's *Mother Courage and Her Children* to the New York stage, starring Anne Bancroft. Zohra Lampert was cast as Kattrin, Courage's deaf mute daughter, and Barbara Harris as the camp follower, Yvette. Robbins discovered in the young Second City actresses, no small thanks to Paul Sills, two unusually knowledgeable and gifted practitioners of Brecht.

After practically begging for a job at The Second City in New York, Joan Rivers, no small thanks to Jerome Robbins, was finally given Zohra's empty place, thus taking over roles in several scenes that she herself had helped to create.

Alan Arkin was cast as the young man from the Bronx who becomes an actor in Carl Reiner's Broadway comedy *Enter Laughing* and got wonderful reviews.

"By the time I joined them in New York, everybody was already a somebody or on the way to being a somebody," Joan Rivers says.

In the improvisational theatre, success in show business was now a golden calf. Within two years of its opening, The Second City, like a designated salmon stream, became "a spawning ground for stars" (a stupid phrase invented for its publicity kits and gushed out again and again by the press), such an illustrious credit for practitioners of comedy that even Mike Nichols would begin to list it instead of Compass in his biographies in *Playbill*.

Because the improvisational actor is trained, against his every acculturated impulse, to relax in the moment onstage without knowing what will happen next, the comedy that emanated from improvisational theatre was one of behavior, not jokes. The acting games derived from Viola Spolin invariably brought a freshness, integrity, surprise, and reality to the work of those who played them. Even in a scripted situation, the improvisational actor revealed a natural, casual quirkiness and a commitment to the irregular and idiosyncratic rhythm of real speech and movement rather than mechanical body language or a fast and snappy recitation of lines. It was soon discovered that the most sophisticated Hollywood comedy projects could be improved by what even Robert Brustein (then Dean of the Yale Drama School) referred to as "that Second City style."

The superficial aspects of any popular art can be dislocated from the gut of it, marketed, and trivialized. That is the inevitable American artistic dilemma. Two decades earlier, "the fervent years" of the Group Theatre had produced our indigenous and revolutionary version of Russian naturalism through the technique of Method acting. The Group Theatre had started out like the Compass, with a view of the theatre as a reflection of the world that surrounds it, an ideological as well as an aesthetic exercise. Its style, not its content, was also absorbed through its most prominent exponents, through other mediums than the ensemble theatre, into the cultural mainstream.

Farther than ever from David Shepherd's dream for an inexpensive vehicle for throwing light on and into the lives of common people, the improvisational theatre had transmogrified into a show-business boot camp, a rung in the short, steep ladder of the funny business.

"Most theatre is slave-market bullshit," Paul Sills once said.

"Of course, you can use improvisation to create television and commercials and the like and you'll get results, but I think it's a little like using a diamond to stop a bottle," Sills also said.

But even in the glory days of the cinquecento (an English scholar Winifred Smith points out), most players of commedia dell'arte reversed to "the precarious hand-to-mouth existence of the unprotected stroller" between engagements with a weekly paycheck at the prosperous ducal courts. In most town piazzas, they were likely to encounter traveling charlatans needing to bring the folks out for a flagon of snake oil with attention-grabbing bits.

So it was not without historical precedent that Madison Avenue was already finding ways to use the unique expressive gifts Sills's personnel had for creation and commentary, hoping the funny dialogue produced by improvisation would improve their pedestrian work.

The ad agency for Milady's Blintzes asked Tony Holland, Andy Duncan, Zohra Lampert, and Eugene Troobnick—the New York Second City cast at the time—to come up with a campaign. When Sills caught his actors onstage one afternoon playing an Irish family eating Milady's Blintzes during a potato famine, Duncan remembers, "He was outraged that we were prostituting our art."

When the advertising awards were given out, the agency writer accepted the trophies for the Milady's Blintzes spots.

On Buddha's 2587th birthday, in the spring of 1963, celebrating Buddhist monks were gunned down by the Diem government's troops in Hue, South Vietnam. "The Dragon Lady," President Diem's sister-in-law, Madame Nhu, sneered at the subsequent self-immolations of the protesting monks as "barbecue shows."

After The Premise had played six months on tour in Washington, D.C., it occurred to Ted Flicker that there was a big difference between being a serious capitalist and a serious improvisationalist. In the nation's capital, he recalls, "We were treated like diplomats from an uncommitted nation." Privileged information might lead The Premise Players to come up with a bit about the president of the World Bank that would "just kill him" when he showed up at the theatre that night. "We really let them have it, and they loved it. They couldn't do enough for us," he says.

Making fun of politicians in mock press conferences and gibberish conversations is not really the same as having a point of view about politics. It is not narrative, writerly, Brechtian. And it is verbally witty: not Violan. Paul Sills disdained political satire. ("It was always very hard for Second City to engage in politics," he once remarked. "It was easier to mention names.")

Ted Flicker loved it anyway. And then, "One day I realized it was bullshit."

There were several British satirical troupes (like The Establishment, The Cambridge Circus, and Beyond the Fringe) that evolved (on the campus of Cambridge University) simultaneously with the improvisational theatre in America. But the improvised commedia dell'arte was a tradition of the romantic countries, not England. In England, it was required that all scripts presented in the theatre be reviewed by the office of the lord chamberlain. Even without a script, the lord chamberlain learned that, in violation of the English law, The Premise Players planned to portray living heads of state. Accordingly, The Premise was banned.

Overhearing the frantic phone calls between London and Washington at The Premise home base in New York was David Dozer, a twenty-two-year-old improviser who had previously performed his own short Dada plays and poems in Pittsburgh at Café Bastille, an off-campus coffeehouse. Dozer learned that JFK himself was sending word that he was perfectly at ease with having himself satirized, even volunteering the endorsement of the First Lady, his wife. Jackie remembered thinking The Premise was "cute" when she saw it in Washington.

" 'We don't care what's okay with you. We don't allow it,' " Dozer recalls the lord chamberlain's office replied. "So in London, we didn't play heads of state. We could have teased them. We could have said, 'Aren't you the King of Roumania?' 'No, I just look like him.' But it never occurred to us. We played Teddy Kennedy cheating at Harvard instead."

Once The Premise was known as the show the lord chamberlain had banned, "The public had the idea that it was dirty," says Dozer. "So a lot of people came." In the English version of Story-Story, the players were provided with audience suggestions that were "eloquent and explicit. Like, 'He took his penis out of his trousers and waved it about,' or 'The archbishop farted and blew the windows out of the loo.' The English love the toidy," Dozer says.

When Ted Flicker saw Prime Minister Harold Macmillan stand up at the Comedy Theatre to applaud The Premise, he said to himself, "We're doing something wrong."

N eil Simon's second play (the first was *Come Blow Your Horn*) was to try out in Bucks County, Pennsylvania, in April 1963, before coming to Broadway. *Nobody Loves Me* was about two emotional opposites in their first weeks of marriage in a New York walkup. *Newsweek* would describe it as "paint-by-the-numbers" or "formula" comedy in which "actors spray each other with Jean Kerr-isms in an unending game of 'Can You Top This?' " Simon's producer, Arnold Saint-Subber, wanted a director for it who was fresh and new. And, along Broadway, the word was out that half a prominent comedy duo was looking to do something without Elaine May. In fact Mike Nichols had already signed to stage a production of *The Importance of Being Earnest* at the Vancouver Festival. (He also performed there in Shaw's *Saint Joan*, in the role of the cranky Dauphin.) "Why don't we just give him the play and see if he's interested?" Saint-Subber said.

Toward the end of his performing days, Mike Nichols recalls being so overwhelmed by "all those performer things . . . anxiety and baby feelings and baby behavior" that "I felt dead." Then *Nobody Loves Me* tried out in Bucks County, and "It was that simple. People liked it and the reviews were very good. It was a promising success. It needed work and changes, which we made," Neil Simon says. After existing for two years as "the leftover half of something," Nichols suddenly rose from the ashes to find his true calling on the other side of the footlights. "All these Daddy feelings came out . . . From the first hour of the first day, I was home."

David Shepherd himself emerged from his self-imposed theatrical retirement in 1963 to direct a summer Compass in the heart of Kennedy compound country, the nonproletarian town of Hyannisport. That year, with a backlog of material and the help of other directors and actors, he used the Compass name to bring to other towns and cities improvisational revues. There would be Compasses in Washington, Boston, New York, Hyannisport, the Catskills, and Bucks County before Shepherd got a full-time job in advertising. ("I need milk to feed my babies," he said.)

The Hyannisport Compass consisted of Ron Weyand, Reni Santoni, Suzanne Shepherd, Alan Alda, and the late Diana Sands. "Shepherd was a great caster," says Paul Sills.*

Not liking actors, Shepherd was better off chasing tomorrow. Since the first Compass closed in Chicago, his ambition was invested in its "replications," not his heart. He had been exhausted by its failure first. He had never been seduced because the audience was pleased. And he had been left gasping hardest in the wave of what Robert Brustein once called "cultural schizophrenia," the phenomenon that occurs when the rebel-artist becomes popularly adored. "For a long time, not only did I think I had invented Nichols and May and improvisational theatre, but I even began to think I had invented nightclub entertainment," Shepherd says.

That summer, under the spell of Camelot and the sailing set, David Shepherd's Hyannisport Compass improvised a presidential press conference from audience questions. "I worked very hard on that. I tried to get a little bit inside his personality instead of doing Caroline jokes," said Alan Alda, who played JFK.

---

*The other Compasses, directed by Larry Arrick, Lee Kalcheim, George Morrison, and George Sherman, included such actors as Jane Alexander, Lloyd Battista, MacIntyre Dixon, Paul Dooley, David Dozer, Tom Erhart, Philip Baker Hall, Larry Hankin, Henry Jaglom, Louise Lasser, Richard Libertini, Paul Mazursky, Leslie J. Stark, and Mary Louise Wilson.

The same summer, following sit-ins and marches in Southern locations like Selma, Greensboro, Nashville, Shreveport, and Birmingham, 200,000 black and white Americans stood before the Lincoln Memorial after a march on Washington and heard Martin Luther King, Jr.'s incantation, "I have a dream . . ."

One thing Neil Simon changed before bringing *Nobody Loves Me* to Broadway (starring Robert Redford and Elizabeth Ashley) was the title, to *Barefoot in the Park*. It opened at the Biltmore Theatre on October 23, 1963, to money reviews. In the *Herald-Tribune*, Walter Kerr said, "Mr. Nichols' eye is a restless absolute, as his ear has perfect pitch" and described his evening at the Biltmore as "two and a half hours of winging it, without ever sloshing into an unfriendly cloud." Others called it "a bubbling, rib-tickling comedy," a "hurricane of hilarity."

Mike Nichols has described the job of the director as "really trying to kiss the audience's ass and please them, because he knows he's got to make them happy to some extent to keep them there." Yet in spite of the simplicity of his aspiration, it was disguised by such wit and stylishness that the reputation he had made with Elaine remained untarnished. When he said, "The trick in attacking the Establishment is not the attack, it's the craft," no one questioned whether he was really on the cutting edge.

Actors who improvise say it is like walking a tightrope or driving Le Mans. At every step of an improvisation there are opportunities to falter, to panic, and to fall. The improvisational actor's obligation to create a coherent piece of theatre out of a mere suggestion makes the actor's nightmare—forgetting lines—seem obsolete, a daydream compared to the improviser's fear of having nothing to say. A great player, Doris Hess, is thinking as Willy Shoemaker as she compares improvisational actors to jockeys: "You fall off the horse. You get mud all over you. You lose. You realize it wasn't part of the job, it *was* the job. Winning a race is a bonus."

Speaking to an audience of college students at Amherst in October 1963, JFK could have been advertising the merits of the improvisational theatre when he said, "In a democratic society, the highest duty of the writer, the composer, the artist, is to remain true to himself and let the chips fall where they may."

On November 22, 1963, he died in Dallas of gunshot wounds, supposedly from a lone assassin's bullets.

It was a moment that begged a connection between the right and left brain.

It may be remembered that without the theatrical chops for the mission, the one comedian who dared to address the blight on the mind of the nation was professionally crucified for it. "He's not funny anymore," it was said of Mort Sahl.

Kennedy's foremost impersonator, Vaughn Meader, had just released his second album. Taking the stage of the Village Theatre on Second Avenue, one of the few in the country from which he and his First Amendment privileges were not banned, Lenny Bruce, the martyr to free speech, paused for a long time and whistled into the microphone. "Poor Vaughn Meader," he said.

In New York, at The Second City at Square East, Roger Bowen wanted to do the Kennedy press conference from heaven. "Not only was my suggestion rejected, the theatre was closed that night."

Assessing the reflexes, muscle, and guts left in the improvisational theatre on that November day of shock and mourning, Ted Flicker reflects that it had long before been decided that "if it wasn't cute and gentle, then nobody would come."

26

Nuclear Winter
and Infrared Spring

"Civilization is over in a lot of different ways," Paul Sills told the *Tulane Drama Review* in 1964. "Our separation from the natural will destroy the inner life of the people—certainly destroy my inner life. I say the job is to turn back and form, in some small way, communities that have a real life." But the cash registers were still ringing, so no one heard.

Mike Nichols's old friend from the dressing rooms of *Camelot*, Sybil Burton (now Richard's ex), was on the board of directors of The Establishment Theatre Company, the group responsible for importing the British satirical troupe. They were turning an empty storeroom near Bloomingdale's into the New Theatre and the Strollers' Club downstairs into Arthur, a chic discotheque.

The first project for the boards was a restaging of a controversial play by Anne Jellicoe called *The Knack*. Jellicoe's writing had been noted for its meandering or disjointed conversation and compared by the London *Observer* to action painting or jazz.* The play told the story of a provincial virgin en route to the YMCA who gets locked into a London house with

---

*The director of the London production, Keith Johnstone, had grown famous himself for using improvisation as a directorial tool in his work with the "angry young" playwrights, (including Jellicoe, John Dexter, Arnold Wesker, and John Arden). At their Royal Court Theatre, "drama beyond the spoken word" was Johnstone's specialty.

three young men. At the virgin's expense, the most cynical and rakish of the three teaches his fellows his own ruthless tactics of seduction, that is "the art of getting girls" (the play's subtitle), that is, "the knack."

It had a great deal in common with Elaine May's 1955 scenario about date rape, *Georgina's First Date*.

Sybil Burton knew Mike Nichols to be an Anglophile who "loved all that was going on" in London, especially the work of the "angry young men." And, as one of her producing partners, Ivor David Balding, said, "He was already hot."

As Mike Nichols sized up *The Knack*, "It's a how-to-do-it play." They hired him.

On Bleecker Street, Ted Flicker was running The Living Premise, turning all the profits over to the three black actors (Godfrey Cambridge, Al Freeman, Jr., and Diana Sands) and the single white one (Calvin Ander) whose scenes about a Jewish maid in a middle-class black household offended even Flicker's mother. But no one in The Living Premise was picking up on Flicker's concept of ensemble: "They all hated each other." The audiences were piling in.

Flicker himself was making a film called *The Troublemaker*, about a New York City cabaret owner who refuses to pay bribes, in which The Premise Permanent Company Players improvised their parts. The film was a hit at the Venice Film Festival, and Flicker anticipated making one satirical film about life in America each year. His expectations for "doing the Ingmar Bergman thing," producing a yearly film while maintaining an active theatrical repertory, ended when the box-office receipts for *The Troublemaker* came in and he sold The Premise, although it was still running successfully after four and a half years.

With Flicker's blessing, the new owner, Michael Brandman, booked Elaine May into The Premise to direct an improvisational revue of her own, *The Third Ear*. She was enthused with Roger Bowen's idea for an evening called "What Have You Done with My Golden Boy?" and by his suggestion for placing a life-size cardboard cutout of JFK torn with three bulletholes outside The Premise door. She asked him to join. "I always thought Elaine was a genius. A brilliant writer, a brilliant actress, a brilliant improviser, a brilliant teacher, and a mediocre director," Bowen reflects. "Four brilliants and a mediocre." He felt more comfortable staying at The Second City. He now had three kids.

In Mike Nichols's version of *The Knack*, one critic discovered that the "intricate patterns of movement" and "knockabout staging" that provided the laughs also tended to "blunt its equally real edge of terror." *The New Yorker* noticed that "the wonderfully ingenious Mike Nichols has directed the play as a breakneck farce when one suspects Miss Jellicoe didn't mean it to be one." The final arbiter was Howard Taubman at *The New York Times*. "Why shouldn't the theatre of the absurd occasionally lean toward hearty laughter instead of bleakness and despair?" he said.

The Knack was a smash hit.

The Third Ear opened downtown on Bleecker Street the very next night. Elaine May's reviews were not kind. Except for a piece about disputative Talmudic students in a Maccabee patrol car in Brooklyn, the critics found the show "more glib than perceptive" and the "improvisations performed without flair." "The tired gimmick of asking the audience for news in the headlines . . . should be abolished," they said.

"Elaine May should have realized how interminable the sketches were." "The skits were not short enough." The cast (Mark Gordon, Renee Taylor, Louise Lasser, Reni Santoni, and Peter Boyle) came in for a tongue-lashing too. "You've got to say one thing for the old-timers," one critic said erroneously. "They knew when to get off."

When Richard Rodgers and Alan Jay Lerner decided to end their unproductive partnership, Lerner took the musical book he had developed for Barbara Harris to another composer, Burton (*Finian's Rainbow*) Lane. In her years in New York under contract for the unproduced musical, Barbara performed in the film version of *Oh Dad*; was nominated for an Emmy for a role in a TV show, *The Nurses*; appeared in two productions of Arnold Weinstein's "comic opera for actors," *Dynamite Tonight!*; and sang in a tribute to Marc Blitzstein with the Philharmonic, under Leonard Bernstein's baton. Between all these projects, she made her way downtown to improvise.

"I don't have a license to practice medicine," Paul Sills once said about improvisation, "but it can cure." Barbara also saw it as restorative: "We could play all the antisocial and rebellious characters we wanted. All the obnoxious people that were aspects of us. We'd do it and it would be over with. If I had a mousy tendency, I'd play mousy women until it went away. I could make fun of myself and the parts of me that were superficial or pretentious. It was a place to ventilate obsession in the whole large scheme of society and politics."

Paul Sills himself had lost all interest in The Second City and once-fresh improvisations that were performed, perfected, and passed on to the new company member like a burlesque skit was passed on to the new blond. During his previous absences, a pool of directors had pitched in for him, including Del Close, Larry Arrick, and Alan Myerson. Even Mike Nichols had once stopped in Chicago to offer a hand. This time the job fell to Sheldon Patinkin, who describes himself as "not much of a satirist, you know."

Since he was no longer an active partner, Sills, like Howard Alk, was obliged by a previous agreement with Bernie Sahlins to sell back his Second City shares. Sheldon Patinkin bought him out.

Sills didn't seem to care. "I wanted to more seriously go back and work on the theater games which I began to see were something to be explored, studied, thought about, worked on. So I helped set up a place with my mother to do that," Sills explained.

Once, as Omar Shapli has pointed out, Sills started "a Brecht fad," once "a liver-for-breakfast fad." Now, while embracing the work of the Jewish theologian, "He started a Martin Buber fad." He talked of the theatre as "a religious expression of the community" and as "a sacred space." During this time, people began to use in connection with Paul Sills the word "priest."

"The sooner the improvisational theatre breaks away from the idea of repeating itself, the closer it will be to a real improvisational theatre. What I'm after is a *total* reversal of values," he said.

According to Sheldon Patinkin, his improbable successor at The Second City, Sills had never liked the writing process. And, as he had set it up himself, his job was really that of the head writer: an improvisation can only be directed after the material is there. "That's why he screams and throws chairs and gets everybody frightened and walks the hell out. The best he can do is throw up a flag and say, 'This is no good,' so people can save their asses for themselves," Patinkin says.

With Sills's departure, Bernie Sahlins was free to begin the transformation of The Second City into what a William Morris agent called the "Superbowl of Comedy" and to justify the deterioration of its originality and taste on the grounds that improvisational theatre belonged to a tradition that is "demotic and burlesque," as the costumed and clowning mug shots of the new companies were supposed to attest. Comfortable with the thought of improvisation as a product, not a process, Sahlins could half jokingly compare Viola's exercises to fencing, "a functional device to achieve a goal other than itself . . . a tool for arriving at Second City material."

At Game Theatre, Spolin and Sills's new creation, Viola's unadulterated exercises—no tricks, no gimmicks, no fail-safe devices, no script, no situation—were elevated to the *ding an sich*. Within the sporting context, the understructure of the games seemed of itself coherent, sufficiently pregnant with artistic possibility to make playwriting obsolete.

Implicit in all the Spolin games had always been Viola's concept of the body as the source of creative intelligence and the idea that space could be used as a substance as creatively as clay. Now these principles were joined to Buber's idea of the stage as "sacred ground": when a player perceives and responds to the space physiologically—as a tangible thing —he or she is capable of sharing it with fellow players, and in the reality of the space, they connect with each other on the sacred ground in a mystical rapport. The grand finale of rapport between the players is expressed by their ability to allow the space they have created together to transform.

In the mystical perception of the universe, there are no beginnings, middles, ends. Viola put forth transformation as improvisation's highest state.

On the cusp of the Youth Revolution, which was now engaging millions of people under thirty in a tumultuous and voluptuary aesthetic of sex, drugs, revolution, and rock and roll, Alan Myerson had taken off for San Francisco and was running an improvisational theatre of his own, with a more visceral connection to the sixties than Sills's chaste, well-bred, and winsome Second City. The political inclinations of its members—Howard Hessman, Garry Goodrow, Peter Bonerz, Carl Gottlieb, Jessica Myerson, and Roger Bowen—were far to the left of the Democrats. When Allaudin Mathieu joined them in 1967, he recalls that their work "really had a gutsy guerrilla street theatre feeling." Then Myerson called for the man who had him banished from Chicago. A former fire-eater fit into The Committee like an index finger on a glove.

Some of Del Close's previous differences with Myerson had stemmed from Close's belief that "comedy is far more dangerous and far more important than politics." He advised one of his workshop members, Ed Greenberg, now a television producer, that "if we're not offending anyone, we're not doing our job." In his search for "wiring diagrams for the gestalt Superman," Close too had become a shaman. In his canon, as in Paul and Viola's, the risks of improvisation had to get higher and higher and the players had to learn to fly without nets. Unlike them, Close was a comedian. "Follow the invisible ball" was not his bell, book, and candle. His was: "Follow the fear. That's where the laughs are."

In the heat of San Francisco's summer of love, he picked up the thread he had left hanging at the St. Louis Compass and invented The Harold, an improvisational long form of jump-cut one-liners, short scenes, and monologues that could be created on the spot by an entire ensemble from an audience-suggested theme.

To be improvising under Close's direction "sometimes was like . . . Nirvana," his old student Ed Greenberg says. "He had a way of inspiring people to feel the power of improvisation, an incredible ability to create an environment, as most geniuses do." He remembers Close conceiving "crazy exercises to get people to express themselves, like Blind Harolds" or Harolds played blindfolded. "We had a sense of changing the world, of going to the edge."

Ed Greenberg went to the edge once in a Blind Harold. And he fell off the stage.

Lerner and Lane's *On a Clear Day You Can See Forever* had finally opened on Broadway in 1965, with Barbara Harris playing the dual role of Daisy, a young woman with extrasensory powers, and Melinda, her eighteenth-century persona in a previous life. By critical consensus, the star was more engaging than the play. *The New York Times* called her "a blithe spirit and a living doll." (During the day, she was playing a social worker in the film of Herb Gardner's *A Thousand Clowns*.)

The next year, playing three singing roles in Mike Nichols's production of Bock and Harmick's *The Apple Tree*, she won many awards, including a Tony, the Drama Desk, and the Cue Entertainer of the Year award. To celebrate, her producers spread her airbrushed likeness across the drama section of *The New York Times*.

Barbara enjoyed the work that success brought her, but she was driven by the desire to participate in the theatre, not the need to generate publicity. She became so shy with the press that Mike Nichols, her boss, volunteered to be interviewed about her in *Life*.

From adolescence, her training had prepared her for the aims and the support of the ensemble, not for the lonely vanities and rewards of being a star. And after all the fanfare, even her appearances at The Second City had become too big a deal. When the limo door closed behind her, she noticed that "I was exhausted. I had no voice. I had no life. I was turning into a total nerd. People were sort of telling me what life was like. And all I saw were the guys who did my make-up and the women who did my hair. All my friends were mad at me."

Among the many Compass Players who played chess backstage, David Shepherd remembers Barbara Harris ranking "right up there at the top."

She took a sabbatical from the spotlight at the height of her fame.

She had already once turned down the lead in a film of musical Lerner and Loewe's *Paint Your Wagon* and almost half a million dollars because "the job seemed disruptive. I was at Hunter, matriculating."

To ground herself when *The Apple Tree* closed, she took a backstage job, reading scripts for the producer David Merrick. After a year, she recommended a play by a young playwright, Elliott Baker, called *The Penny Wars*. Merrick suggested that she direct it herself on Broadway.

While *The Penny Wars* was in rehearsal, she tried to explain her un-conventional moves. She said, "The whole star bit and the kind of public recognition that goes with it gives me the creeps."

As a young man, Paul Sills had brought Brecht and Brechtian acting to life in America. He had given a new and poetic dimension to the performance of comedy and set a new standard for the presentation of satirical humor and social commentary. As the decade turned, his company of Chicago actors were improvising upon fairy tales and myths. "In the oral tradition of Homer, the theatre is concerned with the spoken as opposed to the written word. Theatre has to remain with the spoken word," said Sills. To compress the changes of time and space, Sills was using transformations and the Living Newspaper technique, wherein the actor doubles as narrator and character, weaving in and out of the nar-rative and into the dialogue. "A story is a peculiar kind of journey," he said. Recast with veteran Second City actors, Paul Sills's Story Theatre appeared on Broadway featuring the scenarios of Aesop and Grimm.

With Story Theatre, the academics and the critics looked forward to dramatizations of stories like Kafka's *Metamorphosis*. (Paul Sand, who played a wonderful dog, was urged to take on the role of the roach.)

"The point is to connect the audience today with what has lasted by word of mouth, with *what has been passed down* . . . The gimmick, it's nothing," said Sills.

Reaching into popular rather than literary theatre traditions, directing scriptless plays, Sills was, in fact, still wrestling with those games that had been passed down to him.

The story format answered a number of needs that had been created by the games. It supplied a content for improvisations that pure form had erased. Where else could the magic and the ritual of space be so perfectly paired as with a fairy tale or myth? In what other context could invisible objects and transformations be more appropriate? And stories all have ends.

"My concern with form is what leads me on. You could call it 'the eternal feminine,' like at the end of *Faust*," the author of *The Coming of Bildad* and *The Game of Hurt* once explained.

The essence of Story Theatre was captured in its Broadway logo: a line of seven playful actors, moving forward into limbo in No Motion, in a distanced and dignified silhouette. Sills's imagery—his peerless directorial eyesight—was connected ineluctably to Viola's memory of children playing on an empty street.

I n Hollywood, Ted Flicker made a fine satirical film, *The President's Analyst*, before falling, as one will in an industrial town, into the jaws of the industry. He was coauthor of a television show that made him millions, *Barney Miller*. He prefers to be remembered as the coauthor of the Westminster Place Kitchen Rules. He is now a novelist.

D el Close returned to Chicago as the new artistic director of The Second City in 1971, "hot and smoking from the sixties," he says, to spread his Dionysian word. His new protégés included Bill Murray, John Candy, and John Belushi. He did not have Hollywood in mind when he laid on them the same rune or wanga he had laid on Ed Greenberg: "You have a light within you. Burn it out."

After ten years, due to artistic differences with Bernie Sahlins, he quit. "I got tired of cutting the comedy salami," he says. He began acting and writing comic books again. Following a tenet of Krishnamurti ("We must learn to think together"), he continued to lead players on stage to improvise. (Devotees of The Harold have their own Ivy League.)

E laine May went on to direct plays (mostly her own) that did not appear
on Broadway. She starred in several films, but did not translate as a
movie star. When she set off for her first big Hollywood trip, in 1967, to
film *Luv* with Peter Falk and Jack Lemmon, Mike Nichols predicted,
"Elaine is going to suffer" out there.

In fact, for several years, after directing three films for Hollywood studios,
she became a pariah in the show-business capital charged with stealing
two reels of her movie-in-progress, *Mikey and Nicky*, improvised by John
Cassavetes, Peter Falk, Ned Beatty, Rose Arrick, and others from her
original scenario about friendship and betrayal between two petty gangsters
(one of them Jewish, like her brother Louie). The work had first been
composed on scraps of paper she had with her (along with a baby carriage)
upon her arrival, one freezing cold day in Chicago, onto the set of *The
Dybbuk*, a play about demonic possession, the 1954 offering of the Playwrights Theatre Club.

When, after two years, she had not finished editing the 1.4 million feet
of film she had shot (there were 475,000 feet shot for *Gone With the
Wind*), the studio took away *Mikey and Nicky*. In the dead of an analyst's
night, Elaine's Dr. Rubenfine drove to the studio and took a hunk of it
back, hiding the reels in Connecticut, *Variety* said, in another doctor's
garage. With what was left of the film, Paramount made its own cut and
released it, letting it die their way. The moguls of Hollywood were distressed
by Elaine May's corporate disloyalty. "Why should I be loyal to a big
mountain with some stars around it?" she is claimed to have said.

"It was difficult for me to get directing jobs, because I seemed sort of
crazy," she said when her own approved cut of *Mikey and Nicky* was
shown in New York at a Museum of Modern Art retrospective. Under the
auspices of an old friend, Warren Beatty, her good name was restored in
1978 by a screenwriting credit for a successful remake of *Here Comes Mr.
Jordan* (starring and directed by Beatty) called *Heaven Can Wait*.

Functioning purposely in anonymity thereafter, as a script doctor, she
was well rewarded for her hand in Marlo Thomas's television specials and
in the movies *Tootsie* and *Reds*. After the problems with *Mikey and Nicky*,
she was not being particularly cynical to note that if an artist can help
generate money, "Hollywood doesn't care what you did."

She received more than a million dollars to write and direct *Ishtar*, her
"thinking man's road movie" about a terrible song writing team, two

goofballs who can only get ahead in show business in exchange for doing undercover work in the Moroccan desert for the CIA. She wrote it to star Warren Beatty and Dustin Hoffman (each fiftyish, like herself, each making $5.5 million) as the two jerks.

As a fledgling director, she had spent hours working out the way that Zohra Lampert (playing in Strindberg's *Miss Julie*) should hold a dead bird. With a higher budget for *Ishtar,* Elaine May's famous $40 million disaster, she spent only a commensurate amount of time looking for a perfect camel in Morocco and leveling the Sahara sands.

I n two years, Bernie Sahlins traveled 84,000 miles, commuting to his second house in Belgravia, in London's West End, combing the world's theatres for his various production interests, joining Egyptian archeological digs, and enjoying the profits from the reported $2 million sale of The Second City. The improvisational theatre's most famous, solvent, and enduring institution had indeed become an empire, consisting of touring companies, a branch in Toronto, a syndicated television show, and a salable coffer of twenty-five years' worth of improvised material, now all taped, transcribed, and computerized.

At The Second City's twenty-fifth anniversary reunion, no cherry bombs had dropped when Sahlins stepped onstage to read the congratulatory telegrams of Mayor Harold Washington and Ronald Reagan, the President of the United States. "I don't recognize it anymore," said Paul Sills. Roger Bowen, Andrew Duncan, and Eugene Troobnick had declined to attend. And nervously the lights blacked out to prematurely end the only extemporaneous event in the reunion show, a teaching scene in which Shelley Berman, playing a successful actor, was showing Severn Darden, playing an unemployed one, how to improvise.

S hortly before opening his own sold-out production of *Waiting for Godot* at New York's Lincoln Center in 1988, Mike Nichols shared some of his theatrical acumen with *The New York Times*:

> . . . the Beckett experience is that when the play is over, you sit there and you're utterly depressed because there seems to be no hope at all. And then you walk 15 blocks, and you feel good, and finally you feel great, because somebody has told the truth, and the truth in the end is the best thing we have.

Nichols himself had long enjoyed the acquisitions and the power of a potentate. He was a wildly prolific stage and film director, of apparently limitless facility and range. His name on a project preceded those of his coworkers, who had included many well-known writers and practically all the great stars. As a producer, he sometimes anointed entertainments he had enjoyed in small productions by bringing them to bigger theatres, under more bountiful conditions and brighter lights.

In 1988, he opened an educational institution in New York, the New Actors Workshop, a two-year school. Joining him on the faculty were two University of Chicago colleagues, George Morrison and Paul Sills. He had a blockbuster movie in the can. (Roger Bowen called *Working Girl*, about a low-class woman who succeeds on Wall Street, "a Republican fairy tale.") Nichols also was reported as madly in love, newly married to his fourth wife, Diane Sawyer, a famous television journalist.

The world was indeed his oyster.

But not an empty stage.

For his version of "Sam's play," Nichols delivered two master comedians Steve Martin and Robin Williams, making their professional stage acting debuts as Vladimir and Estragon, the bowler-hatted tramps. F. Murray Abraham and Bill Irwin (as Pozzo and Lucky) rounded out the star-studded cast. For the hottest ticket in town, the Lincoln Center membership was consigned to compete by lottery: the tight schedule of the stars permitted *Waiting for Godot* for only seven weeks. A waste site in an American desert, like Tucson or Las Vegas, was suggested by their stage set, which was full of props and sand.

What with Nichols's famous "knockabout" staging and new business created by the props, here was a *Godot* without the long pauses in which nothing happened. In previews, the laughs were actually unremitting. They filled up Sam's void.

An audience member received a photographic negative of Nichols's own Beckett experience: "When the play is over, you sit there and feel great, because someone has made you laugh. And then you walk fifteen blocks and feel utterly depressed."

D avid Shepherd variously became an "industrial consultant," a "community adviser," a "programmer of group creativity," and "an urban whatever," as one friend says. In or out of these roles he continued to invent and execute new and updated concepts for improvised popular theatres and performance sports. (The most famous is an intermural com-

petition, ImprovOlympic, the most recent is a party game, Shooting Stars!)
Shepherd assembled street kids, old folks, jailbirds, rabbis, computer operators, and buyers from Bloomingdale's, who improvised on his various
formulas on subjects like homelessness, homosexuality, marriage, money,
gentrification, crack. He incorporated all kinds of technological aids into
his projects, such as camcorders, projectors, and videotape. He welcomed
financial contributions from actors to whom he had given a start. He did
not seek out geniuses to be in his casts.

27

The Point of the Compass

The example of Compass and its great players gave great stature to the role of the comedian since it exhibited so clearly the complexity of his or her process and intelligence. It also established the life and concerns of the literate mind as fit sources for comedy. (It is hard to imagine Woody Allen, or Robin Williams, or Steve Martin bringing his braininess to the stage without its precedent.) Most important, it provided a do-it-yourself model and an artistic principle for countless talented vagabonds who would never have otherwise grounded their creativity in the invisible reality of an empty stage. These included graduate students like David Steinberg, salesmen like Jed Mills, and dentists like Alan Euger, all of whom were able to discover on the improvisational stage what they were at the core. In a rather stunning improvement on David Shepherd's expectations, the improvisational theatre also gave to children of the working class, like Bill and Brian Doyle-Murray and John and Jim Belushi, a chance to make a better living in the arts.

In a professional endeavor, Mike Nichols once noted that a hallmark of improvisational actors is "accessible intelligence." Their discipline includes an intimate and extended connection with the public and more than a rudimentary knowledge of all facets of the stage. The habit of responding to audience suggestions and accepting all premises makes improvisational actors curious, informed, and keen to the changes in their cities, their country, their cultural landscape. The practice of tapping into their own supply of subconscious material opens new territory for them as writers, as directors, and as lone performance artists.

Thus, some of our most gifted, daring, and hilarious performers, directors, teachers, and writers have emerged from the improvisational scene. These names and more deserve to be mentioned:

Dan Ackroyd, Peter Ackroyd, Louis Arquette, J. J. Barry, Bernadette Birquette, Karen Black, Ann Bowen, Valri Bromfield, Jack Burns, Hamilton Camp, Sondra Caron, Nancy Cassaro, Jane Curtin, Cassandra Danz, Bob Dishy, Robin Duke, Peter Elbling, Ann Elder, Michael Elias, Nancy Fish, Joe Flaherty, Leigh French, Martin Harvey Friedberg, Michael Gellman, Nancy Giles, Whoopi Goldberg, Gerrit Graham, Judy Graubart, Charna Halpern, Sandy Holt, Tino Insana, Bruce Jarchow, Robert Klein, Tim Kazurinsky, Linda Lavin, Emily Levine, Eugene Levy, Lynn Lipton, Shelley Long, Andrea Martin, George N. Martin, Robin Menken, Ira Miller, Michael Mislove, John Monteith, Mary-Elaine Monti, Catherine O'Hara, Julie Payne, Barry Primus, Gilda Radner, Harold Ramis, Suzanne Rand, David Rasche, Rob Reiner, Eugenie Ross-Lemming, Billy Saluga, Frank Shaw, Martin Short, Betty Thomas, Dave Thomas, Peter Torokvei, Nick Ullett, Marcia Wallace, George Wendt, Debby White, Joshua White, Tamara Wilcox-Smith, Fred Willard, Paul Willson, Alex Zail, and the late John Brent.

Since its birth in Chicago three decades ago, this form of theatre, like psychotherapy and oat bran, has become a regular part of life. And Compass continues to provide a format in which distinctive individuals can play onstage together, as perhaps they never have before or will again, in an atmosphere where it is a virtue to risk and human to fail.

Remembering the improvisational theatre he first saw on Fifty-fifth Street in the back room of the Compass Tavern, Aaron Asher (U. of C. '52) says, "I suppose you always hear this from someone who saw something in its earliest days. But it was better then."

Unlike America's other spontaneous native art form, jazz, there is a paltry recorded history of the early improvised theatre. Most of the great improvisations at the Compass were not recorded on the spot but only after they were "set." The few existing scripts and audiotapes insufficiently document what is essentially a visual form. These artifacts indicate that the Compass had some shortcomings: it was crude. It was loud. The scenes went on too long. It got boring. Not all the actors knew how to act. Yet it seems to have been vastly more thoughtful and complex than its successors, distinguished by its daring, the high intelligence that informed its point of view, its use of an ambitious dramatic form like the scenario, and especially by the fact that in the essential meaning and the spirit of the word, it was really improvised. It was so fearlessly original, experimental, and alive that whatever its shortcomings, thirty years after its closing, it is remembered with reverence and astonishing clarity by the people who were there.

Following their testimony, several of The Compass Players predicted that the story of the first improvisational theatre could be told only as a *Rashomon*, one event seen differently by every witnessing eye or, as Roger Bowen first supposed, "Like asking the seven blind men to describe the elephant. Each blind man describes the part he touched."

But The Compass Players all bear a congruent witness.

Shelley Berman says, "We were doing the best work of our lives." "It was certainly before its time," says Andy Duncan. "It was so raw. It had such energy. It was *so* unusual. And it didn't cost anything."

Severn says, "There was nothing like the Compass."

"There was nothing like it, that's all," says Paul Sills.

"Can you imagine a place like that? Elaine doing what she wanted? All of us doing what we wanted?" asks Barbara Harris.

"Who are we kidding?" Andy Duncan asks. "The early Compass was the best. It was really an ideal that became realized. You rarely see that in life."

Roger Bowen describes The Second City under Paul Sills as "very much like *The New Yorker* magazine, which is not only highly intelligent, very funny, sophisticated, and brilliant, it's quite conscientious too. But from the small point of view: not moving any mountains. The Second City was a more sophisticated form of entertainment than the Compass, but it didn't challenge the fabric of the society we live in. In that sense, all of Second City was not as good as Lenny Bruce."

The philosophy of The Premise, Ted Flicker's creation, is described by David Dozer as "Kennedy Democrat. Flicker saw improvisation as a kind of carny show or con, a public sword-swallowing."

Regarding David Shepherd's politics ("Generically, I would say that I'm a socialist"), various of his associates recall him as "a guy with some fuzzy notion," "an aristocrat who condescends to the people," "crazy," "vague," "rhetorical." "Most likely the FBI closed the files on David Shepherd. They couldn't understand his politics either," Severn sighs.

Yet Compass was the sum of all the worldly attitudes of David Shepherd.

"There's no question. The Compass was his brain child," Roger Bowen says.

Sorting out its special ideology, Bowen refers to a statement of C. Wright Mills, who was writing at the time: "He considered *his* political goal to 'help men connect their private discontents with the public issues.' You see, if you teach people to make this connection, you've got the beginning of the reorganization of society. That was the spirit that was in the air, and that's the principle on which David operated, whether he articulated it that way or not.

"His vision was great, it was authentic, it continued when other people had fallen away, and although it hasn't produced what he wanted, and may never, it produced a lot. We all got a career out of it, and we all made a living from it. Not just ten or twenty, but hundreds of people. Even though he never got there himself, he is the one, he is the Moses who took us out of slavery and brought us to the promised land."

Shelley Berman assesses Shepherd's contribution this way: "I guess if Thomas Alva Edison did not want to sell the light bulb and become rich from it, somebody else would be known as the inventor of the light bulb. The fact is that David Shepherd is the inventor—or at least the discoverer—of this form of entertainment: he regenerated commedia dell'arte. He brought it to earth in America. And we've been basking in the glory ever since. Because he made it possible. And he was *so* young. Just a boy making it possible. And we all leapt from it. But it was *his* dream, *his* energy that made it all come to pass."

As Barbara Harris's memory of David Shepherd zigzags over a long-distance wire, it is July 1954, and he is onstage with Paul Sills at the Playwrights Theatre Club production of A *Midsummer Night's Dream.* She is nineteen years old, dressed to play Puck, and watching from the wings. Paul Sills, who has recently become her husband, plays the lion. Carrying the "lanthorn," Shepherd is accompanied by a dog. He remembers himself chasing the dog, who ran out of the theatre. Barbara Harris remembers him as "a very ro*man*tic man."

"You can call him a dreamer, or a man who didn't find a way to fulfill his dream," an old acquaintance says. "As I see it, he's a man who didn't fulfill his dream. And it was a goddamn good dream."

Since her days as a leading lady on the New York stage, Barbara Harris has been a director and an acting teacher as well as distinguishing herself in such films as *The Seduction of Joe Tynan, Movie Movie, Plaza Suite, Peggy Sue Got Married, Dirty Rotten Scoundrels,* and Alfred Hitchcock's last film, *Family Plot*. For a single scene, as an auditioning actress in *Who Is Harry Kellerman and Why Is He Saying Those Terrible Things About Me?* (starring Dustin Hoffman), she was an Oscar nominee. Her most stunning role in a movie, as Albuquerque, in Robert Altman's *Nashville*, was improvised. In the last scene, as a desperate would-be country music singer, in a frizzy red wig, she is shoved onstage to distract the audience with a song right after the star of the evening is shot. It is, of course, her big break, and as starved as Albuquerque is for attention, her moment follows tragedy. She stumbles into her song.

Remembering her own early days in the theatre and with the Compass, Barbara says, "I didn't mind being relegated to whatever they put me in. It wasn't just the acting part. I liked putting out the programs. I liked sweeping the stage. All of it was important. I liked that it was so democratic, that it was an open forum. Anybody's thought or contribution was valid if it was usable. No one had to listen to one person and diminish himself. It was freedom in the best sense: with great discrimination. I was happy just to be part of it."

One of the Group Theatre's three founders, Harold Clurman, is considered its visionary, its moral and spiritual voice. Writing about the ensemble theatre he helped build when he was young, Clurman reflected on the artist's need for such a theatre, not just as a way station but as "a permanent base." He said,

> The artist builds from the storehouse of his past strength, memory, training and experience almost as much as he does from his present contracts and position. Without some dependence on his tradition, he starts his new work with an always decreasing stock, till he ends with a shadow or a memory of himself, not a consummation. We lack memory. We cancel our experience. That is why for all our effort in the theatre, for all that of our predecessors, we proceed always on the basis of diminishing returns.

There are no "what ifs" in improvisation: the beat goes on. Most improvisers seem to think of it as an activity for which one grows too old. But surely history is not just "full of nonsense," as Viola says. Improvisation thrives on knowledge.

In 1955, after ten weeks at the Compass, Barbara spent two months observing the Berliner Ensemble rehearse Brecht's *Galileo*, watching the author himself direct. Was the Compass his influence? Was it in fact a writer's theatre? Or was it the University of Chicago connection, as Severn says? The combination of Sills and Shepherd? The full measure of Elaine? Or was it urban renewal? The heat of real atomic energy? All those physicists?

"It was a theatre intended for people who had no theatre," Barbara says. "It's interesting that it became so commercial. It went straight to the sophisticates that David wanted to get away from. What happened to it was a total paradox."

NOTES

1: THE HUTCHINS PLAN

p. 4 "a trivialization of our lives": Robert M. Hutchins, *The Conflict in Education in a Democratic Society*, Harper, 1953, p. 19.

5 "When I feel like exercising": Hutchins's biographer, Harry S. Ashmore, attributes Hutchins's most famous quip to McEvoy in *Unseasonable Truths: The Life of Robert Maynard Hutchins*, Little, Brown, 1989, p. 114.

"If a university needs a sport": Hutchins's maxim, mentioned to JC by Eve Leoff ('59), April 11, 1982, and Ed Cook ('29), October 2, 1982.

9 "Place of the wild onion": *Webster's New World Dictionary*, Second College Edition, Simon and Schuster, 1982, p. 246.

10 "the neighborhood pride": Ross Talarico, speaking as panelist on "The Chicago Tradition of Proletarian Writing," American Writers' Congress, New York, October 11, 1981.

"Goin' to Chicago / Sorry that I can't take you": "Goin' to Chicago Blues," words and music by Jimmy Rushing and Count Basie. Published by Bregman, Vocco and Conn, Inc., New York, copyright 1941.

"Peace, pure and simple": From an anti-war speech of Hutchins, Eve Leoff to JC, January 6, 1982.

"more souls were being conceived": Hutchins's quip preceded James Sacks's October 3, 1983 rendition of the Rockefeller Chapel incident (one of eleven).

11 "the only American comic": Paul Carroll, liner notes, for Severn Darden's record album, *The Sound of My Own Voice and Other Noises* (Mercury OCM2202).

12 a "remorseless dissertation": Robert M. Hutchins, *Zuckerkandl!* Grove Press, 1968 (unpaginated). The animated film of Hutchins's tall story by John and Faith Hubley was released before the book and featured a longer version of the text. Portions of Hutchins's reading played on KPFK-FM-Pacifica, Los Angeles, April 5, 1982.

2: TONIGHT AT 8:30: CONNECTIONS ARE MADE

p. 14 "multiplication of trivial courses": Robert M. Hutchins, *The Conflict in Education in a Democratic Society*, Harper, 1953, p. 12.

15 "This is the cast of *Antigone*": Doggerel recited to JC by Omar Shapli, October 8, 1983; Jane Kome Mather, March 5, 1986. Also Edward Asner letter, June 28, 1988.

18 "the people to whom all the good things happen": Nichols to Nora Ephron, "Mike Nichols Raps," *Eye*, April 1969, p. 78.

19 "Please don't kiss me": Ibid., p. 46.
"You're not as funny": Nichols to Barbara Gelb, "Mike Nichols: The Director's Art," *The New York Times Magazine*, May 27, 1984, p. 42.

20 "you could get shrunk for free": Ibid.
"Jesus, the world is full of possibilities": Nichols to Ephron, "Mike Nichols Raps," p. 78.
"weird": Nichols to Gelb, "Mike Nichols: The Director's Art," p. 40.

21 "Grotowski of Comedy": Severn Darden to JC, c. 1981.
"The most striking thing about Paul": Nichols to Jeffrey Sweet, *Something Wonderful Right Away*, Avon Books, 1978, p. 76.

3: THE HIGH PRIESTESS

24 "Everyone can act": Viola Spolin, *Improvisation for the Theater*, Northwestern University Press, 1963, p. 3.

26 Conversation with Involvement: The game described here is hypothetical. Only an ensemble of master players would be likely to make such harmonious moves.

28 "a mental music": Alda to Sweet, *Something Wonderful Right Away*, p. 326.
"once in a while": Nichols to Sweet, *Something Wonderful Right Away*, p. 77.

30 "YESTERDAY'S NEWS": Chicago *Sunday Times*, September 22, 1940.

4: THE GREAT DIRECTOR

33 "a very definite sense of mission": Holland to Sweet, *Something Wonderful Right Away*, p. 254.

34 "a master for being a guru": Roger Bowen to JC, October 21, 1981.

36 "In an age when man should not withdraw": Bertolt Brecht, "Notes on Stanislavsky," *Stanislavsky and America: "The Method and Its Influence on the American Theatre,"* ed. by Erika Munk, Fawcett, 1966, p. 126.

37 "offers no solace": Eric Bentley, *In Search of Theatre*, Vintage, 1954, p. 147.
"invites the eye" Ibid.
"To my mind, Brecht's theory": Ibid., p. 148.
"relieved," "hypnotic state," and "a definite distance between the actor and the role": Brecht, "Notes on Stanislavsky," p. 125.

39 "always into deals": Jeannie Berlin to Sidney Fields, "In Mama's Footsteps," New York *Daily News*, December 19, 1972.

"My mother's a good businessman": May to Marvin Peisner, as told to JC, October 11, 1983.

"quit going to school": May to *New York Times*, May 24, 1959.

"I didn't really like it": Ibid.

"pathetic, awful": Nichols to Sweet, *Something Wonderful Right Away*, p. 73.

"one night there was this evil, hostile girl": Ibid.

40 "it was unwise for people": Ibid.

5: DAVID SHEPHERD'S DREAM

43 "love affairs in Nice": Shepherd to Sweet, *Something Wonderful Right Away*, p. 2.

44 "every surface that could be gilded was": B. Goldsmith, *Little Gloria, Happy at Last*, Knopf, 1980, p. 91.

46 "The Hunt brothers?": From a taped transcription of Shepherd improvising with David Dozer and JC, living room, New York City, August 4, 1980.

47 "I think that any theatre": Shepherd's diary, Vol. I, "The Rolling Stage."

48 "he was a lonely boy": Old friend to JC, January 7, 1982.

"chasing tomorrow": Ibid.

6: SHEPHERD MEETS SILLS

50 "we have routed or at least repulsed": Robert M. Hutchins, speech to faculty and trustees, 1936. Cited in "The Legacy of Robert M. Hutchins," *University of Chicago Magazine*, 69, no. 4 (summer 1977), p. 24.

51 On the University of Chicago campus: Campus activities for Fall 1952 as listed in Frances Gendlin's University of Chicago *Yearbook*, 1955.

"Our mission here on earth": Robert M. Hutchins, Farewell Address to the students, February 2, 1951. Like his students, Hutchins often reused his most pungently worded thoughts. This one appears in slightly different forms in "A Message to the Young Generation," *Freedom, Education and the Fund: Essays and Addresses, 1946–56*, Meridian, 1956; *The Conflict in Education in a Democratic Society*, Harper, 1953; and is cited twice (differently) in "The Legacy of Robert M. Hutchins," *University of Chicago Magazine*, 69, no. 4 (summer 1977), p. 25.

53 "a tall chuckle-headed young man of 24": George Bernard Shaw, *The Man of Destiny*, in *Complete Plays of George Bernard Shaw*, Odhams Press Ltd., 1934, p. 156.

"excite dramatic activity among the Lithuanians": Shepherd's diary, Vol. I, "The Rolling Stage."

"bawling out in the darkness": Ibid.

7: THE PLAYWRIGHTS THEATRE CLUB

p. 55 "playing records": Nichols to Sweet, *Something Wonderful Right Away*, p. 74.

56 "We are not interested": Shepherd to Beverly Fields, *Chicago*, April 1954 (untitled article in Shepherd's files).

57 "There can be no mystery": Playwrights Theatre Club membership brochure, Fall 1953.

58 "strongly syncopated": Roger Dettmer, "Passing in Review," Chicago *American*, June 24, 1954.

"less raunchy": Sheldon Patinkin to JC, December 1985.

"a mobility of expression": Sidney J. Harris, Chicago *Daily News*, from excerpt printed in Playwrights Theatre Club membership brochure, Fall 1953.

"unquestionably the find": Sam Lesner, Chicago *Daily News*, in Playwrights Theatre Club brochure.

"she helped to create": Fields, *Chicago*, April 1954 (untitled article in Shepherd's files).

61 "the off-beat offering": Herman Kogan, Chicago *Sun-Times*, from excerpt printed in Playwrights Theatre Club membership brochure, Fall 1953.

"a didactical comedy": Playwrights Theatre Club program, July 1953.

71 "the simplified view": August Strindberg, Author's Preface, *Miss Julie: Five Plays*, translated by Henry G. Carlson, University of California Press, 1983, p. 66.

"conglomerates of past": Ibid., p. 67.

"people of today": Ibid., p. 71.

". . . avoided the symmetrical": Ibid.

"a talented actor": Ibid., p. 72.

8: PLAYWRIGHTS' SECOND YEAR

74 "a young Fernandel": Kogan, Chicago *Sun-Times*, in Playwrights Theatre Club brochure.

"obvious from his very first scene": Carroll Baker, *Baby Doll: An Autobiography*, Arbor House, 1983, p. 83.

75 "stunning . . .": Sydney J. Harris, Chicago *Daily News*, October 30, 1954.

76 "with amazing exactitude": Ibid.

78 "In a year and a half": Shepherd's diary, Vol. II, 1953–54, entry of May 1954.

79 *Salt of the Earth*: Production and postproduction difficulties of *Salt of the Earth* were recalled to JC in June 1988 by the documentary filmmaker Jules Schwerin, who worked on the film as an assistant director.

81 "no branch of government": George Murray, Chicago *American*, c. February 1955 (from clipping in Shepherd's files).

83 "*Wanted*: Ten scripts": Classified ad copy in Shepherd's diary, Vol. II, 1953–1954 (printed version clipped from *The New Statesman and Nation*, February 6, 1954).

"new types of plays": Shepherd's diary, Vol. I, "The Rolling Stage."

84 "fascinating but slightly bonkers": Omar Shapli to JC, October 3, 1983.

9: ENTERPRISE

87 "Four boys": There were several written versions of *Enterprise*, including Bowen's typed manuscript and several abbreviated (and probably later) handwritten ones. All the quoted scene-by-scene actions for the actors are from Bowen's text.

88 "I must have two hundred": All the set material in *Enterprise* (i.e., the speeches of Crazy Jake, Crazy Sam, and John the Madman) was written by Bowen, Spring 1955.

89 [Original program for the evening of one-acts at the Reynolds Club was provided by Omar Shapli.]

10: VIOLA'S WORKSHOP

94 Mandel Hall workshops: Spolin's own versions and variations on such games as Building a Where and Contact appear in *Improvisation for the Theater*, *Theater Games for Rehearsal*, *Theater Games for the Classroom*, and the *Theater Game File*, all published by Northwestern University Press.

11: THE EARLY COMPASS

100 "every time I see a man": Any quoted dialogue from the Compass scenarios described in this chapter is excerpted from (1) fragments that were "saved" in the outlines found in Shepherd's files, (2) undated tape transcriptions supplied by Shepherd (reel-to-reel) or by Bowen (cassette), or (3) from extended conversations with Roger Bowen, Andrew Duncan, David Shepherd, Bob Patton, Annette Hankin, and Sid Lazard. The only complete extant written transcription of a scenario appears to be one for *The Game of Hurt*. It is subtitled "The opening show at the Compass Theatre, presented June? July? 1955."

107 "the most dramatic material": Viola Spolin, unpublished "Notes for Article," Chicago, 1938.

12: THE SUMMER ENDS

116 "come up with nothing but dregs": David Shepherd, letter to Roger Bowen, August 29, 1955.

120 "slunk back to Chicago": Mike Nichols, "A Show Soliloquy: Mike Nichols and the Midas Touch," *Show*, March 1965.
"if I'd stayed in New York": Ibid.

123 "If we are willing to invest": David Shepherd, letter to Roger Bowen, August 29, 1955.

13: ENTER THE ACTORS

p. 125　"For centuries": This version of Vogelweide's lecture on metaphysics, retitled "A Short Talk on the Universe," appears on Darden's record album, *The Sound of My Own Voice and Other Noises* (Mercury OCM2202). It was recorded live at The Second City on January 30, 1961. As the liner notes attest, the material was originally developed at the Compass. Thus, although the Q&A section of the lecture belonged to the Compass format, the question, "Do fish think?" was actually posed by The Second City pianist Allaudin Mathieu. For asking it, Mathieu was bawled out by Bernie Sahlins, who was afraid the audience would perceive Mathieu as a "plant" or shill.

129　"fooling around," "Come quick!": Nichols to Sweet, *Something Wonderful Right Away*, p. 76.

"wonderful poignant scene": As described by Mildred Goldberger, March 5, 1986.

130　"always intensely verbal": Nichols to Pete Carlsen, "Architectural Digest Visits Mr. and Mrs. Mike Nichols," *Architectural Digest*, February 1987, p. 88.

"We loved to listen": Ibid.

"a certain connection with Elaine": Nichols to Sweet, *Something Wonderful Right Away*, p. 78.

131　"By and large": Nichols to Sweet, *Something Wonderful Right Away*, p. 78. ("She'd fill things, I'd shape them": Nichols to Barbara Gelb, "Mike Nichols: The Director's Art," *The New York Times Magazine*, May 27, 1984, p. 42.)

"I was always very concerned": Nichols to Sweet, *Something Wonderful Right Away*, p. 83.

"forced into": Ibid.

"she had endless capacity": Nichols to Gelb, "Mike Nichols: The Director's Art," p. 42.

"she was a much better actor": Nichols to Sweet, *Something Wonderful Right Away*, p. 83.

"we both had big reputations": Ibid., p. 74.

"her specialty": Ibid.

"somehow safe": Ibid.

132　"SHE: Too many people think of Adler": Mike Nichols and Elaine May, "Bach to Bach," *Improvisations to Music* (Mercury SR60040).

"Pirandello": The third actor was dropped from "Pirandello" after Nichols and May became a duo. Details about the scene in its two versions were supplied by Shelley Berman, September 1982; Jack Rollins, May 1986; Andrew Duncan, April 1986; and Jerry Stiller, September 1988. Other descriptions appear in Sweet's *Something Wonderful Right Away* and in Kenneth Tynan's 1961 review of *An Evening with Mike Nichols and Elaine May*, reprinted in *Tynan Right and Left: Plays, Films, People, Places and Events*, Atheneum, 1967, p. 69.

135　"a group of six or seven people": Nichols to Sweet, *Something Wonderful Right Away*, p. 75.

136　"The Compass is a fraud": Recalled by Severn Darden to JC, February 12, 1982.

14: "DUMP US AT THE COCK"

139 "As of . . . Dump Us at the Cock": Recalled by Andrew Duncan to JC, January 1986.

141 ". . . We accept material": David Shepherd, unsigned, undated brochure, "plans for a popular theatre and an offer to writers, directors, producers, opening 1954–55."

142 "Wanted: Quiet Tenant for Elegant Room": Scenes from *Under Deadwood* described by both scenarists to JC, March 1986. Jane Kome Mather discovered the original manuscript in November 1988.

145 "You can't do that!": Recalled by Mark Gordon to JC, March 1986.
"But that's the whole point": Ibid.

146 "a perfectionist": James Sacks to JC, November 1983; Mark Gordon to JC, March 1986.

149 "the story of a young writer": "This week at The Compass," promotional flyer, 1956.
"I like your book": From an undated audiotape of *Concupiscence and Crucifixion* recorded at the Dock.
"I have made many great films": Ibid.
"Their first attempt at a historical play": Chicago *Maroon*, February 14, 1956.
"the wonderful girls": From an undated audiotape of *PTA Open House and Fun Night* recorded at the Dock, and from fragments of transcripts in Shepherd's files.
"a process at best tenuous": Ibid.

150 "one of the best mediums": Ibid.
"When a painter sees a landscape": Ibid.
"In this case": Ibid.

15: AN ESCALATION OF SCENES

151 "rework the classics": David Shepherd, unsigned, undated brochure, "plans for a popular theatre and an offer to writers, directors, producers, opening 1954–55."

153 "Emma, it's for you": Origins of "The Message" recalled by Severn Darden to JC, June 1983. Retitled "Emma," the scene is recorded on *Comedy from The Second City* (Mercury OCS6201).
"Personally, I've never dated him. . .": Nichols and May, "Disc Jockey," *An Evening with Mike Nichols and Elaine May* (Mercury OCM2200).
"Morgenstern": The substance and stage business of "Football Comes to the University of Chicago" is derived from Roger Bowen's description and from an outline found in Shepherd's files. The dialogue is taken from *From The Second City* (Mercury OCS6203).
"That's not a line, sir": Ibid.
"That's not a circle, sir": Ibid.

154 "The ellipsoids have the ball": Ibid.

p. 156 "She also had a way of sitting": Duncan to Donna McCrohan, *The Second City*, Putnam, Perigee, 1987, p. 24.

157 "The Compass will try to find the fables": "Intention of Compass," Shepherd's diary, Vol. II, 1953–1954.

158 "Did you say a Rosenbusch Krantz?": The plot, stage business, and bits of dialogue from "Mountain Climbing" are derived from descriptions by David Shepherd, Andrew Duncan, and Shelley Berman and from an outline in Shepherd's files.
"Carry on": Ibid.

159 "Do you realize that OTTO": Allaudin Mathieu, diary, as read on phone to JC, September 19, 1986.
"It is hard to compare": Ibid.

160 "the battered elegance": *Christian Science Monitor*, c. 1959.
"disenchanted with the liturgical": Berman to Dom Cerulli. "The Comedy Interview: Shelley Berman," *Comedy* 1, no. 2, Winter 1981, p. 16.
"my parents' and grandparents' ": Ibid.

162 "a bit more vulgar than Mike": Berman to Sweet, *Something Wonderful Right Away*, p. 126.

165 "a nightmare": Allaudin Mathieu, diary, as read on phone to JC, September 20, 1986.
"Dear Friend": Ibid.

16: OUT OF STEP AT THE ARGO OFF-BEAT ROOM

173 "Paul doesn't stratify people": Nichols to Sweet, *Something Wonderful Right Away*, p. 76.

175 "Succeeded in getting L.A.": Shepherd's diary, Vol. II, 1953–1954.

177 "He'd go home and work": Darden to Sweet, *Something Wonderful Right Away*, p. 95.

180 "Straight men have to know": Ibid., p. 94.
"unimaginative": Noted in Shepherd's diary, Vol. II, 1953–1954.
"goof": Ibid.

181 "this beautiful quiet little dandelion": Bobbi Gordon to Sweet, *Something Wonderful Right Away*, p. 111.

182 "Wrote from 1:30–5:30": Shepherd's diary, Vol. II, 1953–1954.

17: ANOTHER ENTERPRISE

198 "one of the greatest plays": Cited by John Lahr, *Notes on a Cowardly Lion*, Knopf, 1969, p. 278.

199 "somewhat pockmarked": The plot of *The Liars* is reconstructed from an undated audiotape and from several scenario outlines in Shepherd's files, some apparently constructed after the performance. Rosenberg's original character descriptions were retained in the outlines.

203 "Happy because": David Shepherd, letter to Roger Bowen, January 12, 1957.

204 "Neither our new director": Ibid.

18: THE ATOMIC COMPASS

207 "a Gibraltar of ineptitude": Eugene Troobnick from memory to JC, May 14, 1986.
"very funny, but": Ibid.

211 "a show place": Jay Landesman, *Rebel Without Applause*, The Permanent Press, 1987, p. 27.
"a promissory note": Ibid., p. 26.

212 "There was something about all the darkness": Ibid., p. 184.

213 "seeking absolution": Ibid.

214 "No one in the audience": Ibid., p. 203.

19: MEET ME IN ST. LOUIS

219 "Isn't it a beautiful first wedding?": Recalled by another wedding guest to JC, March 5, 1986.

220 "sharp, biting satirical commentary": Landesman, *Rebel Without Applause*, p. 203.
"on topical issues or experiences": Ibid.

221 "if only to start a Compass there": David Shepherd, letter to Roger Bowen, April 1957.
"Let's face it, that's my name": Shelley Berman, *Outside Shelley Berman* (Verve MGVS6107).
"All right, here's what I do with you, actor": Ibid.

225 "You've been sittin' on our porch": Nancy Ponder, in character, to JC, July 12, 1988.

20: A HARDER GAME OF HURT

230 "Your motorcycle": Recalled by Del Close to JC, August 29, 1988.

232 "an unnerving display": Kenneth Tynan, *The London Observer*, October 23, 1960.
"In life, you don't decide": May to Joyce Haber, "Very Early for May," *New York*, July 22, 1968.

233 "boundless and frightful capacity for pain": Hermann Hesse, *Steppenwolf*, Frederick Ungar, 1957, p. 11.
"like life itself": Ibid., p. 157.

234 "leaving the company stranded": *Playbill: An Evening with Mike Nichols and Elaine May*, October 8, 1960.
"with $40 between them": Ibid. Also mentioned in unsigned liner notes, Nichols and May, *An Evening with Mike Nichols and Elaine May* (Mercury OCM2200).

p. 235   "the most important booking agent": Shelley Berman, *Inside Shelley Berman* (Verve MGV15003).

"names so big": Ibid.

"Eleanor, sweetheart": Ibid.

21: EXPLOSIONS

239   "The Dean . . . Gentleman Jack": Buddy Morra, Sam Cohn, David Vern, Alexander H. Cohen, Irvin Arthur to JC, c. October 1982, June 1984.

"that hoodlum who handles you": Groucho Marx to Dick Cavett, letter of October 25, 1968, printed in Cavett and Christopher Porterfield, *Cavett*, Harcourt Brace Jovanovich, 1974, p. 217.

241   "a man with no rhythm": Buddy Morra to JC, October 21, 1982.

"That's *right*, de woman is smartah!": "Man Piaba," by Harry Belafonte and Jack Rollins, Folkways Music Publishing Co., New York, 1957.

"over beef stroganoff and cold schav": *Playbill: An Evening with Mike Nichols and Elaine May*, October 8, 1960. Also mentioned in unsigned liner notes, Nichols and May, *An Evening with Mike Nichols and Elaine May* (Mercury OCM2200).

244   "Isn't the lake suicidally beautiful tonight?": As quoted similarly in *Time*, January 27, 1958 and in "Nichols and May's Satire Prickles and Tickles," *Life*, November 21, 1960. (Playing Sugar in Billy Wilder's 1959 movie, *Some Like It Hot*, Marilyn Monroe used the same line.)

245   "It's not the buttermilk": Shelley Berman, *Inside Shelley Berman* (Verve MGV15003).

"You're talking to someone intimately": Shelley Berman, *A Personal Appearance* (Verve V/VG15027).

"Incidentally, if you do buy": Shelley Berman, *Inside Shelley Berman* (Verve MGV15003).

". . . Before departing": Ibid.

246   "Care for a pillow?": Ibid.

247   "If you hit the TV jackpot": Mike Wallace, "Mike Wallace Asks Mike Nichols and Elaine May 'Are You Scared of Success?' " New York *Post*, April 1, 1958.

"We were so spoiled": Nichols to Sweet, *Something Wonderful Right Away*, p. 83.

"The more we became the talk": Ibid., p. 82.

248   "a cross between a church and a movie palace": Landesman, *Rebel Without Applause*, p. 209.

"a church that went bad": Cited by Albert Goldman, *Ladies and Gentlemen, Lenny Bruce!!*, Ballantine Books, 1974, p. 383.

"the times call forth the comedian": Berman to Cerulli, "The Comedy Interview: Shelley Berman," *Comedy* 1, no. 2, Winter 1981, p. 61.

"all bent at the elbow": *Time*, January 20, 1961.

22: AFTERSHOCKS

250   "SHE: Oh, honey": Nichols and May, "Mother and Son," *An Evening with Mike Nichols and Elaine May* (Mercury OCM2200).

". . . All right, Sheldon": Shelley Berman, *Outside Shelley Berman* (Verve MGVS6107).

"a liberal nihilist": Kenneth Tynan, *The London Observer*, October 23, 1960.

251   "I write my own material": Shelley Berman, *A Personal Appearance* (Verve V/VG 15027).

"hate me for having a cavity": Mike Nichols and Elaine May, "Second Piano Concerto," *Improvisations to Music* (Mercury SR60040).

"Do you have moments": Shelley Berman, *A Personal Appearance* (Verve V/VG 15027).

253   "Broadway's first wholly locally created musical": *Variety*, c. May 1959.

"no point of view": Kenneth Tynan, *The New Yorker*, May 23, 1959.

"It was better in St. Louis": Recalled by Jay Landesman, *Rebel Without Applause*, p. 226.

254   "In a nightclub": Anne Meara to Sweet, *Something Wonderful Right Away*, p. 164.

257   "My mother wasn't a clubwoman": Kolb to Sweet, *Something Wonderful Right Away*, p. 204.

258   "on our profounder knowledge": Sills to Charles L. Mee, Jr., "The Celebratory Occasion: An Interview with Paul Sills," *Tulane Drama Review* 9, no. 2, Winter 1964, p. 177.

"backlog of guilt": Ibid.

"he and Elaine": Sahlins to Donna McCrohan, *The Second City*, Putnam, Pedigree, p. 33.

"agonized over": Ibid.

260   "SHE: I told her": Barbara Harris and Severn Darden, "Blind Date," *From The Second City* (Mercury OCS6203).

261   "Monsieur Marceau": Recalled by Eugene Troobnick to JC, October 19, 1983.

263   "members of its growing family": Press kit, *The Second City Twenty-fifth Anniversary Special*.

265   "Let the word go forth": John F. Kennedy, Inauguration Address, *New York Times*, January 21, 1963.

23: FALLOUT

266   "The bigger the nightclub": Nichols to Barbara Gelb, "Mike Nichols: The Director's Art," *The New York Times Magazine*, May 27, 1984, p. 42.

"Monsieur Succès": Unsigned article, "Nichols, 36 ans, Le Metteur en scène du 'Laureat' se plaint: Il a trop de succès," *Paris Match*, October 5, 1968.

267   "She was always brave": Nichols to Gelb, "Mike Nichols: The Director's Art," p. 42.

"I nagged the hell out of her": Ibid.

p. 267　"just something to make a living": Nichols to Sweet, *Something Wonderful Right Away*, p. 80.

"grew up and started our real lives": Nichols to Alice Arlen, "Mr. Success," *Interview*, December 1988, p. 121.

"a big joke": Nichols to Sweet, *Something Wonderful Right Away*, p. 80.

268　"We finally found that the safest thing": Ibid., p. 82.

269　"Everymanic Depressive": *Time*, January 20, 1961.

270　"His records sold like magazines": Mort Sahl, *Heartland*, Harcourt Brace Jovanovich, 1976, p. 43.

"They wanted to turn him into Red Skelton": Sahl to JC, October 2, 1976.

"the greatest actress": F. Murray Abraham, presenting Best Actress Oscar to Page for *The Trip to Bountiful*, 1986.

"He wasn't Red Skelton": Sahl to JC, October 2, 1976.

"and then we stopped": Nichols to Sweet, *Something Wonderful Right Away*, p. 83.

271　"It was also *about* me": Ibid., p. 84.

"The play needed work": Writer to JC, June 1988.

"we were so disoriented": Nichols to Sweet, *Something Wonderful Right Away*, p. 84.

272　"Oh, Mikey": Nichols to Gelb, "Mike Nichols: The Director's Art," p. 42.

24: RADIATION

273　"of inflecting questions": Walter Kerr, New York *Herald-Tribune*, January 30, 1958.

275　"Like a woman asked to marry": Rostova to Robert Higgins, "TV Gives You Time to be Nervous," *TV Guide*, August 29, 1967, p. 23.

"I couldn't bear": Rivers to Sweet, *Something Wonderful Right Away*, p. 291.

"pantomime once a week": Ibid.

276　"Do you guys realize": Recalled by Duncan to JC, September 1988.

"Broadway, Broadway": Ibid.

"not a freeze": Viola Spolin, *Improvisation for the Theater*, p. 190.

277　"I'm so sick": Joan Rivers, with Richard Meryman, *Enter Talking*, Delacorte, 1986, p. 278.

"made me ashamed": Ibid., p. 281.

25: RADIATION BURNS

278　"That funny little face": Rodgers quoted in "A Rainbow Every Evening," *Newsweek*, May 28, 1962, p. 97.

"Since my reviews in *Oh Dad*": Harris quoted in *Esquire*, November 1962.

279　"simplistic": Bernie Sahlins to Sweet, *Something Wonderful Right Away*, p. 182.

281　"that Second City style": Recalled by Larry Arrick (who directed at Yale under Brustein's tenure) to JC, January 5, 1983.

"Most theatre is slave-market bullshit": Sills to Sweet, *Something Wonderful Right Away*, p. 19.

"Of course, you can use improvisation": Ibid., p. 23.

"the precarious hand-to-mouth": Winifred Smith, *The Commedia dell'arte*, Benjamin Blom, 1964, p. 58.

282 "barbecue shows": *New York Times*, May 10, 1963.

"We were treated like diplomats": Flicker to Rocco Landesman, "Interview: Ted Flicker," *Yale/Theatre* 5, no. 2, Spring 1974, p. 69.

"It was always very hard for Second City": Paul Sills in his and R. G. Davis's "A Dialogue," Ibid, p. 52.

"One day I realized it was bullshit": Flicker to Landesman, "Interview: Ted Flicker," p. 69.

283 "paint-by-the-numbers": *Newsweek*, November 4, 1963.

"Why don't we just give him the play": Recalled by Neil Simon to JC, July 1988.

284 "all those performer things": Nichols to Alice Arlen, "Mr. Success," *Interview*, December 1988, p. 156.

"All these Daddy feelings": Ibid.

"I need milk": Shepherd to JC, c. 1964.

"For a long time": Shepherd to JC, "Variations on a Theme," *Yale/Theatre* 5, no. 2, Spring 1974, p. 16.

"I worked very hard": Alda to Sweet, *Something Wonderful Right Away*, p. 324.

285 "Mr. Nichols' eye": Walter Kerr, "The Making of a Big Fat Hit," New York *Herald-Tribune*, November 10, 1963.

"hurricane of hilarity": Ad for *Barefoot in the Park*, *New York Times*, November 1963.

"really trying to kiss the audience's ass": Nichols to Arlen, "Mr. Successs," p. 156.

"The trick in attacking the Establishment": Mike Nichols to Joseph Wershba, New York *Post*, c. November 1963.

"You fall off the horse": Hess to JC, c. 1982.

"In a democratic society": John F. Kennedy, Amherst Address of October 26, 1963, reported in *New York Times*, October 27, 1963.

286 "Poor Vaughn Meader": Lenny Bruce at The Village Theatre, November 23, 1963.

"Not only was my suggestion": Roger Bowen, unpublished "Notes on Tony Hendra's *Going Too Far*," 1988.

26: NUCLEAR WINTER AND INFRARED SPRING

287 "Civilization is over": Sills to Charles L. Mee, Jr., "The Celebratory Occasion: An Interview with Paul Sills," *Tulane Drama Review* 9, no. 2, Winter 1964, p. 171.

288 "He was already hot": Balding quoted by Stuart Little, New York *Herald-Tribune*, May 26, 1965.

"doing the Ingmar Bergman thing": Flicker to Landesman, "Interview: Ted Flicker," p. 72.

289 "intricate patterns of movement": *Newsweek*, June 15, 1964.

"the wonderfully ingenious Mike Nichols": Edith Oliver, *The New Yorker*, June 6, 1964, p. 86.

p. 289 "Why shouldn't the theatre of the absurd": Howard Taubman, *New York Times*, May 28, 1964.

"more glib than perceptive": Newark *Evening News*, May 29, 1964.

"improvisations performed without flair": *Village Voice*, c. June 1964.

"The tired gimmick": *Morning Telegram*, May 30, 1964.

"Elaine May should have realized": Richard Watt, New York *Post*, May 29, 1964.

"The skits were not short enough": *The Villager*, c. June 1964.

"You've got to say one thing": *Morning Telegram*, May 30, 1964.

290 "not much of a satirist": Patinkin to Sweet, *Something Wonderful Right Away*, p. 243.

"I wanted to more seriously": Sills to Sweet, Ibid., p. 15.

"a religious expression": Sills to Mee, Jr., "The Celebratory Occasion," p. 180.

"a sacred space": Ibid.

"The sooner the improvisational theatre": Ibid., p. 167.

291 "a functional device" Sahlins to Sweet, *Something Wonderful Right Away*, p. 188.

292 "a blithe spirit and a living doll": Ad for *On a Clear Day You Can See Forever*, c. 1965.

293 "The whole star bit . . .": Harris to Betty Rollin, "Broadway's All-Female Funnygirl," *Look*, December 14, 1965, p. 142.

"In the oral tradition of Homer": Paul Sills, "Story Theatre," John Hay, ed., *Yale/Theatre* 3, no. 2, 1971, p. 52.

"A story is a peculiar kind of journey": Ibid., p. 53.

"The point is to connect": Ibid., p. 52.

294 "My concern with form": Sills to Sweet, *Something Wonderful Right Away*, p. 19.

295 "Elaine is going to suffer": Nichols quoted by Thomas Thompson, "Whatever Happened to Elaine?" *Life*, July 28, 1967.

"It was difficult for me": May, as quoted by David Blum, "The Road to Ishtar," *New York*, March 16, 1987, p. 42.

"Hollywood doesn't care": Ibid.

297 "When the play is over": Nichols to Mervyn Rothstein, "Nichols Tries to Put the Fun back in 'Godot'," *New York Times*, September 13, 1988.

27: THE POINT OF THE COMPASS

299 "accessible intelligence": Mike Nichols, "A Show Soliloquy: Mike Nichols and the Midas Touch," *Show*, March 1965.

303 "a permanent base": Harold Clurman, *The Fervent Years*, Hill & Wang reprint, 1967, p. 230.

"The artist builds": Ibid.

SELECTED BIBLIOGRAPHY

BOOKS

Adler, Stella. *The Technique of Acting*. Foreword by Marlon Brando. New York: Bantam Books, 1988.

Albee, Edward. *Who's Afraid of Virginia Woolf?* New York: Atheneum, 1962.

Aristophanes. *Four Comedies*. New York: Harcourt, Brace & World, 1962.

Aristotle. *On Poetry and Music*. New York: The Liberal Arts Press, 1948.

Ashmore, Harry S. *Unseasonable Truths: The Life of Robert Maynard Hutchins*. Boston: Little, Brown, 1989.

Baker, Carroll. *Baby Doll: An Autobiography*. New York: Arbor House, 1983.

Beckett, Samuel. *Waiting for Godot*. New York: Grove Press, 1954.

Bellow, Saul. *Dangling Man*. New York: Vanguard, 1944.

Bentley, Eric. *In Search of Theater*. New York: Alfred A. Knopf, 1953. Reprint: Vintage, 1954.

———. *The Playwright as Thinker*. New York: Harcourt, Brace & World, 1946.

———. *The Theatre of Commitment and Other Essays*. New York: Atheneum, 1967.

Berger, Phil. *The Last Laugh: The World of Stand-Up Comics*. New York: Morrow, 1975.

Boucher, Chauncy S. *The Chicago College Plan*. Chicago: University of Chicago Press, 1935.

Brecht, Bertolt. *Baal, A Man's a Man, The Elephant Calf: Early Plays*. Edited and with an introduction by Eric Bentley. New York: Grove Press, 1964.

———. *Brecht on Theatre*. Edited and translated by John Willett. New York: Hill and Wang, 1964.

———. *The Caucasian Chalk Circle*. Revised English version and introduction by Eric Bentley. New York: Grove Press, 1966.

———. *Collected Plays*. Edited by Ralph Manheim and John Willett. New York: Pantheon, 1970.

———. *A Collection of Critical Essays*. Edited by Peter Demetz. Englewood Cliffs, N.J.: Prentice-Hall, 1962.

———. *The Good Woman of Setzuan*. Revised English version and introduction by Eric Bentley. New York: Grove Press, 1956.

———. *Mother Courage*. English version by Eric Bentley. New York: Grove Press, 1963.

———. *The Threepenny Opera*. English book by Desmond L. Vesey, English lyrics by Eric Bentley. New York: Grove Press, 1960.

Bruce, Lenny. *The Essential Lenny Bruce*. Compiled and edited by John Cohen. New York: Ballantine Books, 1967.

———. *How to Talk Dirty and Influence People*. Chicago: Playboy Press, 1965.

Büchner, Georg. *Complete Plays and Prose*. Edited and with an introduction by Carl Richard Müller. New York: Hill and Wang, 1963.

Cavett, Dick, and Porterfield, Christopher. *Cavett*. New York: Harcourt Brace Jovanovich, 1974.

Cheney, Sheldon. *The Theatre: 3000 Years of Drama, Acting and Stagecraft*. New York: David McKay, 1958.

Clurman, Harold. *Lies Like Truth*. New York: Macmillan, 1958.

———. *The Fervent Years: The Story of the Group Theatre and the Thirties*. New York: Alfred A. Knopf, 1945. Reprint: Hill and Wang, 1967.

Cook, Bruce. *Brecht in Exile*. New York: Holt, Rinehart and Winston, 1982.

David, Lester, and Robbins, Jhan. *Richard and Elizabeth*. New York: Funk & Wagnalls, 1977.

DiLello, Richard. *The Longest Cocktail Party: An Insider's View of the Beatles*. Chicago: Playboy Press, 1972.

Duchartres, Pierre Louis. *The Italian Comedy*. Reprint: New York: Dover, 1966. George G. Harrup, 1929.

Faris, Robert E. S. *Chicago Sociology, 1920–1932*. Heritage of Sociology Edition. Foreword by Morris Janowitz. Chicago: University of Chicago Press, 1970.

Freud, Sigmund. *The Basic Writings*. Translated and edited, with an introduction by Dr. A. A. Brill. New York: Modern Library, 1938.

Frodin, Reuben, ed. *The Idea and Practice of General Education: An Account of the College of the University of Chicago*. Chicago: University of Chicago Press, 1956.

Gazzo, Michael V. *A Hatful of Rain*. New York: Random House, 1956.

Gibson, Walter. *The Bunko Book*. Las Vegas: Gambler's Book Club, 1976.

Goldman, Albert. *Ladies and Gentlemen, Lenny Bruce!!* New York: Ballantine Books, 1974.

Goldman, William. *The Season: A Candid Look at Broadway*. New York: Harcourt, Brace & World, 1969.

Goldsmith, B. *Little Gloria, Happy at Last*. New York: Alfred A. Knopf, 1980.

Hendra, Tony. *Going Too Far (The Rise and Demise of Sick, Gross, Black, Sophomoric, Weirdo, Pinko, Anarchist, Underground, Anti-Establishment Humor)*. New York: Doubleday, 1987.

Hesse, Hermann. *Steppenwolf*. Translated from the German by Basil Creighton. New York: Frederick Ungar, 1957.

Hethmon, Robert J., ed. *Strasberg at the Actors Studio*. New York: Viking, 1965.

Hill, Doug, and Weingrad, Jeff. *Saturday Night: A Backstage History of Saturday Night Live*. New York: Morrow, Beech Tree, 1986.

Hodgson, John, and Richards, Ernest. *Improvisation*. London: Methuen, 1966.

Hutchins, Robert M. *The Conflict in Education in a Democratic Society*. New York: Harper, 1953.

———. *Education for Freedom*. New York: Grove Press, 1963.

———. *Freedom, Education and the Fund: Essays and Addresses, 1946–56.* New York: Meridian, 1956.

———. "The Great Conversation: The Substance of a Liberal Education," in *Encyclopedia of World Biography.* New York: McGraw-Hill, 1952.

———. *Some Observations on American Education.* Cambridge, Eng.: Cambridge University Press, 1956.

———. *The State of the University, 1929–1949.* Chicago: University of Chicago Press, 1949.

———. *Zuckerkandl!* Illustrations taken from the film by John and Faith Hubley. New York: Grove Press, 1968.

Ibsen, Henrik. *Peer Gynt.* Introduction by Raymond B. Canon. New York: Airmont Publishing Co., 1967.

Jellicoe, Anne. *The Knack.* New York: Samuel French, 1962.

Johnstone, Keith. *Impro: Improvisation and the Theatre.* New York: Theatre Arts Books, 1979.

Kazan, Elia. *A Life.* New York: Alfred A. Knopf, 1988.

Lahr, John. *Notes on a Cowardly Lion.* New York: Alfred A. Knopf, 1969.

Landesman, Jay. *Rebel Without Applause.* Sag Harbor, N.Y.: The Permanent Press, 1987.

Malina, Judith. *The Diaries of Judith Malina, 1947–1957.* New York: Grove Press, 1984.

McCrohan, Donna. *The Second City.* New York: Putnam, Perigee, 1987.

Mamet, David. *Sexual Perversity in Chicago and The Duck Variations.* New York: Samuel French, 1977.

———. *The Short Plays and Monologues.* New York: Dramatists Play Service, 1987.

Marx, Karl. *Capital, The Communist Manifesto and other writings.* New York: The Modern Library, 1932.

May, Elaine. *Adaptation* (one-act play). New York: Dramatists Play Service, 1971.

———. *Not Enough Rope* (one-act play). New York: Samuel French, 1964.

Mellen, Joan. *Women and Their Sexuality in the New Film.* New York: Horizon Press, 1973.

Morehead, Albert H., and Mott-Smith, Geoffrey. *Hoyle's Rules of Games.* New York: New American Library, 1963.

Morgenstern, Christian. *Galgenlieder: A Selection.* Translated by Max Knight. Berkeley and Los Angeles: University of California Press, 1964.

———. *Gallows Songs.* Translated by W. D. Snodgrass and Lore Segal. Ann Arbor: University of Michigan Press, 1967.

Munk, Erika, ed. *Stanislavsky and America.* New York: Hill and Wang, 1966.

Peake, Mervyn. *Titus Groan.* New York: Reynal & Hitchcock, 1946. Reprint: New York: Weybright & Talley, 1967.

Polsky, Ned. *Hustlers, Beats and Others.* Chicago: Aldine, 1967.

Riesman, David, with Reuel Denney and Nathan Glazer. *The Lonely Crowd.* New Haven, Conn.: Yale University Press, 1950.

Rivers, Joan, with Richard Meryman. *Enter Talking.* New York: Delacorte, 1986.

Sahl, Mort. *Heartland.* New York: Harcourt Brace Jovanovich, 1976.

Sartre, Jean-Paul. *No Exit and Three Other Plays.* New York: Vintage, 1958.

Schuth, H. Wayne. *Mike Nichols.* Boston: Twayne, 1973.

Shakespeare, William. *The Complete Works*. Edited by G. B. Harrison. New York: Harcourt, Brace, 1952.

Shaw, George Bernard. Complete Plays of George Bernard Shaw. London: Odhams Press Ltd., 1934.

―――. *Plays Pleasant*. New York: Penguin, 1985.

―――. *Plays Unpleasant*. Baltimore: Penguin, 1961.

Simon, Neil. *Barefoot in the Park*. New York: Samuel French, 1964.

Smith, Winifred. *The Commedia dell'arte*. New York: Benjamin Blom, 1964.

Spolin, Viola. *Improvisation for the Theater*. Evanston, Ill.: Northwestern University Press, 1963.

―――. *Theater Game File*. St. Louis: CEMREL, 1975. Reprint: Evanston, Ill.: Northwestern University Press, 1989.

―――. *Theater Games for Rehearsal*. Evanston, Ill.: Northwestern University Press, 1985.

―――. *Theater Games for the Classroom*. Evanston, Ill.: Northwestern University Press, 1986.

Stanislavsky, Constantin. *An Actor Prepares*. Translated by Elizabeth Reynolds Hapgood. New York: Theatre Arts Books, 1936.

―――. *Building a Character*. Translated by Elizabeth Reynolds Hapgood. New York: Theatre Arts Books, 1949.

Strindberg, August. *Five Plays*. Translated by Henry G. Carlson. Berkeley: University of California Press, 1983.

Sweet, Jeffrey. *Something Wonderful Right Away*. New York: Avon Books, 1978.

Terkel, Studs. *Talking to Myself: A Memoir of My Times*. New York: Pantheon, 1977.

Thurber, James. *The Thurber Carnival*. New York: Harper and Brothers, 1945.

Von Neumann, John, and Morgenstern, John. *Theory of Games and Economic Behavior*. Princeton, N.J.: Princeton University Press, 1953.

Webster, John. *The Duchess of Malfi*. Edited by Fred B. Millett. New York: Appleton-Century-Crofts, 1953.

Wiener, Norbert. *The Human Use of Human Beings*. Garden City, N.Y.: Doubleday, 1954.

Wilde, Larry. *The Great Comedians Talk about Comedy*. New York: Citadel, 1968.

Willett, John. *The Theatre of Bertolt Brecht: A Study from Eight Aspects*. New York: New Directions, 1959.

Woodward, Bob. *Wired*. New York: Simon and Schuster, 1984.

ESSAYS AND ARTICLES

Ammerson, Jane. "Profile of Bernie Sahlins." *Midway*, January 1989.

Arlen, Alice. "Mr. Success." *Interview*, December 1988.

Berger, Phil. "The Business of Comedy." *The New York Times Magazine*, June 9, 1985.

Biskind, Peter. "Inside 'Ishtar.' " *American Film*, XII, no. 7 (May 1987).

Blum, David. "The Road to Ishtar." *New York*, March 16, 1987.

Brackman, Jake. "Onward and Upward in the Arts." *The New Yorker*, July 27, 1968.

Brecht, Bertolt. "Notes on Stanislavsky." *Tulane Drama Review* (Document Series) 9, no. 2 (Winter 1964).

Carlsen, Pete. "Architectural Digest Visits Mr. and Mrs. Mike Nichols." *Architectural Digest*, February 1987.

Cerulli, Dom. "The Comedy Interview: Shelley Berman." *Comedy* 1, no. 2 (Winter 1981).

Close, Del, and Guare, John. "A Conversation." *The New Theatre Review* 1, no. 3 (Spring 1988).

Coleman, Janet. "Variations on a Theme." *Yale/Theatre* 5, no. 2 (Spring 1974).

D'Aponte, Mimi. "Improvisational Notes." *Commonweal*, September 1986.

Downs, Bernard. "Directing the Metaphoric Mind." *Theatre News* 6, no. 1 (Fall/Winter 1978).

Ephron, Nora. "Mike Nichols Raps." *Eye*, April 1969.

Esslin, Martin. "Brecht, The Absurd and The Future." *Tulane Drama Review* 7, no. 4 (Summer 1963).

Falconieri, John. "The Commedia dell'arte: The Actors' Theatre." *The Theatre Annual* XII (1954).

Feldman, Lee Gallup. "A Brief History of Improvisational Theatre in the United States." *Yale/Theatre* 5, no. 2 (Spring 1974).

Gelb, Barbara. "Mike Nichols: The Director's Art." *The New York Times Magazine*, May 27, 1984.

Gross, Alan. "Improv Central." *Chicago*, December 1982.

Guare, John, and Jones, Laura. "A Conversation with Mike Nichols." *The New Theatre Review* 1, no. 4 (Winter 1988).

Haber, Joyce. "Very Early for May." *New York*, July 22, 1968.

Hay, John, ed. "Story Theatre." *Yale/Theatre* 3, no. 2 (1971).

Higgins, Robert. "TV Gives You Time to be Nervous." *TV Guide*, August 29, 1967.

"Hip Comics and the New Humor: Playboy Panel." *Playboy*, March 1961.

Jennings, C. Robert. "Playboy Interview: Mike Nichols." *Playboy*, June 1966.

Kleinfield, Lenny. "Del Close: Interview." *Chicago*, March 1987.

Landesman, Rocco. "A Conversation with David Shepherd." *Yale/Theatre* 5, no. 2 (Spring 1974).

———. "Interview: Ted Flicker." *Yale/Theatre* 5, no. 2 (Spring 1974).

Levine, Donald N. "Challenging Certain Myths about the 'Hutchins' College." *The University of Chicago Magazine*, 77, no. 2 (Winter 1985).

Liebling, A. J. "Chicago: The Second City," in *Liebling at Home*. Chicago: Playboy Press, 1982. (First published in *The New Yorker*, in three parts: January 12, 19, 26, 1952.)

Martin, Jean. "Letter from Chicago." *The Nation*, May 14, 1960.

———. "Letter from Chicago." *The Nation*, November 3, 1962.

May, Elaine. "*The Real Thing*: A Compass Scenario." *Yale/Theatre* 5, no. 2 (Spring 1974).

Mee, Charles L., Jr. "The Celebratory Occasion: An Interview with Paul Sills." *Tulane Drama Review* (Document Series) 9, no. 2 (Winter 1964).

Merrill, Sam. "Playboy Interview: Edward Asner." *Playboy*, April 1981.

"Mike and Max." *The New Yorker*, April 11, 1964.

"Nichols and May and Horses." *The New Yorker*, November 12, 1960.

"Nichols and May's Satire Prickles and Tickles." *Life*, November 21, 1960.

Nichols, Mike. "A Show Soliloquy: Mike Nichols and the Midas Touch." *Show*, March 1965.

"Nichols, 36 ans, Le Metteur en scène du 'Laureat' se plaint: Il a trop de succès." *Paris Match*, October 5, 1968.

Pooley, Eric. "I've Got the Horse Right Here." *New York*, September 28, 1987.

Rollin, Betty. "Broadway's All-Female Funnygirl." *Look*, December 14, 1965.

——. "Mike Nichols: The Wizard of Wit." *Look*, April 2, 1968.

Rosenheim, Edward. "The Legacy of Robert M. Hutchins." *The University of Chicago Magazine* 69, no. 4 (Summer 1977).

Sills, Paul, and Davis, R. G. "A Dialogue," *Yale/Theatre* 5, no. 2 (Spring 1974).

Thompson, Thomas. "Whatever Happened to Elaine?" *Life*, July 28, 1967.

Tretyakov, Sergey. "Bert Brecht." *International Literature*, no. 37 (May 1937).

Wool, Robert. "Mike and Elaine: Mirrors to Our Madness." *Look*, June 2, 1960.

DIARIES, COLLECTIONS, DOCUMENTS

Bowen, Roger: Performance notes on "The Living Newspaper"; *Enterprise* scenario; notes on scenario construction and staging; *The Show Might Go On* (unpublished novel); correspondence with David Shepherd; notes on Tony Hendra's "Going Too Far" (unpublished).

Close, Del: Notes on improvisation (unpublished).

Dozer, David: *Premise* diaries, New York and London (unpublished).

Lampert, Zohra: Playwrights Theatre Club collection.

Mather, Jane Kome: Authors' manuscript, *Under Deadwood* (unpublished), by Mildred Goldberger and Jane Kome.

Mathieu, Allaudin: Diaries; memoir of Stan Kenton (unpublished).

Moon, Dave: Tapes and album notes for *The Premise* and *The Nervous Set*.

Piven, Byrne: Playwrights Theatre Club reviews.

Shepherd, David: Diaries—Vol. I, "The Rolling Stage"; Vol. II, 1953–1954; Vol. III (untitled); memorabilia; Compass "Newsletters"; Compass scenarios and scenes; "Improvisation Newsletters"; "How to Write a Scenario"; "Working at Play: My Life in Improvisation" (work in progress); Improvisation Olympic Coach's Guide; Faustbook, 1981.

Shepherd, Suzanne: Correspondence.

Spolin, Viola: Clippings, reviews, correspondence, and unpublished notes.

Billy Rose Theatre Collection, New York Public Library at Lincoln Center, Astor Lenox and Tilden Foundation.

SELECTED DISCOGRAPHY

SHELLEY BERMAN

Inside Shelley Berman (Verve MGV15003)

Outside Shelley Berman (Verve MGVS6107)

The Edge of Shelley Berman (Verve MGVS6161)

A Personal Appearance (Verve V/VG15027)

New Sides (Verve V/VG15036)

Sex Life of the Primates (with Jerry Stiller, Anne Meara, Lovelady Powell) (Verve V/VG15043)

LENNY BRUCE

The Sick Humor of Lenny Bruce (Fantasy 7003)

I Am Not a Nut, Elect Me (Fantasy 7007)

American (Fantasy 7011)

To Is a Preposition, Come Is a Verb (rereleased as *What I Was Arrested For*) (Douglas KZ30872)

Berkeley Concert (Bizarre/Reprise 6329)

The Real Lenny Bruce (Fantasy F79003)

DEL CLOSE

The Do-It-Yourself Psychoanalysis Kit (Hanover 5002)

How to Speak Hip (with John Brent) (Mercury 61245)

SEVERN DARDEN

The Sound of My Own Voice and Other Noises (Mercury OCM2202)

FRAN LANDESMAN AND TOMMY WOLF

The Nervous Set (Robert Lantz production. Book by Jay Landesman and Theodore J. Flicker. Based on the novel by Jay Landesman. Henry Miller Theatre, New York, 1959) (Columbia OL5430)

LOTTE LENYA

Sings Berlin Theatre Songs of Kurt Weill (Columbia ML5056)

MIKE NICHOLS AND ELAINE MAY

An Evening with Mike Nichols and Elaine May (Alexander H. Cohen production, Golden Theatre, New York, 1960) (Mercury OCM2200)

Improvisations to Music (Mercury SR60040)

Nichols and May Examine Doctors (Mercury MG20680/SR6068)

Best of Nichols and May (Mercury SR60997)

Retrospect (Mercury SRM2628)

THE PREMISE

The Premise (Vanguard VRS9092)

MORT SAHL

The Future Lies Ahead (Verve MGV15002)

1960: Look Forward in Anger (Verve MGV15004)

At the hungry i (Verve MGVS15012)

THE SECOND CITY

Comedy from The Second City (Mercury OCS6201)

From The Second City (Max Liebman, Bernard Sahlins, Howard Alk: Paul Sills Production, Royale Theater, New York, 1961) (Mercury OCS6203)

Live (Audio Renaissance—cassette)

Writhes Again (Mercury SR61224)

KURT WEILL

The Threepenny Opera (Carmen Capalbo and Stanley Chase production. English adaptation of book and lyrics by Marc Blitzstein. Theater de Lys, New York, 1953), with Lotte Lenya (MGM E3121)

ACKNOWLEDGMENTS

Between 1981 and December 1988, more than a hundred people helped me reconstruct the events that take place in this book. I am first of all deeply grateful to Barbara Harris, Severn Darden, Roger Bowen, Andrew Duncan, Mark and Bobbi Gordon, Shelley Berman, Del Close, Ted Flicker, Paul Sills, and my first of these teachers, David Shepherd, for sharing their time, memories, insights, and artifacts with me so generously.* As long and well as I knew many of them before starting this research, I was continually surprised by the depth and range of their accomplishments.

Viola Spolin was almost 80 when she undertook our series of conversations, arguments, and mutual inquisitions. I thank her for violating her principles about the moment and talking about the past. I also thank her for theater games.

The help and good will of Zohra Lampert, Barbara Anson, Larry Arrick, Mina Kolb, Jane Kome Mather, Allaudin Mathieu, Sheldon Patinkin, Marvin Peisner, Nancy Ponder, Omar Shapli, Eugene Troobnick, David Vern, and Joan Wile were also enormous. I would like to have thanked the late Anthony Holland properly.

It would be hard to dream up more thoughtful and articulate sources than Bill Alton, Rose Arrick, Aaron Asher, Edward Asner, Walter Beakel, Seth Benardete, Peter Bonerz, Michael Brandman, Joy Carlin, Constance Carr-Shepherd, Sybil Burton Christopher, Jerry Cunliffe, John Ecks, Heyward Ehrlich, Tom Erhart, Gwyllum Evans, Judy Feiffer, Ralph Fertig, Frances Gendlin, Mildred Goldberger, the late Max Gordon, Kolmus Green, Ed Greenberg, the late Josephine Gwynne, Annette Hankin, Valerie Harper, Herb Hartig, Calvin Hill, Morris Hirsch, Ted Hoffman, Tresa Hughes, Kenna Hunt, Charles Jacobs, Rocco Landesman, Louise Lasser, Sid Lazard, Mickey LeGlaire, Eve Leoff, Karl Mann, David Margulies, Robert A. Martin, Jean Martin, Saul Mendlowitz, Dave Moon, Buddy Morra, George Morrison, Tom O'Horgan, Jean and Richard Orlikoff, Bob Patton, Byrne and Joyce Piven, Ned Polsky, Peggy Pope, Barbara Probst, the late Catherine D. and George E. Probst, Jack Rollins, James Sacks, Fritzi Sahlins, Paul Sand, Dick Schaal, Jules Schwerin, Evan Shepherd, Suzanne Shepherd, Carol Sills, Robert B. Silvers, Neil Simon, Susan Sontag, Bob Smith, Leslie J. Stark, David Steinberg, Jerry Stiller, Lucille Goldberg Strauss, Studs Terkel, Collin Wilcox, Fred Wranovics, and Sandy Zwerling. I feel honored to have spent even a couple of times with Geraldine Page.

During this same period, I also thought conversations with the following to have added a lot to my knowledge of show business, improvisation, the theatre, and comedy: Peter Boyle, Dick Cavett, Irwin Corey, Dianne Crittenden, Rodney Dangerfield, Heather Dar-

*Despite many entreaties, Mike Nichols and Elaine May declined to be among them.

den, Paul Dooley, Marshall Efron, Bob Fass, Budd Friedman, Silver Friedman, Whoopi Goldberg, Garry Goodrow, Doris Hess, Keith Johnstone, Jon Korkes, Jay Leno, Emily Levine, Mark Lonow, Frances MacKeon, Judith Malina, Garry Marshall, Leonard Melfi, Robin Menken, Alfa-Betty Olsen, Alice Playten, Jack Riley, Bernie Sahlins, Murray Schisgal, Susan Sweetzer, Rip Torn, Nick Ullett, Bruce Wagner, Paul Willson, and Diane Wondisford.

I am indebted to Joyce Sloan for her graciousness at the Second City reunion, to Richard Frankel for making it possible for me to see *Sills and Company* so often, and to Steve Martin for making it possible for me to see *Waiting for Godot*.

Northwestern University Press, *Playboy*, *Billboard*, Richard Pop at the University of Chicago Department of Special Collections, Steve Schur of University Theatre, Mark Hollman of the *University of Chicago Magazine*, Richard Bray of PEN West, the late Blackie Dozer, Joan Ungaro, Erika Munk, Victor Navasky, Iggy Cadillac, Bo Ross, Joshua White, Mickey Midnight, Phil Schaap, and Sylvia Henry helped me track down the most obscure things. The ones who caught mice know who they are.

Through all displays of infirmity, my dear friends Patricia Bosworth, Dante Dincecco, Bruce Hart, Sue Mingus, Robert J. Abramson, and my oracle, Jodi Schneider, were unflaggingly supportive and helpful to my work and to me. Carole Hart performed the deeds of an angel in my behalf. I thank my lucky stars for my enduring conversation with Al Young. Always I was indebted to Ann McIntosh for our collaborations at The Loft. And to Michael Elias for his philosophy of unlimited whitefish and his laugh. Besides answering so many questions on comedy, Jack Winter never once asked, "When are you going to be done?" On all matters of art or reality, Sheila White Samton was my treasured and constant consultant, as she has been since we were both twelve years old.

It was my great good fortune to work on the production of this book with so devoted and sensitive a person as Antoinette White.

Candace Lake had the idea that I write it and Robert B. Silvers directed me to Robert Gottlieb who put a handful of pages into exactly the right hands.

Most of all, I am grateful to my editor, Victoria Wilson, whose taste, imagination, guidance, and confidence in this project were from start to finish my invisible rope.

I thank myself for marrying David Dozer, my beloved partner, teacher, fellow improvisor, and lover of games.

J.C.
New York City
February 1990

INDEX

PHOTOGRAPHIC ACKNOWLEDGMENTS

Following page 82: Page 1: Courtesy the Collection of Robert A. Martin. Page 2: Courtesy of The Chicago *Maroon*. Page 3: Courtesy the Collection of Zohra Lampert. Page 4: Courtesy the Collection of Byrne Piven. Page 5: (above) Courtesy the Collection of David Shepherd; (below) Courtesy the Collection of Zohra Lampert. Page 6: Courtesy the Collection of Zohra Lampert. Page 7: Courtesy the Collection of Paul Sills. Page 8: (above left) Courtesy the Collection of Byrne Piven; (above right) Courtesy the Collection of David Shepherd; (below) Courtesy the Collection of Roger Bowen.

Following page 146: Page 1: Courtesy the Collection of David Shepherd. Page 2: Courtesy the Collection of David Shepherd. Page 3: Courtesy the Collection of Andrew Duncan. Page 4: Courtesy the Collection of David Shepherd. Page 5: (above) Courtesy the Collection of Mark and Bobbi Gordon; (below) Courtesy the Collection of David Shepherd. Page 6: (above) Courtesy William Allaudin Mathieu; (below) Courtesy the Collection of David Shepherd. Page 7: Courtesy the Collection of Andrew Duncan. Page 8: (above) Courtesy the Collection of Mark and Bobbi Gordon; (below) Courtesy the Collection of Shelley Berman.

Following page 210: Page 1: Courtesy the Collection of David Shepherd. Page 2: Courtesy the Collection of David Shepherd. Page 3: (above) Courtesy the Collection of David Shepherd; (below) Courtesy Werner J. Kuhn. Page 4: Courtesy Morton Shapiro. Page 5: (above) Courtesy the Collection of Andrew Duncan; (below) Playbill® is a registered trademark of Playbill, Inc., New York City. Used by permission. Page 6: Courtesy Photofest. Page 7: Courtesy Photofest. Page 8: Courtesy the *Yale/Theatre* magazine.

A NOTE ON THE TYPE

The text of this book was set in Electra, a typeface designed by W. A. Dwiggins (1880–1956). This face cannot be classified as either modern or old style. It is not based on any historical model, nor does it echo any particular period or style. It avoids the extreme contrasts between thick and thin elements that mark most modern faces and attempts to give a feeling of fluidity, power, and speed.

Composed by Crane Typesetting Service, Inc., Barnstable, Massachusetts. Printed and bound by Fairfield Graphics, Fairfield, Pennsylvania.